THE

# **WORTH** Guide to Electronic Investing

# **WORTH** Guide to Electronic Investing

**EVERYTHING YOU**

**NEED TO KNOW TO USE**

**YOUR HOME COMPUTER**

**TO MAKE MORE MONEY**

**IN THE STOCK MARKET**

## JIM JUBAK

HarperBusiness
*A Division of* HarperCollins*Publishers*

HarperCollins books may be purchased for educational, business, or sales promotional use. For information please write: Special Markets Department, HarperCollins Publishers, Inc., 10 East 53rd Street, New York, NY 10022.

FIRST EDITION

*Designed by Jessica Shatan*

Library of Congress Cataloging-in-Publication Data

Jubak, Jim.
    The worth guide to electronic investing : everything you need to know to use your home computer to make more money in the stock market / by Jim Jubak.
      p.  cm.
    Includes index.
    ISBN 0-88730-769-8
    1. Investments—Data processing.   2. Investments—United States—Data Processing.
3. Stocks—United States—Data processing.   4. Portfolio management—Computer programs.
5. Investment analysis—Computer programs.   I. Title.
HG4515.5.J83   1996
332.63'22'0285416—dc20                          96-10717

96 97 98 99 00 ❖/RRD 10 9 8 7 6 5

*For Marie, again and always, and for Finn*

# CONTENTS

## ACKNOWLEDGMENTS

Many people have had a role in bringing this book to fruition. Jim Melloan, Ted Fishman, Curtis Lang, Andy Feinberg, and Tim Middleton all worked with me on the package of magazine articles that started me down the road toward this book. John Koten, editor of *Worth*, gave me encouragement to run with that original project as well as time and support to write this book. Without his commitment and patience I would have never been able to complete this project. Alison Parks and Randall Jones helped this book find a home at the magazine. My agent, Susan Ginsburg, was, as always, a treasured advisor and a valued co-conspirator. A big thanks to my editors at HarperBusiness, Adrian Zackheim and Suzanne Oaks, who believed in this project and suffered through its gestation. And to Marie, who hung out with Finn for more weekends than I can count while I worked on these pages and who kept reminding me that all books come to an end, more appreciation and love than I can put on this page.

# WHAT IS ELECTRONIC INVESTING?

I still remember buying my first share of stock. It was 1964 and I was fourteen. My mother took me down to the local office of a major Wall Street firm, I think it was PaineWebber, in the then-thriving downtown of Plainfield, New Jersey. The office dazzled me—this was the first time I'd ever seen a ticker and I found myself mesmerized by the bright symbols crawling across the wall. The broker gave us a warm welcome, at least partially because my Uncle Eddie, who owned the Studebaker dealership in Plainfield, had a big account with the firm. But in those days, before Charles Schwab & Co. broke up the cozy little world of 6 percent commissions, a broker could also afford to spend a half hour recruiting another soul into the legions of American capitalism. I walked out of his office clutching a handful of yellow Standard & Poor's reports on companies such as RCA and GTE. My mother, always a firm believer in the value of research, helped me send away for the annual reports of the companies I was most interested in. When they arrived, I looked at the pictures of smiling workers and company officials. I finally bought RCA—one share. I watched NBC—it was then the home of Walt Disney, and the broker was positive that color

TV would sweep the country. At fourteen I certainly thought television had a future.

That wasn't the greatest investment I ever made—the Japanese essentially destroyed the U.S. television industry over the next few decades. But my profit or loss isn't the point of this story. Instead I'd like to focus on the process that I went through to pick a stock. It's probably familiar to most investors even today. Sure, most adult investors know more about reading financial statements than I did at fourteen, but many still rely on a broker's recommendation, plus some research from the brokerage firm itself. The more thorough would add data from sources such as Standard & Poor's, and perhaps Value Line. They might even have started out with an idea of what they wanted to buy from an article in *Business Week, Forbes, Barron's*, or the *Wall Street Journal*. And they would certainly have done some rough calculations that looked at price to earnings ratios and projected earnings and growing or shrinking profit margins. But it's safe to say that most investors in 1996 pick a stock or a mutual fund pretty much the way I did in 1964. And many of those decisions don't turn out much better than my selection of RCA did.

But that's not how I pick stocks in 1996, nor how I buy and sell them. The computer—or more precisely the advent of the relatively cheap personal computer—has changed investing for me. And learning how to use a computer to help make my investment decisions has made me a better investor.

Let me show you the difference by describing how I decided to buy 100 shares of Rubbermaid in early June 1995. All the details are real. (And don't worry if some of the analysis or software is unfamiliar to you. Everything will be explained in the chapters that follow. Here I just want to give you a feel for the process I call computerized investing.)

Saturday morning, June 10, 1995. About three-quarters of the way through the *New York Times* report on Friday's market action—"Dow Tumbles 34.58 Points as Hopes Dim for Rate Cut"—an item catches my attention. Rubbermaid, "the household products company, dropped 3 3/4 to 26 7/8." The company "announced yesterday that they expected their quarterly earnings to disappoint Wall Street." That's all.

But I'm intrigued. I've been interested in this stock for a year. While I studied its amazing record of consistent double-digit earnings and sales growth, it ran away from me, climbing from $24 to $30. Now suddenly it's back in my buying range. But should I take the plunge now?

Maybe the company is in serious trouble and I shouldn't buy at all.

I could, of course, wait until Monday and call my broker and ask him. Working for one of Wall Street's biggest firms, he has analyst reports at his fingertips. He can hit a button and immediately see data about the company's sales and financial fundamentals. He can call up a record of Wall Street's expectations for Rubbermaid's earnings and chart its stock price and the number of shares changing hands in the markets. But thanks to my computer so can I.

At 10:20 A.M. Saturday I finish my morning coffee, walk into our second bedroom/office, and turn on my computer. First job: get more news on exactly what the company announced on Friday. I click on eWorld, an on-line information service produced by Apple Computer, and then move to a news database run by Dow Jones, the company that produces the *Wall Street Journal*. I ask for a search for any news stories on Rubbermaid in the last thirty days. In a minute the headlines for three items appear on my screen. Two are market summaries for Friday, which just repeat what I read this morning, but the last is what I want: "Rubbermaid Sees 2nd Quarter Net Near 20 Cents, Below View." I print it out. Wow, the company expects to disappoint analysts by more than a few cents. Wall Street had estimated earnings per share for the quarter ending June 30 would hit 34 cents. On Friday, the company alerted analysts to expect the low twenties instead.

The story also tells me that the trouble is with earnings and not sales. Management blames the earnings shortfall on rising prices for resins, the raw materials in the company's plastic products. Resin prices are near cyclic highs and the company expects them to decline after the middle of the year. Which should mean a return to higher profits.

So far I've spent 9 minutes. To get more details on earnings and sales I leave eWorld and go to Prodigy, another on-line information service, and jump to the Market Guide company reports offered in Prodigy's Strategic Investor area. I type in RBD to call up Market Guide's 12-page report, dated June 8. It gives me 52-week highs and lows—the 52-week low is $24.88 so Friday's plunge didn't take the stock through the support level. (I remind myself that I'd have to get a chart on the stock's movement to see where the support level is.) Revenue growth looks solid: the company grew revenue at a 10.67 percent rate for the last year—ahead of the industry's 6.64 percent. That's actually better than the annual growth rate for longer periods (three years at 9.17 percent and five years at 8.36 percent). The problem does seem to be in earnings, which have trended in exactly the opposite direction: 7.51 percent for one year, 11.75 percent for three years, and 12.55 percent for five. Profit margin figures also confirm the earnings problem: the margin is down to 10.33 percent from 10.79 percent a year ago. But a profit margin above 10 percent seems a historical anomaly for the company—over the eight years tracked by Market Guide, 8 percent or 9 percent has been more usual.

Oddly the stock's price-to-earnings ratio has been climbing—an indication to me that the market either hasn't caught up with the earnings problem or that investors believe that the company's current problems are just a short-term blemish. The price-to-earnings ratio is up from 20.94 a year ago to 21.30 now. I check on the earnings estimates produced by Wall Street's analysts. Well, the direction of the company's announcement didn't come as a surprise to analysts—they've been steadily downgrading their earnings projections for the company. But they're still high—they are now estimating fiscal 1995 at $1.55 a share, down in the last week from $1.58. The consensus is esti-

```
PRODIGY(R) interactive personal service          02/27/96          4:01 PM
                  STRATEGIC INVESTOR COMPANY REPORT

RUBBERMAID INC.                                     Symbol: RBD

INDUSTRY: Personal & Household Prods.

RELATIVE STRENGTH            PRICE RATIOS   Current  Yr Ago   Ind
          Company    Ind     Pr/Earn (P/E)  77.13*   21.69   28.44
4 weeks    -5.5     -3.6      Pr/Sales        1.97*    2.28    1.92
13 weeks   -5.1     -4.0      Pr/Book         3.60     3.86    7.34
26 weeks  -17.5      2.5      Pr/Cash Flow   16.00    15.55   63.30
52 weeks  -31.1     -1.1      Beta            1.31             1.05

RELATIVE STRENGTH RANK       FIN RATIOS     Current  Yr Ago   Ind
          Company    Ind     Debt/Equity     0.13     0.02    0.69
4 weeks     37       14      LTD/Equity       0.01     0.01    0.50
13 weeks    46       22      Quick Ratio      1.51     2.30    0.84
26 weeks    35       63      Current Ratio    2.29     3.39    1.58
52 weeks    23       42      Int Coverage    29.99    43.78   12.80

TRADING VOLUME - NYSE        RETURNS (%)    Current  Yr Ago   Ind
     Avg Shrs(000)    %       ROE (Equity)    4.68*   18.68   23.72
Daily       381      0.2      ROA (Assets)    3.38*   14.14    8.89
Monthly   9,477      6.0      Profit Margin   2.55*   10.52    7.22
```

*The Market Guide database on Prodigy provides twelve pages of fundamental data on*
**Rubbermaid.** *(Courtesy of Market Guide)*

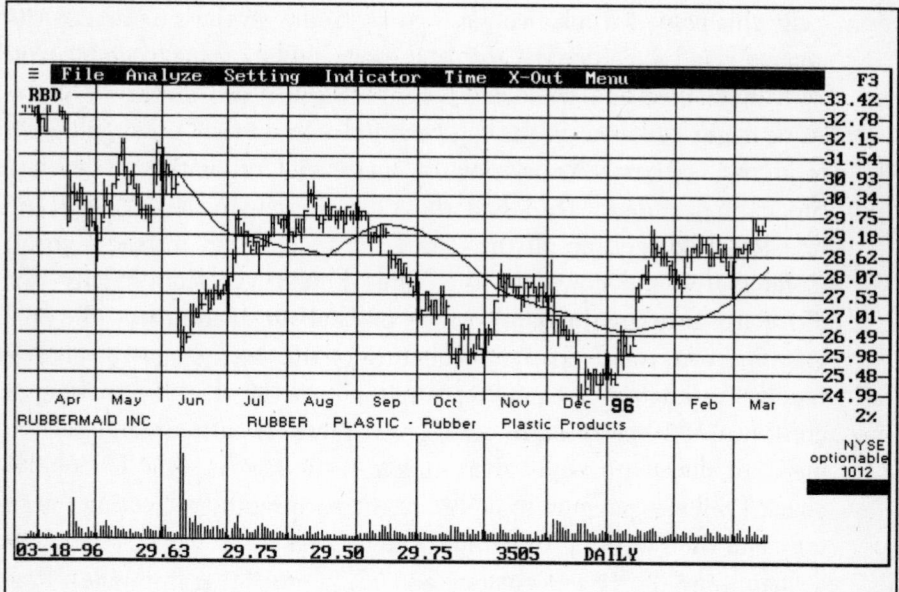

*TeleChart 2000 turns a stock's history into a picture—and then lets an investor draw conclusions.* (*Courtesy of TeleChart 2000® by Worden Brothers Inc.*)

mating $1.82 in 1996. Reassuringly, analysts still believe that the company's long-term growth rate is about 14 percent.

But while buying Rubbermaid will certainly entail market risk, the company looks rock-solid financially. Long-term debt is just 1 percent of equity. The balance sheet is clean as a whistle, as far as I can tell. I've been on Prodigy for 30 minutes.

Disconnecting from Prodigy I remember that I wanted to look at some charts of the stock's price movement in recent weeks. I start up another program, Telechart 2000, and download the most recent price and volume data on the stock using my modem. I've been following Rubbermaid regularly so updating my chart takes just two minutes and costs me $1.12 (which is actually the price for updating all of the 112 stocks that I chart regularly). I create price charts for 50-week moving average, momentum, and volume—all three look bad. This wouldn't seem to be the time to buy. The stock, which rose from October through April, fell off a cliff at the end of that month. To me the charts suggest that if the price falls below $26, the stock might decline further. Creating the charts and studying them takes me about 25 minutes.

By this point I think I've got a good handle on the situation at the company and a feel for the risk in the stock. But I want to understand with more precision what the potential upside and downside of the stock might be based on the fundamentals. To do that I use a program from the National Association of Investors Corporation called the Stock Study Guide. (If I had the time or were near a Value Line newsletter I'd look up all the data I need there, but instead I go on CompuServe and download the Value Line page electronically (for $5). After entering the data—which takes about 25 minutes—the program lets me project different scenarios for the stock simply by changing my estimates of future earnings growth. I start by picking a conservative 10 percent projected growth rate for earnings and sales to see what the earnings per share might be in 5 years. And to double-check I tell the program to calculate the earnings by projecting future sales and then working backward. The two figures are very close: $2.29 a share using the 10 percent rate and $2.17 projecting from sales. Projecting forward, I get a five-year forecast high price of $57.20 and a low of $25.60—about where it is today. There's not much downside risk here. The program suggests buying the stock when it's below $34.80 and tells me that buying at today's price will give me a projected return of 17.7 percent annually over the next five years if the forecast high price turns out to be accurate. This sounds like a buy to me. Working through the analysis takes another 25 minutes—so the total on this program comes to 50 minutes.

But before I buy, I also want to check with my fellow investors. Signing back on to CompuServe, I go first to the Investor's Forum and then to a section, called a forum, run by NAIC. I find ten messages from the last two days talking about the Rubbermaid plunge. Interestingly, the fundamentalists say "Buy"; the technicians see a further decline. That's about where my own analysis wound up. I decide to buy half the position I want now and then see how the market is going. I stay on CompuServe for just 20 minutes.

Armed with my decision, I quit CompuServe and sign on to my electronic broker, a program called StreetSmart that links my home computer with my accounts at Charles Schwab. I place an order to buy 100 shares of Rubbermaid at no more than $27.25 (37.5 cents above Friday's close) when the market opens on Monday. The computer confirms my order entry and tells me that my commission charge will be $49.50 for the trade. Placing the trade takes 10 minutes.

Does this seem complicated? You don't have to master all these programs and every bit of my investment process to put your computer to work for you. I didn't start with something this complicated—and you don't have to learn all these details to improve your investment performance. In fact, the complete novice can probably become a better investor using even a single very simple program. I did. I began by using Quicken, a $50 program that's far simpler to use than any word processor, to track my portfolio. It only took me about an hour to learn enough to use that program to show me which of my investments had done best and which worst. I thought I knew the answer, but I found some real surprises. I discovered stodgy stocks that had earned double-digit returns and "growth" stocks that had returned much less than I imagined once I figured in how long I'd held them. Just that one tool let me weed out the bad and add to my holdings of the best. Only gradually did I discover that what I was doing amounted to electronic investing, and that I was part of a larger trend among investors.

Would you like to learn how to use tools like these and to do this kind of analysis? That's what this book is all about. The tools that I used to buy Rubbermaid might seem complicated at first glance—especially if you're not a computer wizard—but you can learn enough to start using any of these in a few hours. And the costs are very modest— if you trade ten or fifteen times a year the money you'd save from full-service brokerage commissions alone would pay for this software. And that's not counting the additional profits that you'd reap, because using your computer in this way has made you a better investor.

You can put the revolutionary power of electronic investing in your hands. Using the reviews, advice, and hands-on examples in this book, you can gain control over your own financial future. In these pages you'll learn what strategies work and which don't. The novice in computers or investing will find everything he or she needs to start up. The experienced computer user and investor will find tips and tricks, new sources of information, and new programs for manipulating it that can lead to making more money in the stock market. No matter what system you use to invest you'll find suggestions here that will make it work better for you.

## THE GROWTH OF ELECTRONIC INVESTING

This book is your guide to a movement that has already recruited a surprisingly large number of investors. How many? It's hard to tell exactly.

An estimated 7 to 10 million investors actively manage their own money in the United States today. That figure includes both the dedicated trader who runs the family portfolio out of his or her den to the employee who changes the allocations in a 401(k) retirement plan once a year, so not every one of those millions are practicing computerized investors. Almost 7 million people own Quicken. Certainly many of those use that program just to do the household budget, but add in the numbers from the other big "mass market" software packages—Managing Your Money (2 million), Microsoft Money (1 million), Simply Money (1.5 million)—and the river of people practicing some form of electronic investing is impressively broad.

It's also surprisingly deep. Increasing numbers of investors who may have started with one of the mass market packages are moving up to programs that can pick stocks based on their fundamentals, build charts for the technical analysis of stocks and entire markets, sift through the universe of more than 7,000 mutual funds looking for the best, and create investment strategies for increasing returns and minimizing risk. About 30,000 individual investors now use software to analyze mutual funds. More than 150,000 investors use computer programs to pick stocks—either on fundamental (earnings, for instance) or technical (after charting the pattern of a stock's prices over some past period) grounds.

I count more users and more programs—more than 500 programs were on the market when this book went to press—everyday. It's not hard to understand why.

Computers are ideally suited to the kind of repetitive number crunching that produces investment insight. A smart investor would certainly be willing to sit down with pencil and paper to figure out what Wal-Mart should be worth in five years using one assumption for the company's rate of growth. An even smarter investor would like to test more than one growth rate. Or see how much those earnings would be worth on the market if the stock traded at near its high historical price-to-earnings ratio—and near its historical low. Computers can generate that kind of what-if analysis—or charts of a stock's price or sort through thousands of mutual funds—with just a few keystrokes.

It's no wonder that Wall Street, banks, and mutual fund companies have been willing to sink millions into buying huge mainframes and developing proprietary investment software. In the 1960s at Twentieth Century Investors, the Kansas City mutual fund company, founder James Stowers wrote software to identify stocks with increasing earnings growth. In the 1980s programmers at Morgan Stanley created complex "black box" systems that spit out buy and sell recommendations after consulting a computer simulation of the stock market. But these were software programs handcrafted by gifted programmers working with experienced investment managers. They ran on mainframe computers costing upwards of $1 million a piece. This limited these computerized investing systems to money managers running tens of millions of dollars at mutual fund companies, banks, and Wall Street brokerage firms.

The personal computer changed the scale of resources needed to practice computerized investing. Computers capable of running sophisticated investment software now cost $2,500 or less. Instead of producing 140,000 mainframes, as IBM did in 1991, a company such as Compaq, the industry volume leader in 1995, sold 1,450,000 personal computers in the second quarter of 1995 alone. A company such as Intuit, the maker of Quicken, or Equis International, the producer of the MetaStock technical analysis program, does not write custom programs for a handful of clients able to pay six-digit fees. Instead they spread the costs of developing a program across tens of thousands of users and charge $50 to a few hundred dollars. The growing number of personal computers in homes—an estimated 27 percent of all U.S. homes now contain personal computers—and the growing number of electronic investors means that these costs can be spread over an ever larger user base. Programs with ever more useful features cost less and less each day—which of course makes electronic investing attractive to more and more investors.

Growth in any new technology begins slowly and then takes off in the classic hockey stick pattern so beloved by investors in new technologies. And electronic investing has clearly hit the accelerated part of the growth curve. I can see it all around me. I dial in to one of my databases and see that the vendor is offering eight years of historical data on 8,000 stocks for $100. I pick up *Barron's* and see that a competitor is selling its historical data for $49. And a week later I get a notice from the first database that they are now selling eleven years of data for $39. America Online cuts its price for cruising the electronic information highway to $4.95 an hour. Prodigy cuts its to $4.50 and CompuServe follows suit. Morningstar puts all of its mutual fund data on disk for $195 a year. Value Line releases a new product that does the same thing. Morningstar upgrades its product by adding a portfolio manager and keeps the price the same. Charles Schwab gives away Street Smart, its program for on-line trading, to anyone who conducts three trades—and adds data from Standard & Poor's and Morningstar to the package. Reality, whose Wealth-Builder program already supplies mutual fund data, adds the S&P material too.

## THE BENEFITS OF ELECTRONIC INVESTING

Well, maybe electronic investing is the best thing since sliced bread, and maybe more and more investors are joining in and the programs are getting better and better and cheaper and cheaper; still, why should you jump on board?

First, the likelihood is that you, alone, and probably with meager advice from any kind of investment professional, are responsible for all your major investment decisions today. You'll be even more responsible tomorrow. The ranks of people who take an active role in managing their money are being swelled daily by the move in the corporate world away from the company-run defined-benefit pension plan. 401(k) plans, which require the someday retiree to plan how much to save and then to choose specific investments, are gradually replacing the defined-benefit mainstay. Add in vehicles such as IRAs and Keoghs and the number of Americans making their own investment decisions for retirement is even higher.

Second, there's less and less *quality*—remember that word—advice available to the individual investor. Many individual investors have traded a broker's advice for lower commissions by taking their accounts to discount brokerages such as Charles Schwab & Co., Quick & Reilly, Waterhouse Securities, Jack White, and the like. At these firms investors pay lower commissions, but they lose the chance to ask a broker for advice. While many provide research, either their own or from some respected industry source such as Standard & Poor's, an investor with an account at one of these firms can never ask a broker a question such as "What do you think of Rubbermaid?"

Discounters, by not offering advice, have effectively put a price on a broker's advice. If the difference between buying 100 shares of Rubbermaid at Schwab by talking to a human being, and buying at a full-service firm is $15, isn't that the value I should put on the advice dished out by the broker?

That seems awfully little. But even so, if I do more than a few trades a month I can beat the price with my desktop system. On my home computer—which I use to earn my living as a writer—I can get S&P ratings and Value Line's. I can pull up financials—twelve pages of them—and see earnings estimates and analysts' opinions. I can get current news—and if I want to, search the archives for old news stories. If I amortize the costs of my investment software programs over their useful life—three years?—and recalculate my costs for the Rubbermaid trade as a monthly fee, I get a cost of $116.62. If I do eight trades a month I break even when I compare what my information costs me with the higher fees charged by an advice-dispensing broker.

But that analysis doesn't take into account the relative value of the information I get from my broker and from my desktop. I can analyze Rubbermaid for myself in ways that my broker will not. I can project earnings and sales and then see what different assumptions do to the stock price five years down the road. I can scan a chart for Rubbermaid looking for patterns in the data over the last 200 days and then rechart the data for 50-day, 21-day, and 7-day patterns. Sure, I don't have access to the brokerage reports prepared by the firm's own analysts—well, actually I could get them on my home computer but it's very expensive and I'm not sure they're worth the price—but I can trawl the on-line services looking for other investors with opinions on the stock. For my extra dollars I'm getting better information.

It's not that I have better information sources and technology than my broker. It's just that I can afford to spend the time to customize my research to my exact needs. Wall Street is a business like any other business, and as such it's bound by the rules of economics. And the laws of economics as they apply to the Wall Street financial advisor are pretty simple: Time is money. No broker, no money manger, no financial advisor can spend time with an investor without compensation. In the advisor business this compensation is called a commission, and the way to increase commissions is to sell more stuff in less time. Brokers have to earn a living too, and that means they can work only so many minutes on your $1,000 or $10,000 or $100,000. Any more time than that and they lose money.

These economic strictures are getting tighter and tighter on Wall

Street. The financial industry is in the midst of an industry-wide downsizing with no end in sight. The financial sector today employs 50,000 fewer people than it did at the beginning of 1995. Many of those let go have been back-office people, the workers who process orders and keep the books. But brokers feel the pressure to produce as well. They know that performance reviews are stricter than ever and that the office manager is watching the sales numbers. Almost every full-service broker, no matter how well informed or intentioned, is under pressure these days to minimize chitchat and maximize sales.

The full-service firms on Wall Street make a great point of the partnership they offer to investors. The ads on television say, "Your broker will ask the right questions to enable you to retire in a lakeside home. Your broker will pick the best stocks for you. Your broker will spend time learning your risk tolerance and time horizon." Some will even do a complete financial plan for your family, free.

But the reality is slightly different. The financial plan will be a cookie-cutter job designed to make everyone fit into four or five profiles—how could it be otherwise? The marketing department has figured out the cost of this offer. It knows that, say, four out of a hundred people will talk to a broker after this offer and that one of those will become a new client who will bring in $463 in commissions in Year One. So the free plan can't cost more than $5.67 each to produce, advertise, and mail.

You can indeed find a broker who will spend time learning your risk tolerance—if you have enough money to invest or are willing to pay a management fee. Wall Street gives investors who want more handholding various accounts and programs that promise to supply it. These all come with one feature in common—they cost more. For a fee that ranges from 1 percent to 3 percent of your assets, you can get an account with a modicum of financial planning and a broker—now probably called something like an investment counselor—who will spend more time ascertaining your investment needs and goals. That, of course, means that you could spend even more money and/or time doing your own investment planning on your home computer and still come out ahead. Let's face it. No one is going to be more interested in your financial success than you are.

And even if you pay those higher fees, how much individualized investment selection will you actually get? Few brokers and not many advisors do their own investment research. They rely on their firm's analysts for suggestions. But ask yourself about the value of a Wall Street stock pick. I'm not going to argue that the stock pickers of Wall Street are inept or crooked. That's not my point at all. By far the great majority of them work hard at a difficult job and try to call the stocks that they cover as they see them. But I do question the quality and usefulness of that stock pick to you, the individual investor. I'll take a strong recommendation I saw recently as an example: NatWest, a bank with a brokerage business, upgraded clothing retailer The Gap from hold to accumulate.

Well, what's that advice worth to a specific investor? Like the free financial plan, it too is stamped out by cookie-cutter. Most Wall Street research assumes a 12-month time horizon—but I'm a long-term investor. Should I still buy? Is Gap better than the stocks currently in my portfolio? Well, NatWest doesn't know what I hold. What are the tax consequences for me? Is it too risky for someone near retirement or too bland for a young investor who has the time to recover from market dips? And, since everyone knows about this recommendation, how valuable is it as a basis for action now, anyway?

Information like this is cheap—and it always has been—because it is volume information. An investor with an account at Merrill Lynch can call up a broker and say, "I'm just about to put $5,000 in my retirement plan—what do you recommend?" The broker says, "Chrysler." The investor buys. Cost to the firm: 5 minutes. Payoff: $150 in commissions.

Or you could spend a lot more time at your computer analyzing the industries in your current portfolio to see where you are over- and underweighted, comparing the prospects for stocks that you own now (and might want to buy more of) against new securities that you could buy, and weighing the potential advantages and costs of investing in anything right now instead of doing nothing.

Now you've arrived at the third reason to become an electronic investor—your ability to control your own financial future. Each investment decision will be tailored to circumstances that you understand better than anyone. Each strategy can be updated immediately at the slightest change in family circumstance. And each decision you make will be guided by your own self-interest, not by the vagaries of a brokerage commission schedule or a monthly sales incentive for selling a specific stock or fund.

## HOW TO USE THIS BOOK

So you're convinced. But where do you start? There are more than 500 programs on the market. Which ones are the best? How do you combine several programs into an investment system? And what do you need to know about investing itself to make these programs work most effectively? Let's face it, to be a successful electronic investor you have to become comfortable in two different fields: computers and investing.

That's what this book is all about. In the pages that follow you'll find a unique combination of advice. Each of the nine chapters of this book offers concrete information on what programs to buy, what hardware you'll need to run it—and on designing investment strategies that work. I've tried hard not to assume that you know anything about investing—and, because I don't want to lose those readers who do, I've put definitions, examples, history, and the current state of controversy over investing issues (such as book value) in boxes that you are free to read or skip. I've also tried to give the same kind of attention to basic computer technology so that the reader will find boxes discussing issues such as how fast a modem should be. Reading the entire book from start to finish should provide an investor with all the information he or she will need to build a complete investment system, including an investment strategy suited to him or her and the software programs that will implement it.

But you don't have to read the book from end to end. Dipping into only the topics that interest you is another option. Each of the nine chapters is focused on a specific kind of investment task. Chapter 4, for example, is about picking stocks using company fundamentals, such as growth rate and earnings and margins. An investor who buys and sells stocks on their fundamentals can read just that chapter to get a review of the programs that he or she needs and a discussion of how to use them in a favorite stock-picking strategy. Each chapter is relatively self-contained, and at those places where the discussion refers to an earlier chapter, the text notes the page number that introduced the topic. As a whole, the book progresses from simple to more complex software and investment strategies. Chapter 2, for example, should tell even the rankest beginner how to get started and what three pieces of software to buy as a "starter system." The last chapter, on the other hand, is intended for the advanced user who wants to experiment by building a personalized investment system from scratch.

**TIPS ON THE TOOLS**

# A NOTE ON VERSIONS

**D**OS, Windows, Macintosh. All the programs in this book run under one of these operating systems. (An operating system contains the basic instructions for the computer. While all computers execute similar kinds of commands, each operating system "writes" those commands in its own language. Unfortunately, these languages, to date, are mutually unintelligible.)

Where DOS, Windows, and Macintosh versions of a program exist, I have tried to test and review all three versions, since the features may be very different even between DOS and Windows versions. Where the versions are substantially different, I've noted that in my review and tried to indicate important differences. When I have referred to programs in my text, I've tried to make it clear which version I used to produce these specific examples.

The companies that write investment software for IBM-compatible machines lag behind much of the software industry in their adoption of Windows. The simple truth is that many DOS programs are every bit as good as their Windows competitors—and in some cases there are no Windows competitors. No reader should avoid a program simply because it is written in DOS instead of the more "up-to-date" Windows. Learning enough DOS to run a program in that language is a relatively easy task.

As for Windows 95 . . . Very little financial software—Microsoft Money, Intuit's Quicken, and Managing Your Money are the major exceptions—has yet been rewritten to take advantage of Microsoft's most recent revision of its Windows operating system. Some users have reported incompatibility problems between a few existing Windows-based software programs and Windows 95. Managing Your Money, for example, has reported a glitch in the display function when the program is run under Windows 95. The National Association of Investors Corporation has found a printing problem in its SSG Plus program when a user runs Windows 95. Patches and other solutions are available from the software companies.

I haven't attempted to include reviews of every software package currently on the market. Instead I've culled the available software to pick more than 100 packages, data providers, on-line services, and Internet

## TIPS ON THE TOOLS

# DEMOS AND GUARANTEES

You wouldn't buy a car without taking it for a test drive. The same applies to software.

For your software test drive, you can choose one of two methods. The easiest to understand is the money-back guarantee. Many software makers offer a 30- or 60-day period during which you can try out their product and return it for a full refund if you don't like it. Be sure you understand the terms of the guarantee fully when you order. Most companies require you to return all disks and manuals to get a credit. And, especially if the software is expensive, it's a good idea to use a shipper that can provide you with a dated receipt proving that the software arrived at the maker's office.

Demo versions of software are a good way to check out a program without tying up your money in a product that you may ultimately return. Some demos are free, especially those that can be found on-line. Others cost anywhere from $5 to $20.

Since most demos come with preloaded data that you can use to see what the program is like, it's not always simple to tell exactly how easy it is to load data into a program. A good program with a balky routine for downloading data electronically or a cumbersome method for manually entering data is likely to wind up gathering dust on your shelf. If you can't get a good sense of how the data entry works from the demo, get the software maker to explain it to you in detail and go on-line (CompuServe is especially good for this; see Chapter 6) with your questions. You'll undoubtedly find an investor who uses the software (or who tried it) who can tell you what you want to know.

home pages that together provide the building blocks for your investor's tool kit. I've built each chapter around a different investment task, and I end each by reviewing products that can tackle part or all of that task. Rather than recommending just a single tool for each task, I've suggested a number of roughly similar tools so that you can customize your toolbox to your own level of investment and computer skill, to the amount of time that you want to spend at this investment task, and to the specific individual spin that you put on your investment strategy. In my reviews I've tried to indicate both how good a program is at the specific task and sketch precisely what part of the investment job it addresses and what parts it neglects. I've also tried to explain tricks that I've discovered that make some of these programs better tools. I think of these tips as a kind of dialogue: Everyone who uses a good piece of software constantly discovers new methods, functions, and uses. I'd be happy to hear from any of you about what you've discovered. (My e-mail address is polish@pipeline.com). I've run every program reviewed in this book myself—almost always in full versions, but occasionally, in the case of very complex or expensive programs, only in the demo version. (One exception: I haven't been able to open accounts with every electronic broker for financial reasons.) I haven't reviewed anything in this book by simply reading the box that encloses the software. Those claims are advertising, and I certainly don't assume that all programs deliver equally well on what they promise. I've also discovered that often the most interesting—or annoying—feature of a program isn't even mentioned on its packaging.

You'll find relatively few negative reviews in this book. In most cases, bad programs are deservedly obscure. I frankly didn't see the point of making you aware of a program that you've never heard of and are never likely to consider buying for the sole purpose of then slamming it. I have, however, given negative reviews to bad programs that have high profiles—and enough marketing muscle behind them so that they actually show up on investors' software radar. (Needless to say, the fact that something isn't in these pages doesn't mean it's bad. I could have merely overlooked it. If you want to know why I didn't include something—was it bad or did I miss it?—send me e-mail at polish@pipeline.com. I'd like to hear about programs I missed that readers think should be included in the next edition of this book.)

All this, of course, brings us to the question of what is a good or bad piece of software. I think the answer has three parts.

First, the comparative. Programs are always graded on a curve determined by all the programs that exist. We change our definition of what earns a grade of A as investment software gets better.

I've tried to evaluate how well each program does on the jobs a program's creators intended their program to perform in comparison to other programs tackling similar tasks. A program that promises to track a portfolio can't be faulted for not picking stocks—but it should do as good a job of tracking a portfolio as the other programs on the market. A portfolio tracker that stood at the cutting edge one year may wind up lagging the next when some other programmer discovers an easy way to automate data entry or a better way to calculate returns for multiple time periods.

Programs can also lag or lead their peers as software. In each case I've asked how easy a program is to set up, to learn, and to operate. I've tried to judge the quality of the screen—is it easy to read or likely to cause eye strain? I've judged design, albeit subjectively. Does the program "intuitively" group functions and tasks so that the user follows his or her own logic, or does it make the user contort to fit the program? Does the program define unfamiliar terms—and are those definitions easily accessible? Is it easy to toggle back and forth between functions that depend on each other?

(Comparing programs gets complicated when one program performs

---

**BASICS**

# WHAT I USED

I tested all the programs in this book on some rather modest computers. I ran Windows and DOS programs on either a desktop personal computer with an Intel 486/DX2 processor, which runs at an acceptable 66 megahertz or a much slower 486 portable running at 33 megahertz. The desktop PC had 24 megabytes of memory, a 140MB hard drive, and a 2X CD-ROM drive; the portable had 8MB of memory and a 120MB hard drive. That level of memory was fine for everything I tested. But the hard drive size proved a bit small. To make up for it I added a Zip Drive from Iomega, which can store 100MB on a removable disk. I ran all graphics-heavy programs on the desktop PC with its 15-inch color monitor. (I tested Windows 95 programs on a Pentium-based machine running at 75 megahertz.)

I also used two different Macintosh machines, an older Macintosh Centris 610 with 8MB of memory (and a 17-inch color monitor) and an 80MB hard drive and a Power Macintosh 710 (with a 15-inch color monitor) with 8MB of memory and a 500MB hard drive. Both machines were equipped with 2X CD-ROM drives.

With all four machines I used mid-range, 14,400 bits per second modems (Intel and U.S. Robotics on the two PCs and Global Village on the two Macintosh machines) to access on-line services.

only one task and another bundles that function along with several other jobs. I've tried to suggest both how easy it is to link a "single task" program to others and how well the individual parts of a bundle work in comparison to the "single task" competition. The final decision about whether to build a system out of many programs or to use just one or two programs that each perform several tasks will depend on a user's level of computer skill. A user who is comfortable manipulating data formats, for example, would find it easy to mate programs; that task is likely to overwhelm the computer novice. Price is also an issue, and I've tried to provide enough information so that the prospective purchaser can compare the price of getting the job done using different packages against using one package that integrates many investment functions.)

Still operating as a comparative judge, I've tried to get a feel for the company behind the program. Does the program come with a money-back guarantee and does the company seem to honor that guarantee without a fight? Is help readily available over the phone or on-line? What's the attitude of the people who provide technical support to users who are simply confused—or to those more experienced and demanding users who have found a "bug" in the program? To help me judge these qualities, I've spent a lot of time lurking in the on-line forums that discuss software and the company-supported help areas. When I'm reporting a summary of conclusions from observing the on-line traffic, I've indicated that as my source.

Second, the absolute. A superbly designed and supported piece of portfolio tracking software is still a bad program if it uses misleading or wrong formulas for calculating return, for example, even if every other piece of portfolio tracking software on the market uses the same formulas and methods. A mutual fund database and fund picker with a wealth of data is still a bad program if it omits the data items that most investment analysts now believe give investors the best insight into future fund performance. I've tried to keep in mind that this is a book for investors. The ultimate test of a program is its ability to help an investor make money in the financial markets. A program that costs an investor money because of a misunderstanding of conventional financial "truths" or because of biased or missing data is a bad program.

Third, the subjective. You'll notice that I haven't coined my own point system for grading software or issued letter grades or stars. Instead, in my reviews I try to describe the program as much as possible because programs are ultimately used by investors with very different objectives and strategies. No program is equally "good" for all investors. The best program for you is one that combines methods you've found valuable with the kind of effort you can devote to this task, and one that is well-suited to the kinds of assets you favor. You should read the reviews in this book with that in mind: Your goal is to find tools that work for you.

None of this, of course, guarantees that programs that are good comparatively, absolutely, and subjectively will always make money for an investor. A bad investor running a good program is perhaps worse than useless. The combination may be downright dangerous. But then, that's the subject of the next chapter.

# 1

# Five Rules for Building an Investing System

**M**ost of this book is about computers and software. This chapter is about you, the investor. Think of it as a kind of tune-up to get you ready for operating the kind of powerful tools described in the rest of this book.

Buying a computer, some software, and subscribing to an on-line service won't automatically make you a better investor. Computerized investing can put the information you need to make better investment decisions at your fingertips. It can let you run your investment screens far faster and with less effort than ever before. It can help you use complex mathematical tools to fine-tune the mix of assets in your portfolio while never getting your hands dirty with the calculations themselves. It can help you stay a jump ahead of the crowd. And it can locate obscure but profitable investment opportunities.

We haven't yet reached the point where all investment data is available to the individual investor on his or her computer, but we're certainly on the road toward that goal. Already you can find out not just the annual price-to-earnings ratio of a stock for the last five years, but you can also collect a sheaf of the newspaper articles on the chief executive officer and the members of the board of directors. Or find the opinions of the twenty-four Wall Street analysts who cover The Gap, and pull up dozens more opinions on the stock from investors and "experts."

The easy availability of all this information, however, has turned the traditional problem for the individual investor inside out. Once, he or she was handicapped by a lack of information. Now, an investor can be easily overwhelmed by all that's available easily and relatively inexpensively.

The novice electonic investor is likely to collect data simply because he or she can—I know that to be true because of my own experience. The proficient electronic investor, on the other hand, is one who has developed an investment system—some tested and proven, logical and complete way to invest in stocks, bonds, mutual funds, or some other asset class—and has built his or her use of computer, software, and data around that system. In short, this investor has developed an investment strategy first and then found the computer tools to most efficiently implement that strategy.

It takes hard work to make money consistently in the financial markets. (The key word, of course, is *consistently*.) Buying a computer and some investment software won't make that work go away. In fact, many investors discover that they're working harder than before. It's easy to see why. If before you bought a stock after reading a recommendation in a financial magazine and now you buy only after you've studied the stock in the way that I studied Rubbermaid, it's clear which method of investing takes more time.

Of course, most investors won't begrudge that time if it produces higher returns.

To make all this available information work for you and to enable you to focus on just the kinds of work that will pay a dividend, you need to understand the relationship between making money in the markets and information. Let's start with a simple question: Why does a stock go up? Why is a share of Intel, for example, worth $56 in December 1993, according to the stock market, and then worth $104 on May 1, 1995? (I could use other asset classes in a similar example, but I've used stocks because they are relatively familiar to most investors and play a role in most portfolios.)

Many investors, reflexively, would probably say that some news event has pushed the stock higher. The company has announced a new product, a quarterly report showed better than expected earnings, or new orders are running ahead of last year's sales.

But there's a problem with that answer. Let's take a specific event. On May 1, 1995, a New York brokerage firm, Bear Stearns, raised its 1996 earnings projections for Intel to $11 from $10 a share. (All these numbers came before Intel's June 1995 2-for-1 stock split.) It's not surprising that the stock went up on that news, but it is surprising that the stock moved up only $1.75 a share—or about 1.7 percent. Intel, trading at a price-to-earnings ratio of 17 (which says that investors are willing to pay $17 dollars per share to buy $1 per share of Intel's earnings), moves up only 1.7 percent on a 10 percent upgrade in projected earnings.

The market clearly didn't ignore the analyst's announcement; it just chose to take the upgrade with a grain of salt. This was a projection, after all. It isn't certain that Intel would earn even $10, let alone $11 in fiscal 1996. Investors might be willing to pay dollar for dollar for a guaranteed $11 in earnings—which would have bumped the price up, say, $10—but given the uncertainty that these earnings will really materialize, they are willing to pay

## TIPS ON THE TOOLS

# THE TROUBLE WITH PE

PE, the price-to-earnings ratio, is probably the most used term in the investment lexicon, and it is one of the simplest. It measures the ratio between a stock's price per share, say $30, and its earnings per share, say $2. That stock would have a price-to-earnings ratio of 15.

But while the math is simple and the concept easy to grasp, you should be constantly on watch for potential traps when you employ this common measure. First, are you talking about past or future earnings? Price-to-earnings ratios are based either on past, or "trailing" earnings, almost always for the last 12 months, or future projected earnings. It's easy to use projected price-to-earnings ratios to justify the purchase of stocks that are currently overpriced based on their trailing earnings. "Look," an investor might say, "if earnings go up to $4, the price-to-earnings ratio will be just 24, instead of 73." And if wishes were horses, beggars would ride.

Second, price-to-earnings ratios turn into unreliable indicators when the fortunes of a company are about to change direction. A cyclical company (that is, one whose profits and sales rise and fall with boom and bust

*continued*

cycles in the economy) like General Motors will show a high trailing price-to-earnings ratio (and thus seem too expensive to buy) just when earnings bottom as it starts coming out of the doldrums. And such a company will show its lowest price-to-earnings ratio (and thus seem undervalued and a good buy) just as earnings peak and the company heads back down toward the bottom of the cycle. It's important to analyze price-to-earnings ratios in the light of a company's peaks and troughs rather than as an absolute number.

Third, one-time charges (for writing down an unsuccessful product, perhaps) or gains (from the sale of excess real estate, for instance) can seriously distort a company's earnings picture and thus its price-to-earnings ratio. Always check to see that you or your data source corrects for such one-time events.

Unfortunately, not all programs and data sources clearly label and explain their price-to-earnings ratios as trailing or projected. Very few indicate the period used to calculate the ratio—a crucial omission since computerized data comes with varying time lags. Finally, most programs fail to indicate what earnings figures they use—as reported by the company or corrected for one time events, for example. When in doubt, ask. It can make a big difference in your calculations.

only a portion of that premium.

What would happen if, the next day, May 2, an analyst at Goldman Sachs also upgraded the firm's estimate of Intel's future earnings to $11 a share? Intel's price would climb again on the confirmation. That's curious—and revealing. The Goldman Sachs announcement breaks no new ground and adds no new information about the company. But it does change investors' belief in the likelihood of Intel actually earning $11 a share in 1996. And it's that change in belief that leads the price to increase.

And what would happen if, over the next few days, every analyst on Wall Street weighed in changing his or her projection to that $11 a share number? We would certainly expect the stock to continue to rise, but would you be willing to pay $187 (17 times the earnings of $11 a share) for it?

The logical investor who agreed with the analysts wouldn't. If the analysts are right, the stock is fairly priced and buying it won't earn you any money. If you think the analysts are wrong because they are too high, you wouldn't buy the stock, either. Only if you think the analysts are wrong because they are too low in their projections, would you buy the stock.

Derrick Niedermann, a former colleague of mine at *Worth*, loved to remind me that at any given moment, half of the people who trade in any stock are wrong. If I buy Intel at $75.50, or our hypothetical $187, I can only do so because someone else, who has done some kind of analysis, be it scientific or emotional, has decided that this is the time to sell. One of us must be wrong. At this price of $187 one of us wants to own the stock—because of what we see in the future—and the other doesn't—for precisely the same reason.

So let me formulate a set of reasons that explain why stocks go up.

**Expectations.** The prices of stocks—indeed the prices of all financial assets—are based on expectations of future events. Current events change stock prices because of the way that they change investors' projections for the future. We've all seen this happen and probably scratched our heads. A quarterly earnings report of $1.40 a share, up from $1.20, doesn't move a stock at all. Or maybe it even sends it sliding. The announcement won't move the stock's price at all if investors have already correctly projected $1.40 in earnings. They've already paid for the future, which is now confirmed. Report $1.35 a share, however, and the stock tumbles—because the future was built into today's stock price.

**History.** Stocks also have a past that determines their prices. In July of 1994, Intel traded at a price-to-earnings ratio of 11.46. Now 11.5 times earnings isn't a steep price for a company with Intel's growth rate. In fact, it seems downright cheap. At this same point in time, the market was willing to give the average stock in the Standard & Poor's 500 a price-to-earnings ratio of 16. Unlike that average S&P stock, over the last five years Intel had posted almost 30 percent annual growth in revenue and a little better than 38 percent annual growth in earnings. A growth company with earnings like these more typically trades at a multiple greater than its growth rate.

But Intel isn't just any growth company. It's a company that makes semiconductors, an industry with a historical tendency toward boom and bust. In times of booming sales, every company builds new factories. All those factories churning out chips send prices down, and that slide in prices becomes a nose-dive when the boom in sales ends. In 1985, for example, Intel barely eked out a profit, and in 1986 Intel showed steep losses. That put a lid on the price of the stock even as the semiconductor industry racked up the highest sales and growth rates in its history. Few investors thought Intel's growth could be sustained or that the industry had escaped from its boom and bust cycle. At least few believed until 1995, when suddenly Wall Street decided that Intel and a lot of other semiconductor companies had found a way to repeal that boom and bust cycle. With that change in mind-set now working in its favor, Intel gradually climbed from trading at a price-to-earnings ratio of 11.5 to one slightly over 26 by mid-July.

**Uncertainty.** The future and the past are very different beasts. While we can forecast the future, we cannot predict it. And the more complex the system we study, the more difficult even forecasting is. We can accurately forecast that the traffic light at our corner will turn from red to green at 30-second intervals after a relatively short period of study. The logic of the switch that controls the lights is simple and, barring mechanical failure, we can know the future of the traffic light. The financial markets are much more complex. Far too many agents are involved with far too many motives. We cannot specify the exact relationship between the economy and the markets. We cannot foresee how a rate cut by the Federal Reserve will ripple through the stock and bond markets. Sometimes we can't imagine what emotion led investors to rush into or out of a stock.

The past, however, can be known in immense and precise detail. While retrieving the data can be extremely time-consuming for the years before computers, we can know the price and price change of every stock and bond traded on every day and their volume. We can add to that detail about the economy, the money supply, exchange rates, and political events.

We can theorize from this pool of data about the past in an attempt to explain how the future—now the present—came to be. We can say that, all things being equal, some events cause stocks to go up, these send bonds for a tumble, those are irrelevant. Of course, all things are never equal, and we cannot, as we would in a laboratory experiment, eliminate the extraneous variables. No, we have to admit our intrinsic frustration. While it is the future that determines the price of a financial asset, only the past is known. And it is the uncertainty of the future that gives the financial markets the tremendous volume that they have and that makes large profits and losses possible.

**Risk.** A totally certain market wouldn't eliminate all profit. Investors who had put their money into some enterprise for a year or ten years would still demand interest for forgoing their use of that money for the time period.

Investors who buy three-month U.S. Treasury Bills—which are for all intents and purposes risk-free because only if the U.S. government fails do investors lose their principal—earn interest. But the rate is far less than that earned by investors in long bonds. The uncertainty of long bonds, our inability to predict the direction of interest rates and inflation over ten or twenty or even thirty years, earns investors a premium for investing in these assets

## BASICS

## MEASURING RISK

Even though quantifying risk is central to understanding how good an investment a stock, bond, or mutual fund is, there really isn't a single number that adequately measures risk in all situations. First, there are numbers such as *volatility* that measure the up and down movements of a stock, for example. A stock that one month is at 50 and the next month at 40 and the next month at 60 has a higher volatility than a stock that is at 50, then 52, and then 50 again. And investors commonly say that a more volatile stock is riskier.

The obvious problem with volatility, however, is that while some volatility is bad—when the stock sinks in price—and some volatility is good—when the stock goes up—raw volatility numbers don't show the difference. That's why some investors use a number called downside volatility that just looks at a stock's tendency to fall. Or they substitute measures that look at how much a stock or mutual fund has declined in its worst quarter in the last five years.

Second, there are numbers such as *standard deviation* that attempt to look at the pattern of a stock's volatility. Standard deviation is a statistical measure of how closely returns, or any other series of numbers, are grouped together. For example, the returns for the Fidelity Magellan Fund and CGM Capital Development, two successful mutual funds, show very different standard deviations over ten years, 16.62 and 24.70, respectively.

Putting standard deviation together with the average annual return will tell an investor how that average was produced—from annual returns that are relatively similar year to year or from returns that are up one year and down the next.

*continued*

Third, other risk measures attempt to compare the volatility of an investment with the volatility of the market. *Beta,* one of the key numbers in modern financial theory, compares the volatility of a specific stock or mutual fund to the volatility of the market as a whole. The beta of the entire market is defined as 1. A stock that is more volatile than the market earns a beta greater than 1, which means that if the market moves up 10 percent, a stock with a beta of 1.1 will move up 11 percent. The same works on the downside.

Betas of less than 1 can be misleading, however. An international mutual fund, for example, could earn a beta of .35, but that doesn't necessarily mean the fund is stable. Instead it could mean only that the fund is not very closely correlated with the U.S. stock market—that is, its movements could be independent of anything that happens in the U.S. market.

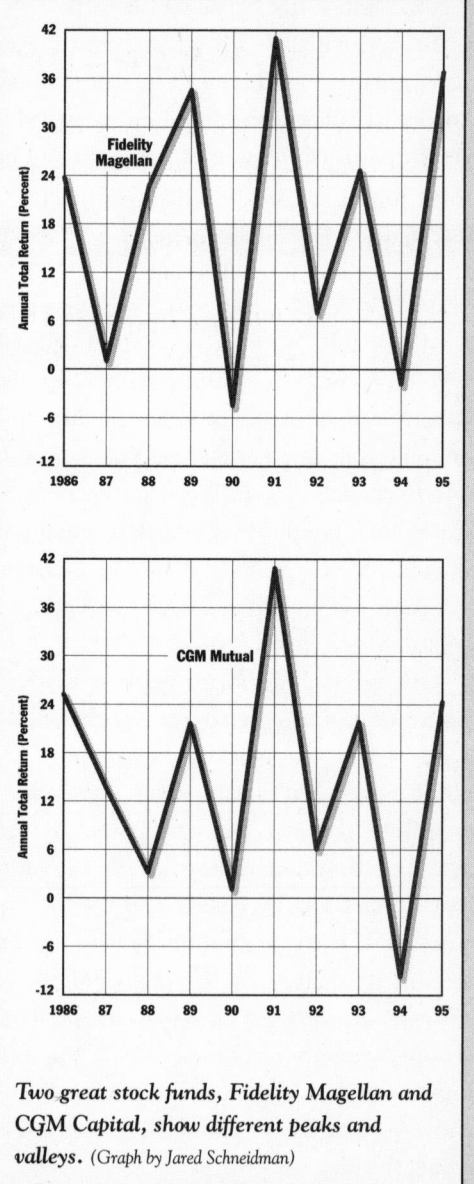

*Two great stock funds, Fidelity Magellan and CGM Capital, show different peaks and valleys.* (Graph by Jared Schneidman)

This is useful to know for investors interested in building a diversified portfolio, but it really doesn't say much about the risk of such a fund in itself. The only way to really get a complete handle on risk is to look at all these measures.

# BENCHMARKS

**A** dairy farmer wouldn't pay much for a cow that didn't give milk, but a chicken that never lactated would be a welcome addition to his barnyard. Smart investors don't expect all kinds of financial assets to produce the same kind of returns, either. From 1926 through 1995, for example, the stocks of large U.S. companies produced a mean total annual return of 10.5 percent. Long-term corporate bonds, in contrast, produced an average total annual return of 5.7 percent. To judge how well an individual stock, bond, or mutual fund is doing, savvy investors compare them to the appropriate benchmarks.

| Benchmark | % Compound Annual Return |
|---|---|
| Large company stocks | 10.5 |
| Small company stocks | 12.5 |
| Long-term Govt. Bonds | 5.7 |
| Treasury Bills | 3.7 |
| Inflation | 3.1 |

Data: Ibbotson Associates

over what they would earn by putting their money into Treasury bills, over and over again, for 30 years. On average, since 1926—a period during which Treasury bills earned an average 3.7 percent a year—that risk premium has been 2 percentage points. Large companies' stocks, whose prices swing up and down with the fortunes of individual companies, are even more risky, and earn an even higher return over time, 10.5 percent a year on average, or 4.8 percentage points a year more than long-term government bonds, from 1926 through 1995 according to Ibbotson Associates.

These four factors certainly don't exhaust the reasons that the market behaves like it does. But together they do tell us what kinds of investment study are worth performing and help us construct our investment toolbox. These factors don't determine what specific tools should be in our toolbox; instead they define the kinds of work we'll want to perform. A carpenter, for example, knows he will need to measure wood, join pieces of wood together, cut pieces of wood apart, shape wood, and smooth it. He can prefer a steel-shanked hammer to one with a wood handle, or replace either with a nail gun, but something that joins wood and joins it well will certainly be in his toolbox.

So what does knowing that profit and loss depend on expectations, history, uncertainty, and risk tell us about constructing our investors' toolbox? I think they identify five basic jobs that should guide our selection of tools. Every investor intent on building a computerized investment system will need to select specific tools that will perform each of these jobs, even though every investor will probably select a different package of programs to make up that system.

**1. Find patterns in the present—by reading the news electronically.** Of course, you want to stay on top of the news. You certainly don't want to be one of those investors who sells only to find out a day later that Wall Street analysts had upgraded the prospects for your stock a week ago. Nor would you like to be one of those investors who buys only to discover that margins at the company started to sag months ago.

But though reading the news is essential, it's not enough. Investors have to understand the direction of news about the overall market or a specific company. Knowing the trend is essential for following it—and for jumping off before it breaks (or on before it rockets upward).

That means constantly sifting through the news of the day, seeing if you can connect two dots and then three. An isolated fact is almost impossible to analyze. Yes, a big competitor of a company you hold in your portfolio issued a bad earnings report that cites falling prices in its industry. Too many of its competitors have built new factories recently. Is that good or bad for your stock? You can't tell.

The next week you notice that your company has confirmed plans to build a new factory. By itself that sounds like good news—your company sees a bright future with growing demand for its product. But the previous story about industry oversupply suggests that its meaning is less clear.

The student of the present isn't confused by this conflict, however. Instead he becomes focused. The specific issues that are critical for his stock emerge. Is the industry suffering from overcapacity across all product lines? Has this company found a critical edge, in technology or in manufacturing, that enables it to keep its prices high or perhaps even to increase profits as prices fall? Sifting though the present tells you what you need to know.

The electronic investor who uses an on-line news reader can do that sifting far more efficiently than a print-based colleague. The best on-line news readers have five advantages over even a great investor's newspaper such as the *Wall Street Journal*. First, you can personalize the contents so that you see stories on just the investments you care about. Second, you will get some information that isn't in the newspaper or get it ahead of the newspaper. Third, you'll be able to check more news sources than you can afford or find time to read in print. A good news reader might, for example, offer news from Dow Jones, the *New York Times*, the *Financial Times*, industry journals, and press releases. Fourth, you will be able to retrieve old stories that you missed when they first ran or that you have forgotten. And fifth, you'll be able to archive stories electronically so that you can pull up that tiny squib about the new factory months from now without looking through a pile of yellowing newspaper clips. (You'll find some information about news readers in Chapter 2 and a more complete discussion with reviews in Chapter 6.)

**2. Study your fellow investors to learn what they're watching—and what they're not.** Since expectations count, find out how other investors value any stock you're considering. Know what worries other investors and how uncertain they feel. The financial markets are too complex for anyone to keep every factor under study at all times. In effect, the market as a whole and investors individually deal with this problem by rotating their attention from one part of the picture to another. On a macro-level, investors pay attention to only part of the global picture at any one time. Interest rates may be rising, but investors may be concentrating on rising earnings. The dollar may be sinking like a stone, but investors may be focused on the growth of the domestic economy. One day the market may change focus and the falling dollar or rising rates may become the center of attention, but until then these very real forces aren't going to move the market as much as the interests du jour. Knowing both what is happening in the real world and what the market is fixated on is critical. The combined knowledge will let an investor buy or sell ahead of the crowd and also gives the investor patience with his or her own investment decisions.

On a micro-level, the level of individual stocks and bonds, the same principal is at work. The Gap may be showing 25 percent earnings growth, but the market may be fixated on the pressure on the company's margins. Nucor Steel may be the industry's most efficient producer and the company most able to thrive in a downturn, but the market may be worried about declining steel prices.

Knowing what makes your fellow investors twitch is partly an intuitive art. But you can learn a lot about the sentiments of other investors by watching how they react to news on the economy and individual companies. Track what's moving the stocks in your portfolio and pay particular attention to signs that the market is starting to discount news it once found important.

And don't forget to keep tabs on the professionals, too. Study the earnings estimates issued by Wall Street analysts and the economic forecasts by Wall Street economists. Set up a shadow portfolio of investments that you are considering for purchase and track news and its effects on them.

Many different types of programs will perform one part of this job or another for you. News readers will help you track events and announcements. On-line services and frequently updated databases will provide crucial information on prices and trading volume so that you can correlate news with market reaction. Those same kinds of services and programs will track analyst expectations and projected earnings as they rise and fall. (You'll find on-line services in chapter 6 and stock databases in Chapter 3.) To help you keep track of real and shadow portfolios you can use a portfolio tracking program. (You can find a descriptive list of some good ones in Chapter 4.)

**3. Study the past—graphically.** Consider these two ways to look at a stock. On May 1, 1995, shares of The Gap, the ubiquitous clothing retailer, closed at $31.875. For the trailing twelve months, the company showed $2.20 a share in earnings, up almost 24 percent over the prior twelve months. (Dividends came to $.40 cents a share.) At this price the company is trading at about 15 times trailing earnings. Should you buy?

Any computer program and many paper sources can give you plenty of data about the stock's past. The stock is well off its 1992 high of $53.50, and that's understandable. While the company earned just $1.62 a share in 1992, earnings grew at 59 percent that year. Investors were willing to pay more for a company with that kind of growth record—presuming, wrongly in this case, that the company would continue to grow at that rate—and The Gap showed a price-to-earnings ratio of 33. The company instead saw earnings fall in 1993. But the last two years have seen growth resume at 21 percent in fiscal 1994 and 24 percent in fiscal 1995. An investor could say that the company seems to have settled into a new pattern and feel justi-fied in projecting 20 percent (if he or she was conservative) or 25 percent growth in 1996. Using 25 percent, the company should see earnings hit $2.75.

Then what's the projected price of The Gap in a year? Well, if the stock traded at the 1993 price-to-earnings ratio, it would be $90.75. At the cur-rent 15, it would be $41.25. That's a whole lot of uncertainty—which of course means that investing in The Gap is both risky and potentially prof-itable.

By drawing pictures of the past, you can discover which possible future outcomes are more likely. For example, I can graph The Gap's past price-to-earnings ratio. Yes, I know that I've already told you that in the past the company has traded at a price-to-earnings ratio of somewhere between 15 and 33. But that doesn't mean the company has traded at 15 as often as it has at 33, nor that it ever traded at 24, the average of those two extremes.

All financial assets show patterns of behavior. They have a range of nor-mal behavior, which circumscribes how they behave much of the time, and they have years of odd behavior where they deviate from their normal range.

Investors often borrow a tool from statisticians called "standard devia-tion" to describe the behavior of a financial asset. For example, many mu-tual fund databases will tell you that fund A has a standard deviation of 2.56 and fund B has a standard deviation of 4.23. From that you can pretty easily figure out that fund B deviates more than fund A. But how much more? And when? And under what circumstances? There's nothing better than a picture to turn that number and other statistics into something that an investor can really grasp.

For example, the graph on the next page shows the earnings per share of Coca-Cola from 1985 through 1994 and the earnings per share of Intel over the same years and the earnings per share for Ford Motor Company. Coke is a blue-chip consumer company—investors are willing to buy it even at a price-to-earnings ratio of 30 because of the straightline pattern of its growth. Intel is the somewhat erratic growth company. It's growing faster than Coke, but look how earnings can deviate from the straight line. Ford is a classic cyclical stock. Its earnings soar when the economy soars and turn sour when the economy does the same. The pictures make these truths easier to grasp and understand than any table of numbers or single statistical measure could.

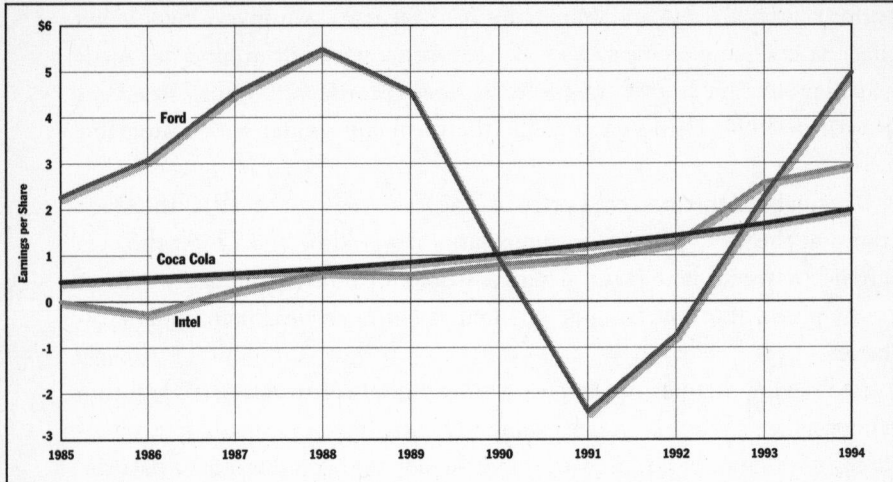

*These lines capture the character of a blue chip, a high-octane growth issue, and a cyclical stock.* (Graph by Jared Schneidman)

Graphs are the best way to see a lot of data at once and understand its significance. To construct one, you'll need good data from the past and tools to draw the graphs. Stock analysis programs and technical analysis programs often come with tools for constructing graphs that bring out the patterns in the past. I cover these types of software in Chapters 4 and 8 respectively. Unfortunately, most of the stock and mutual fund database programs I discuss in Chapters 3 and 5 don't provide adequate graphical tools. But investors can make up for this by using the graphical abilities of spreadsheet programs such as Excel and statistical programs such as Statistica and Mathematica. These programs draw pictures using the data supplied by these databases. I discuss spreadsheet and statistical programs in Chapter 9.

**4. Ask "What if?"** It's not enough to understand the "causes" of the past and to know what constitutes "normal" behavior. It's not even enough to be able to predict when a trend is about to change. If you really want to profit from your knowledge, you need to know what will happen if the change you've foreseen actually comes to pass.

Looking at The Gap, for example, even in a relatively superficial way, an investor can see that times of high earnings growth occur when the sales are rising in existing stores ("Stores that have been open at least a year" is the standard retail definition), when the company is adding new stores, when inventories are not increasing (a sign that merchandise is selling), and when margins are above 13 percent. All these factors can also be charted over time. Profit margins, for example, have swung between 11.5 and 14.7 during 1990 through 1994. A swing above or below that level, even for one quarter, would suggest to an investor that the company might be ready to break out of its normal range of behavior—a sign either to dump the stock or to load up.

But how big an impact on the company's earnings would a change in any of these factors have? Say that you notice that the company announced plans to open 160 new stores next year, up from just 25 this year. Would reaching that goal add 10 cents share to earnings or $1? And what about failure? What would happen to earnings if the company opened just 80 stores—half the goal?

An investor needs to be able to ask "What if?" and see how a change in margins or sales or stores open a year or prices ripples through a specific company. This is exactly the kind of repetitive task that computers are best at.

The best stock-picking, mutual fund, and economics programs all have the ability to build "what if" scenarios and change them quickly—as do good spreadsheets. Project earnings per share five years into the future if sales grow at 12 percent a year and margins drop a percentage point from current levels. Then change the scenario by deciding that sales will grow at 13 percent. And then change it again by specifying a different margin with both the original and modified rates of growth for sales. Not all companies are as equally sensitive to changes in the same variables. This kind of analysis will show you exactly what kind of events are most likely to pose a problem or take the stock straight through the roof.

**5. Make sure you get paid for the risks you take.** Higher uncertainty, indicated either by highly variable patterns in the past or by a "what if" that shows big changes resulting from relatively minor differences in a factor such as sales or margins or interest rates, should earn a higher return. In gambler's terms, if I'm going to bet on the unlikely upset, I want good odds.

Take the example of Arakis Energy, a stock recommendation from Lawrence Auriana that we published in a September 1994 article on high-risk investments. This recently formed oil company had acquired a potentially huge oil concession in the Sudan. Only one problem: The country was locked in civil war and one side or the other could easily blow up the company's yet-to-be-constructed pipeline. The stock was trading at less than $5, but it could easily go to zero. On the other hand, if the company did manage to get oil to market, the stock could run to $70 or $100. Lots of risk, yes. But it's also a lot of reward.

Is the trade-off worth it? To answer that question, an investor needs benchmarks and standardized tools (standard deviation, Sharpe ratio, volatility, and beta are a few) to compare assets. Good programs on stocks and mutual funds should provide a comprehensive list of benchmarks and measures for comparing risk and reward among assets.

And you'll also need enough history to put an investment in context. Bond mutual funds didn't look risky at the beginning of 1994—the first losing year for bonds since 1974—to investors who hadn't studied what happened to these investments the last time the Federal Reserve raised interest rates. Stocks don't look risky now to investors who don't know how painful the bear market of 1973–1974 was or how unexpectedly it began. The best programs on stocks and mutual funds include enough historical data so that you can draw an accurate picture of your risk that includes the unexpected and the infrequent.

That's it. These five jobs obviously don't exhaust the possible tasks confronting every investor, but a toolbox that is filled with programs that can take on these tasks will give you a way to analyze almost any market situation. You'll be prepared to make sense of market history and to see trends in the making. You'll know if you are ahead of your fellow investors, out of step with them, or just lagging behind. You'll be able to assess the risk that you are taking with individual stocks and in your portfolio as a whole—and insure that your potential reward is appropriately high.

There are lots of specific tools that will tackle these jobs in very different ways. A technical analysis program using Japanese candlestick graphs is a very different kind of graphing tool than a statistical package such as Mathematica, for example. The choice of specific tools will depend on your investment strategy, preferred investment assets, individual temperament, and other factors. But that's what the rest of this book is for. Shall we get started?

# 2

# Entry Points: The Two Best Programs and the One Best On-line Service for Beginners

**W**hat would the ideal beginners' program be like?

It would certainly be easy to learn, logically organized, give plenty of help, guide the beginner to commonsense investment decisions, and be so graphically appealing that it would be fun, or at least a pleasure, to work with. I think that's a reasonable definition and, after looking at many of the programs designed for the beginner—Quicken, Simply Money, Microsoft Money, Managing Your Money, and Reuters Money Network—I think that's approximately what the creators of these programs aimed to produce. By and large, they succeeded.

But I think they left out one important rule. A good beginners' program shouldn't be a dead-end. It should serve the absolute beginner, true, but that investor won't be a complete neophyte for long. A great beginners' program should grow with the investor. The first tools, the ones that an investor masters initially, should lay the foundation for more advanced tools and more complex investment strategies. Almost without being aware of the process, an investor should discover new tools and data in the program as he or she learns the software. A beginners' program should enable an investor to perform simple investment tasks and prepare him or her for more complex strategies and software tools.

Of course, the beginner could abandon that first program and buy something entirely new. But it takes too much work to set up one of those "easy" programs for me to be willing to take you down a street that, after a very nice ride of just a mile or two, will leave you facing a road sign that says, "Sorry, that's as far as this software goes—find another program." A beginner, in fact anybody no matter how expert who buys a program, should hope for a long learning curve. We all want to begin using a program quickly, but we don't want to outgrow it within a few months.

Making a program both easy to operate from the beginning and complex enough so that it will continue to reveal new functions as the user progresses certainly isn't trivial. Some of the most popular "beginners'" programs, which in other ways are superbly designed pieces of software, haven't managed to reach both goals. But a few have. I'd like to point them out because they are great programs for getting started—yet good enough to earn a place in even an experienced user's toolbox.

Even the experienced electronic investor can learn something from thinking about the process I describe here. Beginners, after all, aren't the only investors who ever have to master a new program. Experienced users who buy a new program also need to approach that new software with a learning strategy if they hope to eventually get everything out of the program. It's just as easy for an experienced user as for a beginner to get discouraged when facing the complexity of a new program, or to get stuck using only a few tools, usually the first ones mastered, and never finish a thorough exploration of the entire program. So although this chapter is about tools for beginners, it's also about learning how to use any piece of software.

Let's start with a situation that I call the "beginner's trap." I'm going to use Quicken as my example here, not because it's a bad program, but because it's a superb example of the problem. It's also undoubtedly the program most frequently recommended to beginners. (For this example, I'm using Quicken for Macintosh. At the end of this chapter I've reviewed the Windows version, as well as Quicken Deluxe on CD-ROM. Since this is a book on electronic investing and not on computerized checkbooks, I'm going to ignore all the program's features except those that an investor might use.)

Quicken, by Intuit, is easy to use, logical, good at doing what it's supposed to do, and graphically pleasant. By borrowing the format of a checkbook so that a user begins by filling in a register that resembles the one you use to keep track of your checks, the designers of Quicken make it possible for almost anyone to start using the program in less than an hour. These are pretty remarkable achievements. That's why the program has 7 million users.

Call me picky. That's just not good enough.

How would a beginner get started on Quicken? First step: Open an investment account. The program asks you to name it (call it IRA; you're going to use this account to track all the investments in your individual retirement account) and to characterize it (investment account, single mutual fund, money market, and a few more choices.) That's it. The account and its ledger are now set up. That was easy.

But the account is empty. So you begin filling in the blanks of the ledger. Date comes first. Today's is already entered. Then transaction type. A pull-down menu gives you choices: You select "Buy." And then you type in the name of one of your current stocks, Electronic Arts. 300 shares. Price $36.25 today. Commission. You fill in the typical Schwab charge of $55. And you're done.

Well, not really. Before hitting "Record" you survey your work. This can't be right. You bought this stock some time ago at an average price of $18 and change a share. The ledger as you've filled it in so far mixes up current prices with past prices. That won't do. You certainly won't be able to figure out what you made from the purchase unless you enter the historical prices. So you dig into your paper files to find out when you bought these shares and how much you paid. Three lots at three different prices and on three different dates. Three commissions. You enter all that. *Now* you're done. If you click on "Reports" at the top of the screen and ask for "Performance" the program will tell you that you've earned a $5,250 profit on these shares. Neat.

Of course, you still have to enter the same information for the other eleven stocks, bonds, and mutual funds that you own in this account. Entering some of them isn't nearly as simple as Electronic Arts was, either. You own a Time-Warner bond, for example. It pays interest quarterly. Same with some electric utility shares you own. To give the program enough data to calculate performance on the bond and these shares you have to enter every interest payment, every dividend received for as long as you owned the investment. Talk about boring. Unfortunately, you've held these utility shares for a long time—six years. Entering your entire

## TIPS ON THE TOOLS

# SOME PRICES ARE BETTER THAN OTHERS

**M**ost investors know that the stock prices supplied by most investment software—and certainly by all of the mass market packages—aren't current. Most commonly they're delayed by fifteen minutes.

But few investors realize that many programs—Reuters Money Network is one—report composite prices. Many stocks, and certainly most major equities, trade on more than one exchange. You can buy shares of Coca-Cola, for example, on the New York Stock Exchange and on the smaller Chicago, Philadelphia, and Boston exchanges. And since stock prices are essentially set from moment to moment by auction, the prices at the different exchanges can vary.

That's not a problem if all you're doing with these quotes is tracking the day-to-day returns on your portfolio. It can be quite another matter, however, if you try to trade on these prices, since they don't actually exist on any individual exchange. (Don't get mad at your broker, therefore, if he can't find the quote you see.) If you set tight limits when you trade—placing a buy order, for example, for a stock trading at $34.25, for purchase at no more than $34.375)—you should find another source of quotes: the combination of fifteen-minute delays and composite prices makes it impossible to judge the market that finely with these quotes.

(You also ought to make it standard practice to ask your broker where your trade will be placed. Many brokers have started to move trades to the smaller regional exchanges because it helps their firm's bottom line, even though the New York Stock Exchange usually has the most efficient pricing for an investor.)

portfolio of eleven investments takes you four hours.

But finally you're done. Now it's time to put Quicken through its paces and see all the neat stuff your four hours of clerical work has earned you. So you begin cruising through the menu bar; it takes only a few clicks to find the command for automatically updating the prices of the stocks in your portfolio by modem. You're already a CompuServe member so to set up this service all you have to do is enter your CompuServe account number and password, the port that your modem uses, and tell the machine whether you have pulse or tone phone service. But then you have to enter, all over again, not just the names of the stocks and mutual funds that you want to update, but the ticker symbols. (We're talking another hour here of clerical work. Time is starting to add up. Of course, you only have to do all this bookkeeping once.) Quicken comes with a Standard & Poor's Stock Guide, so you can look up each stock and find its symbol and then type it into the Quick Quotes stock list. Then hit "update" and bingo, in a minute you've got all the current prices in a list and in your account. Whoops. You typed in the wrong symbol for the Japan Fund and the price is wacky—it should be $8.78, but instead it's $14.50. You double-check and then correct the symbol.

Okay. What else can you do?

## BASICS

# MODEMS, THE CURSE OF THE ELECTRONIC INVESTOR

**U**nless you really want to spend time in computer hell, don't buy an off-brand modem and cheap communications software. Most investment programs attempt to steer the user past the arcane details of hooking up a modem—so that you never have to look up initialization strings, for example—by allowing you to pick your modem from a pull-down menu of choices. Woe to the those whose modem isn't on the list and have to rely on the hope that a general modem setting will work for them. I'd recommend sticking with the modems produced by companies such as U.S Robotics, Zoom, Supra, Motorola, and Global Village. If you're purchasing both an investment program and a modem at the same time, ask the software company what modem brands their software supports. If they say, "We support them all," rephrase your question (rather than laughing) and ask what brands are listed in their communications setup program.

Don't get a modem slower than 14,400 bits per second (a measure of how fast the modem transmits data)—most on-line data services now support 9,600 bps modems and are on their way to 14,400. Consider a 28,800 (and make sure that the modem uses the V.34 standard) if the price is right and forget about paying up for anything faster if you're communicating over ordinary telephone lines.

*continued*

Most investment software now comes with its own communications software, so you may not even need to install the software that comes with the modem (fortunately, since some of it is pretty minimal)—or buy a third-party communications program. But if you use a lot of bulletin boards or pull up data from a number of different sources, check out a powerful communications package such as Crosstalk from DCA/Attachmate (800-348-3221), HyperAccess from Hilgraeve, Inc. (800-826-2760), Qmodem Pro from Mustang Software (800-999-9619), ProComm Plus, from Datastorm Technologies (314-443-3282), MicroPhone from Software Ventures (510-644-3232), and White Knight from FreeSoft (412-846-2700). Programs like this often come with prewritten routines for dialing in to the major databases, which make it easy to write and save routines for calling up the electronic sources you use most frequently.

But no matter how hard you try, you'll still spend more time wrestling with your modem than you counted on. (And some manufacturers don't do much to take the wrinkles out. I still remember opening the box on my U.S. Robotics Sportster to discover that the modem didn't come with a cable to connect it to my computer. You'll learn a lot about the current state of non-service in computer superstores if you try to get help in one to buy a $10 cable. Fortunately, we still have Radio Shack.) Modem technology relies on matching arcane codes that allow two computers to talk to each other. A line of code in the wrong order or a misplaced prefix can stop you cold. Call the maker of the software package you're trying to use. They have an obligation to help you through the mess (and they're going to be more able to help you if your modem is a brand that they run across frequently.)

The most common and easily fixed reason for a modem to fail to communicate is that the user has specified the wrong communications port on the computer. Remember, many laptops and desktop machines use different ports. The first thing to try if a new modem won't work is changing the "com port" setting from 1 to 2, or vice versa.

You'd love to know how your investments have done. So go to "Reports" and poke around. There's a report for capital gains that lists the realized gains on securities you've sold. This will be useful at tax time. It will give you a list of all the individual buys and sells that you've done and the return/loss on each.

But that's just accounting for the IRS, and you keep moving down the Reports menu to the investment performance report. Here you can get what you want, although first you have to decide what you want. You can get performance calculated in either IRR or ROI. You go to Help for definitions. Help defines ROI (return on investment) as "dollar amount of your investment earnings divided by the dollar amount of your investment, expressed as a percentage"; IRR (internal rate of return) refers you to "average annual total return," which says, "a percentage equal to the interest rate on a bank account that would give you the same total return on your investment." The IRR or the average annual total return, Help continues, "takes into account money earned from the investment (interest, dividends, capital gains distributions), as well as changes in share price and negative cash flow such as brokers' fees." That sounds like what you entered all those quarterly dividends for, so you ask for IRR.

Pretty nifty. Some of the results are really gratifying. Your running position in Electronic Arts, a software company that produces games for Nintendo and Sega and home computers, shows an average annual return of 52.7 percent. Some results are embarrassing. Your return on Merck (which you've owned since 1992) is just 1.7 percent annually, on average.

And some results are really surprising. A run-of-the-mill utility investment such as San Diego Gas & Electric has returned 9.8 percent on average a year—even though the stock is currently in the dumper along with most utility stocks. The investment shows this decent return because you bought the stock in 1986 and 1987 when no one liked it. Might be time to buy more, you think, since everyone hates it again. You hadn't realized that Inco Limited, the world's largest nickel producer, had moved up so strongly in the month you'd owned it—about 20 percent. You make a note to run some numbers to see if it's time to buy more or get out. That was useful, but there doesn't seem to be a way to get an average annual return for the portfolio as a whole. That might be useful in projecting your progress toward retirement.

On to the portfolio value report. Not very useful. It doesn't include dividends, so dividend-bearing stocks show up in a bad light. It's really just a list of unrealized capital gains/losses in the portfolio at this point in time, based on purchase price. It might be useful for planning tax-related selling, but as a long-term investor you try to avoid that kind of investing, so this report doesn't serve your interests.

The newest versions of Quicken (version 5 for Windows and version

6 for Macintosh) have added a feature called "Portfolio View." By clicking on that option under the View command, I can see all my accounts unified into a single portfolio. That's useful for investors who spread positions in a single stock or mutual fund among several accounts, and it lets me see what part of my portfolio is allocated to each instrument. "Portfolio View" also comes with lots of new ways to look at performance, including such measures as market value, return on investment, cost of position, and average cost per share.

And that's pretty much everything the Macintosh version of

## BASICS

# CALCULATING PERFORMANCE

**S**ome methods of calculating performance are, frankly, better than others. None work perfectly in all circumstances.

A few basic distinctions. Performance is either simple—without counting the increased returns that come from reinvesting interest or dividends and getting interest on that interest—or compound. Returns can either be stated as a total for a period, as in "the ten-year total return on the portfolio recommended by the California Technology Stock Letter is 425 percent," or turned into an annual rate, the average annual compounded rate of return. For that same newsletter, the average annual compounded rate of return (usually just stated as average annual return) for the same ten-year period comes to 18 percent.

Performance can also either be total or partial. Terms like *gain* or *appreciation* measure only the returns that come from the price appreciation of an investment. *Total return* counts both price appreciation and dividends or interest, if any.

When reading about the returns that other investors, professional or individual, have recorded, consult the fine print carefully to see not just how the returns were calculated and what they measure, but what they assume about reinvestment. For example, the returns cited by investment clubs that follow the National Association of Investors Corporation rules always include reinvested dividends—and thus take advantage of compounding. If you don't reinvest your dividends, your results will differ from theirs even if you picked exactly the same stocks and invested at exactly the same moment.

Quicken can do for you as an investor. I know. I've used the program since 1988, but I haven't been able to find much more that I want to do with it than calculate the net value of my portfolio, automatically download prices, jigger the portfolio view to track my asset allocation (new in the most recent version of Quicken I bought this year), and figure the return on each stock, bond, or mutual fund I hold.

Each year my data files get longer and harder to abandon. I have some hope of being able to move on whenever I see another program that promises to convert Quicken data, but that promise always turns out to mean that the program will automatically move my budget and household accounts, but not my investment portfolios. I'm actually quite happy keeping that domestic information where it is. Quicken is a great program for tracking my household getting and spending. It's my investment accounts that I want to move, and that never seems possible.

I do have one hope—that my copy of Quicken will simply crash and burn on me one day and I'll have to move. Think it can't happen? I've already been through the experience once, a number of years ago. (And yes, I do keep backup disks. But hey, I'm not that much better than the next guy at keeping backup copies completely up to date.)

Investors who run their software in Windows will find additional features in that version of Quicken (the Macintosh version is now approximately a generation behind). For example, Quicken has added graphs of stock performance to the Windows 95 version that do a far better job at tracking a stock's change in price than the old thumbnail-size graphs in the earlier versions. The charts are also linked to news stories. Once you've set up a list of stocks that you want to track regularly, Quicken will let you download news stories by modem. Those stories are also marked on the graph of the appropriate stock so that an investor can see if there is a connection between a price move and a news event. It's an impressive new feature.

But many investors who've been using another mass market investment program will find these additions old hat. In fact, as a piece of investment software, Quicken is now playing catch-up with one of its competitors—one that I'd like to recommend to the beginners (and even some of the not-so-beginners) in the audience. It's called Reuters Money Network in its Windows version and WealthBuilder in its Macintosh incarnation.

---

**TIPS ON THE TOOLS**

# THE DEPARTMENT OF
# REDUNDANCY DEPARTMENT

It's not enough to know you need to make backup copies of all your programs and all your computer files—you actually need to do it. Regularly. That means developing a routine that will allow you to avoid the worst of any computer catastrophe.

I use a triple-backup system. First, I make a daily backup copy of all my working files every time I make a change in one of those files. Add a stock transaction. Revise a news list. I store this daily backup on my hard disk—the same place that I keep the original.

Now this will protect me if I accidentally erase a file while I'm using it, but it won't save me if my hard drive crashes, wiping out or scrambling everything on it. Second, to protect me from that, I copy the entire drive once a week to an external backup. I use a Zip Drive from Iomega, which stores 100MB on a cartridge. (Syquest makes a similar drive.) If you have bigger storage needs than I do, you'll want to consider a large external hard drive or a tape backup.

Third, I keep extra copies—that means a copy besides the original—of all my applications software on 3.5 inch disks. That way I never have to reload a program from the original. Call me paranoid, but there are a lot of computer viruses out there and if my hard drive got contaminated, the last thing I'd want to do is put an application at risk by using the original disks to reload it.

## WEALTHBUILDER: A FIRST LESSON IN WHY
## IT'S SOMETIMES SMART NOT TO FOLLOW DIRECTIONS

Now, my recommendation may come as a surprise to anyone who has actually tried the WealthBuilder program, since this program comes with the most cumbersome, self-defeating, annoying, time-wasting setup routine that I've ever encountered in a piece of software (and I've run some turkeys). If you follow the program's menu for getting started, you'll never get to the good stuff. In fact, I think you'll probably stuff it back in the box. Which is really too bad because this is, once you get past all that endless introduction, one of the best investment programs going for beginners and more experienced users, too. It's well designed, the communications program—often the weak link in financial software—is sturdy and hardly ever fails, and the entire package puts some extraordinarily powerful tools on your desktop for less than $50.

So I'm going to teach you how to subvert the system and avoid all the steps the program argues are absolutely necessary.

Here's the crucial bit of advice. It's real simple. When, after about four screens, the program gives you the option of filling out all the personal information or going to expert mode—GO TO EXPERT. I don't care if you've never invested before and don't know a hard drive from a bagel. GO TO EXPERT. Otherwise you're going to spend days filling in information about your mortgage and household expenses and the age of your children and the average number of pieces of luggage you took on your last vacation before you get to do anything that is remotely connected to investing. Like Quicken, WealthBuilder assumes that you want a financial planning program. Unlike Quicken, you can void that assumption and go directly to investing. How directly? Select expert, enter a few preferences (remember you can always go back and fill in all this personal data later) to set up your modem, hit "Connect," and whammo, "Look, Mom, I'm investing."

The first thing that the program downloads after you've connected via your modem to the WealthBuilder database is a capsule summary of

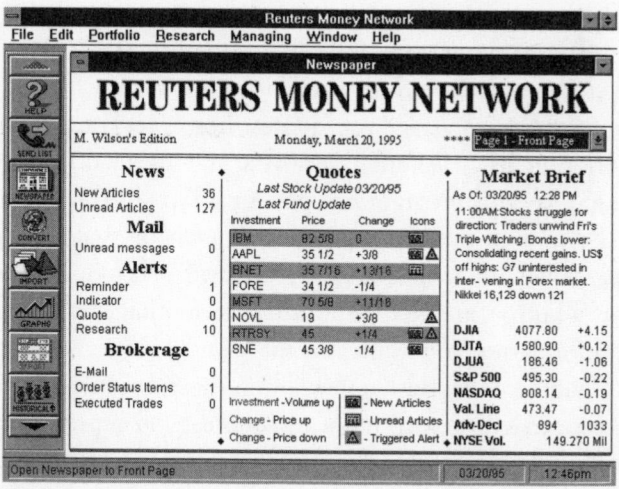

*WealthBuilder uses a newspaper analogy to organize stock news and prices.* (*Courtesy of Reality On-line Inc.*)

today's market activity. Reading how stocks are doing at this moment and about five sentences of explanation will keep you busy while your computer finishes downloading the remainder of your information. A "ding" announces WealthBuilder is finished. Click on "Done" to move to the main screen. (WealthBuilder automatically logged your modem off once it had downloaded all the data. You stay off-line—thus no communications charges—until you want to update your data.)

The WealthBuilder main screen, which is set up like a newspaper page, is the home base for everything you'll do with this program. On page one of your newspaper, you'll find a market brief with the major averages as of 2:57 P.M. (it's now 3:00 P.M.) and a market synopsis: "Blue chips lower. Nervousness tomorrow's jobs report."

This "newspaper" comes with a table of contents (if you click on a button in the upper right). Page 2 is news. It's blank right now, except for a category called "General News" and some samples of investment newsletters. General news lists news digests of the *Washington Post* business section and front page, the *New York Times* business section, and the *Wall Street Journal* and a barrage of other stories on business and economics. The newsletter section includes a sample of James Stack's *InvesTech* technical market letter on the day I signed on.

But you can fill up this newspaper with just the stories that you want to read. Clicking on "News Manager" gives you a "form" for adding the name of stocks (either by typing in the ticker or the name of the company. The program even supplies the ticker automatically if you type in the company name. (If you don't find something that basic impressive, you haven't run other investment programs.)

This news list won't get you quotes, however. For that you have to set up another list. (Damned annoying having to do the work twice, but I didn't say this program was perfect.) Type in the tickers or names of stocks—mutual funds, too—that you own or that you follow with the idea of buying someday. With the two lists—quotes and news—done, hit a button marked "Send List," verify that you're asking for the kind of information you want, and hit "Send."

Downloading takes just a few minutes and while Reuters is busy stuffing your machine with news and quotes, you get the market update screen to study again. A second viewing starts to reveal a few flaws. The top half is okay—the market update is up to the minute—well, actually a fifteen-minute delay—on selected markets and indexes (NYSE, NASDAQ, S&P, Utilities and Transports, Value Line) with volume and advance/decline numbers just for the New York Exchange alone. But market highlights on the bottom of the screen aren't very useful. They're simply not current. At 3:17 P.M. for example, it's still commenting on the 2:10 P.M. market. (That's especially frustrating on a day when something is about to break. One day the news flash told me that the markets are waiting for the International Monetary Fund and Mexico to announce a deal. But the flash was hours behind and I was left to wonder whether the deal was done and every other investor knew it.)

But the graphics are great. Bright color. Big buttons on the side for Help, Send List, Newspaper, Convert, Import, Graphs, Report, Historical. When the download is complete, hit "Done" again. This time the "newspaper" main screen tells you how many news stories are waiting on page 2 and how your portfolio has done since you last priced it (at least it *would* tell you, but you deliberately haven't entered a portfolio, remember?).

The news page begins with general headlines, which range from the useful (to me) to the completely pointless (to me). After using Reuters for a couple of months I learned that I really don't miss anything if I just delete all these general news stories without checking. There is unfortunately no way to customize the headline service.

The real meat of the news page is in the folders on individual companies. When I first started to use WealthBuilder I used it to follow the news of the day on stocks that I either owned or was thinking about buying. So on January 20, 1995, I read Apple Computer's earnings report and reaction to it, "Revenue Growth Called Disappointing." I also got a brief notice that S. G. Warburg analyst David Wu had upgraded the stock. Or on July 13, I read another story on an analyst from CS First Boston upgrading Apple and a story about Trimble Navigation's upcoming secondary offering.

I didn't bother to read a lot of the seventy-five news stories I got on individual companies. From the headline list (WealthBuilder first presents the story as a headline; only if you click on "Read" do you see the full text. Sometimes the story is so long that you have to "fetch" it from the database on your next download.) I can tell that I've already read some of these stories in the *Wall Street Journal* that morning, or that I'm not interested in an announcement about the new advertising agency for Williams-Sonoma. But some stories are items I missed in the *Journal* or that show up on WealthBuilder first. I found myself reading brief notes about analyst upgrades, items on big block trades of a stock, earnings news, and the occasional product announcement.

## CREATING A PORTFOLIO OF STOCKS TO CONSIDER

Why stop with tracking only the stocks that you already own? I've found that closely following the price of a stock I might buy gives me a feel for its price trends and volatility. I can literally watch it dive toward support levels, try to bust through a ceiling, or jiggle in a trading range. Keeping a folder of news on the stock builds a picture of management and strategy. Patterns start to emerge. I notice odd facts that fall into place to form a larger picture.

You can go about building an alternative portfolio in two ways. In the first, the portfolio is just a grab bag of stocks that you find attractive and a device to let you follow each one regularly. After you've checked the stocks you really own, it's time to open the "alternatives" portfolio, update and study their prices, check news on each, and maybe run one or two through one of the stock analysis programs in Chapter 4. Putting these possible investments in their own portfolio means you can easily track their performance and compare each of these stocks with those you already own.

To ensure that this portfolio doesn't become just a dumping ground for random ideas, group the "alternative" stocks together and make them compete against one another for inclusion in your real portfolio. If both Compaq and Hewlett-Packard seem attractive, use the alternative portfolio to make a decision between them. One of these stocks is the best computer maker to put in your portfolio, and unless your portfolio is a lot bigger than mine, you probably don't need both.

Then make each winner compete against one of your actual holdings. Turn it into a shadow investment. If you bought Hewlett-Packard, what stock would it replace? See if its price and the news justify that sell/buy

But as I got more accustomed to the kinds of stories that I saw every day, I began to put several of the parts of WealthBuilder together into an investment system. I often found myself bouncing back and forth between news stories and the quote list of all the stocks and mutual funds that I owned or followed. WealthBuilder's quotes format is clear and concise yet comprehensive. It lists current price, opening price, decision. The competition will keep you fine-tuning your portfolio by adding constantly better stocks—and it will keep you from watering down your returns by owning too many stocks.

The second method takes the alternative portfolio a step further. This time you actually build an entire alternative portfolio with different asset allocations and sector bets and see how it performs against your current holdings. I don't recommend that you employ this method to conduct wholesale switches of strategy, but as a way to discover what's moving into favor and what's cycling out. If a portfolio built around small caps starts to outperform your actual portfolio, it's time to figure out why and perhaps adjust your asset mix.

change, 52-week high and low, and current volume. I found the volume number especially useful as I tried to put news stories together with prices. From the quotes page I could often see heavy volume as someone bought or unloaded. One day, for example, I noticed that the volume on Omega Environmental, a waste-cleanup stock, had been running heavy for days. The price had been inching up, too. Was someone accumulating the stock?

Sometimes I decided to combine current events and prices with historical quotes. That was easy to do—if expensive. If I clicked on the "Historical Prices" icon I could create a list of up to 20 companies and then, for $10 a month, I could download historical charts of price and volume for each of those companies. The graphing is pretty simple—there's only a choice of two time periods (100 days or 52 weeks) and two indicators (50-day moving average and relative strength versus the S&P)—but by looking at those and the bottom graph of volume I could start to see how the stocks I tracked were trending. I now had a context for my daily examination of prices and news. (For more on charting, including programs with far more power, see Chapter 8 on technical analysis. Many of these programs, despite their greater complexity, are easy to operate and generate a chart for far less money.)

Building a news archive on a company turned out to be just as easy and a lot cheaper. Whenever I came across a story that I thought helped me understand the long-term prospects for a company or its industry, I saved it to file from the news story page of the program. I did

**BASICS**

# WHAT'S AN ASK AND WHAT'S A BID? OR WHY DO ALL STOCK QUOTES COME WITH TWO PRICES?

Stocks are sold at auction between buyers who probably never meet face to face. The "bid" price is the highest price that a buyer is willing to pay. The "ask" price is the lowest price that a seller is willing to accept. Presumably a sale can take place either at the bid or the asked or somewhere in between, in that difference called the "spread."

The spread between bid and asked prices varies by security and also by market. Generally, the more trading volume there is in a security, the smaller the spread. Seldom-traded issues tend, therefore, to have very big bid/ask spreads.

The Department of Justice is currently investigating charges that brokers and dealers on NASDAQ routinely refuse to break the spread for small investors. Dealers on that exchange, the charges state, routinely buy between the bid and ask price, but then charge investors the higher bid or lower ask price and keep the difference for themselves. NASDAQ has vehemently denied the charges. Nonetheless the Securities and Exchange Commission has announced a series of new rules that, if they're not changed during the comment period, would require dealers on NASDAQ to offer individual investors the same prices they offer to other dealers.

A good broker should be willing to work to get you a price inside the spread, which can make a significant difference if you're selling or buying a large number of shares, no matter what exchange or what issue you're trading.

the same with earnings announcements. As I did so, icons for company files started to pop up at the end of my news story page.

What kind of things did I save? A few days after S. G. Warburg analyst David Wu upgraded Apple, he downgraded seven of Apple's competitors. I saved that story since I thought it had implications for the entire computer sector. I started to save news on corporate acquisitions as well, and gradually my file on Electronic Arts, for example, began to fill with news of purchases of tiny software developers with hit titles, which gave me a sense of this game software company's corporate strategy. I routinely saved analyst upgrades and downgrades. Sometimes I could see a wave of revisions building, as it did with Intel in January 1995.

Some news, such as earnings announcements, I saved simply for reference. I could use these to update my fundamental study of a stock without ever having to sort through old *Wall Street Journals* looking for those quarterly figures that I just knew I'd seen last week.

What I've described here is the beginning of a simple but effective investment system that will let you follow and interpret news and stock prices, identify trends in the market, and begin to understand what makes individual companies tick. But that's not the end of the tools in WealthBuilder.

For an additional monthly fee (the major criticism I have of this program is that everything comes with an extra fee and the entire package can gradually become much more expensive than an investor thought it would be when initially signing on), I can add stock, bond, mutual fund, and certificate of deposit databases that also include major indexes for comparison. From the database I can create a snapshot report on a company. A typical report, say on Coca-Cola, gives basic information on earnings, price-to-earnings ratios past and present, beta, 52-

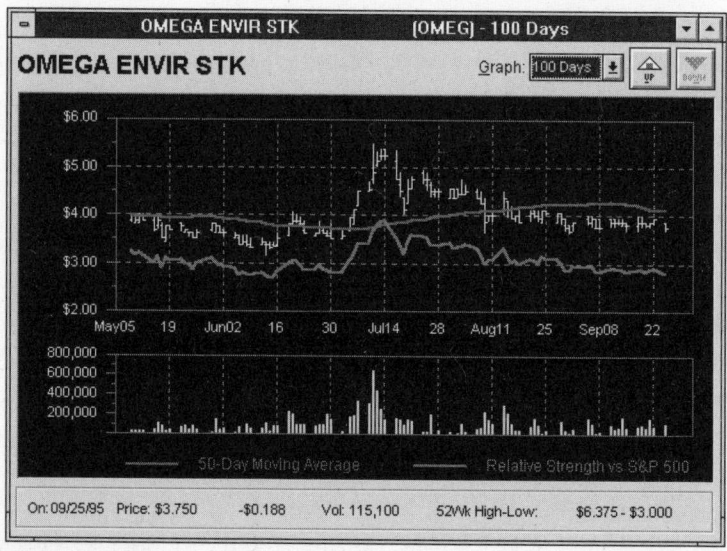

*WealthBuilder can generate simple charts of a stock's price over time.* (Courtesy of Reality Online Inc.)

week high and low, estimated earnings for the current year, historical growth rate and projected growth rate (no source indicated), and some balance sheet and income statement basics.

Or I can build screens to find all the stocks with earnings growth above 20 percent or all those yielding more than 5 percent. Like the rest of the approach in WealthBuilder, the screening function is set up so that the user can choose beginner or expert mode. "Beginner" makes it extremely easy to generate a worthwhile screen with a few terms connected by "and." In "expert" I found I could generate any screen I could create using any of the stock screening programs reviewed in Chapter 3 (except for Telescan, which as I explain in that chapter, has uniquely powerful screening tools).

Will a beginner outgrow WealthBuilder? Maybe. There are problems with many of these tools that will drive some investors to other programs as they become more experienced with computers and investing. Monthly updating, for example, means that the stock database can be significantly out of date. The charting tools are too simple to uncover any significant patterns in stock price data. The news reader doesn't give an investor the ability to search old news stories—if the story hasn't been saved to file, it disappears permanently from the system.

And some of the tools here are truly bad. The portfolio tracking is much worse than on Quicken—I couldn't find a way to generate internal rate of return calculations at all, which leaves an investor with just simple percentage gains based on price as a performance yardstick. The asset allocation system is full of questionable assumptions and the software doesn't offer precise ways to characterize assets.

So don't use these parts of the program. What's left will carry a beginner a long way—and may take some investors as far as they want to go. Particular parts of the program will hold up better for an individual investor than others. Only after using the news reader for a year am I starting to get fed up with its inability to do a historical search. On the other hand, I've only used the charting part of this program once—it just doesn't do the job for me.

But go ahead, outgrow it. The highest praise I can utter about the program is that it will teach many investors enough so that they can leave it behind. If you know nothing, you can operate enough of WealthBuilder to make computerized investing pay off for you. And as it does you'll explore other parts of the program, gradually becoming experienced enough to decide that this tool is good enough for you or to specify exactly what you need from your next tool.

## TELECHART 2000: BETTER INVESTING THROUGH PICTURES

Remember the charts that I mentioned and criticized in Wealth-Builder? Well, Telechart 2000 from Worden Brothers draws charts that can actually show an investor something about where a stock has been and where it might be going. And it's not much harder to operate than WealthBuilder (the program, if not the charts themselves, is even cheaper). As an added benefit Telechart makes one of the most intimidating subjects in investing—technical analysis—accessible to the beginner who knows almost nothing about the subject and isn't very comfortable around computers (Telechart is not available for Macintosh computers).

Start up the program (after having told the program about your modem and after it has dialed the 800-number and downloaded data on the 100 stocks the system charts right out of the box) and the first thing you see is an electronic newsletter, the *Daily Worden Electronic Report*, which comments on the previous day's market and on the stocks in the model portfolio that Worden

## USING QUICKEN FOR ASSET ALLOCATION

**A**cademic research shows that most investment return is a result of the asset class an investor picks rather than specific asset choices in that class. But it's hard to find an easy-to-use, inexpensive program that will break a portfolio into asset classes and calculate returns from each. A simple trick can turn the newest versions of Quicken (version 5 for Windows, version 6 for Macintosh) to just this task. When an investor enters a new stock or other asset into a Quicken portfolio, the program asks for the type and goal of each asset—offering default answers such as stock, bond, etc., and college, retirement, etc. Instead of using the default terms for type, use the "New" command to write in the names of the specific asset classes you want to track: income, large-cap growth, etc. Then, in the program's "Portfolio View," tell Quicken to group assets by type. The program will automatically calculate the percentage of the portfolio in each asset class and apply simple performance measures such as percentage gain. Investors can use the goal menu simultaneously to track assets by, for example, industry. Fill in the sector for each asset and use "Portfolio View" to group assets by goal.

runs. For example, the first day I signed on, the newsletter told me that Worden had bought Barrick Corp., a gold-mining stock, on the previous Friday. The newsletter also gave me tips on stock charts to check out—Staples and Schwab—and sectors—integrated oil. On subsequent days the report told me that Honeywell and Boeing were under accumulation, that the airlines were becoming overextended—consider taking some profits—and that the BOP indicator (whatever that is) recommends a buy on Charming Shoppes. The newsletter is updated every few days.

Telechart comes with an impressive complement of technical tools (see my complete review of the program in Chapter 8 on technical analysis), but remember we're sticking to what a raw beginner can do with this program. Tools such as MACD indicators and envelopes, and stochastics might as well be in Greek. But with Telechart you don't have to read the manual or a book on technical analysis to use the program. Instead click on "Easy Scan." This function will let you quickly view your list of funds and stocks for those that pass specific preset screens. For example, you can try new highs or new lows. That's obvious. Or how about screening for gappers (not too hard to understand—these are stocks that moved strongly out of their trendline, either up or down). On March 15, for example, I got three new lows: Entergy Corp., Kmart, Toys "Я" Us. A few days later I pulled up ten gappers: Monsanto, Xerox, Disney, The Gap, Weyerhaeuser, First Financial, Apple Computer, Bank America, Citicorp, and Automated Data Processing. I think even a beginner could see that something is happening in these charts. The Gap shows a big, obvious break to the upside. First Financial is just running away from the averages. Automated Data Processing is clearly sagging.

This kind of initial success can keep a beginner interested while he or she learns other parts of the system. For example, any of the initial charts that you pull up look much like the ones produced by Wealth-Builder. They chart the price movement of a stock versus some indicator and give you trading volume on the lower part of the screen.

But you can also draw on these charts. If you go to the "Analyze" function and then to "Growth Bar" you can calculate the percentage swing in price visually by drawing a trend line right on the chart. Just use the space bar to toggle between one end of line and the other, use arrow keys to move up and down, left and right, and use "Enter" to save. (Still in "Analyze," a "notepad" function lets you make comments on a stock and its chart.)

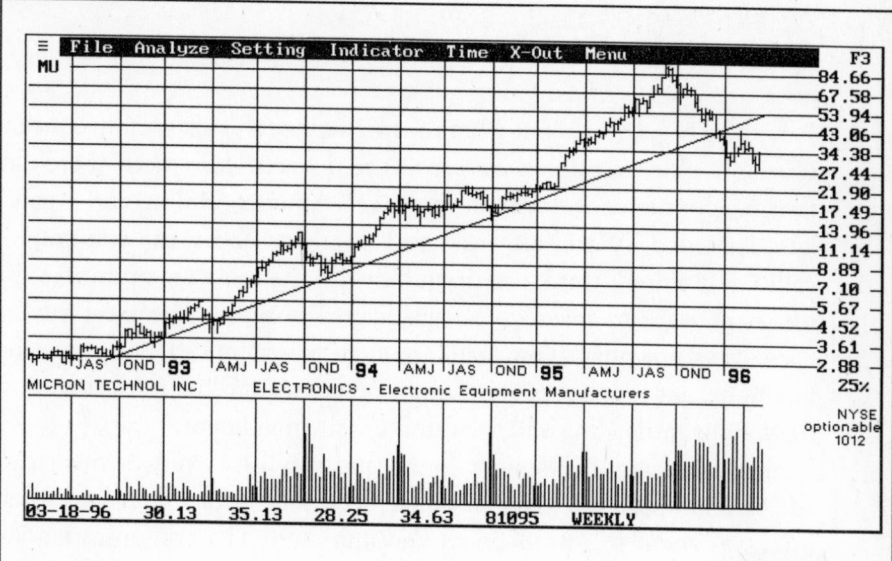

With Telechart 2000®, the beginning electronic investor can analyze stocks by drawing trendlines like this one. (Courtesy of TeleChart 2000® by Worden Brothers Inc.)

It's only a short hop from drawing trend lines to studying charts in more complex ways. Telechart comes with five preset indicators: MACD, stochastics, time-segmented volume, price rate of change, and envelope. A user doesn't even have to know what they mean to grasp one of the key principles of chart study—that the way to find patterns is to look at the same data in different ways over and over again.

At some point an investor will have to learn more than this. The program's extremely thorough and relatively readable manual will take him or her to the next stage. A book like Martin Pring's *Technical Analysis Explained* will fill in even more details. But even if you don't take the next step the program has shown you enough about charts to make it possible to read the charts in a newspaper such as *Investor's Business Daily* or to study the price movements of a stock, looking for a trend up or down before buying or selling. And if you get hooked on technical analysis, it's easy to move up to a more powerful program than Telechart, because many of the more complex programs will read Telechart data.

These programs give any beginning investor two key pieces in building an investment system that's easy to learn, tough to outgrow, and fun to learn from. But I'd like to add one more part—an on-line service.

## AMERICA ONLINE: IT'S WHO YOU TALK TO THAT COUNTS

Advice to beginners about what on-line service to pick usually concentrates on which service is easiest to use. I'm not convinced there's all that much difference anymore (although America Online and Apple's late, lamented eWorld are head and shoulders above the rest graphically), and I don't think user friendliness is the most important feature for an investor to focus on anyway. For a beginner, the most vexing question is not how to navigate around any system's various parts and functions, but how to separate the good advice on-line from the unintentionally misleading and the intentionally fraudulent.

Sign on to any investment forum and you'll be overwhelmed with advice and opinion. I remember the debates that raged on-line when Intel was about to introduce its Pentium chip. The consensus among those on-line who purported to be either insiders or experts was that the design was disastrously flawed. The chip ran way too hot to be put in any computer. I even read a description of a test where a Pentium was said to have melted its way through a motherboard. Was any of this true? I didn't and don't know. Did any of these people have inside dope? Did any of them actually have the credentials they claimed? To me all this was simply noise. I couldn't figure out how to use it because I couldn't separate the good information from the bad.

For an investor's first steps on-line I'm going to recommend a moderated forum, one where someone who knows something puts his or her name on the line and runs herd over the conversation. There aren't many such areas on the commercial systems. The Investors Forum on CompuServe is a good one. The American Association of Individual Investors section on America Online is first rate and so is the National Association of Investors Corp. forum, again on CompuServe. An investor wouldn't go wrong with any of these. Still, I'd recommend the Motley Fool on America Online over any of these. (I've reviewed America Online and all the major on-line services in Chapter 6.)

Hosted by two brothers, David and Tom Gardner, the Motley Fool is irreverent, overflowing with wise-ass character, and, beneath the humor, deadly serious. The Fools have had the courage to go on-line where few have dared to tread. They run a stock portfolio on America Online in real time so that everyone can see their picks succeed or fail. It's this "investing without a net" tactic that makes me take them seriously.

The Motley Fool is divided into a number of sections. The Electronic Fool offers some software for downloading and Internet scuttlebutt such as a list of World Wide Web sites. When I last checked in, the Fool Store was selling a manual to their investment approach and an offer to e-mail their investment decisions. But the two really important sections are the message boards, which contain alphabetized folders of comments on stocks that have generated enough interest among the Foolish (as goes the convention on this board) and the Motley Fool portfolio and comment.

Much of the discussion in the folders is serious and deep, but as you'd expect in a forum that discusses such a tremendous number of stocks, some is totally naive. For example, one week the folder for a small technology company called Brooktrout Technology was chock-full of investors repeating *Smart Money's* recommendation of the stock to one another. Some of the discussion is absolutely enlightened. For example, I read a back-and-forth in the American Power Conversion folder about the quality of the company's backup power supplies for computers and the effect that Hewlett-Packard's entry into the market would have. Another exchange in the Electronic Arts folder took apart Dan Dorfman's pan of the game company. After reading the details laid out by one investor about the big plus that changing from expensive-to-produce cartridges to cheap-to-produce CD-ROM would have on the company's margins, I had to agree with him that Dorfman had got the story exactly backward.

Most impressive, though, are the number of messages that don't either praise or condemn a stock but simply provide information. One investor posted a copy of Bell Sports' disastrous quarterly earnings and then added the company's press release. This was posted on April 28, just a day after it was released.

The Fools' portfolio is relatively small, just nine stocks recently. But they announce all buys and sells as they make them, and then calculate and post their portfolio's performance every day. Additional commentary discusses the latest trade in detail and an archive keeps commentary on past trades. For each stock in the portfolio, the Fools provide an overview, business description, financials, performance, and prospects.

The Gardners haven't been afraid to spell out their methods, either. A file describing their methods for valuing a stock is a model of clarity.

A beginner checking in here everyday would quickly become comfortable in the on-line world—I haven't seen anybody get flamed here or called a blue-haired senile dweeb—and would also be able to watch some serious investors at work. Someday I bet you'd find yourself posting a comment or news to the Motley Fool yourself. That's when you're officially no longer a beginner.

## REVIEWS

### MANAGING YOUR MONEY

Meca Software, 55 Walls Drive, Fairfield, CT 06430, 800-288-6322.

Versions available: DOS (version 12), Windows (version 2.1), Mac (version 7.0), CD-ROM (version 2.0).

Requirements: DOS version requires 640K RAM and 4MB free space on hard drive. Windows version requires 4MB RAM and Windows 3.1 or better. CD-ROM version requires 486 PC or better, 16-bit sound card, 2X CD-ROM drive, 6MB RAM, Windows 3.1 or better, and 14MB free space on hard drive. Macintosh version requires System 6.02 or better, 2MB of RAM, and 3MB of free hard disk space.

Cost: $39.95 suggested retail price of all diskette versions; $44.95 for CD-ROM.

Guarantee: 30-day money back.

Demo or sample: None.

Technical support: Free support at 203-255-7562 (weekdays, 9–6) and on CompuServe (Go Meca). 24-hour fax service (203-256-5195). Plus Plan members get dedicated help phone number. Bulletin board service at 203-256-9474.

User Newsletter or On-line Forum: Plus Plan ($49.95 for 12 months) includes "Managing Your Money Better" newsletter. User forum on CompuServe (Go Meca).

Updated: Annually.

Strengths: The automatic tax lot selection feature, which recommends the best lots to sell—first, last, greatest gain, greatest loss—after studying the tax consequences, isn't matched by any other program at this level. In "Edit Security" function, user can add detail on yield per unit, beta, tax status, risk (high, moderate, low, none, speculative), industry, or add his or her list of attributes.

Weaknesses: The program has suffered years of neglect from its corporate parents—H & R Block now owns Meca. But there have been signs of life recently—especially with the new CD-ROM version—and I sense a new commitment to keeping up with Quicken. That's not unimportant, given the time and effort that it takes an investor to enter a portfolio into a program such as this.

Tricks of the trade: Those investors comfortable with DOS should consider the DOS version with its asset allocation feature. The best description of asset allocation and how to do it ever put on software.

Once the best—and one of the first—of the mass market programs, Managing Your Money now seems just a Quicken clone. Imitation is certainly the sincerest form of flattery. Managing Your Money just proves that if you set out to imitate a competitor you'd damn well better make sure you do it better.

The Smart Desk interface on the newest Windows version of Managing Your Money looks just like the new interface on Quicken.

The program sets up accounts just like Quicken does (checking, savings, credit card, cash, etc.) and then uses a register just like Quicken (for entering dates, actions, units, symbols, etc.) Reports, which include net worth, investment analysis, and investment, pretty much echo the format and calculations that Quicken performs.

The most current versions of Managing Your Money have added several features absent from the last version I owned (the antique DOS version 10). A new "Financial Snapshot" function quickly summarizes your financial status on a particular day. The program will now download prices from CompuServe automatically. But these are features matched by Quicken. (The one exception I could find was Managing Your Money's automatic tax lot selection feature.)

But I find myself missing one feature from the DOS version—the asset allocation feature, apparently tacked on to the earlier version, which gave the best advice on asset allocation that I've ever seen in software. It's gone from the Windows version. And the investment advice from financial guru Andy Tobias doesn't make up for it. Basic topics such as the four-prong approach to investing (liquid money, inflation hedge, deflation hedge, prosperity hedge), handling different types of securities (advice on how to enter different assets into investment register), setting up different kinds of investments (advice on how to set up accounts), bonds (should you buy them, buying at a discount, buying at a premium) are bland and watered down for the complete novice. Only occasionally does Tobias's voice come through—for example, when he dismisses bonds with the comment that "I don't think most people should buy bonds." My favorite section is Tobias's discussion of goals: "If your goal seems unattainable—well, it may be. Some people respond to this sort of news by buying lottery tickets. But unless you're awfully lucky, that just makes your goals all the more distant. Instead, you might want to go to the library and try to find a copy of Marshall Sahlin's *Stone Age Economics*, in which he argues the Zen line. 'There are two possible courses to affluence,' he writes. 'Wants may be easily satisfied by producing much or desiring little.' See also our sister program, Managing Your Mantra."

But such occasional flashes are not enough reason to prefer this program over the commentary-less versions of Quicken.

### MICROSOFT MONEY

Microsoft Corporation, One Microsoft Way, Redmond, WA 98052, 800-426-9400.

Versions available: Windows (version 3.0) and Windows 95 (version 4.0).

Requirements: Windows 3.1 version requires 4MB RAM, 4MB free space on hard drive. Windows 95 version requires 4MB RAM (8MB recommended) free space on hard drive. Modem for quote updates and on-line banking.

Cost: Windows 3.1 version, $29.95; Windows 95 version, $34.95. On-line quotes cost $2.95 a month for six calls.

Guarantee: 90-day money back.

Demo or sample: Demo can be downloaded on the Microsoft Network or Microsoft's World Wide Web page, http://www.microsoft.com/MSHOME/.

Technical support: 206-635-7131 (6 A.M.–6 P.M., M–F), users forum on Microsoft Network (click "Money"), or on the World Wide Web at http://www.microsoft.com/MSHOME/.

User Newsletter or On-line Forum: The Money Forum on Microsoft Network.

Updated: Quotes updated on-line.

Strengths: Easy to use and unintimidating. Appealing graphic interface.

Weaknesses: Basically a home finance program designed for household budgeting and bill paying. Investment features are limited to a portfolio list, a simple chart of asset allocation, and on-line quotes (but for $2.95 you only get six calls a month to fetch quotes).

According to its press kit, Microsoft set out to produce a home finance program for those people who find programs such as Quicken too intimidating. And they've succeeded. Whether any investor will find the result useful is another question.

Most of the program is devoted to household budgeting and bill paying. The budgeting functions are easy to use with lots of shortcuts and automation to make the process about as painless as any that I've used in a home software package. On the bill-paying front, the program has one of the most extensive lineups of bank and financial provider connections of any financial package.

But the investment function? No active investor will find it adequate, although in fairness the program wasn't designed for the active investor. (Who among those of us who manage our own portfolios could get by with only the six on-line quote retrievals a month covered by the program's basic $2.95 a month charge?) You can view your holdings, record buys and sells, calculate a total portfolio value, and see an elementary breakdown of the value of your portfolio by asset classes (although the program seems to think that mutual funds and stocks are each asset classes). But other than updating prices on-line that's about it. Clearly Microsoft Money is still playing catch-up with its personal finance software competitors.

How serious is Microsoft about this product? It's hard to tell. The Windows 95 version is a vast improvement over the old, virtually amateurish Windows 3.1. version—which seems to indicate that Microsoft is determined to be a player. On the other hand, before the Justice Department killed the deal, Microsoft was willing to *give* this product to software competitor Novell in order to complete its merger with Intuit, the maker of Quicken. And for the first few months after this product hit the market, Microsoft was giving it away to build an audience for its new on-line service, Microsoft Network.

Of course, you can't run the new version at all if you haven't moved up to Microsoft's new operating system, Windows 95. And since Windows 95 is a RAM hog—Microsoft says it will run on machines with 8MB of RAM, but users say that running it with anything less than 16MB slows applications appreciably—moving up to that new operating system might require upgrading your entire computer. Money for Windows 95 clearly isn't worth the expense.

But let's say you have already bought Windows 95 for some other purpose. Should you consider Microsoft Money? I'd still have to say no. The program has added even more polish to the great graphics of the earlier version, but the content and the tools haven't gotten much better. From what I've seen, if you simply must have a Windows 95 investment program, Quicken offers a graphic interface that's almost as neat and a whole lot more power for the active investor.

#### QUICKEN

Intuit, P.O. Box 3014, Menlo Park, CA 94026, 800-816-8025

Versions available: DOS (version 8.0), Windows (version 5.0), Quicken Deluxe for Windows (version 5.0), Macintosh (version 6.0), Quicken Deluxe for Windows CD-ROM (version 5.0), and Quicken Deluxe for Macintosh CD-ROM (version 6.0).

Requirements: DOS version requires 640K RAM and DOS 3.1 or better. Windows version requires 4MB RAM, 14MB free space on hard drive, Windows 3.1 or Windows 95. Quicken Deluxe for Windows requires 4MB RAM (8MB is recommended), 20MB of free space on hard drive, and Windows 3.1 or Windows 95. Macintosh version requires 4MB RAM with System 7.0 or 7.1 and 8MB RAM with System 7.5, and 4MB free space on hard drive. Windows Deluxe CD-ROM version requires 8MB RAM, 24MB free space on hard drive, 2X CD-ROM drive, sound board, and Windows 3.1 or Windows 95. Macintosh Deluxe CD-ROM version requires 8MB RAM, 15MB free space on hard drive, 2X CD-ROM drive, and System 7.0 or later.

Cost: DOS version $39.95; Windows $39.95; Deluxe for Windows $59.95; Macintosh $39.95; Windows Deluxe CD-ROM $59.95; Macintosh Deluxe CD-ROM $59.95.

Guarantee: 60-day money back.

Demo or sample: None.

Technical support: DOS support 415-858-6008. Windows 415-858-6004. Windows Deluxe 415-858-6089. Macintosh 415-858-6041. Windows Deluxe CD-ROM 415-858-6086. Macintosh Deluxe CD-ROM 415-858-6087. Among the best in the business. I've never had to wait on hold listening to a recorded message saying, "All our staff is busy." But no 800-number.

User Newsletter or On-line Forum: None.

Updated: Frequently.

Strengths: Quick Quotes, the program's method for updating for prices via CompuServe, is robust, hardly ever suffers a busy signal, and easy to set up. Manual even has number to call to get local CompuServe access number, a sign of exactly how thorough Quicken is. Investment Performance Report offers two ways of calculating performance, including the all-important internal rate of return method. The program handles a full range of transactions—short sales and margin purchases, for example—and events such as stock splits are easy to enter. CD-ROM offers impressive ability to customize reports to include exactly the performance measures the user most wants to see. Most recent Windows versions add news retrieval and Internet access.

Weaknesses: A lot of minor problems. The program lacks a ticker symbol library so that a user must look up every security to download prices. Accounting for batch sales is primitive (but therefore flexible, since it's easy to go back and number various lots as batches for sale). Reports aren't well defined so that beginners may have trouble figuring out which report is best for what investment purpose. But the biggest problem is that this is a great budgeting and family finances program with investment functions tagging along as an afterthought. The CD-ROM version doesn't solve that bigger problem, because the investment advice is so simplistic as to be useless and the stock database is extremely limited.

Tricks of the trade: If you track enough investments (and use Quicken for budgeting, too), you can actually overwhelm the program. I noticed the problem when my portfolio positions began to get increasingly inaccurate after downloading prices every night. For example, while my register was showing I owned 100 shares of Motorola and so would any report that I generated, the portfolio itself showed that I owned 0 shares. Elsewhere I noticed that Quicken had also zeroed out one of my mutual fund positions. I called Quicken and got Megan on the line. She said that sometimes the program gets confused if there are lots of stocks and long histories. She suggested hitting "option/control/U," which updated prices, and "option/control/B," which reindexed accounts. "Option/control/U" worked, but I had to open each account individually to fix the problem. I leave it up to the potential purchaser to decide whether "Sometimes the program gets confused" is an adequate excuse.

I've taken you through the basics of Quicken for Windows and Macintosh above, so here I'm just going to add a few thoughts on these programs and then review the CD-ROM version and all its bells and whistles.

Quicken is a budgeting and expense-tracking household finance program—a great one—that has added more and more useful investment features with each revision. What the program provides is extremely solid. You can calculate returns in both an internal rate of return mode (that accounts for dividends and interest as well as price appreciation) or as a return on investment (that accounts only for price appreciation). Most of what you'll need to do to keep a record of your investments is possible here, and some of the functions have a kind of simple elegance. The program's method for entering splits works well—and the program will adequately deal with short sales, tax-free interest, margin loans, zero coupon bonds, puts and options.

Not everything is well designed or thought out. It shouldn't be possible to delete the name of a security from every account in the program by eliminating its name from the securities list. That's the list an investor uses to ask for electronic prices, so it's easy to make the mistake, as I did, of thinking that if I eliminate a security from that list, all I'm doing is eliminating it from the list of investments I'd like priced each time I log on to CompuServe. Not so. (Use the "Hide" function instead.) And it's quite a shock to start opening portfolios to find that the transactions are intact but the name of the specific security that you bought or sold is gone.

The only real problem that I have with Quicken is that the core program doesn't offer enough for serious investors. An investor can record transactions, update prices, and print simple performance and net worth reports. The newest Windows versions add a decent news reader, an intriguing "Portfolio View," and better charts. But to my mind, that's not enough of a return for the labor of inputting all those transactions, dividends, and interest payments, especially when Reuters Money Network offers more. An investor who wants to track his or her portfolio in more detail and generate more useful performance reports should certainly check out the portfolio management software described in Chapter 4 to see if the added functionality provided by those programs is worth some incremental increase in expense and time spent learning the program.

My suspicion is that Quicken is aware of this "usefulness" problem, too. (They're very smart folks.) And that explains Quicken Deluxe CD-ROM, a version of Quicken that piles on investment advice, extra graphing power, and some stock screening functions. Let me describe what comes in this bundle.

The CD includes Quicken 5 for Windows plus Quicken Home Inventory, Quicken Quotes, User's Guides, 101 Quicken Tips and Tricks, Quicken Tax Guidebook, Intuit Marketplace (stuff to buy from Intuit), Ask the Experts (Jane Bryant Quinn and Marshall Loeb as talking heads on personal finance), Tradeline Electronic Stock Guide (reviewed at more length in Chapter 3), Your Mutual Fund Selector (reviewed at more length in Chapter 5), news stories, and Internet access. (One set of Tradeline data comes free with the program; a subscription, $119.95 for twelve monthly updates on either CD or 3.5-inch disk, with monthly updates is extra.)

Despite all these features, installation was extremely simple, taking all of about five minutes. A prompt in the installation program checks the compatibility of the program with my video card. The program's multimedia functions ran without requiring me to tweak the system at all.

The Quicken Deluxe "Gateway" shows eleven icons after installation. Some of these are items you'll use once, if at all, like the video tours. Others are advice sections of questionable utility—I'll get to them later. Three icons represent the heart of the program for investors: Quicken, Mutual Fund Finder, and Investor Insight. Clicking on the big, yellow Quicken "$" sends you to a graphical version of the standard Quicken menu. From here you can enter investment transactions in your register, and then pull up reports on performance and net worth. Go to Investor Insight to download stock and mutual fund prices, the latest news stories from Dow Jones, and stock charts (unfortunately limited to price and volume). But Investor Insight's charts for comparing the performance of a portfolio, with a benchmark index, are startlingly good for a mass market program. Mutual Fund Finder uses data from Morningstar and Callan Associates, an investment research firm, to create lists of funds that meet risk and return hurdles set by the investor. Once you've put a fund on your search list, you can click to get a report from Morningstar that includes basic returns and style information, and graphs of annual or cumulative returns.

Clicking on the Quicken icon gives me a pathway into Quicken itself. This version has a couple of important innovations not included in the Windows and Macintosh versions I reviewed above. A mode called "Portfolio Review" lets me look at the returns on all accounts and view holdings, performance, valuation, and two user-customized alternatives. For example, I changed the last two columns to read "Last

Price" and "% Gain/Loss." This is roughly equivalent to the portfolio performance report I can generate in the other versions of Quicken, but the fact that I can customize the columns is a definite plus.

Another mode, "Snapshot," lets me customize a quick view of my portfolio. I can create a page that shows a net worth trend line, annual total return by security, net worth, portfolio value by type, average cost, and annual total return by type. A graph called Investment Performance shows monthly portfolio value and average annual return.

These features are definite improvements for Quicken. I'm not sure that most investors will think as favorably about the presence of financial experts Jane Bryant Quinn, currently *Newsweek*'s money expert, and Marshall Loeb, the editor who invented the personal finance magazine when he was at the helm of *Money*. The basic setup puts Jane and Marshall in armchairs and gives the user a list of topics: Financial Basics, Long-Term Goals, Home Ownership, Investments, and Taxes. Click "Investments" and four subtopics (but only four) appear: Risk vs. reward; Should I invest in the stock market?; Are bonds and savings accounts safer investments than the stock market?; and What is a mutual fund?. I don't want to kill all suspense by giving away everything that Jane and Marshall say, so let me just give you the flavor of the risk and reward discussion.

Marshall Loeb gets the task of explaining the trade-off between risk and reward. I think all investors know his spiel by heart: savers don't take risk, investors do; higher risk means higher returns; always have three months of savings for emergencies; conservative investors look for steady risk-free returns. Unfortunately, Marshall never defines risk or takes note of the different kinds. (The implied definition of risk, though, is the worry that you'll lose all your money because the market or the stock goes down.) And there's no talk of the risk in "safe" bonds. The other topics are about as useful. Don't buy this program if you're looking for financial advice. The extreme beginner won't be able to follow much of the discussion—it assumes too much. And for the intermediate to advanced investor, the advice is far too basic and far too debatable.

Tradeline, another major new feature in the CD-ROM version, is also a disappointment. The program will give me limited information and graphs on the S&P 500 stocks, but it omits the data items that a serious investor needs to turn this into a useful program for screening stocks. For example, there isn't any revenue or earnings growth history on any of the companies in the database. And to keep the data current, a user will have to subscribe with Tradeline directly anyway. The data is really just a sample that serves as an advertisement for the complete program. And if you're going to spend the cash to buy a program and data to screen stocks, you can do better. (See review in Chapter 3.)

Quicken has also added an Internet connection in the latest Windows 5.0 Version. Investors can use Quicken's free Internet connection to get in touch with financial vendors such as American Express, and to access the Galt Technology home page (see Chapter 7). And for a small additional fee, a user can gain full Internet access with Netscape's World Wide Web browser. Using Quicken as your main Internet access route is probably too cumbersome for investors who sign on to the Internet frequently, but the low price($1.95 for an hour a month) makes this a good way for a neophyte to explore this part of the on-line world.

### REUTERS MONEY NETWORK (Macintosh versions are called WealthBuilder)

Reality On-line Inc., 2200 Renaissance Blvd., King of Prussia, PA 19406, 800-346-2024.

Versions available: Windows (version 2.5), Macintosh (version 4.01).

Requirements: Windows version requires 8MB RAM, 20MB free space on hard drive, DOS 5.0 and Windows 3.1, and 2400 baud modem or higher. Modem for updating prices and information in investment databases and for downloading news.

Cost: Software plus membership plan. Software: Windows version, $24.95 plus $7.50 shipping; Macintosh, $49.95 plus $7.50 shipping; Windows CD-ROM, $24.95 plus $7.50 shipping. Membership plans: $9.95 Gold or $17.95 Platinum, per month. One month free on-line service with software.

Guarantee: 30-day money-back guarantee on software; cancel at any time and get refund for prepaid unused month of service.

Demo or sample: None.

Technical support: 610-239-0720 or through e-mail function of program (info@reality-tech.com).

User Newsletter or On-line Forum: *Reality Investor* mailed quarterly to subscribers. World Wide Web address: http://www.moneynet.com.

Updated: Databases updated monthly.

Strengths: Very easy and reliable on-line interface—one of the best I've worked with. Extremely useful auto logoff allows a user to download data without being present. Simple menu for telling system exactly what to download—hit "Send List" and you'll see a list of all the items you could download—click to check off the ones you want. Superb quotes format: current price action plus volume along with 52-week high and lows. For a program that, despite all its extra charges, is still reasonably priced, this has an impressive array of deep, well-designed functions—e-mail, alerts, graphing, research, news, and screening of stock, bond, and mutual fund databases.

Weaknesses: No way to customize general news list and no way to retrieve stories more than a few days old. Confusing price structure where many items, such as news, require extra subscription—charges can mount up fast. In contrast to analyst reports from Standard & Poor's ($4.95 each), free reports generated from program's database can be as much as a month out of date. Getting database up to date initially can be frustratingly drawn out process. After purchase, you may need to request disks through the mail to update data, if the data provided with the program is "too old," according to the program, for on-line download. Then, after the disks arrive (and I've had trouble getting these disks the two times I've set up this program), the user must still download the most recent data.

Tricks of the trade: In an effort to make this program easy to use for beginning investors, Reuters has built in many functions that make downloading the monthly updates of the mutual funds, stocks, bonds, and CD databases extremely slow. This is a program that definitely calls for an unattended download strategy. Rather than starting an update when you want to work with the data and therefore have to hang around until the machine is done (an hour to update two of the four databases isn't unusual), try scheduling the update when you really have something better to do. Start the program, check to see that it's connected without a hitch to the database, and then leave it to run automatically. The program will break the phone connection when it's finished, and there's no harm done in letting your computer stay on for a while if you're busy elsewhere.

I've described this product throughly in this chapter, so here I'd just like to highlight some of the most recent changes—and planned changes—to Reuters Money Network. In December 1995—not too long after Quicken added investment news to its menu of features— Reuters Money Network added additional topics to its news coverage:

reports on hot stocks; on ADRs (American Depository Receipts, which allow U.S. investors to buy shares in foreign companies); on the Treasury markets; on precious metals; and on municipal bonds. Beginning in January, news from industry analysts at Standard & Poor's was added to the mix. And, that same month, Reuters and Reality Online started an Internet site, matching Intuit's Quicken offerings. Isn't competition wonderful?

## SIMPLY MONEY

4 Home Productions (a division of Computer Associates International Inc.), One Computer Associates Plaza, Islandia, NY 11788, 800-773-5445.

Versions available: Windows (version 2.0).

Requirements: Windows version requires 4MB RAM, 6MB free space on hard drive, and Windows 3.1 or higher. Modem needed for stock quotes.

Cost: $69.95 in stores or $34.95 by phone.

Guarantee: One-year money back.

Demo or sample: None.

Technical support: 516-342-5466 (9 A.M.–11 P.M. M–F), CompuServe forum (Go Simply).

User Newsletter or On-line Forum: *Simply $ecure* newsletter ($29 a year with offer of free issue with program); CompuServe forum for Simply Money users (Go Simply).

Updated: Quotes by modem either through Simply Money 900-number (don't need account) at $1 a minute or through CompuServe (account required but program comes with one-month free trial account). Version 3.0 was scheduled to ship in the first quarter of 1996.

Strengths: Huge manual that can serve as primer on managing money. For computer novices, the screen is probably the easiest to navigate of any in this category. Huge array of graphs—far more than any competing program offers. Impressive commonsense advice from the editors of *Kiplinger's*.

Weaknesses: Still a family budget program with some investing functions added on. Narrower range of functions than Reuters Money Network: no news, no stock database, no screening capability.

Tricks of the trade: This wouldn't be a bad time to take a long, hard look at your phone bill. Most of us are used to scrutinizing our long-distance charges, but few pay any attention to how local bills are calculated—and that could be a costly mistake for an electronic investor. In New York City, for example, I can choose to pay either a flat monthly fee that entitles me to as many local calls as I want or I can choose a plan where I pay by the unit (each phone call is a unit but the time each call lasts also costs me units.) Many electronic investors and other users of on-line services forget that although they may be dialing a local number to connect with CompuServe to download stock prices, they still may be eating up local phone "units." If you currently pay by the unit, consider switching to a flat fee if you're going to spend much time on-line. The costs of local calls can add up until one day you wonder why your phone bill has doubled.

As a family finance package for someone looking to keep track of spending and prepare a budget, I prefer Quicken. As an investment program, however, Simply Money gives Quicken a stiff challenge. A decision between the two may come down to how much advice you want from your software. The newest version of Simply Money comes with advice on 200 topics from the editors of *Kiplinger's Magazine*, and the quality of the advice is head and shoulders above that dished out in either Quicken or Managing Your Money.

Simply Money doesn't work off a checkbook-style register like Quicken and Managing Your Money, but instead from an "Operations" page that gives an investor ways to indicate interest, capital gains, and dividends; to buy and sell; and to split securities and transfer funds. Buttons on the button of the page can take you to "Help," "Report," "Graph," "Find," and "Advice." Computer novices will probably find this easier to navigate than Quicken's menu bar. More experienced computer users probably won't notice the difference.

There's an amazing amount of power under some of these simple buttons. Hitting "Graph" gets me "Portfolio Value by Account" with more than thirty graph options. Investment graphs include comparative investment performance, portfolio value by account, portfolio value by goal, portfolio value by type, and security price history. A user can also memorize a graph—one step beyond Quicken's ability to create a memorized report.

Adding a new security is not quite as easy as with Quicken. The problem is actually too much freedom: the program gives you space to enter the type of security, but doesn't provide even a suggested menu of types. An organized investor can, of course, create his or her own list of security types for use in allocating assets, but how many of us are that organized?

Tips are mostly about saving money on your home or general advice on topics such as "Kids and Money," but one section concentrates on investing. Topics in "Investments for Today and Tomorrow" include investing in the stock market, investing in mutual funds, bonds, and other fixed-income investments, and investments you don't really need (a category that includes collectibles, commodities futures, diamonds and colored gemstones, gold and silver, and stock options). The advice is good and solid, the kind I expect from *Kiplinger's*, but it also illustrates the limitations of advice that must fit a wide variety of investors. For example, the advice on when to sell a stock says, "Sell a stock when its price appears to be reaching a plateau." And buy low, too.

The software comes with an impressive array of calculators of the type found in Quicken, and the other programs as well. For example, the investment calculator enables you to input initial investment, target amount, periodic investment amount, number of years, expected pretax return, expected inflation, and tax rate to derive an inflation adjusted future value. The calculators also come with advice, in this case a good explanation of why a bank account may not be a safe investment if you factor in inflation.

# 3

# Stock Screens: Finding Not Just Good Stocks, But the Best

Electronic investing can liberate you from the fetters of dubious hot tips, follow-the-leader stocks gleaned from news stories that everyone else has read, too, and the mass recommendations of newsletters and personal finance magazines. Stock screening programs can let an investor generate his or her own investment ideas—ideas whose profit-making potential depends only on the quality of your financial savvy. I'm not suggesting that you need to abandon all the methods that you currently use to generate ideas for your portfolio. In fact, I think the traditional methods are a great place to start if your goal is to find good stocks. Stock screening programs, however, will let you go one step further. With them you can go beyond good stocks to find the very best. Let me show you what I mean.

It's early March of 1995 and I think I've got a hot investment idea. Silicon Graphics, the company whose graphics hardware and software animated the dinosaurs of *Jurassic Park*, has signed a deal to provide the chips and software that will power Nintendo's next generation of video game machines. I've been following the company for a while. I've even visited their "campus" in San Jose where I got a chance to navigate some of their next generation graphics programs. (Including one where I rode on a dragon's back down a narrow, twisting canyon.) I know that the company is producing the boxes that will sit on top of the televisions in Time-Warner's Orlando experiment in interactive television. I know that the company is a hot name among movie producers and scientists, and thinking about the video game–playing teenagers of the world clamoring for this technology pushes me to the edge. I think I want to buy this stock.

How do I decide? I've seen a March 13 buy recommendation by Laura Conigliaro, a Prudential Securities technology analyst I respect. Her report starts off with two pages of text that lay out her reasons for recommending the stock. She doesn't mention the Nintendo deal and instead concentrates on both the trend toward graphic representation of information and computerized manipulation of graphics in everything from movies to home cable. Silicon Graphics has a leadership position in this field now, she points out, and the tests with companies like Time Warner are essentially research and development experiments that will enable the company to outstrip any rivals for a long time to come.

Then the report gives two pages of financial data, first historical, back to 1989, and after that projections for the future through 1996. The report gives quarterly breakdowns of all the data for 1995 and 1996, and then year-by-year historical data on earnings per share, dividends, and book value. The report also includes information on restructuring charges and merger-related expenses, and a condensed form of an income statement that shows sales and expenses for the most recent period. Looking at the data I find myself getting just a little nervous. Silicon Graphics is trading near its 52-week high. The price-to-earnings ratio is 31. I think there's value here even at these levels, but at this price I certainly want to be sure.

If I were doing my research on paper, my next step would be a trip to the library to consult the *Value Line Investment Survey*, the handbook of fundamental stock research that thousands of investors use. But Value Line is now on disk. So instead of settling in at the reference room of the library, I turn on my computer and type "vs" to start up Value Screen III, the software version of *Value Line*.

Value Screen III provides data (updated each month by mail, although quotes can be updated more frequently via modem) on 1,600 stocks. I get a report on Silicon Graphics by hitting the F7 key and then typing in the stock's ticker symbol: SGI. Up come screens of financial data and a blurb on the company that explains what it makes, breaks down the geographical sources of its sales, tells a little bit of company history, and then adds the names of corporate officers, an address, and a phone number (handy for calling Investor Relations to get an annual report). I already notice something of interest. The blurb notes insider holdings and big institutional positions. Fidelity Investments held 10 percent of Silicon Graphics stock as of September 1994. On the one hand that makes me feel good—I'm in savvy company—and on the other it makes me deeply uneasy—Fidelity is not known as a long-term investor, and if the stock's momentum fades the mutual fund giant could well dump its shares and depress the price of the stock.

The data in Value Screen III is both better and worse than that in Conigliaro's report. First, I notice what's missing. Gone are the quarterly financial data and the quarterly and yearly projections. Gone too are the detailed income statements. For example, the Prudential Securities report gives research and development expenses—an important item for analyzing a high-technology company's ability to stay ahead of its competitors—and net and gross margins—important for figuring out if a technology company facing rapidly aging products and intense competition is making enough profit to stay at the top of the heap.

But I also notice information in the Value Screen program that I didn't get from the Prudential analyst. Value Screen projects sales and earnings for three to five years in the future. In addition, the program gives me five-year trend numbers for earnings per share, dividends, and book value that let me put current numbers and projections in context.

Value Screen has also rated the stock for "Timeliness and Safety" and calculated a projected high and low price appreciation for three to five years in the future. Value Screen, unlike Conigliaro, doesn't think much of this stock—it calculates that I'll earn just 7 percent in the worst case and 13 percent in the best over that period—not much of a return for buying a technology high flier with lots of risk.

Is one of these two sources of data on Silicon Graphics better than the other? Not really. Both provide the basic information that most investors look for: past earnings, sales, growth rates, a measure or two of financial strength, some history of past stock prices, and earnings multiples. They both produce the same final result: a projected future price for the stock based on projected earnings. Prudential's buy on the stock—in contrast to Value Screen's rather neutral opinion—results from the brokerage firm's higher estimate for future earnings: a projected increase of almost 54 percent versus Value Screen's 37 percent projected change.

But I can do one very important thing with Value Screen III and all the other good stock screening programs that I can't do with an analyst's report. I can say, "Well, this stock sounds interesting. But can I do better?"

## FINDING THE BEST STOCK ELECTRONICALLY

Stock screening programs let me ask a question that most investors don't routinely consider—simply because answering it had been too hard before the computerized stock database. I really don't want to know if Silicon Graphics is a good stock. I don't even want to know if it is a better stock than any other that comes to my mind as a possible buy. The important question is, "Is it the best stock—among all stocks—that I can buy now?"

Value Screen gives me an easy way to begin to attack this question. Along the top of the screen I see a list of terms. I click on "Reports," which creates a list of further choices. Clicking on "Comparison" gives me a tool that lets me visually compare up to ten stocks. For example, I can eyeball Intel, Motorola, and Silicon Graphics by moving from a screen of data on one company to that on another. (Alternatively, I could simply print out each company's data and look at them side by side on paper.)

Even that simple comparison shows some intriguing differences. SGI might be the riskiest of these three stocks. It earns only a B+ for financial strength, certainly not a bad rating in these days of leveraged balanced sheets, but Intel and Motorola both earn A+ ratings. Price stability (a number that Value Screen's easily accessed on-disk glossary tells me rates a stock's volatility over time on a scale of 1 to 100, with 1 being most volatile) really varies for the three stocks: at 15 Silicon Graphics is far more volatile than either Intel at 35 or Motorola at 55. SGI also has the highest beta of the three at 1.6, versus 1.3 for Intel and 1.25 for Motorola. To compensate, Silicon Graphics shows the highest projected earnings growth rate over the next five years (27.5

percent to 22.5 percent for Motorola and 16 percent for Intel), but the stock's higher risk makes me wonder whether that difference is worth the price. (And we won't even talk about the attractiveness of buying Intel at 13 times trailing earnings versus Silicon Graphics at 31.)

Now an investor working with paper and pencil could still do this three-way comparison—just photocopy the *Value Line* pages and compare them. But that still would only get you to the threshold of answering which of these *three* stocks is better. It doesn't tell you whether Silicon Graphics is the best stock *among all stocks* to buy now. To do that you'd have to look at the entire universe of stocks, comparing each one to Silicon Graphics on whatever measures you thought were important. That sounds like it would take forever. But with a software program I can run that comparison—I can run several comparisons—while you're still trying to figure out how long it would take to do the job on paper. All I have to do is figure out what qualities I want to compare.

My comparison of Silicon Graphics, Intel, and Motorola has set me thinking about risk and return. If I'm going to take on the high risk of a Silicon Graphics (instead of buying Motorola or an electric utility), I'd like to make sure I'm getting the biggest potential bang for my buck. Can I find a high-risk stock that could leave Silicon Graphics in the dust?

Value Line and Value Screen limit their universe to the 1,600 stocks that the Value Line organization follows, so let's switch programs to one with a bigger universe. The U.S. Equities OnFloppy database, which used to be called Marketbase until Morningstar bought the smaller company in 1994, includes more than 7,471 equities. Let's see what stock rockets might lurk in this universe.

## SCREENING FOR GROWTH

I'll design a screen—simply a series of hurdles that a stock must jump—that looks for risky, potentially high-reward stocks. First decision: I'll only look at small companies: they tend to be riskier, but also younger and likely to move up strongly if things go right. The program tells me that the *average market capitalization* of all the companies in the database (that's what the stock market thinks the company is worth; the program calculates it by multiplying the current market price per share times the number of shares of stock a company has outstanding) is $753 million. We'll set our limit at $500 million or less.

We also want fast-growing companies. U.S. Equities easily calculates the average revenue and earnings growth for the companies in the database for the most recent quarter. Revenue grew an average 6.94 percent and earnings a whopping 38.8 percent. But I don't want average companies. So I double these numbers. To pass my test a company will have to show a revenue increase of 14 percent and an earnings jump of 75 percent. Any stock growing that fast might well already have been discovered by investors—and would therefore cost me an arm and a leg to buy. I ask the program to calculate the average institutional holding for the stocks in the database—on average these big investors hold 37 percent of each of these stocks. I tell the computer to throw out any stock where institutions own more than 18 percent.

## SMART STRATEGIES

# FOUR FAVORITE GROWTH SCREENS

Let's start with a basic growth screen and then modify it to build three significant variations.

■ **A basic growth screen.** Most growth screens start by looking at earnings growth over some period of time—a common choice is 12 months. So the first rule of a basic growth screen might be to search for stocks with a percentage change in 12-month earnings per share greater than $x$. An investor should set $x$ after looking at the market as a whole. In periods of high year-to-year earnings growth—the 1995 market was an example—set this hurdle high, say at 100 percent. When earnings growth is hard to come by, set it lower, say 10 percent. Use the screening program to find the average change for the market as a whole and set the hurdle accordingly. Or an investor can use a conventional hurdle rate in all markets—the National Association of Investors Corporation uses a 15 percent hurdle.

Most growth screens also add criteria that make sure that companies with high earnings growth are also reasonably sound financially. For example, an investor might also require (using the logical "and") that the company have a debt-to-equity ratio less than 50 percent and be cash-flow positive (cash flow per share greater than 0). A positive cash flow means

*continued*

that the company is actually generating cash (defined as net profit plus depreciation) after paying for dividends. That's important if an investor is looking for companies capable of sustained growth. (It also rules out companies in industries like cable television that are investing much more than they are earning—and are thus cash-flow negative.)

■ **Screens for long-term growth.** Some investors create a variant on this screen by looking for long-term growth. They require that companies have a high current earnings per share growth—plus a record for past growth. An investor might require, for example, that the company has grown earnings per share at 15 percent annually over the last five years.

Other investors also screen for sustainable growth but define it differently. Instead of looking at the past earnings growth record, they attempt to judge whether current rates of growth are sustainable. Over the long term, a company's growth is constrained by two factors—the amount of profit the company generates and reinvests and the return that it earns on that reinvested capital. It's simple to construct a formula to calculate a company's sustainable growth rate: Sustainable Growth Rate = Return on Equity x Retention Rate. (The retention rate is 100 percent minus the payout ratio. It measures the percentage of earnings that a company reinvests after paying dividends.) An investor looking for sustained growth then would add a requirement like this to the basic growth screen: sustainable growth must be greater than the five-year historical earnings per share growth. Otherwise, such an investor calculates, he or she is buying a company that is about to peak.

■ **Screens for earnings momentum.** Other growth investors don't care about the long term. They're looking to buy companies that are on an earnings roll now. Commonly called earnings momentum investors, they screen for companies where earnings growth is on an upward trend. A common momentum screen (based on the CANSLIM model popularized by *Investor's Business Daily* publisher William O'Neil in his book *How to Make Money in Stocks*) would begin by requiring five-year earnings per share growth of greater than 15 percent and earnings per share growth in the most recent quarter of 25 percent (above the year-earlier quarter). O'Neil's model also requires that the stock is already moving up versus the market as a whole—he requires that the relative strength (a measure that compares the stock's price movement to that of the market as a whole) be greater than 85.

Other momentum investors use more rigorous hurdles. They look for stocks that are showing progressively greater earnings growth each quarter. So to the basic growth screen they would add a requirement that the earnings per share growth of the most recent quarter (over the year-earlier quarter) be 25 percent and greater than the earnings per share growth of the previous quarter (again compared to the year-earlier quarter). Momentum investing with either rule requires ruthless selling discipline—any stock that breaks the pattern must be sold immediately.

■ **Screens for growth at a price.** One last kind of growth screen is called growth at a price. After applying the basic growth screen or the long-term or sustainable growth variants, an investor checks to see what the market is charging to buy this kind of growth. He or she only buys when growth comes at a reasonable price—usually measured by comparing the growth rate to the earnings per share ratio. Peter Lynch in *One Up on Wall Street* proposes that a growth stock should be purchased when its current price-to-earnings ratio is equal to or less than the growth rate of the stock plus its dividend yield. James Craig, the successful growth fund manager who runs the Janus Fund, buys growth stocks only when the earnings per share ratio is less than 80 percent of the growth rate.

I'm starting to get a bit worried that these hurdles are too high—but that's the wonderful thing about running a screen like this on a computer. If it doesn't work out, I can change a parameter in a second, and run the test again. It turns out, however, that I needn't have worried: 279 stocks pass my test so far.

I'm going to narrow down this universe even more, though. I only want companies able to show growth like this over time—I don't want a company that shows this kind of jump in earnings simply because it did so badly one quarter that the next decent quarter makes a nag look like a thoroughbred. One way to get just this kind of company is to demand that it earn a high return on assets (the total value of everything a company owns). This should knock out cyclical, asset-heavy companies that are showing big swings in earnings and revenue because of the economic cycle but still aren't earning much on each dollar of investment. I write a rule that requires all the companies in this universe to show a return on assets of 15 percent or better. And to make sure these companies are reasonably solvent, I also ask the program to rule out companies with a *quick ratio* of less than 1. (The quick ratio is measure of a firm's ability to meet obligations with readily convertible assets on hand. It's calculated by adding up cash, marketable securities, and accounts receivable and then dividing that sum by current liabilities.)

Just thirty-six companies meet this test.

| Company | Market Cap (mill) | Revenue Growth % | Earnings Growth % | Return on Assets % |
|---|---|---|---|---|
| 3D Systems | $173.7 | 42 | 108 | 17 |
| Action Perfm. | 47.2 | 50 | 100 | 16 |
| Alcide | 57.4 | 21 | 89 | 16 |
| Alpha Tech. | 66.4 | 183 | 80 | 16 |
| Anchor Gaming | 269.8 | 78 | 84 | 22 |
| Applied Innov. | 404.7 | 70 | 90 | 36 |
| Cellular Tech. | 263.6 | 188 | 100 | 21 |
| Chips & Tech. | 233.2 | 43 | 248 | 15 |
| Colonial Data | 321.6 | 150 | 373 | 21 |
| Competitive Tech | 34.5 | 57 | 100 | 28 |
| Computer Tel. | 55.8 | 52 | 600 | 27 |
| Cyberoptics | 113.4 | 84 | 220 | 27 |
| Data Measurement | 23.1 | 32 | 200 | 26 |
| Davox | 71.0 | 29 | 100 | 18 |
| Delrina | 340.7 | 96 | 100 | 16 |
| Diodes Inc. | 66.1 | 58 | 91 | 18 |
| Enzo Biochem | 354.5 | 61 | 100 | 15 |
| General Employ. | 12.8 | 23 | 75 | 23 |
| Goldcorp | 338.4 | 14 | 1158 | 16 |
| HEI Inc. | 18.0 | 64 | 143 | 18 |
| Healthy Planet | 17.4 | 54 | 300 | 24 |
| IKOS Systems | 52.0 | 29 | 75 | 16 |
| Interdigital Comm. | 292.4 | 2958 | 100 | 17 |
| Nat'l Home Health | 15.0 | 22 | 100 | 19 |
| Northern Tech. | 29.6 | 33 | 75 | 16 |
| Panatech Res. | 26.8 | 32 | 150 | 17 |
| Penn Nat'l Gaming | 107.5 | 38 | 200 | 18 |
| Pre-Paid Legal | 107.5 | 38 | 76 | 23 |
| Psychemedics | 120.1 | 31 | 83 | 22 |
| Ride Inc. | 137.5 | 1231 | 100 | 20 |

| | | | |
|---|---|---|---|
| Robotic Vision | 194.6 | 62 | 173 | 35 |
| Scandinavia Co. | 9.6 | 2133 | 100 | 62 |
| Scientific Tech. | 216.0 | 43 | 88 | 35 |
| TSX Corp. | 232.6 | 92 | 2025 | 20 |
| UNR Industries | 447.9 | 14 | 118 | 17 |
| Wireless Telecom | 164.7 | 121 | 227 | 23 |

Do I want to buy any of these stocks? To help me decide I can pull up all the information in the database on each one by hitting "Display a stock." Scrolling through the entire list suggests at least one subject for further research.

Applied Innovation, which U.S. Equities tells me is in the business of "manufacturing elec. machinery comm. equipment" (further research in another source tells me that this means the company makes complex switches for the telephone industry), shows steady revenue growth of better than 100 percent stretching back to 1991. Earnings growth is slowing as the company gets bigger, but Applied Innovation still managed 78 percent growth in 1994. The stock isn't cheap, with a trailing price-to-earnings ratio of 45.47, but there are relatively few shares on the market (7.8 million) and institutional ownership is low at 11 percent, leading me to believe the company hasn't yet caught Wall Street's eye. (Confirmed by looking at Nelson's *Directory of Investment*

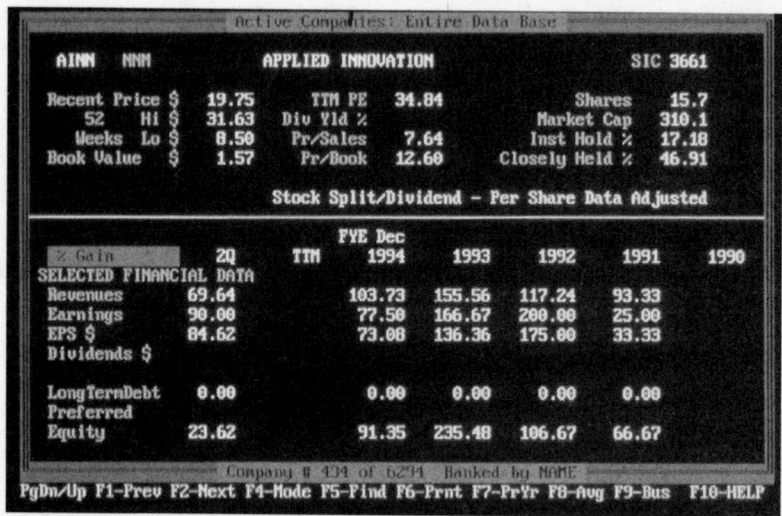

**U.S. Equities** *gives a breakdown like this on more than 7,000 stocks.* (Courtesy of Morningstar Inc.)

# TWO VALUE SCREENS AND SOME INTRIGUING RESEARCH

Value investors don't concentrate on earnings growth. They look instead to buy undervalued assets, and the difference between various kinds of value investing (and different kinds of value screens) comes down to how the value of those assets are calculated.

Frankly, value investing isn't as well suited to computerized screening as growth investing. It's nearly impossible to accurately value a company's assets using the data provided by computers. Stock databases will tell you how much the company's accountants figure its assets are worth, but that's not a figure that the great value investors would have put their money on.

Benjamin Graham, the dean of value investing, made his money by buying a dollar of assets for 50 cents—over and over again. That technique works—and works without much risk—if an investor can accurately calculate the value of a company. Graham figured out what a company was worth by poring over its books and reports. Almost all the computerized methods of calculating value, in contrast, are shortcuts with serious flaws.

**▪ Using book value to find bargains.** The standard value screen starts with book value per share, an accounting measure of the value of a company's assets (machines, inventory, real estate) minus liabilities and preferred stock. A book value screen would, of course, require book value per share of greater than 0, and it might require positive earnings (although some value investors frankly don't care). It would then rank companies on the basis of the ratio of their stock price to their book value per share, looking for stocks with the lowest price to book ratio. (In the cases that delight a value investor's heart, the price of a share is lower than the book value per share, meaning an investor gets more in assets than he or she paid for the share.)

There are two problems with using book value to represent the value of a company. First, in today's economy book value isn't a good representation of the profit-earning capacity of a company. The method was suited to an age when the economy was dominated by asset-rich manufacturing companies. For a company like that, profits were produced by tangible assets. Contrast that to a company like Microsoft, which owns relatively little in the way of tangible assets and whose ability to produce profits hinges most crucially on the quality of its employees—who aren't valued in the accountants' ledgers since they can walk out the door at any moment. Second, the U.S. economy is coming out of a period of intense corporate downsizing. Company after company has sold assets. Exxon sold its New York headquarters building, for example. Other companies, such as Time Warner, have spun off assets—and liabilities—into separate companies. Book value at such a company is not a particularly reliable measure of a company's value. Still, book value is one way to create a list of potential bargains for further research.

■ **Using dividends to uncover value.** Other value investors also screen for companies with low price-to-earnings ratios on the theory that while some of these companies deserve the low price that the market has assigned them, others are just out of favor at the moment. Unfortunately, it's difficult to tell which is which without doing in-depth fundamental analysis of the company.

Adding a rule about dividends to the screen helps with this problem, however. Research indicates that dividends are a reliable source of information about a company's own assessment of its future. The board sets the dividend only after intense study—and using the most conservative numbers. The last thing any corporate board wants to do is raise a dividend and then cut it later. So rising dividends—even if hikes are modest—are a good sign that company management considers its fortunes improving. A low price-to-earnings ratio screen (price-to-earnings ratio less than 12 when the market average is 15) could also require a percentage change in dividends greater than 0.

■ **Does bottom fishing work?** Finally, some recent academic research says, forget all these calculations and just buy the worst companies you can find. Joseph Lakoniskok, A. Shleifer, and R. W. Vishny, in an article entitled "Contrarian Investment, Extrapolation, and Risk" (*Journal of Finance*, December 1994), compared the results of buying a portfolio of companies with horrible sales growth to those with the best growth in sales. Lakoniskok (*et al.*) ranked all the stocks on the New York Stock

*continued*

Exchange on five-year sales growth and then compared the results of buying the stocks of all the companies in the top quintile (the top 20 percent) with the returns from buying all the stocks of companies in the lowest quintile. His portfolio of dogs—almost all of which showed negative sales growth—outperformed the stars over a five-year period by about 4 percentage points a year. Lakoniskok and his colleagues theorize that by buying the completely downtrodden, they were buying a portfolio of cyclical companies headed for better times, companies that were so bad they had to bring in new managers, or companies that looked cheap to potential acquirers. Before anyone tries this at home, however, remember that Lakoniskok's results are based on a very large portfolio and a long holding period. An individual investor without the capital to buy shares of a fifth of the New York Stock Exchange could buy a portfolio of losers by selecting at random from the larger universe of the most downtrodden fifth. Ask your neighborhood statistician to tell you how big a sample you'd need to have reasonable confidence of duplicating Lakoniskok's returns.

*Research*—yes, it's a book, gasp!—which lists only three analysts for the stock.) The company has recently announced a stock split as well, U.S. Equities tells me, which should increase its following. And with a market capitalization of $404 million, the company is not too far away from crossing the $500 million frontier—many institutional investors won't put money in a company that's smaller than that for fear that they won't be able to sell their shares if they need to.

## SCREENING FOR VALUE

I could have just as easily created a screen for underpriced stocks rather than the fastest growers. To build that kind of screen I could again start with small capitalization stocks—the same universe of 783 companies that I used for my super-fast growers run. While I don't care about growth rates, I would still like a reasonable quick ratio and a positive return on assets and equity. I don't want this to turn into a list of companies headed for bankruptcy. So I add requirements that return on equity and return on assets both must be greater than 0, and the quick ratio must be greater than one.

Then, using the averages calculated by the program for my universe I look for value: a price-to-earnings ratio less than half that of the average company (that is, 7.33), a price-to-book ratio of less than .81, and a price-to-sales ratio of less than .33. I'm worried that these tests are too strict. After all, I'm asking the program to look for companies selling at less than 33 cents for each dollar of sales, just to take one example. But the program lets me add only one criterion at a time so I can see the shrinking size of my universe: I get a list of eleven companies that jump these hurdles.

| Company | Market Cap (mill) | price/ earnings | price/ book | price/ sales |
|---|---|---|---|---|
| Ameriwood Ind. | $26.5 | 3.79 | .65 | .25 |
| Burke Mills | 8.8 | 4.62 | .75 | .24 |
| Cerbco | 7.9 | 6.56 | .54 | .21 |
| Douglas & Lomason | 61.9 | 4.92 | .71 | .10 |
| Foster Co. (L.B.) | 47.0 | 7.13 | .80 | .18 |
| Holson Burnes | 20.6 | 3.89 | .60 | .16 |
| Intertan | 80.8 | 3.23 | .68 | .17 |
| Oroamerica | 25.6 | 7.11 | .45 | .12 |
| P&F Industries | 6.5 | 5.93 | .47 | .14 |
| Pitt-Des Moines | 79.3 | 5.51 | .79 | .18 |
| WHX Corp. | 306.5 | 4.98 | .42 | .23 |

Again I look at these stocks in more detail using the program's "Display a stock" function. I see some real bargains here—and several companies that probably deserve to be cheap. Douglas and Lomason Company, which according to the program makes equipment to transport motor vehicles, might be a real bargain. Although earnings are somewhat erratic, revenues show accelerating growth since 1992. And the stock is selling near its 52-week low of 14.75—way below the book value of $20.81. If that's an accurate statement of assets, I could buy $1 of assets for 71 cents. Certainly worth thinking about.

Ameriwood Industries International, on the other hand, is way too volatile to interest me. It can't seem to put two years of earnings growth together back to back. 1992 saw growth of 100 percent, but 1993 showed earnings retreating by 27 percent. In 1994 earnings soared by 67 percent, but the most recent quarter shows a 100 percent decline.

I'm not going to rush out and buy any of these companies without subjecting them to a lot more research (how to electronically research

---

**TIPS ON THE TOOLS**

## CREATING HISTORICAL DATA

Sometimes I'd love to know what a stock looked like one or two years ago. The databases on the market all provide a limited amount of historical information, usually about earnings and sales, but they don't present a history of a company's fundamentals. For example, I can find out about inventory turnover in the most recent year, but none of those programs will tell me what this number was a year ago. But there is a partial solution to this problem—for investors who own big hard disks.

If you subscribe to a program that provides monthly or quarterly updates, you already have this historical information. In March 1994, for example, when I studied inventory turnover for Williams-Sonoma, that was current information. Now it's history. That data is no longer in my current files—when I updated my data, the program wrote over it with the most recent data. But it is still on the disks I received last March. And there's nothing to stop me from retrieving it.

Just reinstall the same program with the old data on your hard drive, being careful to give the file a name that's different from the file holding your current data. You could set up a parallel database that lags your current data by exactly a year. That would give you the ability to do year-to-year comparisons on every item of data in the database. You're free to carry this process to any length your disk space and the history of your subscription will allow. How about one-, three-, and five-year files?

---

and evaluate a single stock is the subject of the next chapter). But I have generated two lists of investment ideas. Any of them might be a better stock at this moment than Silicon Graphics. I've never heard of any of these companies and I would never have even considered them as possible investments if I hadn't run a stock-picking screen on my computer. A few hours of work has generated 47 new investment ideas.

You can order up packages of investment ideas generated in just this way from a variety of sources. Fidelity Investments, for example, offers its account holders monthly lists of stocks spit out by varying stock screens from Standard & Poor's. In May 1995, for example, that package included a list of stocks yielding 4.5 percent or more; a list of stocks that combined slumping prices with upward revisions in analysts' estimates of 1996 earnings; a list of stocks with increasing institutional ownership; a list of stocks with climbing earnings estimates, rising prices, price-to-earnings ratios of less than 20, and insider buying; and a list of stocks selling below their five-year projected growth rates—just to name a few.

You could produce almost any of these screens on almost all of the stock database programs that I review at the end of this chapter. That's important in and of itself: the software frees you from waiting for the mail to deliver the set of screens that Standard & Poor's decided to run a month ago.

## THE BENEFITS OF DOING IT YOURSELF: TURNING HUNCHES INTO STRATEGIES

More important, you can do two things with your software that you can't do at all on paper. First, you can fine-tune each screen. For instance, I can improve, I hope, Standard & Poor's yield screen by asking it to include only companies with a five-year track record of raising dividends by more than the rate of inflation, 3.6 percent annually from 1985 through 1994. Or I could combine several of these ideas into a single screen. For example, I can look for stocks with slumping prices but with rising earnings estimates and, borrowing criteria from other screens, rising insider and institutional holdings.

Second, since the screens are resident in my computer, I can test how these ideas perform over time. These programs let me turn a screen into a portfolio and then track its performance over time. In Morningstar's U.S. Equities, for example, to turn a screen into a portfolio all I have to do is name the screen ("Small Cap Aggressive Growth" and "Small Cap Value," respectively), hit a combination of keys (shift F7) to move to the Portfolio menu within this universe and then type F6 to use this as current active universe.

After saving this portfolio I can go back to the display function and pull up each stock in this portfolio. Next month I can call up these two portfolio functions and see how the market has treated my ideas.

In other words, I can transform these investment ideas into investment strategies. Let me explain the critical difference between the two. An investment idea is close to a hunch. It's an informed guess that a specific stock or stock sector might be a good investment now. An investment idea can be driven by an event at a specific company—Silicon Graphics's deal with Nintendo—or in a group of stocks—my sense, in the late spring of 1995, is that everyone hates retailing stocks. It can also be based on observation of general market trends—utility stocks were at cyclic lows at the end of 1994—or a study of the economy—in a slowing economy I don't want to buy stock in a company that shows rising inventory levels (it's an almost sure sign that the company isn't moving merchandise).

A strategy on the other hand is a long-term approach to the market. It's the extremely unusual investor who can successfully invest using more than one strategy. Warren Buffett is a value investor who throughout his career has remained convinced that the way to make money is by investing in companies that show a good return on capital (and use conservative accounting methods), that show predictable earnings (as a result of low inventory and high turnover of assets), and that own franchises (Coca-Cola and American Express, for example) that give the company freedom to charge a little bit more for their products. Peter Lynch, from the days when he ran the Magellan Fund for Fidelity Investments to his current role as a best-selling author, has believed in buying growth companies that produce consumer goods when the companies are priced at a discount to their growth rate and when they are easily understood and managed. (In Lynch's words, an idiot should be able to run the company, because sooner of later one will.) The phenomenal returns earned by the growth stock investors at mutual fund Twentieth Century Giftrust Investors—a 22 percent annual return over the last 10 years—result from a specific method of analyzing earnings growth called "earnings momentum" that looks for companies with accelerating rates of growth. The Beardstown Ladies and other successful investment clubs all follow a single philosophy that's embodied in the study methods of the National Association of Investors Corporation. What distinguishes each of these successful investors from the unsuccessful is his or her ability to apply a single proven strategy through the ups and downs of the market.

Whether you're a novice or a seasoned hand, you have an investment strategy. I know I do. I believe the best way for me to make money in the stock market is to buy growth when the market is undervaluing it. I have a lot of trouble buying Microsoft at $83 and at a price-to-earnings ratio of 31, even though I know this is a great company with an unbelievable franchise. I can't imagine that the market doesn't know this and hasn't priced the stock accordingly. I can, and

# WHEN TO SELL

When I screen, I don't just look for stocks to buy. I also build screens—very simple ones—that tell me when to sell.

Call this screening for the overvalued. You learn something significant when from one month to the next a basic price-to-earnings screen picks up significantly more stocks (price-to-earnings ratio greater than 1.5 times the stock's earnings growth rate, for example). You can also study the universe generated by such a screen to see if a specific industry is heavily represented or if the stocks on the list have any other common characteristics.

Obviously if a stock you own shows up on an overvalued list, you should seriously reconsider your stake in the company. But you should also look to see if competitors are already well represented on the list. If they are, you may own a laggard in a market sector that's about to peak— not a comfortable place to be.

You can also use screens to identify danger signs. Theoretically you already study all the stocks you own so carefully and individually that you wouldn't miss shrinking margins, but as a double check you should regularly run screens on a few basic items for stocks in each industry you follow—for example, margins, earnings and sales growth rates—and then rank the universe of stocks on each measure. Look for signs that a company you own has peaked and is starting to slide down the ranks in relation to competitors. Also check to see if any of these crucial measures is declining for the industry as a whole. You may believe in Wal-Mart so strongly that you want to hold the retailer's stock even if sales at other retailers are slowing, but you still want to consider your decision to hold the stock in that context.

did, buy Microsoft at $64, at a time when I believed that the market was undervaluing the stock on fears that the company's blockbuster software Windows 95 would suffer delays until it had to be relabeled Windows 96.

My strategy isn't particularly original. It's called growth at a price and counts among its practioners such mutual fund luminaries as Jim Craig, the manager of the Janus Fund. To follow my strategy I look at fundamentals and industry news. And I regularly screen for stocks that might fit my strategy. For example, running my standard screens last spring, I noticed that Electronic Arts, which makes computer game software, had dropped substantially below its 52-week high. Fundamental research told me why: the entire industry was depressed because of a change in technology from the old Sega and Nintendo game cartridge players to the compact disk. Then all I had to do was decide if Electronic Arts was well positioned to successfully negotiate the transition.

Screening programs basically fall into two types: programs that require an investor to build his or her own screens from scratch and programs that come with their own screening process built in. The screens I've discussed, building on Morningstar's U.S. Equities database, fall into the first camp. That program and others like it, such as Tradeline and Stock Investor, give an investor data and logical tools for sorting that information and basically say, "Go to town."

Value Line's Value Screen, on the other hand, applies the investment company's proven method for grouping stocks by risk and reward. (According to Mark Hulbert, the editor of the *Hulbert Financial Digest*, a review of investment newsletters, from 1980 through mid–1992 the portfolio of an investor who bought the 100 stocks rated "1" for timeliness by Value Line—and who bought and sold weekly when those recommendations changed—would have gained 620.7 percent. The Wilshire 5000 stock index gained 432.7 percent during the same period.) Value Screen, while it allows an investor to build his or her own screens, also presents a black box ranking system. An investor can't construct Value Line's ratings for safety and timeliness because the program doesn't state the rules that determine what fundamental factors it looks at or how it weights them.

Which type of screening program is best? Value Line's track record is public and trustworthy. (But remember it is only relevant if an investor buys the entire 100-stock Value Line portfolio and then follows the system's trades.) The screens any individual builds are untested—although they may be based on tested principals. It's up to you.

As useful as all of these programs are, I would never buy a stock without doing some research that can't be performed on a computer. None of these programs can evaluate the quality of a technology company's technology, or a retailer's inventory management, or a pharmaceutical company's research effort. None can tell me very much about a company's management—or even if the track record that an investor is looking at

# COMPANIES THAT GO IN CIRCLES

There's a category of company, called a "cyclical," that's especially hard to evaluate with a computerized stock screen. The fortunes of these companies, the auto makers are good examples, move up and down with the economic cycle. The automobile industry sells more than 14 million cars a year in the United States when times are flush and about 9 million when they're not. The fortunes of General Motors, Ford, and Chrysler go up and down with events inside each company—the hugely successful initial introduction of the Ford Taurus, for example, helped Ford gain a bigger share of whatever market existed—but they also swing with the economic cycle as a whole.

So the price of a cyclical stock describes some kind of spiral (or if the company is completely steady, a circle). A growing cyclical company will still rise and fall with each swing of the economy; the stock price at the top of each new cycle will be higher than at the top of the one before. A declining cyclical will show a lower peak with each top in the cycle.

Depending on where we are in the cycle, a cyclical will show a high price-to-earnings ratio or a low one—neither means exactly what it seems. Cyclicals tend to show high price-to-earnings ratios when they are at the bottom of cycles—earnings are low but investors, looking ahead, are willing to pay for the peak that is to come. In contrast, cyclicals show low price-to-earnings ratios near the top of cycles, when investors start to sell, even though current earnings are high, because they can see the next downturn coming.

All of which makes it hard to evaluate a cyclical. One method with a proven track record is practiced by Anthony Spare, who runs a private money management firm, Spare, Kaplan & Bischel in San Francisco. Spare charts the relative dividend yield of cyclicals and other stocks over time (that is, he divides the dividend yield of a stock by the dividend yield of the S&P 500). When the relative dividend yield is near the top of its historical range (when investors beat down the price of a stock until its yield climbs in comparison to the yield on the S&P), Spare buys. When investors like the stock so much that the relative yield is low, he sells. You can find more details on Spare's system in his book, *Relative Dividend Yield*. It includes sample relative dividend charts for about 40 stocks.

on the screen was compiled by the current management. These programs can't tell me about product cycles or customer satisfaction.

Fundamentally, they tell me what has happened, but they don't tell me why. I can see from the numbers on my screen that Wal-Mart has been a great company—its margins, among other numbers, tell me that. But I don't know what the company has done to create those margins—and that, of course, means that I don't know if those margins are sustainable.

The great investors who invest using just the kinds of data available in systems such as this are the exceptions that prove the rule. They are successful because their strategies require only the kind of numbers that computers are good at spitting out. I remember first meeting Louis Navellier, the editor of *MPT Review*, one of the best-performing investment newsletters (top-rated by the *Hulbert Financial Digest* over the last ten years with a 902 percent return—that's equivalent to an average annual return of 25.9 percent). I asked him what stocks he was buying now. Navellier whipped out a fat computer printout and spread it across the breakfast table. He had run down his first six or seven picks, touting their recent earnings record, before I stopped him. I had never heard of anything he was buying and I asked him what these companies did. He looked slightly, but only ever so slightly, chagrined. "I really don't have any idea," he said. If the numbers looked good, Navellier bought. Industry, management, technology—all those kinds of issues— were unimportant to him.

But Navellier and other number-crunching professionals such as Brad Lewis at Fidelity's Stock Selector and Disciplined Equity Funds or John Bogle, Jr., at the Quantative Funds don't simply look at widely available data, run it through simple screens, and then invest. Navellier, for example, bases his system on a company's ability to generate a sustained but short-term series of earnings surprises. His system works because companies that surprise analysts with stronger than expected earnings in one quarter have a tendency to surprise analysts in the next one or two quarters, too.

No investor can go out and just order up that data from some source. Navellier has built a detailed record of expected earnings for all stocks—and then just as carefully tracked and correlated the reported earnings of each company. Those earnings numbers each have to be studied as well and corrected for extraordinary items such as the sale of a division, a charge against earnings because of a cut in the work force or the acquisition of another company. It's the hard work in creating that data and in figuring out the patterns it reveals that leads to profits.

This kind of data cleaning and the intensive effort to discover meaningful patterns are beyond most individual investors. But there is another way to skin this cat. Investors can use well-constructed screens to narrow the universe to a manageable number of stocks and then do a bottom-up analysis on each of those stocks. Rather than trying to gather reliable and comparable data on 6,000 equities, an investor can study 20 or 30 in detail.

Fortunately several good computer programs now on the market can guide an investor through this task and perform the most time-consuming calculations. The best of them will teach the novice investor the basics of how to use fundamental information about a company to buy and sell stocks, and allow the experienced investor to turn a stock inside out to see exactly what makes it tick. I'll tell you about some of them in the next chapter.

## REVIEWS

### AAII STOCK INVESTOR

American Association of Individual Investors, 625 N. Michigan Avenue, Suite 1900, Chicago, IL 60611, 800-428-2244.

Versions available: DOS (version 2.1a), Windows (version 2.1a).

Requirements: For DOS version, 3MB RAM, 30MB free space on hard drive, and DOS 3.1 or better. For Windows version, 8MB of RAM, 30MB free space on hard drive, and Windows 3.1.

Cost and value: Both versions are $99 a year for members, $150 a year for nonmembers.

Guarantee: Money-back, pro-rated quarterly.

Demo or sample: None.

Technical support: 312-280-0170; fax 312-280-1625. The one time I called (identifying myself only as a user) for help, I got a technician on the phone almost immediately. AAII forum on America Online, e-mail AAIISparky@aol.com or AAIIPaul@aol.com.

User Newsletter or On-line Forum: *Stock Investor News*; AAII forum on America Online (keyword AAII).

Updated: Quarterly.

Strengths: Complete income statement data, distinguishes continued/discontinued operations, perhaps the best data on earnings estimates available on software.

Weaknesses: User must configure DOS version so that the program can find enough memory to run. May require rewriting config.sys and autoexec.bat files. Data updated only quarterly. Newsletter-format manual offers little guidance for using the program.

Tricks of the trade: Combine the project menu with the portfolio function to create a constantly updated screen of candidates to replace your current portfolio stocks. For example, set up a portfolio labeled "Motorola," which consists of stocks capable of beating that stock. Create a screen based on Motorola's key characteristics—the ones that define the company's place in your portfolio and that are important, in your opinion, to the company's success. For example, use Motorola's current growth rate (16.7 percent), projected growth rate for next year (18.0), and return on equity (20.6) to create a list of 80 companies and then rank them by current price-to-earnings ratio. Turn this into a user-defined report (asking for five-year price-to-earnings ratios as well) and look for companies that might be better than Motorola. Update the screen as Motorola's key statistics change—that way you'll be running a continuing test on Motorola, as well as constantly checking the markets for better stocks.

A thorough, data-heavy program for the fundamental investor. (Although the DOS version isn't recommended for the user who isn't comfortable wrestling with DOS's systems files.) Extremely strong set of fundamental data (250 items on more than 8,000 stocks) includes income statement data that will let the user study margins and separates continuing from discontinued operations. Among the best data on earnings estimates available on software. Historical data from Media General and earnings estimates from I/B/E/S, one of the three companies that tracks Wall Street's earnings estimates. Uses a simple menu bar at the top of the screen. The ten screens of basic data include: Company Summary (which lists ratios and compares to industry), Income Statement (with earnings per share for continuing and total operations, dividend, and payout ratio) by for the last eight quarters, Annual Income Statement (sales, cost of goods sold, gross income, net income, gross and net margins, earnings per share, cash flow per share) back to fiscal year ending in May 1990, I/B/E/S Earnings Estimates (with current, previous months, high and low, number up and down), and Ratios (again in comparison to an industry), including beta, 200-day moving average (an unusual number for a fundamental stock screen program to provide but a very useful number), 52-week relative strength, weekly volume, market capitalization, and institutional holdings. Beginners are likely to find the program's multiple valuation models confusing (although the Help function does a good job explaining each method), but more experienced users will find the inclusion of multiple methods a plus, since it allows them to choose the valuation method best suited to a specific stock. For example, several of the valuation models didn't work with Silicon Graphics, since the company doesn't have a useful average price-to-earnings ratio, but the program still used the current price-to-earnings ratio and a calculated projected earnings trend to decide that the company had a fair market value of $37.90. Users can create custom variables (by combining several data items, for example) to use in screens. A project menu allows user to automate regularly performed combinations of tasks, such as loading a specific portfolio and running a defined screen on it each time you open the program.

AAII planned a CD-ROM professional version (again with quarterly updates) for 1996 release. This Windows-only program is scheduled to include expanded financial statements and seven years of historical data. Projected price is $299 for members and $349 for nonmembers.

## MARKET GUIDE AND MARKET GUIDE FOR WINDOWS

Market Guide Inc., 2001 Marcus Avenue, Lake Success, NY 11042, 516-327-2400, ext. 200.

Versions available: On-line through various vendors including Prodigy, StreetSmart, Telescan, or in CD-ROM for Windows.

Requirements: Modem, or 8MB RAM and Windows 3.1.

Cost: Varies with vendor. On Prodigy, it's part of Strategic Investor service at $14.95 a month. CD-ROM version with weekly updates is $9,600 annually.

Guarantee: 30-day money-back.

Demo or sample: Free.

Technical support: Through on-line vendor, or 516-327-2400, ext. 200 (8:30 A.M.–5:30 P.M., M–F).

User Newsletter: None.

Updated: Database updated weekly.

Strengths: Market Guide's attempt to retain the format of the standard company annual and quarterly report makes this database especially useful for fundamental investors. This is the only program that provides both full balance sheet and income sheet statements, plus a cash flow statement. The data even includes an abbreviated version of the footnotes to the company's report so that a user can identify one-time events.

Weaknesses: The CD-ROM version is too expensive for most investors. So while quality, quantity, and freshness make this data the best available electronically, the quality of screening tools will effectively vary widely, depending on the vendor that has repackaged Market Guide's data. Prodigy, the most widely used of these three, offers only limited screening capabilities. Telescan offers the best screening tools (although they require practice to master).

Tricks of the trade: Check the notes to the company's financial statement (listed not on a page or section called Notes, but at the bottom of the income statement highlights-by-quarter screen on page 8. Notes give an investor information on any one-time events that might have affected the reported numbers and critical clues to the character of the company's accounting practices. Both conservative and aggressive accounting methods are legal and acceptable—but it's important for an investor to understand which a specific company practices.

It's hard to imagine needing more fundamental data than this source provides in a typical twelve-page report on a company. Data includes price, full-year earnings estimates, revenue, earnings, dividends, book value, cash flow for the last four quarters, plus revenue and earnings for the last four quarters, and revenue, dividend, and earnings growth rate for one, three, and five years on more than 6,000 companies. Year-by-year financials for most recent eight years list high and low price and price-to-earnings ratio, earnings per share, revenue, net income, profit margin, payout ratio, and effective tax rate. Market Guide compares price and financial ratios—price to earnings, price to sales, price to book, price to cash flow, beta, debt to equity, quick ratio, return on equity, return on assets, and profit margin—of a company to those for its industry as a whole. Analyst estimates and recommendations from Zacks Investment Research, Inc., and information on insider activity, short interest, and institutional activity reports complete the package. (In 1996 the company plans to add earnings estimates from First Call.)

Since Market Guide is a data provider, the quality of the screening tools that come with this data will vary depending on what program or vendor is supplying you with it. Prodigy's Strategic Investor feature provides a decent combination for the beginner. It links screening tools called Stock Hunter to the Market Guide database. Stock Hunter comes with predefined models, labeled: Graham/Dodd, One Up on Wall Street, CANSLIM, WallFlowers, Sustainable Growth, Consistent Dividends, Low Price/Book Value, High Price/Book Value. Each is thoroughly and very technically described—Graham/Dodd, for example, tells who these two investors and theoreticians were, and then gets technical immediately by reciting a formula: Price = Earnings x [8.5 +(2xGrowth)], and then notes that this formula is based on a period when a Corporate AAA bond yielded 4.4 percent and suggests adjusting the formula by using 4.4/the current AAA yield. You don't have to follow the discussion to use the screen, however. Simply hit the Graham and Dodd button and up pops a list ranked by percentage undervalued. Cigna heads the list with value at $120, price at $73 for an estimated 66 percent undervalued.

Options for creating custom searches are much more limited. Possible criteria include only four items: industry, dividend yield, five-year earnings per share growth, and price-to-earnings ratio.

Market Guide data is also available through Telescan and Schwab's StreetSmart.

### U.S. Equities OnFloppy (Formerly Marketbase)

Morningstar Inc., 225 West Wacker Drive, Chicago, IL 60606, 800-876-5005.

Versions available: DOS (version 4.1).

Requirements: For DOS version, 512K RAM, 6.3MB free space on hard drive, and DOS 3.1 or better.

Cost: $55 for one time, $145 per year for quarterly updates, $295 for monthly updates, and $995 per year for weekly updates.

Guarantee: 30-day money back. After 30 days pro-rated refund of subscription.

Demo or sample: One time version available for $55.

Technical support: 800-866-3472 (8 A.M.–7 P.M., M–Th; 8 A.M.–6 p.m., F; 10 A.M.–3 P.M., Sat.).

User Newsletter: None.

Updates: Weekly, monthly, or quarterly.

Strengths: A compact program that requires only 512K of memory. A toggle, hitting the F4 key, switches the form of company data from percentage gain, to millions of dollars, to dollars per share. Opening screen gives averages for all data for all companies, a useful tool for investors looking for reference points to use in building screens.

Weaknesses: Hidden commands (not visible from the menu bars) require constant reference to manual, which is organized as a tutorial—good for learning, poor for continued reference. Once you've generated a list of stocks, truly aggravating procedures for printing out a screen require creating a separate report format listing all the data items to be printed out. (See Tricks of the trade below.) Confusing and complicated system for specifying time period for any data item (such as 1993 earnings per share) when creating a screen.

Tricks of the trade: Displaying the results of a screen is complicated. Once you figure it out, write it down—the instructions are buried in the manual. Remember that after you've constructed and run the screen (and saved the criteria so that you can run it again), you need to hit Shift F4 to display the results. Although you would expect the display to list all the data on the companies in the screened universe, it won't. You'll need to ask for the data categories you want to display one by one. Remember to save this report, too. Screening criteria and display reports are saved in totally different files.

One of the best fundamental database and stock screening programs, U.S. Equities is also irritatingly difficult to navigate and sometimes frustratingly cryptic about the date of specific items (more than 100 variables) on the 7,471 companies it tracks. The program is strongest and easiest to operate as a source of fundamental data on an individual company. "Display stock function," a choice in the opening menu, lists recent data on top of the screen and on the bottom a balance sheet with selected financial data. A simple toggle (hitting the F4 key) lets the user see data either in millions of dollars, as percentage gain, or as dollars per share. Another (F7) switches the presentation of the annual data between most recently completed prior year and trailing twelve months. A third (F8) toggles between data items on the specific stock and averages for the database as a whole, making comparisons of price-to-earnings, price-to-book, and similar ratios simple.

There's good and bad news about the data. Morningstar provides all the expected standards—dividend yield, price-to-earnings, price-to-book, and debt-to-equity ratios, sales, earnings, etc., plus some useful items sometimes missing from computerized databases—percentage of institutional holdings, cash flow, and price-to-sales ratio, for instance. But no analyst estimates, no data on the number of analysts who follow a company, no trading volumes. Some fundamental investors will find the lack of profit margin numbers and inventory data a critical flaw. Also the numbers can be old and it is hard to tell what months and quarters numbers refer to. In the Morningstar tradition, charts are few and rudimentary.

As a screening program, U.S. Equities is powerful but idiosyncratic. The program comes with several predefined screens—Good Price Ratios, Decent Price Ratios, Earnings Growth, Dividend Income, and Undervalued Growth with Strong Balance Sheets—that will give beginners ideas on how to build screens. (See this chapter for details on what building a screen is like in this program.) Constructing custom screens is easy—all a user needs to do is type in the category of data, price-to-earnings, for example (but only in the correct format to be found under F5), the value, an operation (greater than, less than, equal to), and then move on to the next data category. Logic is, however, limited to and/or for connecting items—which makes optimization impossible.

Stocks surviving a screen can be turned into a new stock universe, the set of stocks that the program will now use, for further study, or into a portfolio, but since there is no way to track initial and subsequent prices, there is no way to study the performance of a screen over time, an important tool for testing screening criteria. The process of creating a portfolio is typically quirky. A user must create a screen or retrieve an already created set of screening rules, run the screen, hit Shift F7 to move to portfolio menu (while staying in the stock universe created by this screen), type F6 to use this as current active universe, type "1" to make this portfolio active, and then finally save the portfolio. After this, however, I can access this portfolio without having to rerun the screen.

Morningstar is in the process of updating U.S. Equities OnFloppy. At the end of 1995 the company added data on another 1,250 small companies (those currently trading on the NASDAQ SmallCap market). A "substantially enhanced" Windows version is scheduled for 1996 or 1997.

## TELESCAN ANALYZER AND PROSEARCH, AND TELESCAN INVESTOR'S PLATFORM

Telescan Inc., 10550 Richmond Avenue, Suite 250, Houston, TX 77042, 800-324-8246.

Versions available: Analyzer DOS (version 3.8), ProSearch DOS (version 4.0), and Telescan Investor's Platform Windows (version 1.1).

Requirements: For DOS version, 2MB RAM, 5MB free space on hard drive. For Windows version, 4MB RAM, 6MB free space on hard drive.

Cost: Software for Telescan Analyzer, the basic DOS module, costs $99; Analyzer plus ProSearch software costs $295. In the Windows version, the Telscan Investor's Platform Analysis Module costs $199; the Analysis and Screening Modules together sell for $349. On-line data charges vary from as little as $9.95 a month for one hour of use (additional hours cost $4.80 each) to $49 a month for unlimited analysis plus $18 a month for unlimited use of ProSearch. Other Telescan modules, such as Mutual Fund Search ($100) and ESearch ($149), require additional fees.

Guarantee: 30-day money back on software. Subscription refund prorated.

Demo or sample: Users can preview the service using Telescan's Internet site (http://www.telescan.com).

Technical support: 800-324-4692.

User Newsletter: Free quarterly newsletter, *Telescan News*.

Update: On-line service. Updated daily.

Strengths: Every piece of information—and most of the analytical tools I can think of lusting after—are in one place: fundamental and technical data on stocks; technical charting and stock screening; mutual fund performance numbers and earnings estimates from Wall Street analysts; access to company reports from Market Guide; MarketScope for Standard & Poor's; and mutual fund news and analysis from Morningstar. And, of course, a portfolio manager to let you count up all your gains.

Weaknesses: Pricing, pricing, pricing. Telescan data is expensive and the company's pricing scheme penalizes investors who want to use the full power of the Telescan system. Unlimited access to just Telescan's analysis service costs $45 a month—but you still have to pay extra for Prosearch, Mutual Fund Search, and ESearch. Charges for those three services are $18, $12, and $12 a month, respectively.

Tricks of the trade: Use all the tutorials. Take advantage of every free minute that comes with your initial software. If you learn the Telescan system—and how to download information so that you can spend most of your time off-line—you can radically minimize the hours you pay for, which can actually make Telescan affordable.

Are you ready for a major commitment? Telescan isn't for the casual electronic investor—it's too expensive and too tough to master. If you don't use tons of fundamental data in picking stocks, regularly consult technical indicators, run complicated screens for stocks and mutual funds, or feel compelled to keep up with the latest thoughts from Wall Street, then Telescan is not for you.

But for the very active investor, one who's never met a datapoint he didn't like, the program amply rewards the effort. Some of Telescan's features clearly outdistance the competition.

Let me give you an example of both the program's power and the demands it makes on an investor. ProSearch is Telescan's stock screening module and, short of building your own spreadsheet, the most powerful program I've discovered for finding investment ideas. Programs such as Morningstar's U.S. Equities limit the kinds of searches an investor can run by supplying very limited logic—I can search for stocks with growth rates better than 20 percent *and* a price-to-earnings ratio below 20. But I can't look for stocks with the best combination of those two factors—nor can I weight them so that the program considers high growth 50 percent more important than price-to-earnings.

With ProSearch, I can—if I'm willing to master the commands and procedures. Using ProSearch in the absolute mode, I can build screens just as I do with U.S. Equities. I can enter values and commands for greater than, less than, or equal to. In relative mode, however, I can weight each criteria—exactly what I want to do. But Telescan's ProSearch doesn't begin this process with anything as simple as the spreadsheet-style, pre-loaded, and formatted data that U.S. Equities presents. Instead, since Telescan uses an on-line database, a user has to specify what fundamental information he wants on which stocks, download the data, and then use the commands unique to Telescan to construct the screen. It's easier to do this in the Windows version (with its pulldown menus) than in the DOS version, but I still wouldn't call it easy. Building my first screen took me more than three hours of fumbling, mistakes, reloading data, and constant reference to the Help screen. At the end I had a better screen than I could have built with any other product—but the time I spent learning this system is only justified if I use it frequently.

I've reviewed Telescan as a technical analysis program in Chapter 8, so let me finish this fundamental investing review by mentioning a second Telescan feature that I also haven't found duplicated in any other program for the individual investor. ESearch, an add-on module that will cost you an extra $149 for software and $12 a month for non-prime-time access, will let you build stock screens based on Wall Street earnings estimates. I/B/E/S Express does this, too—but at $10,000, it's intended for the professional market. For more on I/B/E/S Express, see Chapter 9.

I think it's difficult to tell if Telescan's unique mixture of power and complexity is for you without trying it first. Fortunately, the company has set up a World Wide Web site (http://www.telescan.com) that will let you get the flavor of the program. Take it for a ride.


### TRADE LINE ELECTRONIC STOCK GUIDE

IDD Information Services, 2 World Trade Center, New York, NY 10048, 212-323-9107.

Versions available: Windows (version 2.0) and CD-ROM (version 2.0).

Requirements: Windows version requires 4MB RAM and 10 MB free space on hard drive. RAM requirements for CD-ROM version will vary depending on user's choice of how much of the program will be run off the hard drive instead of directly from CD-ROM (the more on the hard drive, the faster the program will run). Standard installation, which combines hard drive and CD-ROM requires 1MB of RAM. (Speed was not unpleasantly slow in this configuration.) Also requires Windows 3.1 or higher.

Cost: $159 for an annual monthly subscription or $74.95 for quarterly updates.

Guarantee: 30-day money back.

Demo or sample: Demo costs $25. Users can also try Tradeline's data at IDD's World Wide Web site: (http://nestegg.iddis.com/).

Technical support: 212-323-9107 (9 A.M.–5 P.M., M–F). Customer service wasn't impressive. Tradeline's telephone order-taker miscopied my credit card number and then took weeks to correct my order.

User Newsletter or On-line Forum: No newsletter, but World Wide Web site at: (http://nestegg.iddis.com/).

Updated: Available in monthly or quarterly versions.

Strengths: Easy to navigate. No manual is supplied with the program, but user won't miss it. Decent onscreen help suffices. Menu limited to File, Edit, Security, Window, and Help. A dialog box lists the options under "Security": search, screening, compare, and charts. Includes data on dividend-paying preferred issues and other securities of interest to the income investor not found in any other stock database that I reviewed.

Weaknesses: Scanty data on each issue and extremely limited screening and graphic abilities. Missing key fundamental data.

Tricks of the trade: An investor may not need this program when the market is soaring, but it could be very useful for nervous investors seeking to hedge their bets. This program is the best I've found to explore the nooks and crannies of the market for preferred and other high-dividend-paying shares. In a bear market, the high dividends on preferred shares will support the price of the stock, making them an attractive alternative to the common shares of the same company. Unfortunately, in bull markets, preferred shares don't match the big upside moves of common stock.

Investors familiar with the wealth of quality data that IDD, the publisher of industry journal *Investment Dealers Digest*, provides in other formats will find this CD-ROM disappointing. While the program is extremely easy to operate, its designers have achieved that goal only by sacrificing depth of data and limiting the power of the program's analytical tools. Typing in a ticker symbol and hitting "OK" produces thumbnail charts of a stock—high/low/close, volume, and return on the individual security versus S&P, plus data boxes on performance (including beta and earnings per share) and pricing (one-year and five-year change, 52-week high and low). But that's the limit of the data available here.

The "Compare" function will let the user compare two price charts—but no other charts or data. To get a total return comparison, a user would have to print out bar charts of total return for each security and then put the paper version side by side. Still, this is one of the few database programs to chart total return at all.

The screening function is cluttered with vague and useless criteria. I find it hard to imagine why, for example, I would want to use "exchange" as one of my criteria for building a screen. The preset screens on total return, dividend yield, price-to-earnings ratio, and payout ratio are easy to operate but logic is limited to "and" for the connecting criteria of a screen. The lack of basic fundamental data such as sales or earnings per share growth rate makes it impossible to execute most standard screens for growth stocks. The program can't rank stocks in a universe except alphabetically.

### Value/Screen III

Value Line Publishing, Inc., 220 E. 42nd Street, New York, NY 10017, 800-654-0508.

Versions available: DOS (version 3.009), Macintosh (1.1).

Requirements: DOS version requires DOS 3.0 or higher, 640K RAM, and 2 MB free hard drive space. Macintosh requires 640K RAM. Modem for weekly quote update.

Cost and value: Monthly $465, quarterly $325.

Guarantee: Only with purchase of annual subscription.

Demo or sample: Free.

Technical support: 800-654-0508 (9 A.M.–5 P.M., M–F).

User Newsletter: None.

Updated: Quarterly by disk. Weekly by modem only. Monthly by modem or disk.

Strengths: 52 screening variables clearly defined in glossary at end of manual. Ability to track a portfolio over time. Inclusion of time-tested Value Line ratings for timeliness and safety makes it possible to build and manage a portfolio that follows the Value Line rankings. Lists projections for growth in earnings, price appreciation, dividends, earnings per share, and book value from Value Line analysts. Users can download data to spreadsheets such as Lotus and Excel. Program will give onscreen definitions of variables if user hits Alt F1. (This and other key commands refer to the DOS version.)

Weaknesses: Data only on Value Line universe of 1,600 stocks. Lack of quarterly sales and earnings numbers means that this program can't be used to replace paper Value Line newsletter for investors who use Value Line data to build their analysis of stocks.

Tricks of the trade: Even investors who don't follow the Value Line system for rating stocks may be interested in tracking the company's changes in timeliness ratings. It's not simple. The program has no key or function for picking up changes. To do it each month, you'll need to set up a portfolio for stocks rated 1 for timeliness, sort that alphabetically, and compare it to the portfolio you set up and alphabetized for last month's 1-rated stocks. Or download the ratings into a spreadsheet each month.

Your opinion of this program will probably depend on whether you use the paper Value Line investment newsletter—and on what you use it for. Investors who use the Value Line system and its recommendations to buy and sell stocks will probably love this piece of software, since it makes it easy to track Value Line's recommendations. Investors who use Value Line as a source of data for their own stock-picking system will find this software frustrating since it omits crucial data now found in the newsletter.

Data items (52) on a universe of 1,600 stocks include the usual financials plus timeliness and safety, financial strength, and technical rank ratings from Value Line. A thorough set of projections for future earnings growth (next quarter to next year), three-to-five-year price appreciation, dividends, and book value. Historical data limited to last quarter and trailing twelve months earnings per share change, five-year earnings per share, dividend, and book value growth. Lists current price-to-earnings ratio but not historical range. Substitutes a number called "return on net worth" for return on assets or equity.

The program operates off a straightforward menu bar. To screen, the user hits "S" from the main menu. A window in upper left then defines seven categories of screening data: ratings and estimates, market data, historical measures, growth projections, fiscal year data, identification, user-defined data. Each one of these has subcategories that appear once the user has selected the category. For example, if I type "M" (for Market), 4 (for current P/E), then the program prompts me to fill in relationship ("less than"), and value ("15"). Hitting F2 to put the screen in action tells me that 848 of the 1,600 stocks in the program pass. To save a list the user hits F4 and gives the list a name for future recall.

Hitting F7 pulls up a single ticker report, which gives all the data on a company listed above, plus a blurb that tells what it makes, where sales are, who its officers are, and what insiders hold.

"Comparison Reports" feature enables the user to enter symbols for up to 10 stocks, and then, by hitting F2, get data for the companies under comparison arranged in columns for easy cross-company study. ("Comparison Reports" can also be customized to include particular variables.) A user can compare the values for any company to the entire database by going to "Statistical Summary" under "Reports." The program will also graph the value of a data item for a single company or sample of companies against the value of that data item for the database as a whole.

# 4

# Analyzing a Stock: A New Way to Conquer Uncertainty

So far, I've concentrated on telling you about some very real benefits of computerized investing. I've told you about programs that can get information to an investor faster, or that can help an investor look at more alternative stocks than would be reasonably possible on paper, or that can sort and rearrange data more easily. But the tools of computerized investing offer another kind of advantage as well. They make it possible to think about investing in radically different ways. You haven't tapped in to all the power that this software can put in the hands of individual investors until you've learned a different way of thinking about how to analyze an investment.

Successful electronic investing requires a shift in how you think. You can use these programs as more powerful versions of the tools that you've used before as an investor and they will indeed automate and speed up retrieving information, keeping records, tracking performance, finding new investment ideas. You will, however, still be thinking about investment decisions in pretty much the same fashion as you did before you put a computer on your desktop.

Computerized investing changes a crucial ratio: that between the amount of effort required to think intelligently about an investment decision and the amount of effort required to do the often complex calculations that underlie much of modern financial theory. While thinking intelligently hasn't gotten any easier or harder (much evidence to contrary), calculation has gotten massively easier. Where it once might have taken me two hours to look up the formula to compute the fair market value of a stock with an earnings growth rate of 18 percent and a yield of 6.3 percent when interest rates on a one-year Treasury bill are 5.7 percent, it now takes me about five minutes, using Quant IX's Stock Analyst program, to do the computation and record the results in a fashion that I'll be able to read tomorrow.

Why is that change in how much time a task takes important? It means that I can change the variables and run the analysis again and again and again. In the last chapter, I mentioned how this approach would let me fine-tune stock-picking screens. But the effects of this change go well beyond fine-tuning. You can now approach uncertainty—whether it's uncertainty about earnings or sales or expectations—in an entirely different way. Using your computer and this kind of thinking you will be able to understand the uncertainty—and therefore risk—of individual stocks in new and much more precise ways, and to make sure that you get well paid for all the risk you take.

I could natter on about paradigm shifts and the like, but instead let me show you what I mean with a case study of three stocks that illustrates the electronic investor's way to think about how to use the fundamental facts about the company and its business in order to predict stock prices. The basic question is simple: Which of three stocks—computer-maker Hewlett-Packard, utility Enova, and retailer Williams-Sonoma—should I buy? (The list comes from the "To Buy" list that I keep; see Chapter 2 on setting one up; prices and other details are as of mid-1995.) To demonstrate the computerized way to think about fundamental stock analysis, I used two programs—NAIC's Stock Selection Guide and Quant IX's Stock Analyst.

## The "Paper" Way of Thinking

Let's start by doing a computer analysis of Hewlett-Packard using NAIC's Stock Selection Guide. But even though I'm using investment software, I'll stick to "paper" thinking.

When I started my analysis, Hewlett-Packard had just been ham-

# THE DATA LAG PROBLEM

Speedy delivery of out-of-date numbers is a fact of life for the computerized investor. The data that arrives on disk with a monthly or quarterly update can be as much as two quarters out of date if a company's reporting period breaks the wrong way. Even on-line data isn't as fresh as it should be. The Standard & Poor's company reports on-line through sources such as Schwab's Street Smart can be weeks old—and the data is often a quarter behind.

Two ways around this problem: with your news reader, save to file the two most recent quarterly earnings reports on each stock you follow. If you start following a new stock, immediately search for the most recent earnings report (remember that many news readers delete news more than 60 days old).

Second, don't forget that you can still call the company's investor relations department. Many now offer automated services that will mail or, even better, fax you the most recent quarterly income statement. Most, automated or not, are happy to send a potential investor the most recent news on the company. For example, from phone call to receipt, it took me six minutes to get a faxed quarterly income statement from Enova.

mered in a technology rout set off when Intel disappointed Wall Street analysts by reporting 99 cents a share when predictions had called for $1.03. In sympathy Hewlett-Packard fell by $9 a share in two days.

I start by opening up the quarterly data file that NAIC sends me on disk to see if I need to update any information on Hewlett-Packard. The most recent earnings and sales data, from the quarter ending April 30, are already entered. I decide that I'm close enough to the end of the second quarter to use the analysts' consensus estimates as data. Waiting until I've got the real report could consume another month and I want to know if I should buy now. (I'll enter the real numbers when they become available. I feel relatively comfortable using the consensus of $1.00 because the company is followed by nineteen analysts and there's relatively little spread between the median estimate of $1.00 and the average estimate of $1.01. The consensus is also conservatively below the high estimate of $1.18 for the quarter.)

Updating the data by hand involves typing in three numbers—revenues, earnings, and dividends. I also adjust the stock price entered into the program to include the stock's price on July 19 of $77.875.

By using some complicated mathematics to find the line that most closely fits all the annual data for sales and earnings, this program charts a trend line for Hewlett-Packard (see illustration below). The trend line for sales is rock solid—the line passes right through the points that indicate the annual sales for the company with hardly a quiver. Hewlett-Packard has grown sales at 15.9 percent annually from 1988 to the present, the program calculates. The earnings line is more erratic, and the trend line fits between the curves of a shallow S. Historical earnings growth averaged 11.2 percent.

The graph has already flagged one crucial question about Hewlett-Packard. The last three annual data points for earnings clearly put earnings on a growth path above the historical rate. The three recent quarterly figures suggest an even more rapid acceleration of growth. In

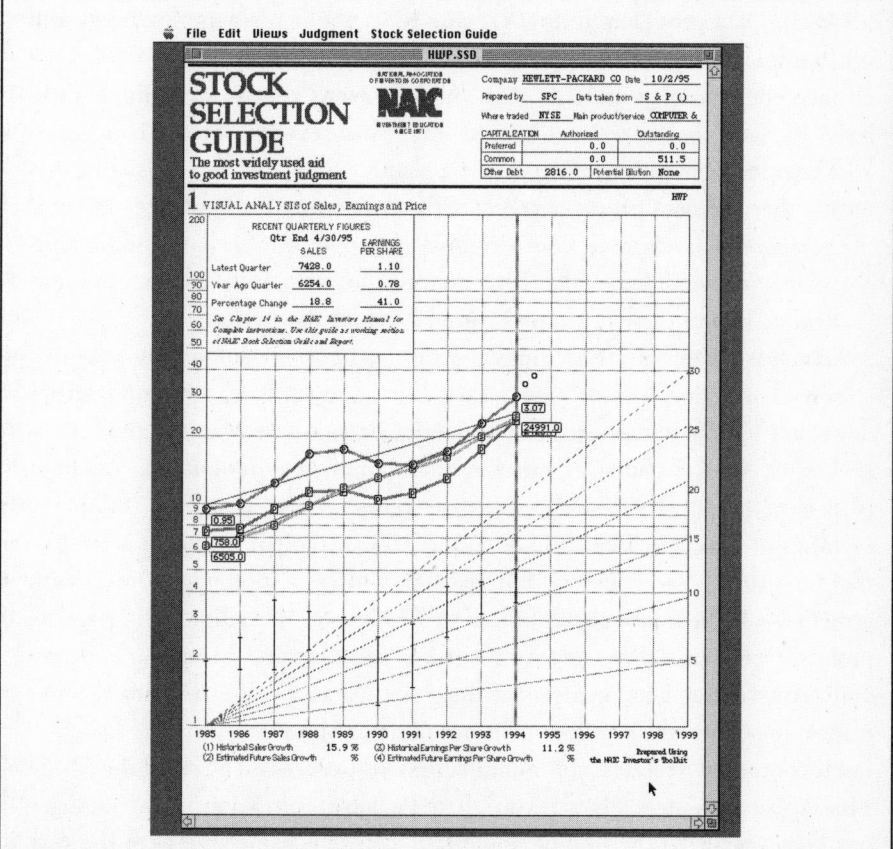

*Hewlett-Packard as pictured by the NAIC Stock Selection Guide. The recent acceleration of earnings and sales is clearly visible. (Courtesy NAIC)*

case I've missed this on the graph, the program expressly asks me about growth. Blanks at the bottom of the page ask me to fill in "estimated future sales growth" and "estimated future earnings per share." The sales numbers seem easy. Just follow the solid historical trend and type in 15.9 percent. Earnings are the major problem: Will the future price of the stock follow the historical trend or will it reflect the new and higher trend line of the last three quarters?

## WHAT ARE EARNINGS?

**N**ever put anything in your ear smaller than your elbow and never plug an earnings number into a value calculation until you know where it's been. Data providers follow varying rules about reporting earnings and other financials. Data can be presented exactly as the company does. Disclosure and Market Guide do this. Which means that raw earnings numbers haven't been corrected for one-time events or a company's idiosyncratic accounting practices. Or data can be modified—usually this means that the data provider corrects the data using the footnotes in company reports. Standard & Poor's follows this practice. Or data can be both corrected and modified. Value Line analysts sometimes revise data to more accurately match their interpretation of accounting events.

Which is preferable? Raw numbers can lead an investor seriously astray, so some correction is clearly necessary. For example, Intel took a big write-down in the fourth quarter of 1994 to straighten out problems with its Pentium chip. Market Guide, rightly but misleadingly, reports full-year earnings of just $2.62 for 1994—reflecting the charge. Using that data (following earnings of $1.24 in 1992 and $2.60 in 1993), though, makes it seem like the company's growth has faltered. But there's nothing wrong with growth—sales rose from $8.8 billion in 1993 to $11.5 billion in 1994. The problem was a one-time expense related to recalling and fixing the Pentium chip. Any fundamental analysis of the stock needs to take that into account rather than using the reported earnings number blindly.

How much correction and modification you use—the S&P or the Value Line approach—depends on you. Just be sure you know what changes have been made to the numbers and that you're comfortable with the reasons behind the changes.

Now I know from experience how to approach this question using paper, pencil, and printed resources. I know that the company has been steadily moving up in the ranks of the computer industry. Standard & Poor's analyst, for example, wrote on May 26 that the company "is emerging as the dominant computer vendor in the world." The company has aggressively cut prices on its line of computers based on Intel's industry-standard Pentium chip; Hewlett-Packard intends to grow market share. The company's dominance of the market for desktop laser and ink jet printers gives its brand name a cachet that should ease the company's penetration of other segments of the business market. And the company has a strong product line in servers and networked machines, the fastest growing part of the computer industry. So a higher growth rate certainly isn't impossible.

The historical 11.2 percent therefore seems too low, but does that make the 14.7 percent growth rate, which my research tells me is the consensus on Wall Street, right?—14.7 percent seems a very big jump. Looking at the graph I can see one other period (1985–1989) of rapid earnings acceleration like what I'm seeing in the quarterly numbers

---

**TIPS ON THE TOOLS**

## ALL THOSE TOUGH CALCULATIONS IN ONE BOX

There's a handy little book, the *McGraw-Hill Pocket Guide to Business Finance*, that I rely on when I'm trying to remember how to do one of the calculations that bedevil investors (such as turning a cumulative total return into an annual rate). Now that book has been turned into a software program called McGraw-Hill Financial Analyst. This $69.95 package contains 201 formulas for calculating everything from the required return on an investment using the capital asset pricing model to the value of a stock using Gordon's Dividend Growth Model to the value of options.

The program is set up like a book with a table of contents entry for each formula and pages that explain how each calculation is performed. The math can get pretty dense, but each calculation comes with sample spreadsheets—all you have to do is find the sample that best fits your case, click on the sample button on the page, and fill in the blanks on the spreadsheet.

For example, let's look at chapter 145, "Portfolio Theory," which will help you compute the expected return
*continued*

and risk on a portfolio holding different assets. In that chapter I can enter five years of returns for three different securities, and then calculate which two securities produce the best combination of risk and return. I don't have to even understand the math or the notation, as long as I grasp the investment principles.

(Windows only. Requires 4MB RAM and 12MB free space on hard drive. $69.95 from McGraw-Hill, 800-722-4726.)

so far. If I use the program to isolate just that period (by telling it to ignore the other data points), the computer tells me that growth for that four-year period averaged 14.2 percent. That's three percentage points over the current long-term historical growth rate and not too far below the analysts' projections of 14.7 percent for future growth.

So maybe 14.2 percent is the best number to use; it's pretty conservative—it leaves me below the sales growth rate of 15.9 percent and below the analysts' consensus earnings growth rate of 14.7 percent. Projecting earnings growth at this rate, out to 1999, gives me $5.96 a share in that year.

Taking my earnings growth projection of $5.96 I move to the second "page" of the program. Here the program will attempt to turn a projected earnings figure into a buy/sell/hold recommendation. It begins by setting up a table that charts the pretax profit on sales and the return on invested capital going back to 1985. I'm looking here for confirmation of my earnings growth projections and to see if I can detect problems in how the company is managed that might derail Hewlett-Packard in the future. I find a gentle slump in the middle of both data series and then a rising trend line. Pretax profit, for instance, went from 11.7 percent in 1985 to a low of 7.8 percent in 1991 and then rose in 1992, 1993, and 1994 to 9.7 percent. This data certainly makes me feel better about my projected earnings growth rate.

The next table lists the high and low price-to-earnings ratios for Hewlett-Packard since 1990. (The Stock Selection Guide uses S&P data, but Value Line also provides the information.) The stock has ranged on the low end from 8.1 to 14.4 (an average of 11.6) and on the high end from 16.5 to 24.2 (an average of 19.2). I note that even after the recent slaughter the stock is priced at a price-to-earnings ratio of 20.8.

The computer now tells me that I've reached another decision point. The program will project the five-year price targets for the stock using

# UNIT GROWTH

I haven't been able to find a computerized data source that reports unit growth, but that's no reason to leave it out of your analysis. In my opinion it's one of the most important indicators of a company's long-term prospects.

Most companies grow by selling more units of whatever they make, but that growth is imperfectly reflected in the standard sales numbers. A company that has raised prices can show rising sales, even though it hasn't increased the number of printers or shirts it sells. A company that cut prices can show rising sales, too, but only if the number of units it sells rises.

A company that raises prices isn't necessarily one I want to own. I only want to buy shares in a company that can raise prices when the price hike doesn't depress the number of units it sells. (That's why I need to know how many units the company is selling and has sold in the past.) A company like this has obvious pricing power. Consumers want what it produces enough to pay more for it without complaint. That's an impressive sign of the quality of the company's goods and its cachet on the market. This pricing strategy also tends to attract competitors that see an opportunity to steal customers by offering lower prices, however. I worry about a company that raises prices in the current global economy—I suspect that its success won't last.

What I most want is a company that cuts prices and sells more units—so many more units that sales revenues climb. (And I obviously don't want this to be a one-time phenomenon, because that could mean the company is in deep trouble and is resorting to fire-sale prices to move goods. To double-check that I also want to take a look at margins and make sure they aren't falling drastically.) For example, on July 25, Silicon Graphics reported net income for the second quarter of $72 million (after correcting for special items related to two acquisitions), up 57 percent from $46 million in the year-earlier period. Sales revenue went up 44 percent. But unit growth went up even more, 55 percent, well above the industry average. That's a company that knows how to protect its market lead—drive down prices so that competitors won't be able to grab market share on price.

high and low price/earnings figures, but I have to decide how to calculate those highs and lows. I can use the average, the high or the low price/earnings multiple, or some other method. Using the high price-to-earnings average, for example, and multiplying it by my $5.96 earnings estimate gives me a five-year projected price of $114.30. Using the low price-to-earnings average (11.6) and assuming that the company fails to grow earnings at all (and they stay at the $3.07 of 1994), yields a low price five years from now of $35.60.

---

**TIPS ON THE TOOLS**

## CREATING COMPETITOR COMPARISONS

I can easily create competitor comparisons with any of the stock screening programs that allow me to sort companies by a Standard Industry Code (SIC) number. Unfortunately, the comparisons aren't very useful.

SIC numbers lump together companies that aren't actually in the same business. For example, in the U.S. Equities program, Hewlett-Packard, which makes computers, printers, and test equipment for engineers, is grouped with Pitney Bowes, which makes postage meters and mailing systems, in SIC 3570 (manufacturing computer equipment).

The electronic investor doesn't have any real option except to create competitor comparisons by hand. Fortunately, you don't need to track every competitor to make this exercise worthwhile—in fact, all you really need is a set of benchmark companies. First, decide what questions you want the comparison to answer. If you are studying retail stocks, pick an industry-leader known for its inventory management (and track inventory turns), pick an upscale store (and track margins), pick a thriving established company (and track same-store sales). Add a couple of retailers that are currently in favor with Wall Street analysts. They'll be comparing your stock to these companies so you should, too. Picking the companies doesn't need to be very sophisticated. Call up a couple of brokerage houses and ask for their current buy-lists or skim analyst buy recommendations electronically from sources such as Standard & Poor's. Download the fundamentals on four or five companies into a single file so you can pull them up when you study the retail stocks you're thinking of buying.

How to decide? I go back to my research to try to choose a number. I know that Hewlett-Packard's proper future p/e is a hot issue among analysts. The computer industry is intensely competitive. Price-cutting is rampant. Margins are under pressure. Compaq, a major competitor, trades at a price-to-earnings ratio of just 13.6. Given my belief in Hewlett-Packard's growth potential I certainly would give the company a premium to Compaq, but how much?

I frankly don't think there is any way to know precisely. I could assume a conservative case and be surprised if the future turns out better. On the other hand, if I'm too conservative, I'll decide against buying Hewlett-Packard even if that is the right decision. So I decide to assign the company a price-to-earnings ratio above that of Compaq, and above its own growth rate.

In effect, I'm borrowing a pricing tool from Peter Lynch. Lynch's formula suggests that an investor buy a growth stock only when its price-to-earnings ratio is less than its growth rate plus its dividend yield. So I'm willing to pay 14.2 (growth rate) plus 1.5 (the yield). I fill in 15.7 where the program asks for high p/e. That gives me a forecast high price of $93.

The default value of 11.6 for the low price-to-earnings ratio also needs a hard look. The program gives me four choices for figuring the low price. I can use the low price-to-earnings ratio times 1994 earnings ($35.60), or the average low of the last five years ($24.10), or the serious market low ($25.10), or the price that the stock's dividend of 80 cents a share will support ($47.40). Since this is my conservative scenario and since, despite the dividend, I believe investors buy Hewlett-Packard as a growth stock, I use the low price-to-earnings estimate of $35.60.

Continuing with my scenario, the program finishes by dividing the range between $93.60 and $35.60 into thirds and labeling them buy, sell, and hold. Hewlett-Packard falls into the bottom category, a sell. The stock would have to break below $74.30 to become a hold and below $54.90 to become a buy.

There's absolutely nothing wrong with this approach to valuing Hewlett-Packard. The program has urged me to carefully consider each number that is crucial to reaching a final decision and I've rigorously studied each of those decisions. I've done a reasonable amount of research on what each of those numbers should be and I certainly think the result is defensible and reasonable. In fact, I feel proud of the quality of this analysis. But as solid as this analysis is, it represents a continuation of pencil and paper thinking. With a computer I can do better.

## THE ELECTRONIC WAY OF THINKING

On paper, I'm under constant pressure to pick one number as *the* number and move on in my analysis. Maybe, if I'm very ambitious, I will take a single question, such as the future rate of earnings growth, and model it two or three times. But I certainly wouldn't do that with multiple variables—it's just too much work and too complicated. But thanks to the computer I don't have to pick just a single scenario. Software makes it easy for me to generate alternative "earnings futures." That's the simple key to a new way of analyzing stocks.

To my first scenario outlined above I add a radically more optimistic one. I decide to choose a rate that reflects the most recent slope of the line, or 19.5 percent. Projecting earnings growth at these rates out to 1999 gives me $7.48 a share. Now, instead of looking at research and picking one of these over the other, I'll treat each earnings estimate as an alternative "what if" and examine both. I've already constructed my first "what if," the one for $5.96, in my prior analysis, so I can move on to the $7.48 a share scenario. That will involve taking each alternative assumption, filling in the rest of the blanks using that data, and then going back and doing the same with the other sets of assumptions. I'll then compare the results.

## RULE ONE: DON'T JUST CHANGE SINGLE VARIABLES— BUILD BEST AND WORST SCENARIOS.

Thanks to the computer there's no reason to reexamine the effect of changing only a single variable—the five-year projection for earnings per share. Instead I can—and should if I'm to exploit this way of thinking to the fullest—create whole new, consistent scenarios. For example, since I'm building a best case scenario by using the $7.48 earnings projection, I also want to use 19.2, the historical average high price-to-earnings ratio, instead of the 15.7 I calculated using Lynch's rule. If the company actually grows earnings at 19.5 percent, it would certainly command this kind of premium. That gives me an estimated high price of $143.60 and an estimated low, the same as before, of $35.60. Dividing that into thirds Hewlett-Packard still manages to rate only a hold.

The stock would have to break below $71.60 to rate a buy.

What scenario would make the stock a buy? Well, if I change the estimated low price by using the price that the dividend will support—$47.40—the stock becomes a marginal buy at $77.875, since the program recommends a buy below $79.50.

## RULE TWO: COMPARE THE REWARD AND PROBABILITY OF SCENARIOS.

None of these three scenarios alone tells me if Hewlett-Packard is a buy at $77.875, but all three together do. If the conservative view of future earnings and price-to-earnings ratio and the optimistic view of earnings and price-to-earnings multiple both say this stock isn't a buy at its current price, that's pretty convincing to me. It suggests that the market has already figured in Hewlett-Packard's rosy future into the price of the stock. Only if I'm willing to accept both the most rosy scenario and assume a roughly 50 percent higher floor under the stock can I justify a buy at this price.

I can still buy the stock after all this analysis, but the program has forced me to examine why I want to buy the stock at this price. It has led me through the data and the connections between the data in a way that has made the future of this stock clearer to me.

## RULE THREE: TRY DIFFERENT METHODS FOR FIGURING A STOCK'S VALUE—ONE SIZE DOESN'T FIT ALL.

Okay, so I don't want to buy Hewlett-Packard. How about Enova, formerly San Diego Gas & Electric?

This electric utility stock is a very different kind of investment than a growth stock such as Hewlett-Packard. No investor looking for growth would turn to a utility operating in the tough California regulatory environment. Growth of sales has averaged just 1.1 percent since 1985, and earnings turned sharply downward in 1994.

In 1995, the company, with cost-cutting and higher returns on capital due to a new rate-setting scheme, looks like it has rebounded. Including 1994's loss skews the earnings growth line below what seems to be the modest short-term trend. By eliminating that year—using the program's edit function—I get a much more accurate trend line. I feel that the historical growth rate and even the analysts' consensus is a little low, given all the changes that this utility has made. I enter a growth rate of 2.5 percent for earnings (still below inflation). That takes earnings to $2.10 a share in 1999. That's only marginally higher than the level analysts are projecting ($2.09) and that calculated by the program's own procedure for projecting earnings ($2.03). Utility earnings just aren't as volatile as those for growth stocks.

Turning those earnings into a projected price is pretty simple—this stock doesn't have the price-to-earnings volatility of Hewlett-Packard, either. Historical high price-to-earnings ratios vary only between 13.1 and 21.4, so after discounting the 21.4 of 1994 (a result of the company's poor performance that year), the average high price-to-earnings ratio is 13.9. Which yields an estimated high price of $32.40. The estimated low, using the average low price-to-earnings ratio of 11.6, is just a few dollars below the stock's current price of $21.375 at $14.40. Not much price appreciation here—the stock could go up approximately 50 percent in five years. But not much risk, either.

Of course, without the potential appreciation on the upside, this stock falls into the sell category according to this program. And since there isn't much wiggle in earnings, developing best and worst case scenarios like I did with Hewlett-Packard isn't going to change the bottom-line result—or tell me much about the stock.

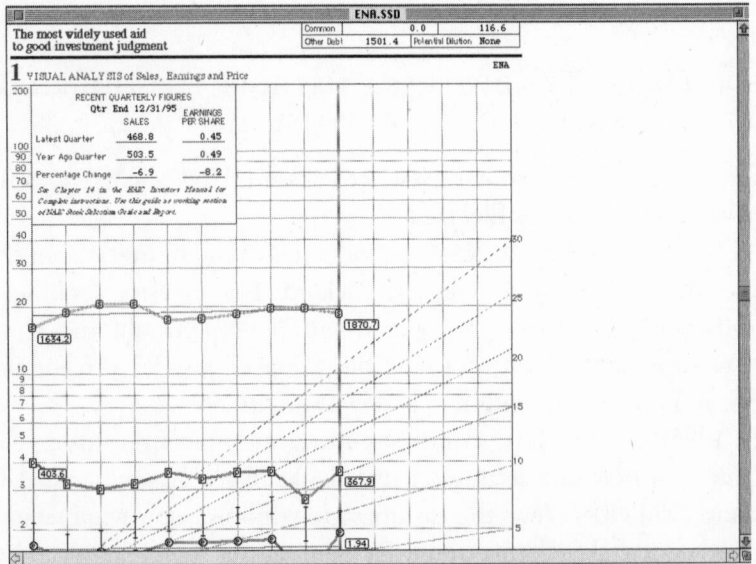

*No big surprises in the history of Enova: earnings at utility stocks just aren't very volatile.* (Courtesy NAIC)

While building alternative scenarios isn't appropriate here, using alternative methods for calculating the value of a stock is. The NAIC Stock Selection Guide is designed for growth stocks. It follows the organization's emphasis on picking stocks that can appreciate at 15 percent for five years. No utility is likely to meet that goal.

The methods that are perfectly appropriate for valuing one stock are often misleading for a different type of company. For example, the method I've used so far to calculate the possible low for Hewlett-Packard and Enova is based on price-to-earnings ratios, but that's the wrong method to use for a stock that I'm buying not for growth, but mostly for income. The dividend, as long as it's safe, puts a floor under the price of the stock.

So besides figuring alternative scenarios, for Enova I need to calculate alternative valuations. The Stock Selection Guide offers me several. One method for figuring the possible low price for the stock—the low price supported by the dividend—calculates that floor at $20.80, just 50 cents below the current price of the stock. Using this number, Enova becomes a very strong buy according to the program, with a downside risk of only 50 cents a share and a potential total return of 14.6 percent for the next five years.

Can that be right? When I find this kind of fairly obvious bargain in the market I double-check my logic to see what I've missed. I certainly want to consider how safe this dividend is, for one thing. The Stock Selection Guide does give me one way to gauge this—a ratio called "payout," which measures what percentage of a company's earnings are being paid out to cover the dividend. Obviously payout ratios of greater than 100 percent aren't sustainable, and payout ratios close to 100 percent suggest that dividends aren't going up very soon. Enova's payout soared to 130 percent in 1994, but the company seems to have returned to a level of earnings that will bring the payout ratio back down to around 80 percent.

But that's really as far as the analytical structure of the Stock Selection Guide will take me. There's nothing wrong with the Stock Selection Guide. It's just geared to analyze growth stocks, not utilities. It doesn't give me an easy way to consider other factors that I'd like to make a part of my step-by-step analysis of this utility stock. In fact, such items as Enova's market risk (if I'm comparing this to a bond, I'd like to know how much riskier it is) and its sensitivity to higher interest rates, which could drive down the price of the stock, can't be included in my analysis at all if I use this program. For that I need a different kind of tool and a different kind of fundamental analysis.

## RULE FOUR: CONSTRUCT SCENARIOS THAT CONSIDER ALTERNATIVE MACRO-ECONOMIC EVENTS, SUCH AS RISING AND FALLING INTEREST RATES.

Stock Analyst from Quant IX takes the opposite approach from NAIC's Stock Selection Guide (which is interesting since the two companies work together and Quant IX produces the portfolio-tracking software that NAIC sells to its investment club members). The Stock Selection Guide chooses a single method of evaluating a stock and then guides an investor through it. Stock Analyst provides tools to value stocks using five different methods. The program guides an investor through the data for each one and offers help to explain each, but leaves the choice of which valuation to believe up to the investor.

For Enova, I start by spacing across the menu bar to "Operations" and then select "Update asset list manually" and "Update a single asset" from the pull-down menu. Typing in "ENA" gets me the data entry screen for Enova. I type in today's price from the *Wall Street Journal* of 21.375, the dividends per share $1.56, earnings per share for the last twelve months $1.89, beta (a measure of how the stock reacts to

```
F1=HELP                QUANT IX STOCK ANALYST v1.0          07/25/95
ANALYSIS        OPERATIONS        REPORTS        UTILITY         QUIT

 Symbol SDO    Mkt Price 21.375

 Asset Name     San Diego Gas & Ele.   Last Revised        07/25/95
 Asset Type     Common Stocks          Dividend-Interest/Share 1.56
 Industry/Size  Utilities/Medium       Earnings/Share          1.89
 CUSIP Number                          Beta                    0.50
 Modem update? Yes

                      STOCK ANALYSIS VARIABLES
 Projected Dividend        1.60     Earnings Grow Rate     2.500 %
 Projected Earnings        1.94     Book Value per Share   13.05
 Dividend Growth Rate 1    2.50 %   Cash Flow per Share     4.35
 Dividend Growth Rate 2    2.53 %   Normal P/E             12.00

 VALUATION RESULTS    CAPM REQUIRED RETURN   8.70%      FUNDAMENTAL
 MODEL   V(0) V0/P0   GORDON IMPLIED RETURN  9.99%    RATIO ANALYSIS
 ---------------      ALPHA                    +      ---------------
 CGDD $ 26   22%                                      CURR PE   11.31
 VGDD $ 26   22%                                      PROJ PE   11.02
 NPE  $ 23    8%                                      EG/CPE     0.22
 ED   $ 26   22%                                      EG+DY/CPE  0.87
 EG     NM+   NM+                                     CF/DIV     2.79
                                                      MKT/CF     4.91
                                                      ROCF %    20.35
                                                      MKT/BOOK   1.64
                                                      ROE %     14.48
```

*Stock Analyst calculates the value of a stock using five alternative methods. (Courtesy Quant IX)*

market moves that I find in Value Line) .50, projected dividend (using the projected 2.5 percent growth rate in Value Line) $1.60, projected earnings of $1.94 (using my 2.5 growth rate), earnings and dividend growth rates, book value per share $13.05 (from Value Line), cash flow per share $4.35 (from Value Line), and median p/e of 12. Then I save and move to "Analysis" on the menu bar and "Analyze an asset." Again I type in "ENA."

The valuation results are in line with those produced by the Stock Selection Guide, although somewhat more conservative. Going down to the box of numbers under the heading "Valuation Results," I see three columns. The first, "Model," lists the five different methods, abbreviated cryptically, that Stock Analyst uses to calculate the fair value of a stock. The next, "V(O)," lists the fair value price, and the third the percentage the fair value is above or below the current market price. Most of these models say that Enova is undervalued by about 23 percent.

I'll explain these models in a moment, but first I want to point out several features that reveal the very different analytical structure that underpins Stock Analyst. Right above the table of Valuation Results the program has printed out a set of data it labels "Model Constants." Here you'll find data that was simply irrelevant to the analysis conducted by the Stock Selection Guide, such as the price level of today's market, the entire market's price-to-earnings ratio, and the market's yield. The middle column, which may be the hardest to interpret on the page, is actually the most important. RFRR stands for the "Risk-Free Rate of Return." Here an investor enters the current yield on the one-year Treasury bill, a standard benchmark. One-year bills are almost risk-free—an investor can easily hold them to maturity so that his or her principal is safe from the potential ravages of interest rate hikes, and a year is so short a time period that inflation is not likely to climb rapidly higher. (Of course, this assumes that the U.S. government will be good for the debt when it comes due in a year.)

The number right below that represents the extra return that an investor requires for taking on the extra risk of stocks. If I can make 5.70 percent guaranteed, how much more return do I require to make up for the potential ups and downs of the market? (I filled in the one-year Treasury bill yield from the data in the back pages of Barron's.)

The risk premium is somewhat subjective. One-year bills are yielding 5.7 percent. Long bonds around 7 percent. The market is very high and, I think, risky, so I want more of a premium to invest in stocks. The Stock Analyst Help function says that the risk premium for equities has historically been between 5 percent and 6 percent. Choosing the high side of that range, I add 6 percentage points to the risk-free rate to set what's called a hurdle rate of 11.70 percent. I require that the average stock promises me that much before I'd be willing to put it in my portfolio.

But very few stocks are average. If the market index as a whole fell 1 percent, many stocks would go down more than that and some less. Over time, financial analysts have charted the propensity of each stock to move with the market, giving each a rating called *beta*. A stock with a beta of 1 moves, historically and on average, in lockstep with the market. A stock with a beta of less than 1 moves up and down less than the market. Stocks with betas greater than 1 move up and down more than the market does.

Once an investor knows a stock's beta he or she can adjust the risk premium and the hurdle rate. A stock with a beta greater than 1 should compensate an investor with greater return. A stock with a beta of less than 1 comes with less risk and an investor should expect less of a total return in exchange.

That relationship has been turned into precise numbers by a formula called the Capital Asset Pricing Model, or CAPM. Corporate executives regularly use this to decide whether to build a new plant or buy a new machine. Investors can use it to figure the required return for a specific stock with its particular risk characteristics. Quant IX's Stock Analyst uses this system to value stocks.

At this point, you really don't need to know much about the Capital Asset Pricing Model or Modern Portfolio Theory. In summary CAPM is simple. It says that an investor who takes on more risk wants more return in exchange for that risk. A risky investment in a new factory or in a stock is only worth making if the potential return is high enough to compensate for that risk. To get precise numbers from the CAPM formula, therefore, an investor needs to know two things—the potential return from an investment and the potential risk.

Risk, it turns out, is easy to measure, at least as long as we believe that the future will resemble the past. Beta, among the most common measures, works well with CAPM, and Stock Analyst uses it to calculate a required return for each stock. For example, the CAPM required return for Enova, with its very low beta of 0.5, is just 8.70 percent.

Since the stock is less risky than the market as a whole, an investor should expect less of a premium return to own it. (By contrast, the beta on Hewlett-Packard is 1.89.) An investor buying Enova should aim for more of a return than he or she would get on a one-year Treasury bill, but less than he or she would get from buying an index fund that mirrored the market as a whole.

Stock Analyst lets an investor enter and revise interest rates and inflation—in effect, creating alternative macro-economic scenarios—to see how they might change the attractiveness of an investment. I click on the program's "What if" function, call up my data on Enova, and then change only the values I want to study—in this case I decide to see what would happen if interest rates went up 0.5 percentage points to 6.2 percent. The program quickly recalculates the required return on the market—now 12.2—and the CAPM required return on San Diego Gas & Electric—now 9.2 percent, up from 8.7.

But this is only one part of the formula—the return I should look for. The second part of the formula, the potential return on Enova, is a lot harder to estimate. Stock Analyst, in fact, offers five different methods for the investor to choose from. They're listed by their abbreviation in Valuation Results.

Why didn't Peter and Matt Willms, who manage about $40 million at their company the Willms Group, simply pick the best method when they wrote Stock Analyst? Because different kinds of stocks need to be valued using different methods. Some stocks with meager dividends, such as Hewlett-Packard, are attractive to investors because they will grow earnings. Others that are growing earnings slowly can still be worthwhile investments because of the high dividends they pay. Other stocks are valuable because of combinations of both. The five valuation methods offered by Stock Analyst cover a lot of the bases, although they basically break down into two camps: models for stocks that pay dividends and models for stocks with no or small dividends but with growing earnings per share.

For example, CGDD, which stands for the Constant Growth Dividend Discount model, calculates the value of Enova today by dividing the dividends projected for next year ($1.60) by the difference between the CAPM required rate of return for Enova (8.70 percent) and the constant annual expected growth rate in dividends (2.5 percent) or 6.2 percent. Which equals $25.80. The second model, VGDD, which is the abbreviation for Variable Growth Dividend Discount model, takes into account changes in dividend growth as a firm matures. The program uses the company's return on equity (what it is earning on its invested capital) and the historical payout ratio to determine what the long-term dividend growth rate should be, and then factors that dividend growth rate into a formula like that used by the constant growth model. For Enova, which is already a mature firm, the two models yield the same $26 valuation.

What's the logic behind these methods of valuation? Simply, they attempt to figure out what an investor should pay today for a dollar of dividends next year—given the risk of the specific asset. Enova will pay $1.60 next year—we hope. We demand a return on this stock of 8.7 percent, which is equivalent to what we could earn on a risk-free investment plus some premium for the risk of this stock. Following this logic we'd be willing to pay $18.39 for this stock today to get that $1.60 in dividends tomorrow. On a risk-adjusted basis this is exactly the same as paying $18.39 for a one-year Treasury bill that pays $1.05 in interest next year. Dividends on the stock are going up, however, at 2.5 percent a year (we hope) and therefore we should be willing to pay more for a stream of dividends that begins at $1.60 and then goes to $1.64, $1.68, $1.72, and so on.

The three earnings-driven models attempt an analogous valuation, but based on earnings not on dividends. The first earnings model should be familiar from the Stock Selection Guide program. NPE, the Normalized Price/Earnings model, calculates the estimated future price of a stock by multiplying future earnings per share times the estimated future price-to-earnings ratio. That's exactly how the Stock Selection Guide arrives at its five-year price target. This method puts the value of a share of Enova at just $23.

The earnings discount model, ED on the valuation results table, expands the basic normalized price/earnings model to make it useful for valuing stocks when the historical price-to-earnings ratio doesn't accurately reflect the likely future price-to-earnings ratio of the stock. The program looks at current earnings, dividend projections and growth rates, and the required return for the stock to calculate a price-to-earnings ratio that may be higher or lower than the stock's historical ratio. In the case of Enova, the program calculates that the company's historical ratio understates future expectations and gives the stock a slightly higher valuation of $26 on that basis.

The last earnings model looks further into the future. It focuses on estimated earnings growth rates three to five years from now on the theory that investors buy stocks looking at future growth rates. This model doesn't produce a meaningful result in the case of Enova.

The next step is to combine these valuation models and the program's "What if" function. The valuations produced by these five different models don't change in precise tandem as I alter the risk-free interest rate or the future earnings growth rate for the stock. For example, if I set interest rates at 6.2 percent, Enova is worth only $24 a share, instead of $26, according to the dividend models. This stock, I can see from the "what if," is extremely sensitive even to small changes in interest rates. I certainly want to factor my expectations about rates into a buy/sell/hold decision on this stock.

And it only takes a hike in interest rates of another 0.5 percentage points to 6.7 percent to pretty much wipe out any reason for buying Enova. The forecast price drops to just $22 and the gain to 4 percent. I'd eat up this kind of gain in brokerage costs.

The stock's valuation using the earnings models takes much less of a hit from rising rates. The normalized price-to-earnings model stays exactly the same, for example, at $25.

## TIPS ON THE TOOLS

# HOW'M I DOIN'?

**F**iguring out how your picks do is as important as picking stocks in the first place. There's a lot of portfolio-tracking software on the market, but getting performance numbers that accurately reflect performance isn't as easy as it should be. Many programs only give you gain and loss, and that isn't enough. You'll need to figure total return unless you want to bias your picks against dividend and interest bearing securities. Try one of these programs to track how your picks are doing.

### FOLIOMAN
### (DOS VERSION 1.6) (A WINDOWS VERSION WAS PLANNED FOR THE FIRST QUARTER OF 1996.)

*From E-Sential Software, 213-257-2524, $89. Free demo.*

It's harder than it should be to find portfolio management software that can accurately calculate investment returns. FolioMan does a solid job of giving an investor both a capital gains and a total return calculation for income investments. The program also does a particularly good job at tracking the cost basis of an investment. Its graphic presentation of returns doesn't offer anything to write home about, but will be enough for most investors.

*continued*

## OWL PERSONAL PORTFOLIO MANAGER (DOS VERSION 6.0C) AND OWL PORTFOLIO PRICE LOADER (DOS VERSION 3.2)

*From Otto-Williams Ltd. 301-306-0409. Portfolio Manager $45, Price Loader $15, Demo $10.*

Owl combines portfolio management and technical analysis. It can maintain 5,000 securities in 500 portfolios. Report formats include net worth, performance, transactions, unrealized gains, stock/bond summary, stock list, bond list, options list, savings list, capital gains, other assets, liabilities, interest, dividends, and other income reports.

The program can create two types of charts—technical (relative strength, three kinds of oscillators, on-balance volume, and others) and portfolio (net worth, asset allocation, and more). Asset allocation breaks down classes only into stocks, bonds, cash, etc.—too general for portfolio optimization. Extremely useful correlation function that will calculate correlation coefficient between two securities or security and index. Price loader is not a standard downloader, but instead software that will let the program read quotes that have already been downloaded from a quotes service such as America Online, Prodigy, CompuServe, or Dow Jones.

## CENTERPIECE (DOS VERSION 4.0) AND CENTERPIECE PERFORMANCE MONITOR (DOS VERSION 2.0)

*From Performance Technologies, Inc., 800-528-9595. Centerpiece $895, Centerpiece Performance Monitor $595.*

Extremely expensive and needlessly difficult to use, Centerpiece nevertheless is one of the few packages that gives an investor the ability to judge the returns on a portfolio against an appropriate benchmark. Designed for the professional, this software can generate an audit trail of capital flows, track matched sales between accounts, short sales, and lot buys and sells. Performance Monitor module computes monthly returns for each portfolio or portfolio group and saves returns in performance history file. The program can generate 20 different reports using either time-weighted return or IRR. It can also compare market indexes (again, time-weighted or IRR) against portfolios, including the impressive ability to compare a portfolio to a blended index that matches the asset allocation policy of the portfolio. Returns are reported gross or net of fees. Price downloads from Dow Jones, Dial Data/DTN, and Signal. For advisors who want to downlink account transactions, the program provides import connections with Schwab's Financial Advisors Service, Fidelity, First Trust, IM&R, National Financial, T. Rowe Price, Vanguard, Wachovia, and Waterhouse for an additional fee.

## NAIC PERSONAL RECORD KEEPER (DOS VERSION 1.0) (A WINDOWS VERSION WAS SCHEDULED FOR RELEASE IN FEBRUARY 1996.)

*Produced by Quant IX. Available from National Association of Investors Corp., 810-583-6242, $79 for nonmembers, $59 for members.*

A simple to use portfolio tracker that keeps solid performance numbers and divides the portfolio into more asset classes than most: cash, U.S. government, tax exempts, corporate bonds, preferred stocks, mutual funds, common stocks—but still too general for effective use in true asset allocation. Performance report gives the user choice of time-weighted return or annualized performance.

## CAPTOOL (DOS VERSION 5.0) AND
## PFROI (DOS VERSION 6.9). (WINDOWS VERSION OF CAPTOOL WAS PLANNED FOR RELEASE IN FIRST HALF OF 1996.)

*From Techserve Inc., 800-826-8082. Captool $149, PFROI $79. (Captool incorporates PFROI, which is the portfolio manager part of the program.) Demos available on CompuServe and America Online.*

PFROI tracks investment costs using specific lot, FIFO, LIFO, and average cost methods, computes estimated taxes, and calculates returns on investment using IRR method—in short, everything a portfolio tracking software program should do. Stepping up to Captool links PFROI with another set of tools: a share evaluation program called Stockpar, which uses the Capital Asset Pricing Model to generate valuations; Bondpro, which evaluates bonds and calculates yield to maturity; and a module that graphs price history against moving averages. Not an easy program to navigate in the DOS version (maybe the Windows version will be easier), since the relation of screen to screen is often perplexing and the manual can be frustratingly opaque, but Captool and PFROI is an intriguing combination of solid portfolio management with some interesting tools for fundamental analysis. Captool can import quotes from Prodigy, DTN, Metastock, Telechart, and FastTrack.

## Rule Five: Put all these scenarios together to understand a stock's sensitivity to change.

What I've done with Hewlett-Packard and now Enova is a kind of sensitivity analysis. I certainly wouldn't claim that this rough-and-ready system is equivalent to the extensive testing that the big Wall Street firms do, but it is the same kind of analysis. While Wall Street's money mangers use complex computer models to test what would happen to a security if interest rates went up or down, if the economy sputtered or surged, if the dollar plunged or soared, an individual investor can use the "what if" capabilities of programs such as Stock Analyst and Stock Selection Guide to get a feel for the risk and reward of an investment under different economic and corporate scenarios.

Sticking with Enova for a moment longer, I can also check to see what my potential reward would be if earnings and dividends grew at 3.5 percent a year instead of at 2.5 percent. The stock would move up to somewhere between $28 and $31, the program tells me, tacking on anywhere from an extra $2 to $5 a share. I don't have to imagine a tremendous improvement in the company's fortunes to see a substantial addition to the potential upside of this investment. Measuring that potential reward from increased earnings and the potential downside from rising interest rates certainly helps me see this investment more clearly.

These two programs don't, of course, include every tool that can be used to value a company. Macro*World Investor (see reviews at the end of this chapter), for example, attempts to calculate a private market value for the company (what a similar company with similar assets would bring in a private sale), a useful tool for the value investor. And not every valuation tool used by investors is available in software for the individual investor. I haven't been able to find a program that values a stock on the basis of a company's free cash flow, a fairly common measure used, again, by value investors.

## Rule Six: After figuring how change would effect a stock's price, figure the probability of that change.

Valuation is really only half of fundamental analysis. Besides calculating what a stock would be worth if a specific fundamental trend turned out to be true—what Hewlett-Packard would be worth if earnings grew

# FINANCIALS ON-LINE

**A**s this book went to press, the Securities and Exchange Commission had stepped in to save Edgar from extinction. Edgar, an experiment funded by the National Science Foundation, put company quarterly and annual reports (10-Ks, 10-Qs, and others) on the Internet's World Wide Web. While the database was frustrating since it didn't include SEC forms filed prior to Edgar's inception, information was posted reasonably promptly and accessing a company report was free. (Quite an improvement over the $50 or so that it costs to receive one of these public reports electronically from commercial ventures.)

But the NSF decided not to fund the pilot project any further, and the SEC had momentary second thoughts about picking up the costs. (Not surprising, given what the current Republican Congress has done to the agency's budget.) In mid-October the agency decided to keep Edgar running at a new address on the World Wide Web: (http://www.sec.gov).

One interesting alternative to Edgar deserves a look. Cambridge Interactive (http://www. money.com ) on the World Wide Web is experimenting with corporate advertising as a way to fund a similar service. The site's "Investor In Touch" page mixes data from Nelson's *Directory of Investment Research* (basically, earnings estimates, lists of analysts who cover each company, and  lists of analyst reports) with additional pages sponsored by individual companies, which provided copies of recent annual reports, press releases on recent financials, daily high/low/volume charts, and a list of SEC filings. (Check the World Wide Web indexes, such as Yahoo, to catch any new sources for SEC documents.)

at 19.5 percent a year–fundamental analysis also attempts to gauge the probability of this wish actually coming true. How likely is it, for example, that Enova will be able to increase earnings by 3.5 percent instead of the historical 1.1 growth rate since 1985? I can guess or I can look at the fundamentals of the utilities business that determine profitability.

Unfortunately, no program I've been able to find will answer this for an investor, or even guide him or her through the process. And good data of this sort are hard to come by electronically. Even good databases such as Morningstar's U.S. Equities and Value Line often don't have enough detail or the kind of presentation that investors need. It's certainly beyond the scope of this book to teach you what data to look for to assess every sort of company, but I can set out some guidelines that will help you tell if a software program that promises fundamental data really delivers. I can also give you some tips on how to conduct this kind of analysis. For this last example, I'm going to use a combination of the Market Guide Inc. database, available through Prodigy's Strategic Investor package and through other sources, and U.S. Equities to analyze upscale kitchen goods retailer Williams-Sonoma.

Most electronic databases take the information the company reports and condense it into summaries that omit exactly the data I now need. Market Guide, however, gives me both a detailed recent income statement and balance sheet, and annual summaries of important categories for the last eight years—year by year.

I've had retailer Williams-Sonoma, which operates the Williams-Sonoma, Pottery Barn, and Hold Everything stores and catalogs, on my

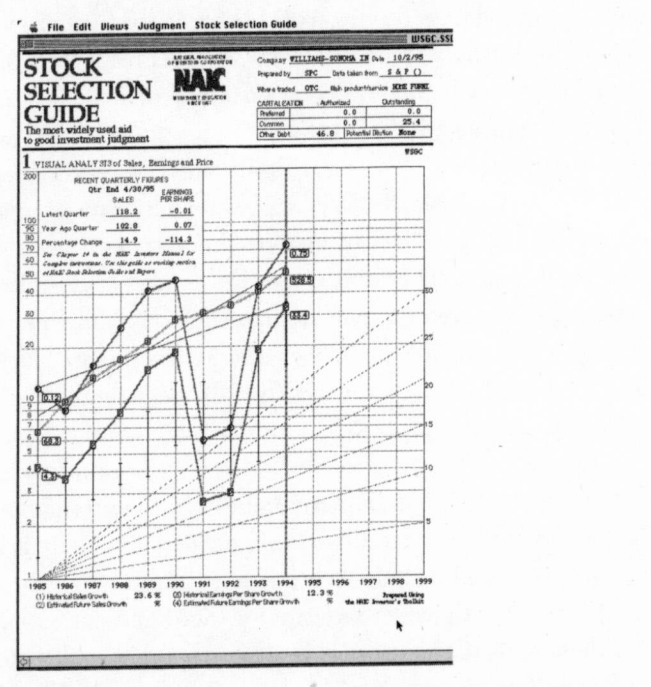

*The Stock Selection Guide shows exactly how erratic the stock of Williams-Sonoma has been.* (*Courtesy NAIC*)

"to buy" list for a while now, but the company is a tough one to figure out. It has a relatively short track record—1985 was the first year it did business and the company went public only in 1990—and its earnings chart is extremely erratic (see illustration). This potential growth star ran totally off the track in 1991 and 1992. The quarter ended in April 1995 undermined hopes that Williams-Sonoma was back on course—the company lost $.01 a share—far below the $.07 a share in profit recorded in the first quarter a year earlier. As of the middle of 1995, Value Line gave the company its lowest rating for timeliness and next to lowest for safety. Is this a great buying opportunity built on investor disappointment?

Going through an analysis of Williams-Sonoma in Stock Analyst or the Stock Selection Guide is almost pointless. The important issue isn't how the company should be valued, but how well this company is being run. What can Market Guide tell me?

Page two of the report on Williams-Sonoma, which compares key company ratios to those at other retailing companies, gives me pause. Everything looks good—this is a financially solid company—until I get near the bottom of the page and notice profit margin—at 3.21 percent it seems low, but maybe that's normal for retailing. Nope. Market Guide tells me Williams-Sonoma trails the industry average of 3.94 percent. In 1991 and 1992, the "bad" years, margins fell to just 0.5 percent. The company has never done a whole lot better—1989's 3.9 percent is tops. This isn't a company where high margins can make up for a momentary lapse of attention by management.

On the balance sheet I find other troubling items. Accounts receivable—what the company is owed by others—has climbed by about 50 percent quarter to quarter for the April 1995 period and is up just slightly less for fiscal year 1995 to fiscal year 1994. That's troubling when sales are up only 15 percent quarter to quarter. Inventories too are climbing. They're up 35 percent quarter to quarter. The company seems to be both slow in collecting its debts and lax in controlling how much unsold merchandise sits on its shelves.

One other item also bears thought. On the last page Market Guide prints a cash-flow statement. This very useful but overlooked financial report tracks how much cash, after correcting for accounting fictions, the company is actually consuming or generating. Roughly, calculating cash flow begins with net income, then adds any depreciation (a paper expense that doesn't require the company to spend any cash), then subtracts capital expenditures and dividends, and adds in any money received from raising capital. Williams-Sonoma is deeply cash-flow negative before adding in new capital because of its spending on renovating stores and expansion. Considering its margins, growth can't be financed internally. As an investor I have to worry about possible dilution if the company has to issue new shares to finance its expansion to 294 stores in 1996.

## RULE SEVEN: PUT IT ALL IN CONTEXT BY LOOKING AT COMPETITORS.

I want to double-check my impressions about Williams-Sonoma by comparing it to another retailer. For that, while I can use Market Guide, I prefer U.S Equities. That program compiles a single page of important ratios and allows me to toggle quickly back and forth between two or several companies to create comparisons. The program lists a number I'm especially interested in for a retail company—inventory turns, the number of times a year a company manages to sell out its inventory, restock it, and sell it out again. I'm going to compare Williams-Sonoma and The Gap, another then-struggling specialty retailer but one known for the quality of its management, and Home Depot, another retailer positioned to take advantage of the home-improvement nesting trend.

I call up Williams-Sonoma by typing in its ticker WSGC and then hit the page-down key three times. On the bottom half of the screen I see a table called "Selected Relations". There I see the troubling return on revenue of 3.22 percent and some new numbers: return on equity (14.84 percent), which measures how much the company earns as a percentage of what shareholders have invested in the company; return on assets (7.36 percent), another measure of profitability, which looks at how much the company earns on its assets; and the item I mentioned above, inventory turns (5.14 times). I print out this table for easy comparison to The Gap and Home Depot.

Hitting F5 and typing in "GPS" gets me a similar table for The Gap. The ratios are higher across the board. Return on revenue is 8.03, nearly three times Williams-Sonoma's current figure and more than twice the best that Williams-Sonoma has ever done. Return on equity at 22.17 is 50 percent higher, and return on assets at 15.86 is twice as high. The Gap turns its inventory 9.34 times a year—again almost twice as often as Williams-Sonoma.

What can I make of all this? Here I have a company, Williams-Sonoma, that earns only half as much on each dollar of assets—which includes the goods it sells—and turns over its inventory only half as often. No wonder that The Gap earns almost 3 times the return on each dollar of revenue. The amazing thing, after this analysis, is why The Gap sells for a price-to-earnings ratio of 16 times trailing earnings and Williams-Sonoma for a trailing price-to-earnings ratio of 32. Especially since both companies are in the midst of major expansion efforts.

Just in case I've been unfair to Williams-Sonoma by comparing it to a clothing retailer—the company sells a mix of food, pots and china, and small appliances—I call up the same set of ratios for Home Depot. Now I'll be comparing Williams-Sonoma to a high-volume, low-margin store. As I expected, Home Depot turns its inventory more frequently—6.60 times annually—than Williams-Sonoma, but a 1.5 difference really doesn't strike me as too bad. But the return on revenue number is actually shocking. The high-volume, low-margin Home Depot actually earns 1.5 percentage points more on each revenue dollar. Home Depot earns a little less on equity—my guess is that it costs more to build a big Home Depot than it does to build a Williams-Sonoma or Pottery Barn store, but the big retailer earns a higher return on assets. I know that Home Depot is building stores everywhere. Again, I can't see a reason to pass up its shares and buy those of Williams-Sonoma.

No program has guided me through the last part of this fundamental analysis. I'd love to find one, but I can't imagine how anyone could ever write one. No one set of steps and data would fit every industry. Insurance companies, for example, don't even report a number called sales. Instead they list net premiums collected and investment income. A program that tried to help an investor decide whether to buy American International Group would have to examine an entirely different set of numbers and ratios than we've looked at for Hewlett-Packard, Enova, or Williams-Sonoma.

Maybe that's why there are so few computer programs that help an investor tackle fundamental analysis. I count no more than a half-dozen serious efforts. Which is actually shocking when I consider that the disciplined study of the past performance of companies in an attempt to predict their future value is, in theory at least, at the heart of most investing. (And certainly at the heart of all intelligent investing, except for those investors who practice some form of technical analysis.)

# A QUICK TOUR OF IDIOSYNCRASIES

**M**easures such as earnings per share and debt to equity apply to virtually every company that an investor wants to analyze. But individual industries also have their own key benchmarks. Here's a list of some of them:

Bank and finance: Return on equity or assets. How much income the bank produced by lending out its available capital expressed as a ratio of income to capital.

Cable TV: Revenue per subscriber. How else could an investor compare companies with radically different markets? (Also see revenue per potential subscriber below.)

Cellular: Revenue per potential subscriber. A related item to revenue per subscriber. It measures dollars of revenue per potential customer in the service area, which gives an investor a good measure of market penetration.

Insurance: Loss ratio compares the company's payout to cover insured losses versus premiums collected. Insurance companies make money not just by collecting premiums, however, but by investing them—investment return measures how good an insurance company is at this crucial part of its business.

Retail and restaurant: Same-store (or same-restaurant) sales compare sales for the current period at stores open at least a year with the sales at those same stores a year ago. The measure is a good way to tell the difference between a company that's showing growing sales because it's adding stores and one that's seeing more business at existing stores. The number cuts slightly differently for restaurants because restaurants have limited seating and therefore a limited ability to grow same store sales.

Manufacturing: Factory utilization measures current output versus potential output. This is a good way to judge where a cyclical company, such as an automaker, is in the cycle and to examine potential upside. A company running at a low utilization rate will be able to make more widgets without building a new factory (which takes time and costs money).

Part of the reason is that fundamental analysis is so damned hard to implement on a computer. On the surface, fundamental analysis would seem ideally suited to this technology. Take data on sales and earnings and dividends and margins—and anything else an investor can think of—and plug it into a time-tested formula. *Voilá!* an accurate valuation of any stock.

But that surface simplicity and accuracy is a thin layer hiding frustrating depths of complexity. Data can't be accepted at face value—one company counts sales only after the money is in the bank while another records the revenues as soon as the product leaves the shipping dock at the factory. Cash flow is a useful measure for assessing the health of a manufacturing company, but insurance companies don't even calculate such an item on their financial statements. One company keeps all its debt on a single balance sheet; another stashes billions off-balance sheet by spinning off debt-laden subsidiaries. Dirty data plugged into the best program will produce nothing but garbage.

And no program can tell an investor what fundamental factors are the crucial ones to examine. Predict a future value for a stock based on earnings growth and ignore sales growth? Study sales, but which sales number?—the dollars in revenue that the company brings in or the number of units of its product that the company has sold? The decision is crucial if the company is in a highly competitive industry where prices are under constant downward pressure. If sales are increasing, is the company producing too slowly to meet future demand or are goods piling up in retailers' warehouses faster than those companies can move them? The first will squeeze sales and earnings when the company can't meet consumer's demands. The second could produce a disaster when all those retailers fail to reorder.

Fundamental analysis programs put a tremendous burden on the investor. Since no program can automatically clean data or even identify the data that needs to be cleaned, the investor must be able to recognize potential problems. Since no program can tell an investor how to balance all the fundamentals, the investor must be able to build a coherent structure for himself or herself from all the available pieces.

The best fundamental analysis programs recognize their dependency on investors. They are designed not to lull the investor to sleep by mechanically producing buy and sell recommendations. Instead, by their structure, they flag the questions that an investor needs to answer about each company. As an investor works through the step-by-step analysis scripted by one of these good programs, he or she will have to decide what factors drive a company's success.

In effect, these programs are a kind of scorecard against which any investor can measure the state of his or her own customary fundamental analysis. Most investors will find that the program makes them think harder than they do now about why earnings will grow, about the relationship of earnings to sales, about the way that good management is reflected in financial ratios, and about the way the market values a company. These programs will make most investors work harder at the basics that should underlie sound investing. They are valuable at least as much for the discipline they teach as for the buy/sell/hold recommendations they generate. Even if you don't end up using one of these programs to pick and sell stocks, they are the best tests I know for grading the quality of your investment thinking.

## REVIEWS

### MACRO*WORLD INVESTOR

Macro*World Research Corp., 4265 Brownsboro Road, Suite 170, Winston-Salem, NC 27106, 800-841-5398.

Versions available: DOS (version 4.0).

Requirements: Requires 640K RAM, 8MB free space on hard drive, DOS 3.1 or higher.

Cost: $899.95 plus $399.95 a year for update after the first year.

Guarantee: 30-day money back.

Demo or sample: None.

Technical support: 800-841-5398 (9 A.M.–5 P.M., M–F).

User Newsletter: With monthly disk.

Update: Monthly on disk (by Internet sometime in 1996). Bulletin feature in program gives news digest on trends and a recommended asset allocation for the next nine months.

Strengths: A complete investment system where each of the functions is good enough to stand on its own. I'd recommend every single one of the package's functions—asset allocation, stock picking, economic analysis, and valuation—if they sold as stand-alone programs. This program will make an investor think about individual decisions and investing as a whole in new ways.

Weaknesses: A tough learning curve. The program's recommendations are likely to be virtually incomprehensible to the beginner, and its various report formats will initially seem a maze of overlapping and contradictory information. The investor without some basic understanding of how economics works will face perhaps insurmountable obstacles to getting maximum value from the program. An ugly and antique DOS interface disguises the program's real strengths.

Tricks of the trade: Note that this DOS program installs not with an "Install" command but with "Copy." Use the housekeeping function in the main menu to turn off the annoying flashing cursor.

The manual calls this an "expert forecasting system," and there's no other program quite like it. Designed to be a "black box" stock-picking system, Macro*World Investor has soundly beaten human stock pickers in public and impartially judged competitions. Following the Macro*World system will limit an investor to a portfolio of about 100 stocks, certainly enough to give a broad and flexible exposure to the market. Investors who find that universe too restrictive can still gain valuable investment insight from unique examinations of economic, financial, and market trends.

Doug Graham built this program around the idea of constantly combing through economic, financial, and market data to find projectable trends (using a statistical technique called regression analysis). Each night the computers at Macro*World look at the last thirty to forty periods—the program studies both the short-term past of the last forty days and the long-term past of the last forty years—to find statistical patterns that could forecast the future. Macro*World then gives each of these forecasts a probability that indicates the likelihood that this future will come about.

Macro*World looks at data ranging from auto sales to interest rates to the money supply and then produces forecasts ranging from the unemployment level in a year to the price of a share of The Gap in three months. Predictions are listed by the probability that they'll come true (there's an 88.5 percent probability that industrial production will go up for the next twelve months, for example, and a 69.3 percent probability that the price of a share of The Gap will go down to $29.63). The manual notes that, generally, a probability above 80 percent is significant and probabilities below 60 percent are really meaningless ("indeterminate" in the manual's language).

An investor who doesn't want to use that forecast as a buy or sell signal can instead study the interconnections between economic and market factors. It will take some time before you learn how to read the tea leaves, though. For example, the program firmly predicted in December 1994 that within twelve months the S&P 500 Index would hit 535.83

(88.9 percent probable), an 88.4 percent probability that interest rates on one-year notes would fall to 3 percent, and an 88.3 percent probability that NASDAQ would climb 218.30 points to 973.5. It's not really too surprising that falling rates are really bullish for the market, but the program also reminds an investor that historically The Gap thrives in economic climates like this. Over this longer period there's a 69.5 percent probability that The Gap will go up to $48.80 from $32.50. But the program is actually waving a warning flag here. An investor ought to wonder why this rosy scenario, which has such a strong probability, generates only a moderate probability that shares in The Gap will thrive.

The program can chop and dice its data and forecasts into some very useful types of reports. For example, the "Turning Point Report" lists the date when each major data series will most likely experience its next major change in direction. At the end of 1994, for example, profit margin hit the top of the list: the program was pointing to a high in the fourth quarter of 1994. The report also forecast that interest rates on three-month Treasury bills would peak in the third quarter of 1995, and that the NASDAQ and Russell 2000 indexes would hit their highs for this cycle in March and April 1996. Looking through the data, an investor would have to conclude that the program was suggesting a recession in 1996.

The "Exception Report" is equally useful: it lists all the series where values are at extraordinary levels relative to historical trends and relative to past high or low points. The first part of the list shows series likely to be at exceptional levels in the latest period: the price of The Gap shows up on this list as extra low. The second part looks for exceptions in the next period, and the third part looks at exceptions that are now moving back to more normal levels. The stock prices of AT&T and Safety Kleen were at lows, for example, and Hewlett-Packard was at a high.

A user can then analyze any of these data series in detail. For example, I can look at the data for The Gap. The program predicts (69.5 percent probability) that the stock will climb to 48.80 from 32.50 in January 1995. But the fact that the stock is at an exceptional low suggests caution—the manual tells me—since an exceptional low means that the stock could be breaking its past pattern. Using page up and page down I can look at the past behavior of The Gap's share price. The stock looks as if it climbed from $20 to $60 after the recession of 1990 and was essentially flat during it. With a recession looming in 1996, do I want to hold the stock?

Besides information on individual stocks and trends, the program generates a portfolio of specific securities and issues buy/hold/sell signals. Macro*World adds its own wrinkles here, too, since it considers not just historical risk and return, but also expected future returns and future risk (based on the program's confidence in each forecast). The asset allocation system is designed to let an investor construct an efficient portfolio—one that has the lowest risk for a given rate of return. (For more on asset allocation programs, see Chapter 9.) Macro*World uses its forecast to create projected rates of return and then assesses the probability of that return exceeding the risk-free return on three-month Treasury bills. An individual investor can customize the portfolio by choosing an acceptable probability range and a target beta.

Macro*World's valuation function includes the usual culprits—an investor can rank the program's 100-stock universe on earnings outlook, earnings and price growth, yield and dividend growth, and an extremely interesting Graham and Dodd–based attempt to figure the economic value of an enterprise. Basically this method seeks to value the company's ability to earn high returns (above market rates) on retained earnings and estimate how long this period of excessive returns will last—how long it will be before the company matures and begins distributing excess capital as dividends, since it can't earn a higher than market return internally. By this method, The Gap would have to grow at pre-maturity rates for twenty years to justify its price and McDonald's at only nine. Which is the better long-term buy? (Before you call your broker to buy McDonald's, note that Coca Cola's price is justified by only seven years of pre-maturity growth rates.)

No review can end without a nod to the ugliest interface in investment software. I think DOS is certainly an acceptable operating system for financial software, but there's no excuse for the program's ghastly green background with black type. And whoever suggested that brown cursor bar?

## QUANT IX STOCK ANALYST

Quant IX Software, 11516 N. Port Washington Rd., #206, Mequon, WI 53092, 800-247-6354.

Versions available: DOS (version 1.0). Windows version scheduled for late 1996.

Requirements: Requires 640K RAM, 4MB free space on hard drive, DOS 3.1 or higher.

Cost: $69.

Guarantee: 30-day money back.

Demo or sample: None.

Technical support: 414-241-3990 (8 A.M.–3 P.M. CST); Bulletin board (via modem) 414-241-4652; CompuServe (Go Vendors) and CompuServe e-mail to 76703,4415.

User Newsletter: None.

Update: Quotes and some fundamentals are available via CompuServe. Stock Analyst comes with a download routine for CompuServe. (Warning: it can be buggy, but the fix is easy if you call Quant IX.)

Strengths: Extremely personal support—I was able to reach Peter or Matt Willms by phone almost immediately each time I had a problem. The simple menu makes it easy to get up and running quickly. A great manual explains the basics of the various methods for valuing a stock in detail and is complemented by an outstanding help function: pressing F1 while an item is highlighted gives explanation and instructions on that item. "What if" function can model sensitivity of any valuation to changes in earnings and dividends. This is the only program I've found that lets the fundamental investor consider the effects of interest rates on potential investments.

Weaknesses: Installing this program will present memory problems for most users. DOS has this nasty built-in 640K memory ceiling: your machine may have 24MB of RAM, as one of mine does, but DOS will treat everything except that first 640K as extended memory and will require you to make enough of that 640K available to run this program. It should be possible to rewrite your autoexec.bat and config.sys files to get around this problem—the process is described in the manual that came with your copy of Windows. If you want a text written in something closer to English, you'll have to buy one of the many books with a name like *DOS for Idiots*. Fortunately, you'll only have to do this once. (The company's Windows version should avoid this problem.)

Tricks of the trade: Takes a while to load, so don't get nervous. That completely blank screen is normal and will go away. (I promise). Use the time to read the manual—not to learn how to operate the program, but for a crash course in finance. You can update prices and fundamental data on the stocks you study automatically via CompuServe, but you're probably better off sticking to prices and entering the fundamentals by hand so that you can control the quality and time period of the data.

Easy to operate, yet theoretically sound and rigorous, Stock Analyst will let an investor turn a stock inside out using five different valuation methods. If only its DOS operating system didn't require the user to dip his or her hands into the slimy entrails of computer code, this program would be close to perfect.

The first screen simply lists "Analysis," "Operations," "Reports," "Utility," and "Quit" in a menu along the top. That bar controls the entire program—no hidden commands or codes to learn, since everything works from pull-down menus from that bar.

You'll find a thorough description of the two tasks under the Analysis command ("display an asset" and "what if"), so let me concentrate on a few other features. "Operations" lets the user update assets manually or by modem, using CompuServe, to update constants such as the interest rate on one-year Treasury bills from either a paper source such as *Barron's* or by modem from the Stock Analyst bulletin board, and to set price alerts. The "Reports" function produces summary reports that compare all the stocks in a user's list on the basis of several different systems of analysis— dividend analysis, earnings analysis, ratios analysis—and valuation systems. Ratio analysis, which the program calls a snapshot of the company, lets an investor examine all the standard measures (dividends/projected dividends, payout ratio, earnings growth rate/current price-to-earnings ratio), and throws in a few extra (such as two Peter Lynch formulas).

I can't say enough good things about the manual. It's short, so a user might actually read it, but it thoroughly explains the theoretical methods that the program uses. The theories at work here aren't unusual or cutting edge, but instead represent the bread-and-butter methods of modern financial theory. The math-phobic will have problems following the examples in the manual, but anyone who isn't sent into total shock by an algebraic equation should experience few problems.

The manual contains one of the best brief descriptions of risk and what to do about it that I've seen. The text breaks risk into market and asset-specific risk and notes that asset-specific risk can be reduced with a portfolio—sixteen stocks is sufficient, they say. To aid the user in achieving diversification Quant IX lets the user divide common stocks into one of nine industries and one of three market capitalization sizes.

Quant IX promises a Windows version for 1996.

### STOCK SELECTION GUIDE (PART OF NAIC INVESTOR'S TOOLKIT COMPLETE)

National Association of Investors Corp., P.O. Box 220 Royal Oak, MI 48067, 810-583-6242.

Versions available: Windows (version 2.5), Windows 95 (version 1.0), Macintosh (version 2.5). Complete program includes Stock Selection Guide, Stock Comparison Guide, Portfolio Management Guide, and the PERT (Portfolio Evaluation and Review Technique) form. Parts are available individually and in varying configurations.

Requirements: Windows version requires 4MB RAM, 4MB free space on hard drive, Windows 3.1 or higher. Windows 95 requires 8MB RAM, 6MB free space on hard drive. Macintosh version requires 2MB RAM, 5MB free space on hard drive, System 6.05 or higher.

Cost: Investor's Toolkit Complete, $159 for nonmembers, $139 for NAIC members. Stock Selection Guide module alone is $69 for nonmembers and $49 for NAIC members.

Guarantee: 30-day money back.

Demo or sample: Demo $5. You can also download demos at NAIC's World Wide Web page (http://www.better-investing.org).

Technical support: From Triple-I (the company that wrote the software), 305-829-2892 (9 A.M.–5 P.M., M–F), fax 305-829-5121.

User Newsletter or On-line Forum: Published monthly, *Bytes* is available to dues-paying members of NAIC who choose to join the computer users' group. It's not very useful. Much more useful is the NAIC forum on CompuServe (Go NAIC). There you'll find other users and NAIC staff who often post and discuss examples of individual stock studies. You can also find NAIC on the World Wide Web at http://www.better-investing.org.

Update: Quarterly update of stock data on disk from S&P costs $119 for annual subscription.

Strengths: An extremely thorough manual will guide the beginner through the first analysis in detail—it will tell him or her precisely where on Value Line or Standard & Poor's sheets the right data can be found (with diagrams and arrows) and where to put it in the form generated by the program. The graph that tracks historical earnings and sales is perhaps the best single fundamental tool now available for grouping the character of a growth stock.

Weaknesses: Program lacks any method for guiding an investor to understand risk. As long as an investor sticks to solid growth stocks with predictable patterns of earnings growth (the category that the program is designed to analyze, in fairness) that's probably not a problem. But investors who attempt to analyze younger, unpredictable emerging growth stocks may be in for some expensive surprises. In an ideal world the program would come with a calculator/form that would help investors understand how future changes in profit margin will affect earnings per share.

Tricks of the trade: Don't be dismayed by how long it takes you to do the first stock using the Stock Selection Guide—the effort drops dramatically as you learn your way around the data sources (Value Line's and Standard & Poor's both work equally well) and figure out where it all goes. I spent two hours doing my first stock, an hour and a half on the next, and an hour on my third. If you plan to analyze a lot of stocks, the quarterly data disks with data from S&P are a good buy. They supply historical data and you'll only have to update them between quarters. Be warned, though, that the data can be very late—a lag of two quarters is possible if the company's reporting period breaks in the wrong place. And be sure that you put any stock selection guides that you've altered (by entering new numbers) or completed (by filling in the calculations for growth and price) in a separate file. Otherwise, the quarterly data update will overwrite your changes.

This program won't help an investor analyze every kind of stock, but if you believe in buying solid, predictable growth stocks, the kind that grow earnings 15 percent a year, then this is the program for you. The Stock Selection Guide manages to crunch numbers in a way that tells the investor a lot about how they fit together to determine a stock's future.

This program is based on the NAIC philosophy: invest regularly in high-quality growth stocks and reinvest the dividends. The theory works—thousands of investment clubs across the country have built respectable portfolios on it for years.

The program therefore concentrates its fundamental analysis on predicting earnings. As the manual puts it, "A company's earnings determine the price of its stock" despite short-term fluctuations. "If we can predict how much a company will earn, we should be able to take a pretty good guess at what its stock will sell for based upon the relationship between its past earnings and the p/e at which its stock normally sells."

The Stock Selection Guide is the master program in the Investor's

Toolkit. It's built around an easy-to-complete data form (earnings, sales, dividends, shares outstanding, debt, historical high and low prices, and price-to-earnings ratios) that will accept data manually or from quarterly disks available by subscription from NAIC. Basically this program calculates a ten-year earnings and sales growth trend line that is used to estimate future growth of sales and earnings. The program then evaluates management using consistency and trend of profits and return on invested capital as benchmarks. (One caveat: a rising trend may mask problems at the company if the level of profitability is below industry norms.) Finally, the program uses the stock's price-to-earnings ratio history to calculate high and low prices for the stock five years into the future. A buy, hold, or sell range, upside/downside risk ratio, and potential annual return complete the evaluation of the stock.

While this reads like a cut-and-dried exercise, the program clearly flags crucial points where the results depend on an investor's judgment and interpretation. The clear insistence on investor judgment is one of the greatest strengths of the program—it makes it extremely hard for an investor to go to sleep and assume that the raw numbers will determine a future stock price without any application of the investor's gray matter.

Other parts of the program seem useful afterthoughts. Stock Comparison Guide creates forms that list crucial data items for several stocks in side-by-side columns for easy comparison. PERT attempts to calculate when to sell a stock. The Stock Selection Guide remains the reason to buy this program.

# 5

# A BETTER WAY TO PICK THE BEST MUTUAL FUND

**A** t first glance, anyone who can use a computer to screen stocks and then evaluate its fundamentals (in other words, anyone who read the last two chapters) knows everything he or she needs to pick a mutual fund. Mutual fund computer programs combine a database strikingly similar to that in stock programs with the by-now familiar tools for creating a screen that will sift through the more than 6,000 existing mutual funds to find the right one for a portfolio.

Evaluating a fund seems like it should be even easier than picking a stock. The amount of data far exceeds that available about any stock. Performance, for example, is sliced and diced to a fine puree.

But that simply isn't so. The scads of data available for any fund tell an investor exactly where the fund has been. It tells you very little about where the fund is headed in the future. This chapter is all about how to apply intense and idiosyncratic bending, folding, and spindling upon these reams of numbers from the past to reveal something about the future.

Take a simple category like performance. Look at all the data available in just one of the financial newspapers. The *Wall Street Journal*, for example, lists the entire mutual fund universe of more than 6,000 funds. During the course of a week, the paper reports on the performance of each fund for the year to date, the last four weeks, the last thirteen weeks, the last twenty-six weeks, the last thirty-nine weeks, the last twelve months, the last three years, the last four years, and the last five years. The tables note any charges for buying the fund—"loads" in the terminology of the mutual fund industry—and the expenses—management fees and the like—that investors pay to the company that runs the fund. The tables even categorize the funds, labeling some growth and others international, so that investors can compare funds with similar investment objectives to one another. To aid in that process the *Journal*'s tables give each fund a grade for performance compared to its peers for the one-, three-, four-, and five-year periods.

A software program, Alexander Steele's Mutual Fund Expert, provides even more information about performance. For each of 5,361 funds the program lists one-, three-, five-, ten-, fifteen-, and twenty-year returns. There are annual returns back to 1975. Yield, beta, alpha, R2, standard deviation, Sharpe ratio, Treynor ratio, volatility—all these for three, five, and ten years. Fees, expenses, a return rating, a risk rating, and an overall risk-adjusted return rating.

| | Name | Detailed Objective | Overall Rating | Risk Rating | 1-Month Return | SEC Total Return | St. Dev 5-year | 3-Month Return |
|---|---|---|---|---|---|---|---|---|
| 831 | Fidelity New Millennium | Growth U.S. | A | E | -1.70 | 83.82 | 3.54 | 7.10 |
| 832 | Benham Target Mat 2020 | Govt General | A | E | -1.75 | 114.93 | 5.12 | 7.91 |
| 833 | Seligman Frontier/A | Small Company Growth | A | D | -1.91 | 493.97 | 4.69 | -0.71 |
| 834 | United New Concepts/A | Small Company Growth | A | C | -2.02 | 357.77 | 4.33 | -1.05 |
| 835 | AIM Aggressive Growth | Small Company Growth | A | D | -2.33 | 485.69 | 5.12 | -1.32 |
| 836 | Putnam OTC Emerg Grth/A | Small Company Growth | A | E | -2.46 | 1113.94 | 4.85 | 5.50 |
| 837 | Seligman Commun & Info/A | Technology | A | E | -2.46 | 731.40 | 6.62 | -16.28 |
| 838 | Waddell & Reed Growth | Growth U.S. | A | D | -2.69 | 112.87 | 3.33 | -0.59 |
| 839 | Franklin Tmpl Gl:Hard Cur | Currency Money Market | A | C | -3.05 | 72.90 | 2.89 | -4.27 |
| 840 | Phoenix Srs:US Stock/A | Aggressive Growth | A | B | -4.28 | | 3.25 | 4.39 |
| 841 | PBHG Growth | Small Company Growth | A | E | -4.47 | 650.96 | 6.20 | 2.10 |
| 842 | Twentieth Cent:Giftrust | Small Company Growth | A | E | -5.29 | 957.45 | 6.34 | -4.06 |
| 843 | Govett Small Companies/A | Small Company Growth | A | E | -9.48 | 196.70 | 5.32 | -3.31 |
| 844 | Blanchard Precious Metals | Gold/Precious Metals | B | C | 24.93 | 35.91 | 7.52 | 37.14 |
| 845 | PIMCO Adv:Prec Metals/A | Gold/Precious Metals | B | D | 20.74 | 84.40 | 7.53 | 29.31 |
| 846 | Van Eck Intl Investors/A | Gold/Precious Metals | B | E | 19.25 | | 8.17 | 28.70 |
| 847 | Fidelity Sel:Amer Gold | Gold/Precious Metals | B | B | 17.75 | 156.61 | 6.96 | 31.40 |
| 848 | Vanguard Spect:Gold & PM | Gold/Precious Metals | B | B | 17.45 | 103.57 | 6.97 | 25.39 |
| 849 | United Serv:World Gold | Gold/Precious Metals | B | C | 16.16 | 132.62 | 7.55 | 29.61 |
| 850 | Colonial Newport Tiger/T | Pacific Equity excl. Japan | B | E | 9.72 | 168.34 | 5.62 | 14.52 |
| 851 | GT Global High Income/B | Global Emerging Market Bond | B | E | 8.64 | 56.12 | 4.89 | 17.55 |
| 852 | GT Global High Income/A | Global Emerging Market Bond | B | E | 8.61 | 54.75 | 4.90 | 17.60 |
| 853 | Franklin Strat:Gbl Hlth | Health | B | D | 7.39 | 93.62 | 4.95 | 23.36 |

Ranked by Overall YTD — 7730 Records — 0 Tagged — 1-31-96 — Equity/Fixed - Pro Plus

*Steele's Mutual Fund Expert shows performance data in the familiar spreadsheet format.*

(*Courtesy Steele Systems*)

## What Exactly Does the Past Tell Us About the Future?

But how should I use this data? All the information in these programs is about past performance and I want to predict the future. Is there any way to do that? Let's use one of the mutual fund programs, Morningstar's Mutual Funds Principia, to find out. (You can do the studies that follow with Steele's Mutual Fund Expert as well. I find that Morningstar's hypothetical portfolio feature is ideally suited to doing this kind of "what if" calculation. For the relative merits of all these programs see the reviews at the end of the chapter.)

### Experiment #1: Do above average funds stay above average?

Here's the first experiment. How many funds with above average performance for one five-year period beat the average for the next five years? In other words, if on January 1, 1990, I invested in the best funds of 1985–1989, how would I have done by June 30, 1995?

I started with growth funds, a big mainstream category since I wanted a significant sample of funds with ten-year track records. Morningstar lists 824 funds in that category and 164 have ten-year track records. Morningstar's "fund universe average" function calculates the average performance data for the funds in this universe. For my experiment I demand that each fund outperform the average in 1985, 1986, 1987, 1988, and 1989. I will then see how those funds compared over the next five years to the average growth fund.

To do that I go to the screen function and add performance hurdles—in Morningstar this works much like it does in one of the stock screening programs. A fund had to beat the 29.60 percent average return in 1985 (what a great year for mutual fund investors), the 14.62 percent average in 1986, the 3.02 percent average in 1987, the 14.21 percent average in 1988, and the 27.03 percent average in 1989. Just four funds managed to be better than average in all those years: Dreyfus Appreciation, Fidelity Exchange, IAI Regional, and State Street Exchange.

Now, how did those funds do in comparison to the average growth fund over the next five years? Not great. The five-year average annual return for the average fund was 11.33 percent. Only Fidelity Exchange beat that, with a 11.51 percent annual return. Dreyfus Appreciation (10.70), IAI

Regional (10.33), and State Street Exchange (10.02) all trailed the average growth fund.

Interesting. What's going on here? Using Morningstar's performance graphing function, I also compare each fund with the performance of the Standard & Poor's 500 index for the period beginning January 1, 1990 through June 30, 1995.

Dreyfus Appreciation, for example, fund returned 10.70 percent—but the index returned 12.08 percent. I would have been better off investing in an index rather than in one of my "best" funds.

### CONCLUSION #1: YES, THEY DO, IF WE FIGURE RISK INTO PERFORMANCE.

But so far, we've left out one important element: risk. Sure, these "best" funds slightly trailed the average growth fund for the period, but they also showed less risk. The five-year standard deviation, for example, was 13.16 for the 164 growth funds with ten-year track records and 12.09 for Dreyfus and just 10.81 for IAI Regional. That compares with a stan-

---

### Fund Detail

**Dreyfus Appreciation**
08-31-95

| | | | | | |
|---|---|---|---|---|---|
| **Rating** | ★★★ | **Assets** $325.7 mil | **NAV** 18.34 | **Objective** Growth | |

#### Performance

| | Total Rtn | +/- S&P 500 | +/- S&P 400 | %Rank Obj | Load Adjusted Return % | |
|---|---|---|---|---|---|---|
| YTD | 21.09 | -3.04 | -4.71 | 70 | 12 Mo | 21.34 |
| 1 Mo | -0.65 | -0.62 | -2.31 | 93 | 5 Years | 13.64 |
| 3 Mo | 3.84 | -1.84 | -7.48 | 97 | 10 Years | 13.96 |
| 12 Mo | 21.33 | 0.25 | 1.07 | 38 | Inception | 391.59 |
| | | | | | | |
| 3 Yr Annlzd | 9.49 | -4.23 | -6.62 | 89 | Yields | |
| 5 Yr Annlzd | 13.64 | -1.40 | -5.98 | 70 | SEC | — |
| 10 Yr Annlzd | 13.96 | -1.20 | -2.49 | 48 | 12 Mo | 1.53 |
| 15 Yr Annlzd | — | — | — | — | | |

#### Risk and Return

| | 3 Yr | 5 Yr | 10 Yr |
|---|---|---|---|
| Morningstar Risk | 0.98 | 0.83 | 0.93 |
| Morningstar Return | 0.53 | 0.92 | 1.10 |
| Std Deviation | 8.96 | 11.31 | 16.38 |
| Mean | 9.50 | 13.48 | 14.54 |
| Sharpe Ratio | 0.62 | | |
| | | | |
| Alpha | -3.91 | | |
| Beta | 1.03 | | |
| R-squared | 82 | | |

Average Historical Rating over 104 Months: 3.7★s

#### Performance History

| | 1985 | 1986 | 1987 | 1988 | 1989 | 1990 | 1991 | 1992 | 1993 | 1994 | 08-95 |
|---|---|---|---|---|---|---|---|---|---|---|---|
| Total Return % | 35.19 | 15.03 | 4.54 | 16.61 | 27.20 | -1.83 | 38.43 | 4.28 | 0.71 | 3.62 | 21.09 |
| +/- S&P 500 | 3.45 | -3.65 | -0.72 | 0.00 | -4.48 | 1.29 | 7.95 | -3.34 | -9.35 | 2.30 | -3.04 |
| +/- S&P 400 | -0.39 | -1.18 | 6.57 | -4.26 | -8.34 | 3.29 | -11.64 | -7.62 | -13.22 | 7.21 | -4.71 |

Close

---

*In this format Morningstar's program gives a snapshot of the Dreyfus Appreciation Fund.*

(Courtesy Morningstar Inc.)

dard deviation of 20.3 for the S&P 500 itself. These funds would be perfect for an investor looking for solid performance with less risk.

**EXPERIMENT #2: BUT WHAT IF "ABOVE AVERAGE" ISN'T GOOD ENOUGH? CAN WE FIND TOMORROW'S SUPERSTARS BY LOOKING AT PAST PERFORMANCE?**

How about using another strategy, an often publicized one that's the antithesis of buy and hold. For five years, each January I'll simply buy the best performing five funds (starting with $50,000 divided equally and then dividing the remainder equally each year) from the previous year. (For the first year, we'll use the best performing fund from the previous year.) To make our results comparable to the study we just did, we'll limit the study again to growth funds. Two hundred and sixty-two funds have the six-year track record we'll need (1989 through 1994).

The portfolio starts out with a thud. Of our five funds (Eagle Growth, up 51.72 in 1989), Janus Twenty (up 50.85), Berger 100 (up 48.31), Janus (up 46.32), and Idex II Growth (44.41), only Janus Twenty manages a positive return in the next year, 1990— and that was just 0.59 percent. The year of the invasion of Kuwait, 1990 was a tough year for

## TIPS ON THE TOOLS

# WHAT PERFORMANCE NUMBERS DO AND DON'T COUNT

How, exactly, do the big firms that provide the numbers every mutual fund investor uses—Morningstar, Micropal, Iverson Financial, IDD, Lipper Analytical, and the rest—calculate performance? Any investor who uses a software package ought to quiz the data provider carefully so that he or she knows the ins and outs of the performance numbers.

Let's take Morningstar, since its data is all over the newspapers and the on-line services. The simplest way to describe their performance numbers (and I think they're among the best in the business, don't get me wrong—I'm just suggesting that you understand them thoroughly) is that your returns will not, ever (well, hardly ever), match those that the company publishes. First, Morningstar's returns assume reinvestment of all income and capital gains distributions. In other words, if you take a dollar of dividends out or don't put every cent of the end of the year distribution back into the fund, your returns will be different

*continued*

(in most cases they'll lag due to the power of compounding). Second, Morningstar does not deduct front-end sales charges (or delayed sales charges, either) before calculating performance. The company's numbers (and this is true pretty much throughout the industry) have not been adjusted for the 3 to 8 percent fees that many funds charge to sell you shares (usually split with the broker who does the actual selling).

How important is that? Well, it depends on how long you hold your shares. Let's say an investor writes out a check for $10,000 to a fund with a 5 percent sales charge that goes up 10 percent the first year and 10 percent the year after. According to Morningstar that investor should have $11,000 after one year and $12,100 after two. Of course, the investor really has only $10,450 (after paying that 5 percent sales charge, only $9,500 actually got invested) the first year and $11,495 the second. As you can see, no matter how long the investor holds, he or she will never catch up. But only if that investor sells the fund quickly and invests in another load fund does the damage really start to mount up.

I've never heard a reasonable defense of the practice of not adjusting performance numbers for loads. Most of the excuses boil down to "It's too hard."

the market. Eagle Growth certainly suffered—it was down 20.95 for the year. Our portfolio isn't a pretty picture at the end of a year. Thanks to an 8.5 percent sales charge on Eagle Growth and a 5.5 percent charge at Idex—and the fund's negative return—my $50,000 is down to $46,052 on December 31, 1990. I've got just $9,210 to put into each of five new funds in 1991.

No highfliers make the 1991 list—remember that 1990 was a tough year. Still, Mathers (up 10.43 in 1990), Wasatch Growth (up 10.32), Anchor Capital Accumulation (up 8.57), Northwest Investors NW Growth (up 6.32), and Phoenix Growth (up 6.05) all managed to hit positive turf—and then explode into the double digits in 1991 (except for Mathers at 9.45), with Wasatch Growth leading the way at 40.8 for the year. I finish 1991 with $56,014 (or $11,203 for each fund in 1992).

Logically, if 1991 was hot, 1992 ought to be even better. At least it looks that way when I list the top five of 1991: CGM Capital Development (up 99.08 in 1991), Berger 100 (again, up 88.81), Mim Stock Appreciation (up 76.97), Vista Capital Growth (up 70.74), and Janus Twenty (again, up 69.21). But looking at how these funds did in 1992 makes me long for a time machine instead of a rearview mirror. CGM sinks to a still respectable 17.48, Janus Twenty ekes out just 1.97. Every fund is off its blistering pace of 1991. I do okay—finishing the year with $60,651 (or $12,130 per fund for 1993).

And so on. In 1993, I invest in 1992's winners, Parnassus, Merrill Lynch Phoenix, Dreyfus Special Growth, Gintel, and First Eagle Fund and end the year with $71,016 ($14,203 per fund.) In 1994, I invest in 1993's stars, Warburg Pincus Growth and Income, Merrill Lynch Growth, New Economy, Merrill Lynch Phoenix (two years in a row), and CGM Capital Development (again), and end the year with a loss (that year's market wasn't kind to these funds) of $6,212.

(A disturbing pattern is starting to emerge. This strategy is eating me alive on fees. About $2,300 of my 1994 loss is due to sales charges.)

One last time: I invest in 1994's winners for the first half of 1995 (again dividing my $64,803 portfolio into five $12,960 shares) among Parnassus, Vanguard/Primecap, Fidelity Blue Chip Growth, Longleaf Partners, and Cornerstone Growth. Thanks to the rally in the first half of the year I finish the experiment with $74,135.34, a profit of $24,135.34 in five and a half years.

Let me directly compare that to the results of buying and holding my four "above average" funds of the same period. The original $50,000 invested in them ($12,500 each) on January 1, 1990, and cashed out on June 30, 1995, comes to $87,761.64. The "above average" funds beat the annual winners by $13,626.30. I don't have to look far for half of the reason, either. None of my four "best" funds had, so chance would have it, any front-end sales charges or redemption fees. Every dollar I had to invest went into a portfolio returning 10.64 percent on average every year. In contrast, I paid $6,588 in sales charges in the high-turnover, highfliers portfolio. That accounts for about half under performance. (The results would be even worse for the highfliers portfolio if I took taxes into account, since I would have had to pay capital gains taxes when I cashed out each December 31 to put money into new funds.)

But it's not all of it. The highfliers portfolio earned only an average annual total return of 7.43 percent.

## CONCLUSION #2: IN PREDICTING FUTURE PERFORMANCE, LOTS OF THINGS BESIDES PAST PERFORMANCE COUNT—FEES AND FUND STYLES, FOR EXAMPLE.

In the highfliers portfolio each year I was picking funds whose portfolios were perfectly suited to the year that had just passed. These funds had made big bets on a style, an industry, or individual stocks that a fund was paying off. But there was no guarantee that it had paid off because of talent or knowledge on the part of the managers who ran these funds. I had picked a group of funds, some headed by skilled managers and some by lucky managers—and my screen didn't separate the two.

**Any system for picking a fund has to begin by analyzing what's behind its performance.**

Let's bring these portfolio experiments down to the muddy fields where most investors do battle. Can I apply any of this knowledge to the most common question mutual fund investors ask—should I dump a fund for something better? I'm going to use Harbor International Fund as an example. The fund, a long-time star, didn't do especially well in the first half of 1995—up 6.38 percent. This was especially disappointing because the fund returned only 5.43 percent in 1994. That was well below the fund's five-year return of 10.76 percent annually.

I know that 10.76 is good long-term performance and I know that a lot of short-term trading will eat my profits alive. But the short-term slump bothers me. To diversify I want to keep an international fund in my portfolio—that's why I bought Harbor International in the first place (and because I saw its manager, Hakan Castegren, profiled in some money magazine). But maybe some other international fund will give me a better combination of long-term track record and recent success. I certainly don't want to hold on to this fund if Castegren is starting to coast on his long-term record. So I build a screen with Morningstar's Principia.

From the program's opening screen, which simply lists funds alphabetically and then runs data in ninety columns across the screen and beyond, I click on "Screen" in the main menu bar and then on "Create Screen." That brings up another list of choices. I scroll down to "Investment Objective" and ask the program to give me a list of all international equity funds. That gives me 632 funds. I hit another command on the menu bar, "Rank," and ask the program to relist the funds from high to low according to their five-year annualized returns.

Harbor's 10.76 percent average annual return over the last five years turns out to be a tough benchmark to beat—which in itself makes me feel better. Looking at Morningstar, I find just nine funds that jumped this hurdle: Keystone American Global Opportunity A (16.36 percent average annual return), Colonial Newport Tiger (15.93), GAM International (15.24), Founders Worldwide Growth (13.42), Templeton Global Opportunity (12.84), Smallcap World (12.84), Templeton Growth , Templeton World (11.75), and New Perspective (11.72).

To check on short-term performance I add terms to this screen to make these 10 funds (including Harbor) my new universe. I require a fund to show five-year returns of 10.76 or higher and then rank them by year-to-date return. All nine beat Harbor International so far in 1995—some by a lot. GAM International shows a 19.90 percent total return for 1995 so far. The worst, Smallcap World, beat Harbor by more than four percentage points (10.99 to 6.38).

It seems like a significant difference. But is it? Let me use some of what my two previous experiments showed to put these results in context for you (actually several contexts) and see what you think.

### FIRST, CORRECT PERFORMANCE FOR SALES CHARGES AND OTHER FEES.

How long am I going to hold this fund? Yes, yes, I know everyone is a long-term investor. But, really, how long am I going to hold this fund? I'm considering abandoning Harbor International after only five years. Several of the funds I'm considering as alternatives have large, very large in fact, sales charges. If I put $10,000 into Keystone American Global, for example, the mutual fund company takes 5.75 percent for its own coffers and I actually invest just $9,425. Harbor International, on the other hand, doesn't collect a sales charge. My entire $10,000 would go to work.

That can make a big difference for a short-term investor. Even if Keystone returned 11.58 percent for the full year and Harbor just 6.38 percent, at the end of the year I'd still have $10,638 in Harbor and just $10,517 in Keystone. I don't want to start too far in the hole, if I switch, especially if the year-to-date returns don't hold up. But I don't want to rule out all the funds with sales charges—some are showing great numbers.

I decide to knock out any fund that hasn't beaten Harbor International by enough—assuming that the fund's performance for the whole year matches its six-month number—to offset its sales charge. For a fund with a 5.75 percent load to jump that hurdle it would have had to return more than 12.9 percent for 1995. That knocks out all the funds except for GAM International (19.9 percent), Templeton World (13.62), and New

## STRANGE NUMBER #1: R-SQUARED

Investors shouldn't overlook this unfamiliar number that shows up in both Morningstar and Steele. R-squared is a statistical tool that measures how much of a fund's price movements are explained by the movements of its benchmark index. For example, an S&P 500 index fund would have a very high R-squared (approaching 100), which indicates that its return is almost completely explained by the movements of the S&P 500 index itself. Actively managed funds tend to have lower R-squared numbers. A fund such as the Third Avenue Value Fund, which has an R-squared of just 50, dances to its own tune and not to that piped by the index.

Why does this matter? A fund's R-squared number tells an investor how relevant a fund's beta is. Beta, which measures a fund's volatility in reference to a benchmark index and thus measures market risk, is only a useful measure of risk for a fund with a high R-squared. For a fund with a low R-squared, which doesn't correlate to the index or the market very highly to begin with, beta is meaningless, and investors have to look to other measures of risk.

Perspective (13.65). Founders Worldwide Growth also makes the cut at 11.82 percent since it doesn't collect a sales charge.

### SECOND, CORRECT PERFORMANCE FOR RISK.

My definition of the "best" fund to buy also needs to consider risk. Risk can be measured in a lot of ways. If I were looking at domestic stock funds, I'd consider the beta, so that I could compare the volatility of each of these funds to the stock market as a whole. But international funds don't follow the movements of the U.S. market very closely, so this measure isn't very useful in this case. Instead I'll look at standard deviation.

The volatility of these funds varies significantly. Harbor International shows a standard deviation of 15.25—about the middle of the pack. Colonial Newport Tiger is the highest at 21.92—but we've already ruled this out on the basis of return and sales charge. Of our survivors, GAM International (15.88) is roughly as volatile as Harbor. Founders (12.56), Templeton World (12.58), and New Perspective (11.76) are all less volatile. Looking at this group of funds it's easy to see what standard deviation, which sometimes seems very abstract, means in practice. Colonial Newport Tiger, the most volatile fund, had the biggest annual rise in the group (75.24 in 1993) but also the biggest drop (15.14 in 1990). Founders Worldwide, in contrast, shows 34.79 as its largest gain and 2.16 percent as its biggest drop. Putting return and standard deviation together suggests that maybe I do want to move out of Harbor. The risk-adjusted returns are even less in its favor than the raw performance numbers.

### THIRD, REMOVE "LUCK" FROM PERFORMANCE.

Remember that when I created my highfliers portfolio and studied the dismal results, I theorized that a large part of the problem was that I couldn't separate lucky managers from good ones. I'm not sure that the technique I'm about to suggest solves the problem, but it certainly does address it.

While the ten funds in my original international sample all earn the same label "International," they had very different investment agendas. The Morningstar function labeled "Investment Objective," which breaks down fund categories in more detail, gives me a clue to that. GAM International and Harbor International are both classified as "foreign" mutual funds. According to Morningstar's definition that means they invest only in non-U.S. equities. GAM's largest holding, according to Morningstar, is Fortis AMEV, a U.K. insurance company, and Harbor's is Gencor, a Dutch drug maker. Colonial Newport Tiger is a "Pacific" fund: its portfolio is limited to Asian companies such as Hong Kong and China Gas and the Thai Farmers Bank. The remaining funds are all "world" funds. They're free to invest inside and outside the United States. Founders Worldwide Growth, for example, owns shares of Nokia, the Finnish maker of cellular phones, and U.S. airplane giant Boeing.

At least 25 percent of a world fund's portfolio must, by Morningstar's definition, consist of non-U.S. stocks. But the percentage can vary widely. Keystone was only 38.5 percent invested in foreign stocks, according to Morningstar, on June 30; Templeton Global, 64.7 percent; and Founders, 72.7 percent.

Adding a foreign fund gives me 100 percent exposure to non-U.S. markets, but adding some world funds may give me as little as 25 percent non-U.S. exposure. This means I can't use just any of these funds to diversify my portfolio, but it also puts the performance numbers in a new light. If these funds must invest in different markets by their charters, at least some of each fund's performance is attributable to the kind of assets that it must invest in. A Pacific fund that is in Pacific market stocks when those markets soar should earn fabulous returns. If it doesn't, that should be a strike against the manager since it certainly demonstrates a lack of skill. Conversely, a fund that prospers with the markets it must invest in, but does no better, shouldn't impress me. Again, there's no skill here. Measuring performance in this way actually can take some of the luck out of performance numbers.

So, a smart investor benchmarks fund performance against the *appropriate* index. That's a little more work than simply looking to see how a manager compares against a standard benchmark such as the Standard & Poor's 500, but it's also a lot more accurate. For a domestic fund, I'd like to compare a small company growth fund, not to the large stocks in the S&P 500 index, but to an index that tracks similar stocks, such as the Russell 2000 Small Cap Growth Index. We have to do exactly the same kind of matching in the foreign realm. In this case, we need to look at returns for a foreign stock index: 5.58 percent for the five years and 3.69 percent year to date; a world stock index: 7.45 percent for five years and 10.65 year to date; a Pacific index: 3.43 percent for five years and 2.18 year to date; and a U.S. index, such as the S&P 500: 12.08 for five years and 23.52 year to date. The extremely high returns for the U.S. stock market certainly explain why world funds, with their exposure to that market, so readily beat foreign funds.

Now, I can redo the performance ratings for the five funds still in the running, ranking them by how much they beat the appropriate index over five years.

Notice anything rather astonishing? For most of these funds, the superior performance that initially attracted our attention has just about disappeared. Most of the difference between Harbor, an international fund, and Founders Worldwide, Templeton World, and New Perspective is due

|  | Original 5-year return | Original ytd return | New 5-year return | New ytd retrn. |
|---|---|---|---|---|
| GAM International | 15.24 | 19.20 | 9.66 | 15.51 |
| Founders Worldwide | 13.42 | 11.82 | 5.97 | 1.17 |
| Templeton World | 11.75 | 13.62 | 4.3 | 2.97 |
| New Perspective | 11.72 | 13.65 | 4.27 | 3.0 |
| Harbor International | 10.76 | 6.38 | 5.18 | 2.69 |

*To correct returns for luck, compare funds to the appropriate index.*

to fund charters that require these three to be invested in the U.S. market and a charter that prevents Harbor International from sharing those gains. If I still believe in building a diversified portfolio, I certainly wouldn't abandon Harbor International in favor of one of these three funds. I'd essentially be selling Harbor International because it is an international fund.

## TIPS ON THE TOOLS

# WHO HAS THE BEST BENCHMARKS?

The only funds I want to compare to the Standard & Poor's 500 index are funds that invest in exactly the same kind of large market capitalization, established companies that make up that index. I want to compare every other fund with the index that is closest to the composition of the fund in question. And I want my mutual fund software to give me the indexes I need. Morningstar and Steele have both developed relatively complete libraries of indexes. Monocle's package is also first-rate. Here's a table of the indexes you'll need:

| Index | Asset class | 5-year annual total return | Best annual return | Worst annual return |
| --- | --- | --- | --- | --- |
| S&P 500 | Large cap stocks | 17.23 | 37.51 | -3.15 |
| Russell 2000 | Small cap stocks | 17.11 | 46.04 | -19.53 |
| Wilshire 5000 | Entire market | 15.45 | 34.20 | -6.18 |
| Morgan Stanley EAFE | Foreign stocks | 6.97 | 32.95 | -23.32 |
| Financial Times World | World stocks | 9.76 | 22.49 | -17.08 |
| Lehman Bros. Corporate Bond | Corporate bonds | 10.10 | 22.25 | -3.35 |
| Lehman Bros. Govt. Bond | U.S. treasury bonds | 8.69 | 18.34 | -2.38 |

Other indexes to consider for less common asset classes include the Morgan Stanley Pacific Index, the Lehman Brothers Mortgage-Backed Securities Index, the Lehman Brothers Municipal Bond Index, and the National Association of Real Estate Investment Trusts.

# STRANGE NUMBER #2: SHARPE RATIOS

All investors should know about William Sharpe. He won a Nobel Prize in Economics for his work on the relationship between risk and reward. He's even got a number named after him, the Sharpe ratio, that you'll find in several mutual fund programs.

What is the Sharpe ratio? As you'd expect from the rest of Sharpe's work, it's an attempt to quantify the relationship between risk and reward for a specific asset—in this case a specific mutual fund. It's calculated by subtracting the 12-month risk-free rate of return (the 12-month return on the 3-month Treasury bill) from the fund's 12-month return. The number that's left over—the amount by which the fund outperformed 3-month Treasury bills—is called the "excess return." That's the extra return that an investor gets by taking on the risk of the fund. That excess return is then divided by the fund's standard deviation to calculate the amount of extra return per unit of risk. The higher the Sharpe ratio, the better a fund's risk-adjusted performance.

GAM International is another issue. The fund has significantly outperformed its benchmark index *and* Harbor International. The two funds have just about the same standard deviation, so one is not significantly more volatile than the other. GAM International has beaten Harbor International's five-year performance by about 50 percent and its year-to-date performance threefold. The only strike against the fund is its 5 percent sales charge. If I really will hold this fund for five years, I should sell Harbor International and buy GAM International.

**FOURTH, PRETTY MUCH THROW OUT PAST PERFORMANCE WHEN A NEW FUND MANAGER TAKES OVER.**

I want to check two more bits of information on these two funds before I make my decision. Managers come and go at mutual funds. The manager who built a track record may be dead, retired, or at another fund by the time I discover the fund he or she used to manage. That would make using a past performance record to suggest future performance an exercise in futility. Neither of the funds I'm considering has this problem. John Horseman has managed GAM International for five years—all the track record I considered in my screens belonged to him. Hakan Castegren has been at the helm of Harbor International for eight years. (But other funds in the group have changed managers during my five-year study period. Christopher Ely has run Keystone America Global for less than a year, for example.)

**FIFTH, FUNDS HAVE FUNDAMENTALS, TOO—FIGURE THOSE INTO YOUR EVALUATION OF PERFORMANCE.**

Morningstar's CD-ROM version is currently the only mutual fund program that gives a detailed breakdown of all the stocks a portfolio man-

---

**TIPS ON THE TOOLS**

## THE TEAM MANAGEMENT SCAM

Some mutual fund companies have gotten wise to investors who check to see how long a manager has helmed a fund and who then avoid funds with new untried managers. (This is easy to check with mutual fund software. Just look at the data column labeled "Tenure.") The companies have moved to obfuscate the issue by claiming that their funds are "team managed." That way managers remain mostly anonymous and investors not only can't follow the comings and goings, they can't even tell when a departure or arrival is significant.

This said, I also need to note that some funds really are team managed. Decisions are made by committee. The management company has set up rules and procedures, implemented research strategies, maybe even written software that picks stocks. In this case, team management isn't a ploy. A team really is responsible for the fund's performance.

There's no simple way to separate the real teams from the pretenders. Be skeptical of any fund that suddenly changes from an individual manager to a team. Look twice at any team fund at a management company that lists individual managers for the rest of its funds.

Finally, though, realize that team managers should be able to explain the strategy that guides a team and its process just like an individual manager should be able lay out how he or she runs a portfolio. If a team can't do that to your satisfaction, remember that with more than 6,000 mutual funds now on the market, you have plenty of choices. You don't need to put your money with a fund that can't or won't answer your questions to your satisfaction.

ager holds (I'll look at this in more detail in a moment), but all the Morningstar versions, Value Line Fund Analyzer, and Steele's Mutual Fund Expert give a general picture of a fund portfolio. In comparing GAM International and Harbor International even an overview is revealing. GAM International has the lowest price-to-earnings ratio and price-to-book ratio of any fund in this ten-fund universe. GAM International is heavily into utilities—they make up 44.3 percent of the portfolio—and financials—35.3 percent—and stocks in both of those industries tend to have lower price-to-earnings and price-to-book ratios than technology stocks do. Horseman owns nothing in the technology sector at all.

The fund is different in one other way. Just over 47 percent of the portfolio is in bonds instead of equities. (Harbor International has no bonds in its portfolio.) With the emphasis on utilities, financials, and bonds, this fund has a strong interest rate exposure, which any investor ought to think about before jumping on board.

Now I can do this kind of analysis on any domestic equity fund—and on any bond fund, too. I don't need to start with a screen, either. I can use one of these programs to analyze a single fund to see what makes it tick.

## PUTTING IT ALL TOGETHER I: TAKING APART FIDELITY MAGELLAN

At $56 billion, Fidelity Magellan is the biggest fund in the industry. To get to Magellan from the opening Morningstar screen display you can either page-down the name column—as if running your finger down the data in the newspaper—or call up the function "Find a Fund" (by hitting F8 or pulling down the Function menu and clicking on the item) and then typing in the name Fidelity Magellan.

There are two ways to read all the data on Magellan—straight across from the name of the fund to its investment objective and so on to "Brokerage Availability," the last column, or by going to the Options menu and clicking on "Display a fund." That puts all the Magellan data on two screens. According to Morningstar, Magellan was up 35.18 percent year-to-date for 1995 (as of July 31—which put it in the top 5 percent of similar growth funds—and in 1994 it was down, –1.81. The program confirms that over the last five years this fund has been a superb performer, returning an annualized 18.24 percent.

The computer also lets me put those returns in a precise context. I can compare Magellan to all similar mutual funds and to the market as a whole. Part of the comparison makes Magellan look good. In 1994 Magellan's down performance still beat the returns of the market as a whole, which, measured by the Standard & Poor's 500 index, went down even more, –3.13 percent. On a five-year basis, Magellan beat that market measure by 6.73 percentage points a year.

But the program also shows exactly how different the fund has been under its three managers: Peter Lynch (from Magellan's 1981 inception as a publicly sold mutual fund to June 1990), Morris Smith (July 1990 to July 1992), and Jeffrey Vinik (August 1992 to the present). Everyone

## TIPS ON THE TOOLS

# WHY THE NUMBERS DON'T ALWAYS AGREE

**S**hortly after I did my first stint as editor of *Worth*'s annual mutual fund survey, I got an irate call from a reader. He had just picked up *Money*'s end of the year fund issue and, looking up one fund he owned, noticed that the five-year performance number that *Worth* and *Money* reported were radically different—something like 9 percent versus 11. Who was wrong? he wanted to know.

Off the top of my head I couldn't answer. I suggested that the only obvious difference in the two magazine's surveys was the time period of the data. Our November issue had used a five-year period that began in August 1990. *Money*'s December issue used a five-year period that ended in September 1990. He dismissed my explanation with a snort—a month couldn't make that kind of difference. I said I'd do my homework and call him back.

To my surprise—and the skeptical reader's, too—one month did make that kind of difference. The market plunged in July of 1990 and then rallied in August. Our performance numbers started off with a low base (which didn't matter in our rating system since we compared all funds to the appropriate benchmark for the period). *Money*'s began at a higher initial level.

This example has a significant take-home lesson, however. If we had been comparing funds across categories, we would have wound up with serious distortions that might have in fact rewarded more volatile funds for their

*continued*

volatility—since they would have fallen further and therefore started from an even lower base than steadier performers. It always pays to learn a few facts about the performance of the market during the period of any study.

For example, I know of one study that compares the risk and return of convertible bonds (more return and less risk, the study concluded) and common shares, and just happens to take 1973 as its starting date. Remember what happened in 1973?—the summer of that year saw the beginning of a bear market that took the S&P down 40 percent. Any guesses why the study turned out the way it did?

is familiar with the Peter Lynch legend, but pulling it up on the screen in detail is still amazing. For his entire tenure as a manager, Lynch averaged an annual total return of 23.83 percent—beating the Standard & Poor's 500 index by 8.17 percentage points a year. The average growth fund trailed the S&P in this period by 1.26 percentage points a year. (So Magellan beat the average growth fund by 9.42 percentage points.)

Magellan came back to the pack in the two years Smith ran the fund. Magellan returned 14.11 percent a year, but that only beat the S&P by 2.78 percentage points (*only!*) and the average growth fund by 3.16 percentage points. These "declines" are what started everyone talking about the effect of the size of Magellan. Lynch had racked up his returns when the fund was comparatively small (it had $14 billion under management when he retired), and Smith was struggling under the load of a $22 billion portfolio. Returns had to come down, every pundit said.

Along came the Vinik years—now three and counting—and returns popped back up. For the Vinik period Magellan has returned 19.90 on average annually—6.95 percentage points above the S&P 500. Interestingly, the average growth fund beat the index for this period, too (a highly unusual occurrence), by 0.55 percentage points. Magellan still beat the growth fund average by 6.4 percentage points annually.

The Morningstar program can tell me something about how Vinik earned those results. If I create a screen for the 831 growth funds in Morningstar and then ask for an average on that universe, I can compare the portfolio composition of the average growth fund with Magellan's. Significant differences: Magellan has 43 percent of its portfolio in technology stocks compared to the group average of 19 percent. Vinik has also underweighted such growth fund staples as health (he's got 3 percent of his portfolio in that sector while the average growth fund has 11 percent), utilities (no meaningful exposure in Magellan, while the average growth fund has 5 percent in the sector), and consumer staples (nothing in this favorite Peter Lynch category versus 5 percent for the average growth fund).

Because of those sector choices, Magellan seems riskier than the average growth fund, but the numbers say that it isn't that much riskier. Beta for Magellan is 1.12; for the average growth fund it's 0.99. Three-year standard deviation at Magellan 11; at the average growth fund 9.99. Roughly, Magellan seems to be about 10 percent riskier by these measures. Not bad, since annual returns are 47 percent higher on average for the three Vinik years.

But what about the fund's risk in a downturn? Vinik hasn't confronted more than the slightest dip—1994—in the general stock market during his three-year run. The last crash took place in 1987 and that was short-lived. The last serious down market came during the Iraqi invasion of Kuwait in 1990. An investor really can't tell from the numbers in Morningstar how Magellan would fare in a serious down market. All I can con-

## TIPS ON THE TOOLS

# THE HISTORICAL DATA PROBLEM AGAIN

Despite all the historical performance data these programs provide, the investor is still missing key historical data on the fundamentals of mutual funds. For example, there's good evidence that excessively fast growth in assets under management can seriously erode a manager's future performance. I would certainly like to know if a fund that otherwise shows great performance numbers has suddenly added a bundle of assets.

Similarly, I'd like to be able to check to see if a fund has changed style since it built its track record. To do this I might compare the average market capitalization of the companies in the fund's portfolio three years ago with the size of companies in the portfolio now. I might do the same with beta and price-to-book to see if a fund had gone from small cap to mid or large cap, from less risky than the market to more risky, or from value investing to growth.

Unfortunately, none of the programs I looked at give an investor past data on items like this. The diligent investor has only two options, neither particularly attractive. One option is call the fund company and

*continued*

grill them about the characteristics of the fund in the past (three years is a good period). A second option, keep those old mutual fund data disks. Someday you will be able to set up a parallel database for funds that trail your current data by three years. Then you'll be able to get the historical perspective you need. (And, of course, we can all hope that before that date, someone will start selling historical data about fund fundamentals on CD-ROM.)

clude from this is that the fund will probably fall at least slightly further than the average growth fund and than the market as a whole.

Is any of this enough to make an investor run for the hills on Magellan? Of course not. But the computer does give an investor a chance to look with the same degree of attention at some alternatives. If we're worried about the fund's risk under its new manager of three years but attracted by his performance, we can look for some possible replacements. For three years Magellan beat 92 percent of the funds in the growth category. Well, do any of the 8 percent that beat Magellan look attractive? Let's use the Search function to find out.

Keeping the universe set for the 831 growth funds, let's add some more criteria. First, we want funds that beat Magellan's 19.89 percent annual return for the last three years. By typing "and," and picking "Tot Ret Annlzd 3 Yr," ">," and "19.89 percent" from the menu choices, I get a list of thirty-two funds that all fit the bill. Now, I don't want to take on more of the kinds of risk I'm worried about with Magellan, so I'll also screen out funds with managers who have tenures of less than three years, where turnover is more than 120 percent, where technology makes up more than 42.6 percent of the portfolio, and where the price-to-earnings ratio of stocks in the portfolio is higher on average than the 20.7 in Magellan's portfolio. I also don't want to pay a sales charge to transfer my money, and it's pointless to look at funds that aren't accepting new investors. All those conditions give me a final universe of 3: Longleaf Partners, Neuberger & Berman Focus, and Oakmark.

## PUTTING IT ALL TOGETHER II: FINDING AN ALTERNATIVE TO MAGELLAN

None of these funds have matched Magellan's eye-popping returns for 1995, but then that's expected, since I screened out funds that might have loaded up even more heavily on technology than Magellan did this year. But all three funds beat Magellan on a three-year basis: Longleaf at 21.54, Neuberger & Berman at 20.04, and Oakmark at 24.74. And most important for our current effort, all of them outperformed Magellan in the tough market of 1994: Longleaf at 8.97, Neuberger & Berman at 0.87, and Oakmark at 3.32. Both Longleaf and Oakmark show betas below Magellan's (0.76 and 0.90, respectively) and below the average growth fund. Three-year standard deviation confirms the solidness of these two funds: Longleaf at just 7.92 and Oakmark at 9.57.

One further way to study these three funds against one another is to chart them against one another. The graph shows the three funds climbing steadily, but also clearly illustrates the greater volatility of Magellan. The fund had fallen behind the other two in 1994 and only the steep climb in 1995 brought the three even.

Now, does this make me sell Magellan and buy Oakmark or Longleaf? Of course not. You'd want to consider your view of the future of the market and for the technology sector—are they set for a period of turbulence?—and your attitude toward risk. If you stay with Magellan, you're signing on for a high-octane ride.

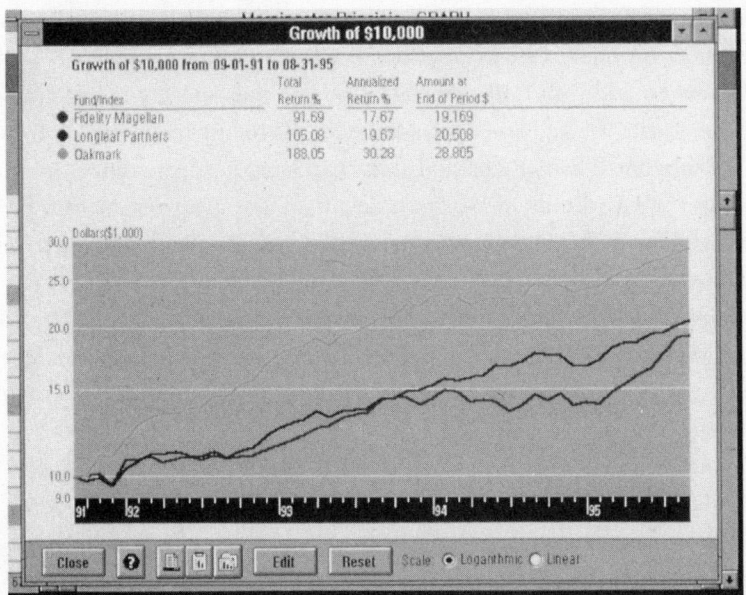

*Magellan, Longleaf, and Oakmark are all great funds—but Magellan is clearly more volatile. (Courtesy Morningstar Inc.)*

## TIPS ON THE TOOLS

# FUND CATEGORIES

Is your portfolio balanced? Do you own an equity income fund? How about a growth and income fund? (And how are those two different?) How about a small cap fund? And an aggressive growth fund? Morningstar divides the mutual fund universe into more than 30 different categories, and the other software programs aren't far behind. Is any of that important?

Simply, no. The categories are arbitrary. So Gen International is listed by Morningstar as an asset allocation fund, for example. Beyond that, they aren't useful.

The theory behind this kind of slicing and dicing is that it will let the investor judge a fund against absolutely the right peer group of funds. The fact that it also makes the fund industry happy by giving more funds the chance to be at the top of their categories is just an added bonus. But so what? An investor trying to build a balanced portfolio doesn't need a fund from each of 30 groups. He or she needs exposure to five equity styles and possibly the same number of income styles—at most—to create a diversified portfolio.

Think about what diversifying a portfolio means for a moment. An investor wants to add different asset classes, but not just any asset classes. He or she wants to add asset classes that move independently of each other. We mix small cap stocks and large cap stocks, for instance, because historically the two kinds of stocks tend to get hot at different times. An investor who owns both will earn more than an investor who owns one alone, and with lower risk, because of that independence.

Therefore, it's only important to add mutual fund types to a portfolio if the types show significant independence. We know bonds move independently of stocks—but do corporate bonds move independently of government bonds? An investor should know before deciding to put both in a portfolio. (Research suggests that all types of bonds, with the exception of junk bonds, move pretty much in sync. Maturity, the life of a bond in years, is more important than type in building a diversified bond portfolio.)

What categories perform with enough independence to make a difference to a portfolio? Large and small caps. Value and growth stocks. International and domestic equities. Bonds and stocks. Maybe add a spoonful of precious metal stocks or real estate equities—although these tend to be interest rate and inflation sensitive just like bonds. That's it. Who cares about equity income funds in this context? If I want equity, I'll buy a stock fund. If I want income, I'll buy bonds. If I want equity income, I'll mix the two simpler categories.

An investor can deconstruct the categories used by any of these programs by building screens that divide the universe the way he or she wants. If large cap growth funds are an important category for your portfolio, screen on market cap, price-to-earnings, and earnings growth to create a list of true large cap growth funds.

The great thing about these programs is that if an investor doesn't like the mousetrap the software company has built, it's pretty easy to build a better one. Or at least one that fits the investor's purposes more closely.

## Extending This Method: Bond Mutual Funds

Mutual fund software programs work just as well for bond funds as they do for equity funds, but an investor has to learn a new type of analysis to take into account the difference between stock and bond funds. Let me show you how, using a case study that I ran for one of my co-workers at *Worth* in late 1994. Bob (not his real name and not a reference to the trademarked Microsoft program of the same name) came to me with two bond funds. One, Vanguard Fixed-Income Long-term Corporate, he'd found in the bond fund ratings in our December 1994 issue. The other, Fidelity Intermediate Corporate, he'd simply heard about. So we pulled up each fund on Morningstar.

First, we looked at the Vanguard fund. The year-to-date numbers for 1994 didn't look good. Vanguard Fixed-Income Long-term Corporate had lost 6.61 percent so far in 1994, not surprising since the Federal Reserve rate increases that had begun in February 1994 had kicked the stuffing out of the bond market. But the Vanguard fund's return was especially bad—the loss put it in the 91st percentile for group (meaning that 91 percent of all funds in this bond fund category did better).

But the fund had a much better long-term record. For three years it was in the top 2 percent of the category—with a 7.28 percent annual return—for five years it was in the top 1 percent—with a 8.58 percent annual return—and for ten years it stayed in the top 1 percent-with a 10.31 percent average annual return.

But 1994's returns shouldn't be dismissed. It was the first real down market for bonds in more than ten years—and therefore an important year for judging the risk in a bond fund. Vanguard's returns for that year suggest that the fund might be riskier than its long-term record seemed to imply.

If I look at a new number, one important for bond funds but not for stock funds, I can see where that risk may reside. The average maturity (the time until a bond's maturity date—when the issuer pays investors their principal) is a whopping 19.3 years. All things being equal, the longer the term of a bond, the more sensitive it is to interest rate changes. An average maturity of almost twenty years makes this fund very sensitive.

The comparison to Fidelity Intermediate Bond Fund, which is also a corporate bond fund, is stark. The 1994 year-to-date total return on this fund is a negative 2.33 percent, just about a third of the loss Vanguard showed. That puts the fund at the 44th percentile for the year, solidly in the middle of the pack. In fact, all the fund's returns are solidly middling. The ten-year average annual return of 9.24 (almost a full 100 basis points, or one percentage point lower than Vanguard's) puts the fund again in the 44th percentile.

This fund is also far less volatile than the Vanguard fund. The average maturity of the bonds in the fund is only 6.70 years, which explains the difference between the two funds. The Fidelity Fund is also 33 percent in cash, compared to 4 percent for Vanguard, which also damps volatility.

Well, so far I know a lot about the interest rate risks of these two funds, but that isn't the only kind of risk a bond fund can take. There's also credit risk—the possibility that the borrower won't be able to pay back the loan—and currency risk—the chance that the value of our bond will fall because of a decline in the value of the foreign borrower's currency. For information like this, I'll have to go deeper into the portfolio of each fund.

What's in the portfolio? "Composition" will tell us. Eleven out of the twelve largest holdings in the Fidelity fund are U.S. governments issues, or Ginnie Maes (mortgage-back bonds issued by and backed by the Government National Mortgage Association). But below that foreign issues dominate—Korea Development Bank, Province of Mani-

# CASH AND THE BOGUS BOGEY

Every once in a while, the financial press rediscovers indexes and index funds. Suddenly the pages of the money magazines are full of stories about how most funds don't beat the indexes most of the time and how, therefore, investors should put their money in index funds.

In case you haven't noticed, we're in such a time now. Probably because in the 1995 market run very few managers have outperformed the good ol' Standard & Poor's 500. So what are we paying them those big fees for?

Well, I got news for my brethren. The observation is 100 percent accurate. The conclusion is downright, 100 percent wrong.

Most mutual funds do trail the indexes in an up market as supercharged as this one. That doesn't mean an investor should pitch them aside in favor of an index fund.

Let's take a look at the differences between an index and a mutual fund. The index is always, by definition, 100 percent invested. (It also never deducts a transaction charge when it trades—"rebalances" in the lingo of the indexers, but we'll ignore that point.) It never takes in new cash that sits inactive until the manager can figure out how to deploy it. It never puts any cash aside as a reserve to pay for redemptions in case shareholders get antsy.

All that means that mutual funds should trail the index in an up market—the cash in the fund acts as a drag on performance since in an up market stocks are earning way more than the money market is paying in interest. And it means that mutual funds should outperform—or actually in this case not lose as much—in a down market where the same cash keeps paying a steady positive return while everything else turns negative.

So once again, the crucial question is how does a fund perform versus the index on a risk-adjusted basis? A fund can't match the index in an up market unless it takes on more risk than the index (to make up for the drag of cash) and a fund should outperform in a down market, unless it took on extra risk to try to outperform the bull market. Indexes aren't absolute targets, but relative ones. The smart investor always adjusts returns—even index returns—for risk.

toba, Kingdom of Denmark, Kingdom of Thailand. Makes an investor wonder what would happen if international markets came under stress.

How does this compare to Vanguard? The portfolio looks quite different than Fidelity's. Five of the seven largest holdings are U.S. government issues or Ginnie Maes. The two others are Bank of Boston and ATT. But the portfolio as a whole contains far fewer foreign issues and more U.S. corporates: GE Capital, Arco Chemical, United Parcel Service. The first foreign holding is Nippon Telephone and Telegraph.

There are ways to study the risks of bonds and bond funds in more precision, but not with any of the existing mutual fund programs for the individual investor. I'm left to weigh the two funds in a relatively subjective manner. Do I think, going forward, that interest rate risks (Vanguard) are more or less likely to expose me to big losses than credit and currency risks (Fidelity)?

## ANOTHER KIND OF BEAST ENTIRELY: PROGRAMS FOR TRADING MUTUAL FUNDS

You'll notice that in this entire discussion I haven't talked about one kind of data—daily prices—and one kind of investing—trading. Much mutual fund software is designed for the buy and hold investor with a relatively long-time horizon. While the programs make it possible to compare performance on a month-to-month basis, they implicitly assume that the user won't be trying to market time, that is to attempt to buy funds when the market is headed up and sell them when it's ready to fall, using mutual funds.

For an increasingly large minority of mutual fund investors, that assumption is dead wrong. For these investors mutual funds are nothing more than baskets of stocks. And just as individual stocks can be traded on the basis of technical signals—patterns in a stock's price over time that technicians believe can generate buy and sell signals—so, too, can mutual funds.

The mutual fund industry, by and large, claims to be appalled by this practice. They continue to tout their products as long-term vehicles for investors saving for retirement, college, a second home. The managers who run mutual funds certainly don't want to see money sloshing in and then running out of their funds by the millions or billions whenever the 90-day trend line says "Sell."

Yet, mutual fund companies have created the conditions necessary for short-term trading of mutual funds. They've added telephone switching among the funds in their family so that an investor can move among all the Invesco Funds or all the Fidelity funds with a phone call and without charge. First Charles Schwab and then Fidelity created mutual fund marketplaces that let traders move among funds or different families with a single phone call—and often without charge. Several fund families, most conspicuously Fidelity, have marketed funds that seem designed for in-and-out traders. Think auto stocks are about to get hot?—buy Fidelity Select Automotive. Ride them till the indicators suggest a top and then sell in order to buy Fidelity Select Energy.

You can of course trade mutual funds on their fundamentals—moving from Founders Worldwide Growth to Fidelity Blue Chip when you think international stocks have faltered and the U.S. market is looking up. But fundamentals change only slowly. To be an active trader of mutual funds, you need frequent price information so that you can build the charts and graphs necessary to see when to switch.

A program to do this kind of mutual fund analysis is a very different creature than the fundamental and performance databases such as Morningstar's Principia or Steele's Mutual Fund Investor. On a first glance at a program of this sort, such as American River's Mutual Fund Investor and its associated database Fundscope, that isn't apparent. Mutual Fund Investor appears to be a stripped-down version of the data in Morningstar. Instead of eighty columns of information on a fund, the program lists just twenty-four.

But data isn't the point of a program like this—graphing is. If in Mutual Fund Investor I scroll down the list of funds until I get to Fidelity Magellan, and then hit two keys simultaneously, "Alt" and "G," I get a graph of the price behavior of Magellan.

The first graph I get in Mutual Fund Investor, the default graph, shows the actual price of Magellan from 1986 through the present and also graphs an average of those prices called the 39-week moving average. (I can set the time period of the average to virtually any period. See Chapter 8 on technical analysis programs for more detail on why this is important.) Once I've got the graph up, I can easily add another fund to the graph, say Fidelity Contra Fund, by hitting "C" and then picking Contra out of the database list. The graphs show that the prices of the two funds have moved in virtual lockstep. I can also compare, graphically, any fund with the S&P 500 or some other index.

But most important, and here's the difference at the heart of trading programs like this, the computer will generate a buy or sell signal for me on the basis of a fund's price trend. For example, as of January 27, the program said that if Magellan dropped to a NAV of 66.717 from its current NAV of 66.940, I should sell. The price trend would have decidedly turned to the downside.

Whether you believe a signal like that probably depends on your feeling about technical analysis. But let me suggest several intriguing ways to use one of these timing programs, even if you don't believe in trading mutual funds, market timing, or technical analysis. For my example I'm going to use Monocle from Manhattan Analytics.

Monocle is organized around the concept of fund groups, a set of funds with a defined benchmark, which can be either another fund or an index. The fund group can be a fund family (Fidelity), an investment objective (growth), or, intriguingly, user defined.

I'll start by choosing a simple fund group, the Fidelity Investments family. After clicking "OK", I get a tiled screen with price history (benchmarked against S&P 500), relative strength crossover, relative strength active, and short-term performance, each graphed for the first fund in the group, Fidelity Advisor Growth Opportunity. Using a sim-

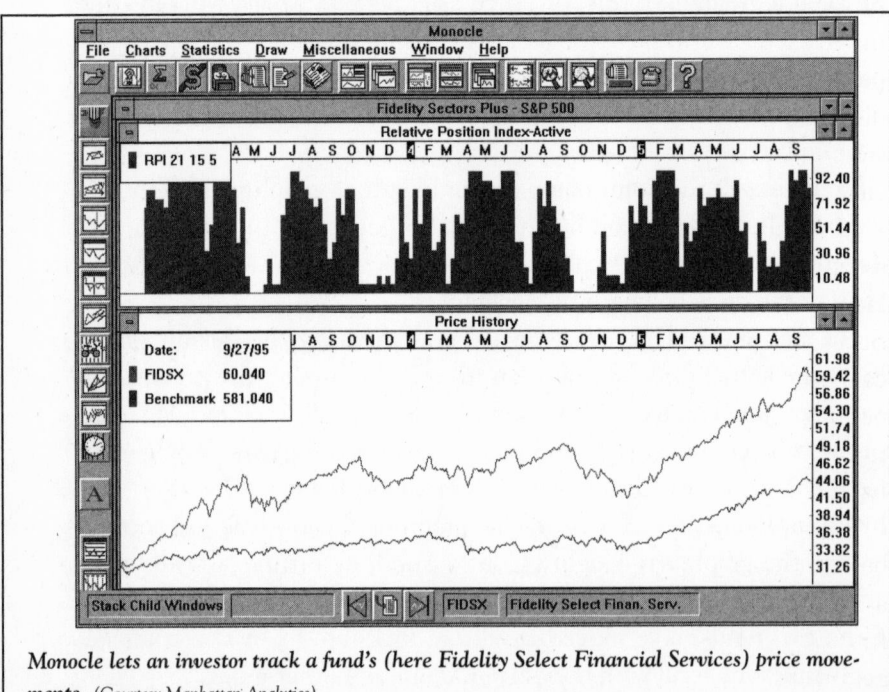

*Monocle lets an investor track a fund's (here Fidelity Select Financial Services) price movements.* (Courtesy Manhattan Analytics)

ple icon for "Select current fund" at bottom of the page, I change the current fund to Fidelity Stock Selector.

I eyeball the price graph, but it's hard to tell if the fund has been outperforming the S&P 500 benchmark since a big fall in both in March 1994. So I turn to the "Choose Indicators" menu to get a list of other ways I can look at this fund. I pick "Relative Strength" and several periods—50 days for medium-term trend and 200 for long-term trend. Then click "Display" and "Edit" to change what statistics get displayed below the charts. I choose alpha, beta, standard deviation, Sharpe ratio, annual return for fund and benchmark, and year-to-date return for the fund and a benchmark. Then I click on "OK" (which also saves, a nice touch that I wish more programs included) and that produces a chart with three relative strength indicators: blue (very jagged and very short term), purple (50-day and somewhat smoother) and green (200-day and smoothest). All three seem to show that this fund is basically flat relative to the S&P recently.

I haven't done anything nasty (like trade on the basis of this analysis) that might offend any investor who doesn't believe in technical analysis, but I have turned a lot of data into an easily comprehended picture. In Monocle I can easily compare a fund to a number of benchmarks (in a much more useful format than the "growth of $10,000" and performance bar charts I am limited to with Morningstar.) Instead of discussing the details of technical analysis here (turn to Chapter 8 instead), let me show you what can be done with pictures and a graphically powerful mutual fund program.

I can graph Fidelity Magellan against an up-and-coming fund such as Fidelity Stock Selector. Interestingly, the graph shows that Magellan and Stock Selector are extremely similar funds after a big bump in Stock Selector in late 1992 and early 1993. Here, in one picture, I can see that I really don't need to have both of these funds in my portfolio. They behave in lockstep. Owning one is sufficient. The picture has replaced the need to compare beta and R-squared, or to analyze fund portfolios.

I can also use pictures to create a diversified mutual fund portfolio and benchmark it against a single fund or an index. For example, I can create a custom fund group that includes Magellan, Third Avenue, and GAM International, and compare that portfolio to an index. If it doesn't outperform, I've got the wrong mix and I can go back and tinker. Trial and error. All in pictures. Look, Ma, no math.

Which is a great segue to the subject of the next chapter, on-line investing—another part of our subject that's in an interesting transition between words and pictures.

## Reviews

### AAII Quarterly Low-Load Mutual Funds

American Association of Individual Investors, 625 N. Michigan Avenue, Chicago, IL 60611, 800-428-2244.

Versions available: DOS (version 2.1), Macintosh (version 1.3).

Requirements: DOS version requires 3MB of RAM, 6MB free space on hard drive, and DOS 3.1 or higher. Macintosh version requires 3MB RAM, 6MB free space on hard drive, System 4.2 or higher.

Cost: DOS and Macintosh versions $50 annually for nonmembers, $39 annually for members.

Guarantee: Money back pro-rated quarterly.

Demo or sample: None.

Technical support: 312-280-0170; fax 312-280-1625. The one time I called for help (identifying myself only as a user), I got a technician on the phone almost immediately. AAII forum on America Online (Keyword AAII) and e-mail (AAII Sparky@aol.com).

User Newsletter or On-line Forum: AAII forum on America Online.

Updated: Quarterly by disk.

Strengths: All the basic information is here, plus an interesting bear/bull performance record that charts the fund's performance in the last bear and bull markets. Relative performance screen makes finding funds in top quarter of a category extremely simple.

Weaknesses: User must configure DOS so that the program can find enough memory to run, which may require rewriting config.sys and autoexec.bat files. Data updated only quarterly. Newsletter format manual offers little guidance for using the program. No information on portfolio holdings or sector composition.

Tricks of the trade: When an investor finds a program with good data like this one but inadequate screening tools, try downloading the data into a spreadsheet program such as Excel or Lotus 1,2,3. Most mutual fund and stock screening programs, including this one, make it pretty easy and there are good reasons to go to the trouble.

Even the best stock and mutual fund screening programs come with only a limited range of logical tools to use in building screens: "and/or" pretty much exhausts the list. With a spreadsheet, on the other hand, an investor can create customized formulas that attempt to optimize combinations of factors rather than using several values as a hurdle. For example, with only "and/or" at a user's disposal, an investor can screen for funds with returns greater than 15 percent and standard deviations of less than 12 percent, but he or she can't ask for the best combination of reward and risk. With a spreadsheet, an investor could try for that best combination or even give risk more weight (double weight, for example) and look for the fund with the best combination of return and low risk.

Simple to use. Cheap. Adequate but not great data. So-so screening tools. This program doesn't really give you enough information to do the kind of in-depth analysis that this chapter outlines, but it will let you look for new funds to consider buying, and its bull/bear funds information can help you to manage your risk.

### CLOSED-END FUNDS

Morningstar Inc., 225 West Wacker Drive, Chicago, IL 60606, 800-876-5005.

Versions available: DOS (version 1.20) until early 1996 only; Windows (version 1.0), called Principia for Closed-End Funds, due February 1996.

Requirements: Windows version requires 4MB RAM (8 recommended), 25MB free space on hard drive, Windows 3.1 or higher.

Cost: One-time $95, one-year subscription with quarterly updates $195; one-year subscription with monthly updates $395.

Guarantee: 30-day money back.

Demo or sample: None.

Technical support: 800-866-3472 (8 A.M.–7 P.M. CDT M–T, 8 A.M.–6 P.M. F, and 10 A.M.–3 P.M. S), e-mail tech@mstar.com.

User Newsletter or On-line Forum: None.

Updated: Quarterly or monthly.

Strengths: The only product that tracks these funds.

Weaknesses: With monthly updates the most frequent schedule available, it's hard to use this program to buy and sell funds on current discounts and premiums.

Tricks of the trade: Try combining Morningstar and *Barron's*, which lists discounts and premiums for closed-end funds weekly.

This is a program for the specialist—Morningstar's Closed-End Funds is a tool designed for the very peculiar world of closed-end funds. It provides a database, including the standard Morningstar data and ratings—and screening tools for 520 closed-end funds.

Most mutual fund investors put their money into open-end funds. An open-end fund such as Founders Worldwide Growth takes in money from an investor, issues shares in the fund to the investor, and buys securities with the investor's cash. When more investors want to put money into the fund, it issues more shares. The value of those shares is simply the daily value of the securities held by the fund divided by the number of shares issued by the fund. An investor who wants to sell shares sells them back to the fund at a price set by the value of the assets.

Closed-end funds work very differently. They issue only a set number of shares in an initial public offering. (Never, never buy a closed-end fund at the initial public offering. The offering price always includes commissions and fees to the underwriters that get deducted from the money raised from investors. So an investor who buys a share at $10 in the initial offering, winds up paying 50 cents to the underwriter, and only $9.50 gets invested. An investor who waits a day can often buy the fund for that $9.50 a share net asset value.) An investor who wants to buy shares after they've all been sold to the public has to buy them from another investor. The price of that trade is set not just by the value of the assets held by the fund but also by investors' eagerness to buy shares. Closed-end funds thus trade at a premium or discount to their net asset value, which reflects their popularity with the investing community at the moment.

So when Mexico hit the skids in 1995, the price of closed-end funds invested in Mexico and in other Latin American countries fell not just because the value of the stocks held by each one of those funds fell, but because investors didn't want to hold shares in the funds and dumped them. The funds quickly moved to a discount to net asset value. Astute investors—who believed that this selling was overdone—bought. They followed the one rule of closed-end fund investing—buy at a discount, sell at a premium.

Morningstar's program tracks the performance of 520 closed-end funds and notes both the current discount or premium to net asset value and the historic range of those discounts or premiums. (Unfortunately, the time lag imposed by the monthly update means that an investor who finds a promising fund to buy will have to update the premium or discount from another source. *Barron's* gives weekly premiums and discounts. The *Wall Street Journal* publishes the same information on Mondays.

Here's an example of the kind of data and analysis an investor can do with this program. The first screen is the by-now familiar Morningstar alphabetical list of funds. Using the "Find a fund" function I go to Morgan Stanley Emerging Markets. The program tells me the objective of this closed-end fund (investing in markets such as Brazil and Turkey), rates it (four stars out of five), lists a current price, and gives me the all-important premium/discount figure (premium of 3.6 percent—used just for reference, the three-week lag of this data is certainly significant here). *Barron's* lists the premium at 10.3 percent. The most useful information—largely because it isn't in *Barron's*—is the average premium/discount over the last ten years. From this I know that the fund hasn't been at a discount in its history since 1992 (for a full year, anyway, since these are average numbers). Of course, the program gives total returns for one, three, and five years—plus shorter periods. I can figure out that this is a very volatile fund from its price-to-earnings ratio of 42.3 and its standard deviation of 20.7. I get some information on the composition of the fund's portfolio: it's got only 5 percent exposure to bonds, but a big exposure to financial stocks—33.6 percent of portfolio.

I can graph the fund against two benchmarks/funds of my choice. I pick the Morgan Stanley Capital International Emerging Markets Index and Asia Tigers Fund. The fund beats Asia Tigers cold, but slightly trails the index. In fact, in the last month of 1994 and first month of 1995 its performance increasingly lags the index. (Hmmm ... ) My graphs are limited to the standard inadequate Morningstar pair—a line tracing growth of $10,000 or annual performance bars.

All in all a useful tool for the investor who works this part of the mutual fund universe.

**FUNDGRAF**

Parsons Software, 1230 West 6th Street, Loveland, CO 80537, 970-669-3744.

Versions available: DOS (version 2.1).

Requirements: 384K RAM, 1MB free space on hard drive, DOS 3.1 or higher.

Cost: $100.

Guarantee: 30-day money back, less $15 restocking charge.

Demo or sample: Demo $10.

Technical support: 970-669-3744 (10 A.M.–6 P.M. MST)

User Newsletter or On-line Forum: Parsons publishes *Fundgraf Advisory Newsletter*.

Updated: Program comes with data on limited number of funds. Supplemental disks (8 with 32 funds each) with four years of historical data, cost $20 each. Alternative is downloading data from Compuserve. Supplemental program, Fundgraf Downloading, for downloading data from Compuserve ($25) will download current quotes from Compuserve free and historical data at cost ($.05 a quote).

Strengths: What seems like an idiosyncrasy—building the analysis around groups of four funds—is actually a good foundation for a trading strategy that relies on moving in and out of funds that move independently. An investor would only have to follow a few groups to execute such a strategy.

Weaknesses: Loading data could well stump the DOS-challenged. First, a user makes a directory called c:\Funds, then, to load data, creates a subdirectory for the data (a and b), then copies to c:\funds\a using command copy a:\a:*.*—and then does the same with b.

Tricks of the trade: Many trading strategies founder on trading costs, and while many fund families and brokerage firms with mutual fund programs permit telephone switches from one fund to another at little or no cost, most restrict the number of such switches or add fees for frequent switches. That's something to keep in mind when you decide which funds to use as part of your trading strategy. And, of course, using funds with significant initial sales charges makes turning a profit that much more difficult.

An investor looking to apply technical analysis to mutual funds can find a cheaper, better integrated, easier to install, and more powerful alternative. Still, Fundgraf will get the job done.

Fundgraf is actually a group of nine programs that make use of common data: Add-Data program, Add-Name, Graphs, Moving-Average, Printout, Rating, ShiftData, Signals, Redate. (Additional add-on programs include a downloader for Compuserve data, one to move data to Lotus 1,2,3 and other spreadsheets, a checking program to make sure dividends are entered correctly, and another that shows the growth of $1,000 if investor had used signals generated by Fundgraf.)

The basic goal, however, is to produce buy and sell signals using a variety of technical indicators—and then to track the results. The system approaches the task from its own idiosyncratic direction.

The graphs program, for example, serves up funds in groups of four to graph against one another (with a little practice a user can create different groups) and then gives you a choice of indicators to use in comparing the funds. For instance, Fidelity Contra, Fidelity Equity Income, Dreyfus Third Century, and Evergreen all fall into one group. To graph one or all of these funds you pick a period for the moving average (say 50 weeks) and then decide between crossover and trend signals. (*Crossover* is when price and moving average cross. *Trend* is when trend of moving average changes direction from up to down. It's all explained in a decent manual.) A small green tick indicates a buy, a small red one a sell.

The rating subprogram generates other buy and sell signals by deriving a strength rating. Rating is calculated by dividing percent gain/loss by number of weeks ago, multiplying result by 2, and then adding sum to 70. A rating above 70 indicates positive growth.

The signals subprogram, on the other hand, doesn't produce a different set of signals, but instead shows the current status of buy and sell signals obtained by crossover or trend of price and moving average. (That's what the graphs subprogram graphs.)

The program will also produce a reported return number: what you would have made if you had bought and sold on the signals. The profit or loss doesn't include trading costs, a significant omission since some of these indicators produce frequent trades.

### MONOCLE (ORIGINAL VERSION WAS CALLED FUNDPRO)

Manhattan Analytics, 912 Manhattan Avenue, 2nd floor, Manhattan Beach, CA 90266, 800-251-3863.
Versions available: Windows (version 4.0).

Requirements: 4MB RAM, 18MB free space on hard drive, 2400 bps modem or better, Windows 3.1 or higher.

Cost: $149 (with trading system $249). Annual quarterly data subscription $75, annual daily data subscription via modem $240.

Guarantee: None.

Demo or sample: Demo $10.00.

Technical support: 310-374-2142 (8 A.M.–5:30 P.M. PST, M–F); fax 310–374–3142: e-mail TechSupport@ManhattanLink.com.

User Newsletter or On-line Forum: World Wide Web page http://www.ManhattanLink.com.

Updated: Quarterly or weekly data.

Strengths: Manual includes good discussion of each indicator and its uses with a chapter of definitions, although some are a bit circular— "The relative strength statistic displays the relative strength of a fund over the time period specified." Combination of technical analysis charting and performance and fundamental data makes it possible to design trading strategies that fit within an asset allocation plan.

Weaknesses: Graphics are the most important feature of a technical analysis program and, while Monocle's are good, they aren't great when compared to those found in the best programs reviewed in chapter 8. Good selection of standard indicators, but difficulties in programming a customized indicator will limit the program's appeal for hard-core fans of technical analysis.

Tricks of the trade: I haven't tried this long enough to see if it works well, but I can't see why it wouldn't. It should be possible to use the program's timing indicators to move in and out of entire style classes of mutual funds. For example, an investor could set up a growth portfolio and a value portfolio and move in and out as the indicators show the market swinging for and against an entire style.

A full-featured technical analysis program for mutual funds with enough tools of high quality to stay in the ballpark with the best programs designed for the technical analysis of stocks.

The Windows group shows three icons—Monocle, Downloader, and Update. Monocle is the main program; the other two are for adding data (current data is from Signal Data; historical data from Iverson Financial Systems).

The Monocle screen is laid out clearly with function icons across the top and drawing icons for drawing charts along the left side, a typical layout for a technical program written for Windows.

Funds here are organized in fund groups, which the manual defines as either a set of funds with a defined benchmark, a fund family, funds with a shared objective, or anything a user can make up. To start I choose a family, Fidelity Investments, which gets me a tiled screen, a graph with price history (benchmarked against the S&P 500), relative strength crossover, relative strength active, and short-term performance for the first fund in the group, Fidelity Advisor Growth Opportunity. It's easy to use the icon on the bottom of the screen to change the current fund to Fidelity Stock Selector.

I've already described the process of retrieving and customizing a graph in this chapter, so let me take you a step deeper into Monocle. While the program can't match the depth of data in a screening program such as Steele or Morningstar, Monocle can combine current and historical data with its "Statistics" function to create and graph custom fund groups. For example, I can screen for low beta funds with year-to-date returns greater than 5 percent by simply selecting beta, less than 1, year-to-date return, greater than 5, and hitting "OK" in the "Select fund" window. Only twenty-two funds made the cut—I can now turn that list into a fund family for analysis, graphing, and comparison.

An investor can use the program's "fund portfolio" functions to create and evaluate hypothetical portfolios and the "trading systems" function to design and test trading systems based on the buy and sell signals generated by any indicator.

## MUTUAL FUND INVESTOR

American River Software, 1523 Kingsford Drive, Carmichael, CA 95608, 916-483-1600.

Versions available: DOS (version 6.0). A Windows version is planned for late-1996.

Requirements: 640K RAM, 2MB free space on hard drive, DOS 3.1 or higher.

Cost:$295.

Guarantee: Demo converts to full program with payment, so user can thoroughly test the program before purchase.

Demo or sample: Demo, with all features of program except ability to update data, is $10.

Technical support: 916-483-1600 (11:30 A.M.–8 P.M. M–F).

User Newsletter or On-line Forum: None.

Updated: Manual data entry as well as Compuserve and Investment Company Data downloads.

Strengths: Charts are clear and the use of a simple indicator (where the moving average crosses the graph of a fund's daily price) makes it easy to identify buy and sell signals and impossible for the program to fudge the results of its calls.

Weaknesses: My inability to reach the company by phone, ever, makes me concerned about support and other amenities. They do respond to messages left on their phone machine, however. Limited technical tools for generating buy/sell signals—basically just moving average indicators. Other mutual fund trading programs provide a wider range of indicators. Limiting the user to moving averages will make it somewhat easier for a beginner to get up and running on this system, but he or she will probably soon want a better tool set.

Tricks of the trade: Compare two funds that you think are similar or alternatives to see if they really are. The program's use of corrected net asset value prices makes these comparison charts much more useful than the "what $10,000 would be worth now" approach in Morningstar. For example, looking at Magellan and Acorn shows that these funds track each other almost exactly, but that Magellan moves up more strongly in a bull market.

Only traders or market timers who switch among mutual funds frequently could use Mutual Fund Investor and its related database program FundScope as their sole mutual fund programs, but fundamental buy-and-hold investors might want to consider adding it to their toolbox to take advantage of some strong features found in very few other programs (and certainly not in Morningstar or Steele).

Mutual Fund Investor will let you graph mutual funds against each other for comparison, compare funds to market indexes, and generate buy/sell signals based on moving averages, a common technical indicator. The program's portfolio function will then keep track of your trading and compute your performance.

Mutual Fund Investor comes already loaded with free data on thirty popular funds, among them Acorn, Magellan, and Mutual Shares. (Others can be downloaded by modem or from a related database program from American River, FundScope. Fundscope provides a statistical and graphical database for the entire mutual fund industry. It won't do portfolio management but rather gathers daily net asset values and fund distributions that can be uploaded into Mutual Fund Investor.)

Hitting F3 from the main menu takes the user to the graphing and performance function. Here I can easily pull up a chart of Fidelity Magellan, for example, showing the daily price of the fund (net asset value) and the 39-week moving average. More options include a toggle that changes the chart from 39-week moving average to 195-day moving average. I can also customize the moving average for periods from 1 to 999 days. Both are corrected for distributions. Below that chart a data table lists net asset value of the fund and the total return on the fund during the period of the chart.

I can clearly see the past dates on which I would have wanted to buy or sell as the moving average and price lines crossed. I can see a buy signal in late 1990 just a few weeks after the price started to climb off the October 1990 floor. The program also indicated a sell in mid-1994. Hitting the page-down key gives me performance comparisons over this period for all the funds in my current master list in all categories. I can tell that Magellan beat Acorn (76.0 to 70.1 percent), beat Vanguard Index (which returned 48.3 percent), and far outdistanced the S&P 500's 32.8 percent return. The page-up key gives the performance for funds on my designated watch list by period—last week, last two weeks, last four weeks, last twelve weeks, since end of 1993, just 1993, and a momentum score. It's easy to change time periods.

The "Portfolio" function has a wide range of options for calculating and displaying returns. A user can display the performance of a specific fund versus an entire current portfolio to visually examine a fund's fit with a current portfolio. The program calculates performance using the internal rate of return model. An extremely useful calculation lets an investor compare the results of a buy-and-hold strategy versus switching at buy and sell signals. Back-testing is relatively simple to perform: set up a separate portfolio with an earlier beginning date and see how the fund did.

**FUNDSCOPE**

American River Software, 1523 Kingsford Drive, Carmichael, CA 95608, 916-483-1600.
Versions available: DOS (version 3.1). A Windows Version is planned for late-1996.

Requirements: 512K RAM, 2.5MB free space on hard drive, DOS 3.1 or higher.

Cost: $25 with monthly disk. Also see Updated below.

Guarantee: Demo converts to full program with payment, so user can thoroughly test the program before purchase.

Demo or sample: Demo, with all features of program except ability to update data, is $25.

Technical support: 916-483-1600; 11:30 A.M.–8 P.M. M–F.

User Newsletter or On-line Forum: None.

Updated: Manual data entry as well as Compuserve and Investment Company Data downloads. Data updated each month on disk or daily from Compuserve (which would require manual input of distributions) or Investment Company Data, Inc., by modem. The latter option costs $50 to set up, plus $10 minimum a month, plus $12 communication time fee after first 30 minutes a month. A daily net asset value costs 6 cents during day, 2 cents at night. Distribution info is 15 cents during day, 6:01 A.M. to 6:00 P.M. SDT every day the markets are open, and 12 cents at night. Disk updates from Planners Edge (206-451-8755) are $39.95 monthly or $289 for annual subscription with quarterly updates.

Strengths: Computes the volatility of a fund over any period you choose—which is certainly superior to the fixed three-year periods of Morningstar and Steele. The data includes one bit of historical information not available anywhere else—three-year asset growth year by year—an important tool for judging how much faith to put in a fund's past performance as an indicator of future results.

Weaknesses: Less data than Morningstar or Steele. Data items include turnover, yield, beta, fees, and all necessary returns up to ten years. Standard deviation, Sharpe ratios, R-squared, and such fundamental data as manager tenure and even manager name are absent.

Tricks of the trade: Try the "Leaders and Laggards" performance report. This lists, for your choice of period, 15 leaders and laggards. Setting the period for one year might pick up currently out of favor funds that might be poised for a comeback. For example, in early 1995, a lot of Latin American funds showed up on the one-year laggards list.

This program provides data on more than 5,200 mutual funds for use with Mutual Fund Investor. The data itself is a mixture of strengths and weaknesses. As you'd expect from the database that goes with a program

that emphasizes technical analysis, FundScope is light on such fundamental data as manager tenure. But it does offer compensating goodies—besides the ability to compute volatility over any period the user
chooses and three-year asset growth data year by year mentioned above,
it provides an extremely wide range of indexes and indicators, such as
the Nikkei and European averages, currencies such as yen and mark,
money market yields, and the consumer price index, all useful in judging
why a fund is performing the way it is. The Market Watch feature (hit
the "M" key) gives the user this month, last month, one-month percentage change, and year-to-date percentage change for S&P 500; Dow Industrials, Transportations, and Utilities; Tokyo Nikkei, Frankfurt Dax,
London FT 100, Gold (Comex spot), Oil (W. Texas Intermediate), Yen,
Mark, money market yield, and CPI (year to date and last year).

(I found one of the two display modes particularly useful for comparing a fund to the S&P 500. This mode gives the fund performance in
one column, the S&P without dividends in the next, and the S&P
with dividends in the third.)

### MORNINGSTAR MUTUAL FUNDS ONDISC.

Morningstar Inc., 225 West Wacker Drive, Chicago, IL 60606, 800-
   876-5005.
Versions available: DOS CD-ROM (Version 3.0) to be phrased out in
   1996 or 1997 in favor of Morningstar Principia.
Requirements: DOS version requires 8MB RAM, 25MB free  space on
   hard drive, DOS 3.1 or higher. Windows version requires 8MB
   RAM, 25MB free space on hard drive, Windows 3.1 or higher.
Cost: $295 for one-time subscription, $495 for one-year subscription
   with quarterly updates, $795 for one-year subscription with monthly
   updates.
Guarantee: 30-day money back.
Demo or sample: Free
Technical support: 800-866-3472 (8 A.M.–7 P.M. CDT, M–T, 8 A.M.–6
   P.M. F, and 10 A.M.–3 P.M. S), or e-mail tech@mstar.com.
User Newsletter or On-line Forum: None.
Updated: Monthly or quarterly on disk.
Strengths: More data than any other mutual fund program. Analyst re-
   ports, a feature standard with the CD-ROM version, provides useful
   context on a fund's past and current performance. Currently this is

the only Morningstar program that not only breaks down the portfolio of each fund by asset class and sector, but also provides a list of
the fund's complete holdings.

Weaknesses: As with all Morningstar products, a really aggravating
print function that makes it terribly difficult to print out just the
data you want (and some users report having problems getting it to
print at all). Graphs are few and underpowered.

Tricks of the trade: Try using the hypothetical portfolio function to recalculate fund returns after front-end sales charges. The program will
automatically deduct the sales charge from an initial lump sum investment so that by setting the time period for one, five, and ten
years, an investor can calculate the load-adjusted returns that he or
she will actually collect from investing in a specific fund. (Be careful
how you account for taxes, however!)

As far as I'm concerned this is still the cream of the Morningstar
crop—although Principia has added some features not found in
OnDisc. The few flaws in the program—a really lousy printer driver
(the software that lets a user print out what's on the screen) and woe-
fully underpowered graphing tools—are overwhelmed by a depth of
data that can't be found anywhere else.

I used this program to illustrate many of the concepts in this chapter,
so I won't repeat all of them here. Instead I'll mention some additional
features.

I gave what I hope is a rather full description of one of the features
that sets this program apart from the rest of the Morningstar universe,
the data on what fund managers hold in their portfolios. But I only really mentioned the second major feature built-in here but that costs
extra in other versions, the analyst reports.

Morningstar's analysts don't review all 6,000+ funds in the Morningstar universe—some never get reviewed at all—and they don't review each fund monthly, once or twice a year is more like it. But even
though these reviews are almost always out of date by the time an investor reads them, I still find them valuable. In twenty to thirty lines an
analyst who follows the fund regularly can point out changes in manager and philosophy, compare the fund to its peers and to its own past
record, and draw some conclusions about the fund's portfolio. I don't
always agree with the analyst but I always read these reports as part of
my due diligence on a fund.

**MORNINGSTAR MUTUAL FUNDS ONFLOPPY WITH PORTFOLIO DEVELOPER.**

Morningstar, 225 West Wacker Drive, Chicago, IL 60606, 800-876-5005.
Versions available: DOS (version 1.0).
Requirements: A real space hog—requires 15.5MB of disk space without portfolio developer, which requires an additional 10MB.
Cost: $165 per year for quarterly updates, $335 for monthly updates.
Guarantee: 30-day money back.
Demo or sample: One-time trial for $75.
Technical support: 800-866-3472 (8 A.M.–7 P.M. CDT M–T, 8 A.M.–6 P.M., F, and 10 A.M.–3 P.M., S); e-mail tech@mstar.com.
User Newsletter or On-line Forum: None.
Updated: Quarterly or monthly by disk.
Strengths: See above comments about OnDisc.
Weaknesses: See above comments about OnDisc.
Tricks of the trade: None of the mutual fund screening programs have very good logical tools. For example, the ability to build screens in Morningstar products is constrained by the program's limited logic of *and/or/not, greater than, less than,* and *equal to.* But an investor can expand this limited tool kit somewhat by combining those functions with the "Find average" function under Options. At any point an investor can run a screen, get the average value for a data item, insert that into the screen, and then resume building. It's even possible to take two averages and manipulate them on a calculator or on paper and then use that new product in building the screen.

For example, let's say I'm building a growth at a price screen. I've screened for earnings per share growth rate in the companies owned by each fund, requiring a 15 percent growth rate to jump this hurdle. I then go to "Find average" to check on the average price-to-earnings ratio in my new smaller universe. It's 24—much higher than the 15 in the entire 6,000 fund universe. I also look for funds with a price-to-earnings ratio that is 80 percent of the new average growth rate. That will still be an approximation. (Of course, I could do even better by downloading the data into a spreadsheet.)

This is the DOS version that Morningstar Principia for Mutual Funds, the Windows-based product, is supposed to supersede in early 1996. Which is too bad. This workhorse is simple to operate with its outdated pull-down menus. Its data are comprehensive enough to stand up against the other Morningstar products and Steele's Mutual Fund

Expert, although the program does come without such tools as analysts' reports and portfolio holdings.

## Morningstar Principia for Mutual Funds

Morningstar, 225 West Wacker Drive, Chicago, IL 60606, 800-876-5005.

Versions available: Windows (version 1.0).

Requirements: Windows 3.1 or higher, 4MB RAM, 20MB free space on hard drive.

Cost: $195 annually for quarterly updates, $395 for monthly updates.

Guarantee: 30-day money back.

Demo or sample: One-time trial for $95.

Technical support: 800-866-3472 (8 A.M.–7 P.M. CDT, M–T, 8 A.M.–6 P.M., F, and 10 A.M.–3 P.M., S); e-mail tech@mstar.com.

User Newsletter or On-line Forum: None.

Updated: Monthly or quarterly by disk.

Strengths: See comments about OnDisc above. Includes utility for converting screens written for OnFloppy to Principia. This is the only mutual fund program to offer load-adjusted performance for funds—crucial for investors seeking to compare a no-load fund to a fund with a sales charge. Additional indexes and style box help investors more accurately categorize funds.

Weaknesses: See comments about OnDisc above. Increased graphing capabilities let user chart total return, standard deviation, rolling returns—but the program still needs more.

Tricks of the trade: Ignore "blend" as a category on the fund style box. It tends to be a catchall description for funds that don't quite fit in the other groups. Besides, when was the last time anyone recommended that you add more "blend" funds to a portfolio? (And what index should a blend fund be measured against?) But don't ignore the funds in the category. Just try to use the data in Principia on market cap and price-to-earnings ratio and the like to recategorize the fund and pick a reasonable index for a benchmark.

If I was going to name a piece of software after Sir Isaac Newton's *Principia*, I'd certainly make sure it was a sleek model of efficiency. Instead this program confirms the doubts that many investors have had about Morningstar's software: the data is great, but can't they hire some better programmers?

Why does everyone producing programs think that icons are easier to use and understand than words? If hieroglyphics were so wonderful, why did alphabets clean their clock 2,000 years ago? This program is less easy to use with its cryptic icons than is the DOS version with its clunky pull-down menus. Before a user had to look for a function called "Find a fund." Now he or she has to search for an eye.

That said, Morningstar has added enough new features so that this program now gives the CD-ROM OnDisc a run for the money. For example, finally someone is publishing load-adjusted returns. Investors in Principia will find them alongside the raw returns for twelve months, five and ten years.

Morningstar has added more indexes to the pages that profile each fund. Now when I look up Crabbe Huson Special, I get the returns for the fund compared not just to the S&P 500 but to the midcap S&P 400 index as well. The profile now also includes the investment style box that used to be available only in print versions of Morningstar. For Crabbe Huson it tells an investor that the fund is a blend of value and growth and specializes in relatively small cap stocks. In fact, the program gives you enough information to see if you agree with Morningstar about how the fund is categorized.

And, while I think the program still needs more graphing punch, Principia has added graphs for total return, rolling period return, and standard deviation to the usual "what $10,000 would be worth now" picture.

But Principia comes with a set of trade-offs. For example, the current version of Principia doesn't list individual stocks and bonds in a fund's portfolio—instead an investor gets a portfolio breakdown by sector (such as the percentage of technology holdings). To get any individual holdings—and then only the top 25 for each fund—you'll have to buy an extension called the Electronic Binder. Besides the short list of portfolio holdings, the Electronic Binder also includes reviews of the funds from Morningstar's analysts—exactly what you now get with OnDisc. But the price isn't the same: Principia plus Electronic Bind is $295 for one-time use, $495 for quarterly updates, and $795 for monthly data. Other extensions will follow the same pricing model: Portfolio Developer (scheduled for mid-1996) will duplicate the portfolio developer function on OnDisc, and Advanced Analytics (scheduled for late 1996) will let an investor get deeper into Morningstar's data, although it's not clear to me that the user will get any deeper than is currently possible with OnDisc.

**CHARLES SCHWAB FUNDMAP**

Charles Schwab & Co., 101 Montgomery Street, San Francisco, CA, 800-334-4455.

Versions available: Windows (version 1.0d)

Requirements: 4MB RAM, 9MB free space on hard drive, printer will need 2MB of memory to print out worksheets, Windows 3.1 or higher.

Cost: $25.

Guarantee: 30-day money back.

Demo or sample: None.

Technical support: 800-334-4455.

User Newsletter or On-line Forum: None.

Updated: Quarterly, $5.

Strengths: Easy to operate and sharp, colorful, and inviting in design— I wish some of the other mutual fund software companies would hire whoever designed FundMap. Although limited fund data and screening capabilities make this program an also-ran for anyone who wants to pick funds, the superb material on asset allocation (from Ibbotson Associates) and saving for retirement (from Deloitte & Touche) make this a great financial planning tool. One of the best explanations of risk I've seen on software.

Weaknesses: Mickey Mouse. Only includes funds available through Charles Schwab, making it impossible to create meaningful screens to identify the best fund available in a category. Most categories, in fact, have fewer than ten members.

Tricks of the trade: Think of this as the prize in the box of Cheerios and get it for free from Schwab if you can. Then you won't feel guilty that you never use it for its intended purpose of picking funds (it's useless), and instead use it as a useful tool for visualizing the returns and risk of different classes of assets over different time periods. In other words, use the Ibbotson graphs and let the rest of the program molder.

A beginners' program that someone really put a lot of thought into is thoroughly sabotaged by the decision to include only those mutual funds available through Schwab. It's a shame, really.

Fund selection is only one of five topics—the program is set up as a wire-bound book with five chapters: Welcome, Investing Basics, Savings and Retirement, Asset Allocation, and Fund Selection. Only the last is a letdown.

Investment basics starts with the most basic advice: "Before you start building your investment portfolio, you might consider setting aside three- to six-month's living expenses in a money market fund or other liquid investment." But definition of risk, while just the standard text-book stuff—goes a step beyond the advice in most beginners' programs to note that risk comes in many types—inflation, market, and that associated with individual securities—and is dependent on holding period. A volatile stock may be risky in the short run but lower risk if held for several years.

In explaining returns the program actually gets creatively interactive. Instead of just the standard "stocks returned an average of blah, blah," the program creates graphs that show the average maximum and minimum returns over different time periods. I can see that one-year returns varied between 54 percent (1933) and −43 percent (1931) and that five-year returns varied between 24 percent and −12 percent. Ten-year returns were between 20 percent and −1 percent and twenty-year returns between 17 and 3—that's a graphic illustration of the effect a longer holding period has on risk and volatility. The program can also create another version of these graphs for bonds and cash equivalents that pretty clearly demonstrates that high returns and volatility go together.

After a savings and retirement chapter built around the ubiquitous questionnaire format (How much income do I want when I retire?), which leaves far too much up to the investor, the asset allocation chapter at least forces me to break down my portfolio to the right level of specificity. I can look at my initial moderately aggressive portfolio recommendation of 20 percent bonds, 5 percent cash, and 75 percent stocks in more detail. The program suggests that I break down stocks into 35 percent large company, 20 percent small company, and 20 percent international. The best feature is a separate box that lets me see the historical performance and volatility of each of five suggested portfolio stances—"moderately aggressive" has an average annual return of 12.28 with upside return of 35.22 and a downside return of 18.05 from 1970 through 1993.

The program attempts to move the user seamlessly from asset allocation to funds that will fulfill each goal. I click on "International" to get more information on the possible alternatives for this part of my portfolio. The data is from Morningstar, but the choices are limited—just three, in fact: Strong International, 20th Century International, and

Warburg Pincus International. Only Warburg Pincus has the five-year track record I like to see before I invest.

The program lists only five small company funds—Invesco Dynamics, Founders Discovery, Heartland Value, PBHG Growth, 20th Century Ultra; eight large company funds—Invesco Industrial Income, Berger 100, Crabbe Huson Equity, Crabbe Huson Special, Stein Roe Special, Strong Opportunity, Neuberger and Berman Guardian, Warburg Pincus Growth & Income; and five bonds—Dreyfus Short-Intermediate, Strong Government Securities, Benham GNMA, Federated Income Trust Institutional Shares, and Federated Short-Intermediate Government Trust Institutional Shares.

The problem isn't just a lack of selection here, either. The funds grouped in each category are hardly alternatives to each other. PBHG Growth, for example, is one of the most volatile aggressive growth funds available, while Heartland Value is exactly what the name says, a value fund. I can't imagine a scenario where I'd have to choose between the two.

### ALEXANDER STEELE'S MUTUAL FUND EXPERT

Steele Systems Inc., 12021 Wilshire Boulevard, Suite 340, Los Angeles, CA, 90025, 800-237-8400.

Versions available: DOS (version 2.1), Windows (version 4.5).

Requirements: DOS requires 560K RAM, 4MB free space on hard drive. Windows requires 4MB RAM, 5MB free space on hard drive, Windows 3.1 or higher.

Cost: Personal edition, $95 for quarterly updates, $185 monthly; professional edition $399 quarterly; $599 monthly.

Guarantee: Pro-rated refund of unused subscription.

Demo or sample: Free demo available.

Technical support: 310-478-4213 (7:30 A.M.–6 P.M. PST).

User Newsletter or On-line Forum: None.

Updated: Monthly or quarterly by disk.

Strengths: More data on performance and ways to slice it than anyone can possibly use—and solid presentation of risk measures, too. The 75-minute tutorial that comes with the program will get any user up and running quickly. Much easier to customize display and printing than on any Morningstar product. Requires only 3MB of hard drive space—about one-fifth of the space you'll need to hold Morningstar's data.

Weaknesses: Graphing is weak—investors are basically limited to versions of the "growth of $10,000 from then to now" format. Database is missing fundamental information on contents of fund portfolios.

Tricks of the trade: Rewrite some of the screens that you like best using logical "or." Most investors build their first screens using nothing but "and"; for example, by screening for funds with five-year performance greater than 20 percent and standard deviation less than 10 percent—and keep on writing them that way. But it's hard to optimize (to get the best combination of high performance and low standard deviation) a combination of factors with an "and" screen.

Try combining less than optimal hurdles with logical "or." For example, instead of the "and"-based formula above, screen for funds with five-year performance greater than 20 percent *and* standard deviation less than 12 percent (thereby loosening your standards enough to let some borderline funds slip in that are slightly riskier than you'd prefer) *or* five-year performance greater than 15 percent and standard deviation less than 10 percent (thereby letting in some funds with a little less performance than you'd prefer but with a little less risk as well).

Steele's Mutual Fund Expert doesn't have anywhere near the name recognition that Morningstar commands for its mutual fund products, but the company has decided to take on its bigger rival head-on, and Morningstar is taking the competition very seriously. That's great for investors. The two companies are busy adding features to their flagship programs at a furious pace.

Steele beat Morningstar to market with its Windows version by almost six months. Morningstar added a "what if" portfolio function that allowed investors to create and track hypothetical portfolios of funds—nine months later Steele added a similar feature. In July Steele pumped more data into its program—monthly returns for all the funds in its universe now go back thirty-three years.

Here's how I'd assess the competition at this point. Morningstar's CD-ROM product is the better of the bunch by a nose—the company has used the space provided by CD-ROM technology to add a wealth of data about what individual stocks and bonds fund managers hold in their portfolios and to append reviews by Morningstar analysts to about 1,500 funds. In the Windows battle between disk-based versions, however, I'd give the nod to Steele, at the moment, on programming, and a slight preference to Morningstar's Principia on data (largely for its use of load adjusted returns). I don't think there's more than a hair's worth of difference between the two in terms of data—both are very good— but Morningstar's Windows interface is clearly not as easy to operate as Steele's. I don't think you can go wrong with either choice, however.

Double-clicking on the Mutual Fund Expert icon calls up the notebook analogy that Steele uses to organize its data. But what a notebook—7,000 funds (including money market funds) at last count. One-, three-, five-, ten-, fifteen-, twenty-, and thirty-year returns (the last two seem like competitive overkill—Morningstar doesn't yet go back this far). Annual returns by year back to 1975. Yield, beta, alpha, R-squared, standard deviation, Sharpe ratio, Treynor ratio, volatility rating—and each for three, five, and ten years. Includes the standard data on fees and expenses. Some fundamental data included in Morningstar is missing, however. No price-to-earnings average, no price-to-book, no breakdown of a fund portfolio into asset classes. Morningstar's data in these fields is proprietary and I'd guess that Steele hasn't yet put the effort into collecting this portfolio data from the fund companies.

So if this program and Morningstar run essentially the same data, what are the differences? Well, in Steele it's easy to choose what columns to display (the program uses drop and drag techniques much like a spreadsheet). In Morningstar it's hard to customize the display on screen and even more difficult to do for printing out on paper. (If I had my pick of the one feature that I'd like to improve in all of Morningstar's programs including U.S. Equities, it would be the way it handles printing.) It's slightly easier to look for a specific value in the column in Steele and to rank—again because the program works on a spreadsheet model.

On the other hand, Steele's "filter" function, this program's equivalent to "screen" is less convenient and harder to learn than Morningstar's pull-down menu. To screen on Latin American funds, for example, I had to go to Help frequently to figure out the names of the fields I wanted or shuttle back and forth to "Pick values," which gave me a menu like Morningstar's.

The programs handle other tasks in strikingly similar ways. Click on "Fund" and then "Single fund report" at the bottom of the page and Steele will produce a view of all the data on a single fund that is virtually identical in format to Morningstar's treatment. Graphing is also frustratingly similar in the two programs. I wish that both companies would go to the trouble of collecting net asset value data and then make it possible to graph it the way that Monocle and American River's Mutual Fund Investor do.

## VALUE LINE FUND ANALYZER

Value Line Investors Corp., 220 E. 42nd Street, New York, NY 10017, 800-654-0508.

Versions available: Windows (version 1.10), Windows CD-ROM (version 1.10).

Requirements: Windows 3.1, 1MB RAM, 35MB free space on hard drive.

Cost: $295 for standard version or $395 for CD-ROM with full-page research reports from Value Line.

Guarantee: 30-day money back.

Demo or sample: 3-month trial, $49.

Technical support: 800-654-0508.

User Newsletter: None.

Updated: Weekly by modem.

Strengths: Reports from Value Line's analysts on 1,500 funds supplements more than enough data on performance to make any but the most number-crazy investor happy. (If you want more numbers, Steele Systems has them.) For investors who are serious about asset allocation, Value Line's numbers tracking the correlation of a fund with one of four asset styles will be invaluable. Neither Steele Systems nor Morningstar currently match this feature.

Weaknesses: The smallest universe of funds among mutual fund databases, just 3,600. Analysts' reviews, very similar to Morningstar's in format, cover an even smaller group of funds, 1,500. Although the library of preformatted graphs that comes with the program offers more formats than Mornigstar or Steele, and I found creating custom graphs more complicated than I expected.

Tricks of the trade: While the ability to use style correlation gives an investor an important tool in putting together a portfolio, be careful how you handle the numbers. Correlation will, first of all, give you only a relative degree of match. You have to decide whether a .60 correlation, for example, is enough for you. And second, a fund can correlate strongly with more than one style. So always check out all of a fund's correlations—with the four style groups—before using it as a building block in your portfolio.

With this program Value Line joins the data competition with Steele Systems and Morningstar—and ups the ante. While this program only tracks 3,600 funds, the smallest universe among these three, it offers new types of data on each fund. While Value Line doesn't match the historical depth of either Morningstar or especially Steele—Value Line's performance data goes back only ten years—the company has added several new numbers on risk-adjusted performance (including one that ranks a fund manager on this basis against managers of similar funds), more data on such portfolio measures as alpha, beta, and R-squared, and calculations such as persistence, which attempt to rate the consistency with which a fund beats its peers.

In the battle of the data, Value Line has also enlisted time on its side. Rather than waiting for a monthly data update to arrive in the mail, users of Value Line's system can download new data weekly. I question whether weekly fund data is of any real use to investors and frankly I find Value Line's inclusion of one-week performance numbers a dismaying invitation to short-term trading of what should be long-term investment vehicles.

But on one front I think Value Line Fund Analyzer offers a glimpse of the future of mutual fund software. Future programs, if I read Morningstar's plans correctly and understand the implications of Value Line's offering, will compete on the power of their analytical tools. Here's where I find Value Line unmatched by Steele Systems or Morningstar: a data set called correlation.

Here's how it works. Value Line lists a fund's correlation—that is, the likelihood that the fund will zig when a particular part of the market zigs as well—to four different investment styles: large cap value, large cap growth, small cap value, and small cap growth. The Acorn Fund, for example, has −.20 correlation with large cap value and an equally negative correlation, −.14, with large cap growth. This fund, these numbers say, zigs when these styles zag. But exactly the opposite is the case with small cap growth (correlation .71) and small cap value (correlation .67). An investor who wants to build a diversified portfolio can use these numbers, rather than misleading fund labels, to pick one fund from column A and one fund from column B. You can also use the filter function to create a universe of funds with high correlations to a style—I built a list of twenty-six funds with a correlation to small cap value greater than .60—and then sorted them on five-year performance. Here are top funds that strongly follow a small cap value style—Montgomery Small Cap Fund, MAS

Small Cap Value, Strong Common Stock Fund, Fidelity Low-Price Stock, DFA US9-10 Small Company, Vanguard Explorer, and Acorn Fund.

Style analysis is probably currently the hottest new analystical tool among professional money managers. I'll tell you more about some of the more poweful programs that specialize in this method in chapter 9.

### YOUR MUTUAL FUND SELECTOR

Intuit, P.O. Box 3014, Menlo Park, CA 94026, 800-624-6930.

Versions available: Windows CD-ROM.

Requirements: 4MB RAM, 3MB free space on hard drive, 2X CD-ROM drive, sound card, Windows 3.1 or higher.

Cost: $40 for program plus cost of quarterly data updates, $39.95 annually.

Guarantee: 60-day money back.

Demo or sample: None.

Technical support: 505-896-7160.

User Newsletter or On-line Forum: None.

Updated: Quarterly (data from Morningstar) by disk.

Strengths: Great for the manual-phobic. The manual is short, just five pages. A user doesn't really need more because the video instructions on the CD-ROM (which shares the well-built Active Books shell with other programs such as the Wall Street Guide to Personal Finance) will take him or her through the rest of the program. Chapter 7, "Researching Your Funds," defines all the terms—what is a beta, for example. The program goes interactive at this point and lets a user change the beta and graphically see the change in return versus the market.

Weaknesses: Extremely small universe of just 1,000 funds. The program emphasizes three-year performance numbers. That's too short a period for reliably judging a fund's volatility. Only one general stock index to use for measuring a fund's performance.

Tricks of the trade: Try page 48. After lots of dull advice about setting goals and expected returns, the Bull and Bear dinner menu graphically shows the power of inflation using prices of food items. The user can change the years of the study.

This is a product designed for people who don't know very much about mutual funds—but I don't think it does them any favors. By limiting the funds in its universe—just 1,000—to those that earn at least a three-star rating from Morningstar, the program pretty much assures that a user can't go too far wrong. But the program's reliance on three-year performance is troubling. That short a time period may give the beginning investor a false read on exactly how volatile each fund is.

Double-clicking on the Mutual Fund Selector icon in Windows immediately produces a talking head in a three-by-four window in the corner of the screen. A woman with curly brown hair and talking in that odd way that computer video does (caused by a lack of sufficient frame refresh) says, "To learn more about the book click one of the following topics: Getting Started, Why This Book, How to Use an Active Book." (I did nothing to customize the video installation, by the way, and it worked without problems.)

As you might expect from Intuit, the makers of Quicken, "Getting Started" immediately plunges the user into the familiar worksheet format. "To make intelligent mutual fund recommendations, we need to know about your financial goals and needs," the talking head says. This section starts with a video of a couple talking and bantering: What makes a stock price rise or fall? What should I do if the market is overheated?—and quickly segues to a worksheet that asks about age, annual household income, federal tax rate, combined state and local tax rate (does anybody really know this off the top of his or her head?), planned age of retirement, and more. After this the program tries to determine a risk profile of the user by asking questions such as, Do you gamble frequently? (giving the user a higher risk tolerance if the answer is yes). The whole exercise is pointless.

The advice that follows is extremely simple. To judge performance, for example, it urges the investor to look at either consistency or compare funds to similar funds in group. Look at one-year, five-year, and ten-year performance numbers and see whether the fund took advantage of up markets and weathered down markets well. In chapter 7, where I can look up my funds, the program gives me very little except pap about the fund's strategy and the bare bones of returns—nothing about what the fund holds.

One final caveat. The risk calculator and the asset allocation function will change how much of a portfolio an investor should put into a sector such as growth funds (I couldn't find any way to jigger my risk profile and financial goals to get the program to put me in aggressive growth funds, by the way.) But it won't select different funds in that category to reflect higher risk tolerance. That seems puzzling since funds in a single category can have very different risk/reward ratios.

# 6

# Lost in Cyberspace:

# Investors On-line

Starbucks, the Seattle-based coffee retailer, just opened a store two blocks from my house. In fact, it's the fourth Starbucks to open in my neighborhood in the last year. All the stores look crowded at virtually any hour I pass by. The demand for a $3 cup of coffee seems insatiable. Still in the midst of an aggressive national expansion, Starbucks might be a growth stock I'd like to own. But at a price-to-earnings ratio of 57, the stock is risky. If that expansion doesn't rapidly translate into growing earnings, the stock will plummet. I'd sure like to know how busy older Starbucks stores are. Once the novelty has worn off, do the crowds move elsewhere?

If I covered Starbucks for a big Wall Street firm or one of the mutual fund giants, I'd answer the question by hopping on a plane and visiting a few of the company's older stores. As an individual investor, however, I can't afford that kind of in-person research.

But I do have an alternative. I can walk into my home office, sit down at my computer, and, by dialing in to one of the major on-line services—America on Line, CompuServe, Prodigy—or the amorphous world called the Internet—I can put the community of 20 million people who exchange information, discuss problems, and share resources electronically to work on my problem.

To talk to only the most knowledgable investors about Starbucks, I decide to put the insomnia of heavy coffee-drinkers to work for me. At 3 A.M. I dial in to the Investors Forum on CompuServe and post a query about business at other Starbucks across the country. The coffee fanatics are awake in Portland, Seattle, Denver, and Dallas and ready to chat on-line about how many cups of java Starbucks is pushing. They are remarkably in agreement about the persistence of the stores' popularity. The only dissent comes from a disgruntled Bostonian, who laments the decline in quality at the Coffee Connection since Starbucks bought that small Northeast chain.

Want a reaction to Merrill Lynch's downgrade of Intel? Dial in to an investors' forum for an analyst-by-analyst breakdown on what all of Wall Street thinks about the company. Want to join a three-year-old running argument about the value of technical analysis or ask how to get Federal Reserve data or how to find a specific mutual fund? Want the dope on obscure emerging markets from seasoned international analysts? It's all available on-line, and everyday some company that you've never heard of is inventing—and then virtually giving away—a new souped-up hot rod for cruising from forum to forum, from information source to information source with ever more ease and ever more speed. And best of all, you can join an international community of investors that shares insights and information about investments—a kind of global investment club where everyone pitches in to help each other beat the market.

But let's get right down to the bare-assed truth. All this does indeed exist on one of the increasingly interconnected computer systems that make up the river of electronic information. Five years ago—well, to be honest until about twelve months ago—it was so difficult to sign on and find anything that someone who could navigate these waters was accorded a status next to godhood. (And was instantly in the business of churning out articles and books touting the wonders of this electronic world.) Whether or not he or she had even actually managed to find and use any useful information in all this navigating was beside the point. Have you ever wondered why almost all the articles in the press on the information superhighway tell the reader in detail about all the neat places that exist in this electronic world—but stop short of giving any great examples of useful things the author has done with this data?

Well, navigation hasn't exactly become easy, but it is now easy enough so that the average computer user does stand a reasonable shot at actually signing on and getting to the stuff on the network. The big three—and other kin such as Apple's eWorld, Delphi, Genie, and the Microsoft Network, the new gorilla on the block—have all upgraded their software so that it's relatively painless to connect with their networks and get to the features on their system. Even Dow Jones, the producer of Dow Jones News Retrieval, one of the most frustrating information systems ever sold to the general public, has upgraded to a point-and-click Windows interface.

All the big commercial networks have added doorways to the Internet—or will have by the time this book goes to press—that don't re-

---

### BASICS

## BULLETIN BOARDS, ON-LINE SERVICES, AND THE INTERNET— WHAT'S THE DIFFERENCE?

Once upon a time, there was no Net. Instead there were hundreds of electronic bulletin board systems, connected by modem to anyone who knew the phone number to dial and who had paid the subscription fee, if any. A bulletin board subscriber could download data or "talk" to other members of the board by typing messages to them. There were bulletin boards about cars, and Japan, and investing, and hundreds of other topics. There still are. Sign on, for example, to Donoghue's Money Letter, which is described in the box "Don't Forget About Bulletin Boards" in this chapter.

The commercial on-line services are actually just collections of bulletin boards, all operating from the same phone number. Dial in to CompuServe and connect with an area on bed-and-breakfasts operated by the author of a set of guidebooks on the subject, or an area about beer, or with the Official Airline Guide. The great advantage of the network is that I can get all these bulletin boards by dialing just one number and I can talk to anyone on the service no matter what bulletin board drew them on-line initially. I can now leave e-mail messages for anyone who subscribes to CompuServe. I don't have to wait in hope that the person I want to talk with will sign on to my bulletin board.

The Internet grew out of a computer network (called DarpaNet) funded by the U.S. Defense Department and was intended to let all the scientists working on government research projects talk to one another and share data by computer. Computer nodes were established at major research sites, most corporations and universities, and then joined together by a backbone of high-speed data connections.

While the Internet long ago outgrew that rather limited community of users, its node and network structure still derive from that period. An individual user can't simply hook up a modem and dial in to the Internet in the same way that he or she can dial in to CompuServe. To connect with the Internet you have to either become a node in the system—which requires a special communications line and special communications software—or sign on with a service provider that is itself a node on the system.

Unlike the commercial on-line services where a single company owns the network, controls the traffic, and regulates who gets on and how, the Internet is decentralized. It has no administrators and no owner. Anyone who can either afford to become a node or who pays someone for access can get on what is now a globally connected system. That's one of the glories of the Internet.

The World Wide Web, the current hot technology in the on-line world, isn't another network. Instead it's a technology for writing, distributing, and then reading interactive graphical messages and databases on the Internet. (See "So What's This World Wide Web Thing?" in this chapter.)

Now the Internet presents an interesting problem for the commercial on-line services. They each connect only their own subscribers, but the Internet can connect everyone—so all the services added tools that allowed their subscribers to e-mail people on other networks or on the Internet through the Internet. But their subscribers wanted more. They wanted to connect with the Internet. So now America Online, Prodigy, CompuServe, and the newcomer Microsoft Network all have gateways to the Internet. Which raises the interesting question of whether these services are on the path to becoming just providers of Internet gateways. At the moment these networks are loaded with proprietary content—content that Morningstar created for America Online, for example. But it doesn't make long-term sense for content providers to limit their wares to only one service and one part of the on-line market. Morningstar data, for instance, can be found all over the World Wide Web. One way, of course, for the on-line services to respond is by beefing up their efforts to provide unique content by offering content developers better deals and more development support. It will be interesting to see how they answer the Internet challenge.

quire anyone to master either a software language such as UNIX or install a dedicated phone hookup. To compete, the dedicated Internet companies have cut prices and upgraded their software. I can now get unlimited Internet access for $20 a month. I don't expect that price to stay even that high for long, since the big three commercial networks are now engaged in a price war for the mass audience.

So it isn't enough anymore to talk about navigating the net as if it was an end in itself. It's time to move on to the issue that the consumer of electronic information cared about all along: content.

So how good is the content for investors? Frankly, only a handful of the information sites available through one of the commercial services or on the Internet can compete on the basis of quality and comprehensiveness of information—and price—with the average good piece of investment software. Even the best sites can't compete for ease of use, depth of material, graphics, and power with the best programs reviewed in this book. That's not surprising. The on-line world is still in its infancy, and expecting even the best on-line vendors of investment information to match up with a program that's been around for years and been fine-tuned through a half-dozen revisions is unrealistic.

To show you what I mean, let's compare the information on mutual funds that Morningstar, Inc. provides on-line (through America Online), and on its software that arrives every month through the mail. Let's say that I want to check out a specific fund, Twentieth Century Ultra Investors, for example. On-line I get a brief synopsis of the fund's purpose, annual returns stretching back to 1991 (versus the S&P 500 index, too), three- and five-year performance, such risk measures as beta and standard deviation, the fund's top ten holdings, and statistics on expenses and fees, and such ratios as turnover and the median market capitalization of the fund's portfolio.

Not bad, and not a bad set of basic data. But it can't compare in depth to the information Morningstar sends out on disk. Morningstar's software gives me ten- and fifteen-year returns, as well as annual returns stretching back equally far—an increasingly important advantage to investors worried about how a fund will perform in a downturn as the last bear market slips further and further behind us. On software, I'll find statistics such as the Sharpe ratio, a measure of the relationship between risk and return, and a breakdown of the fund's holdings by industry so that I can judge how concentrated this fund's holdings are in a particular sector of the market.

And perhaps even more important, on the software I can screen to find funds that meet a particular set of requirements—say, no load, low expenses, and performance in the top decile of all funds over the last ten years. Although I can look up an individual fund on-line, I can't do this kind of screen. Nor can I rank funds or track hypothetical portfolios over time or test investment theories.

But this kind of comparison really underemphasizes the true advantages of the on-line investment world. The strengths of the best on-line vendors are not in supplying vast quantities of standardized data or years of historical data—that's more cheaply and efficiently accomplished in media such as the floppy disk and the CD-ROM. Distributing powerful analytical programs is also probably better accomplished through the static media of disks and CDs.

So what is this technology good for?

## THE THREE TRUE BENEFITS OF ON-LINE TOOLS

First, on-line services are great at providing access to time-valuable data. Part of what I mean by that is obvious. If a investor is a trader, he or she wants to see real-time quotes—or at worst, fifteen-minute delayed quotes. Waiting a month for a disk is unacceptable. But I think other, less obvious, kinds of data also fall into this category. For example, there's data whose very appearance in the world is unpredictable—such as, for example, a press release announcing the resignation of Phil Knight, the leader/guru of Nike. (Relax, Nike investors. This is a hypothetical example.) Getting access to data like this is a major problem for an individual investor who in the past often didn't even know it existed until the data's usefulness had passed.

Second, for many of the one-time research tasks that investors face regularly, going on-line is far more efficient than trekking to the library and more cost-effective than subscribing to expensive journals or data services. For example, if I'm constructing an investment model that relates the movement of automobile stocks to interest rates, I want a historical record of interest rates and auto sales and auto stock prices. I'm not going to need this data again—I simply want it for one-time use. On-line can be the way to fulfill this kind of need. If I want to know about manufacturing activity as a way to gauge the strength of the economy, or I want to get analyst estimates on earnings for Home Depot, or I want to read an economic analysis of Japan before I plunge into the Tokyo stock market, I can find all of that on-line.

Third, the on-line world is good for the interactive exchange of information—a conversation, if you will, where each participant—and there can be many—has a chance to add information, ask questions, and answer them. On-line an investor can find communities of other investors and experts for interactive dialogues on topics ranging from the prospects for individual stocks to the validity of particular investment theories to how to fix specific technical glitches in a piece of investment software.

But the on-line world is, in many crucial ways, far less easy to use than a library—and that situation is getting worse as it becomes possible to get almost anywhere in the electronic world with reasonable ease. You have been let loose in the world's largest candy store and it's hard to know where to go first—especially because there is no central index, card catalog, or Dewey decimal system. Want stock prices? There are dozens of sources. Want a discussion of stocks by other individual investors? I know of a dozen discussion forums. Sample copies of newsletters? Software to download? Mutual fund ratings? All available in a dozen places. And the list doesn't get a whole lot shorter if you're looking for technical stuff. There are dozens of economics bulletin boards, competing forums discussing unpublished papers on finance, and alternative sources of the Federal Reserve's monetary data.

Some of this is sludge—barely processed refuse that's not even good for fertilizing a garden. Some is the purest cream skimmed from the investment world. Some is easy to use. Some is impossible. Some is efficiently organized. Some wastes more time than it's worth. Some that you've never heard of is wretched and some unexpectedly superb. Some brand names used to be good and aren't anymore. Some places are so crowded with mindless drivel that the best investors, the ones who earned a place its reputation don't show up anymore. In Yogi Berra's phrase, "It's too crowded. No one goes there anymore."

## A SYSTEM FOR MASTERING ON-LINE INVESTING

Learning to use the electronic world isn't just a question of picking out the good stuff and leaving the bad behind. There's even too much good stuff available—often from competing vendors at very different prices. The task confronting the investor who wants to get an edge from this electronic flow of data—and still wants to have some time to actually

BASICS

# GETTING ON THE INTERNET

To get on the Internet, you'll need to find a gateway and there are plenty of companies that will sell you one. Basically, this will allow the modem on your home computer to dial the modem on the gateway provider's computer which will connect you to the Internet. I'm assuming here that most investors don't need a direct Internet connection. Information on such a direct connection is a little beyond the scope of this book.

Not all gateways are the same. If you pick up some books about the Internet, it's easy to get lost in arcane discussions of SLIP versus PPP connections and the need to telnet and ftp. Fortunately, most of the major Internet service providers have pretty much standardized the kind of connection they sell to the general public. You should get e-mail, the ability to open an ftp connection, to telnet (to log on as a terminal), and to run searches using gophers, archies, and veronicas, to sign on to Usenet news groups (important, since that's where the misc.invest newsgroups are located), and a connection to the World Wide Web.

With connections relatively standardized, the real difference is ease of use. Early Internet connections required users to master an unfamiliar computer language called UNIX and type in arcane codes and commands. Now the best Internet services provide easy to use point and click navigators. At a minimum, a good interface should allow you to subscribe to

*continued*

invest—is how to edit out all the vendors and sites and overlapping information you don't need while learning where to find exactly the information you do need. That involves constructing a system tailored to your investment needs.

Let me show you what I mean, using the on-line availability of financial news as an example. All investors want news about the markets, about their stocks, about companies and industries. That's why we subscribe to the *Wall Street Journal*, *Investor's Business Daily*, and *Business Week*, and *Barron's*, *Forbes*, and *Worth*. Well, you get the idea. An investor can never have enough news and he or she lives in constant fear of missing some crucial event. The news can never be fresh enough, either. The morning paper is already hours behind the news when it ar-

Usenet newsgroups with a simple click (and to set up a list of the groups that you use most frequently), and it should allow you to keep an address list (sometimes called a "bookmark" of the places that you go most frequently) and to navigate to any address on the list with a click. It should be easy to tell when you have new e-mail, to retrieve it, and to compose it off-line and then send it. And finally, with the increasing importance of the World Wide Web, your internet connection should come with a good Web browser or be compatible with one. The Web is in the middle of one of those periodic computer wars about who is going to set the standards for writing a Web page (with Netscape and Microsoft the leaders so far), so there really isn't a single standard for Web browsers yet. At the moment, Netscape's browser probably is the closest thing there is to a standard. Many pages are written with specific commands (in the language that governs how a Web page, and especially its graphics, are decoded) that only a Netscape compatible browser can fully read. Even if your internet service doesn't come with a Netscape-compatible browser, it should at least support browsers that use Netscape's code.

rives, so we flip on CNBC or CNN for the morning's events and then tune in to Bloomberg Business Radio.

The most serious investors—and that includes everyone with a terminal on a desk on Wall Street—get constant news feeds during the day. That's long been too expensive for most individual investors—a Bloomberg terminal costs $1,000 a month, for example. But the marriage of the personal computer and the electronic distribution of information has helped bridge that gap. For as little as $9.95 a month, I can get my news on-line.

That's all it costs to get one of the major electronic services—CompuServe, Prodigy, or America Online—delivered to your desktop. And for that price—about what ten days of the *Wall Street Journal* now costs on the newsstand—you don't get some amateurish, hard to use, and impossible-to-read piece of computer hacking. Signing on to America Online, for example, is a visual delight. While the modem makes its way through the telecommunications protocols, you get to watch not some mundane bottom of the screen message saying "Dialing" or "Trying to Connect" but instead a lightning bolt in full color that gives way to a key when the connection has been made. A computerized voice announces "You have mail," if anyone has sent you a message. The initial screen lists the day's headlines and hypes the sections of special interest today. If you skip these enticements and go to the main menu, full color graphics again present buttons for travel, personal finance, and news, among other choices.

Clicking on "Personal Finance," a wealth of interesting topics parades in front of you. AAII on-line, Morningstar, Investor's Business Daily, Investor's Network, Decision Point Timing/Charts, Market News, Motley Fool, Quotes and Portfolios, Software Center, Telescan Users Group, Top Advisors Corner, Vanguard on-line, Wall Street SOS forum. Click on any of these and the software moves you to a lushly designed screen that offers specific choices on each of these goodies. You haven't even searched for it, but already you've had a screen full of headlines and the offer of news from *Investor's Business Daily* and a selection of market news.

If I want to concentrate on news, I can click on "Business News." Calling up this function gets a list of headlines (preselected by Reuters,

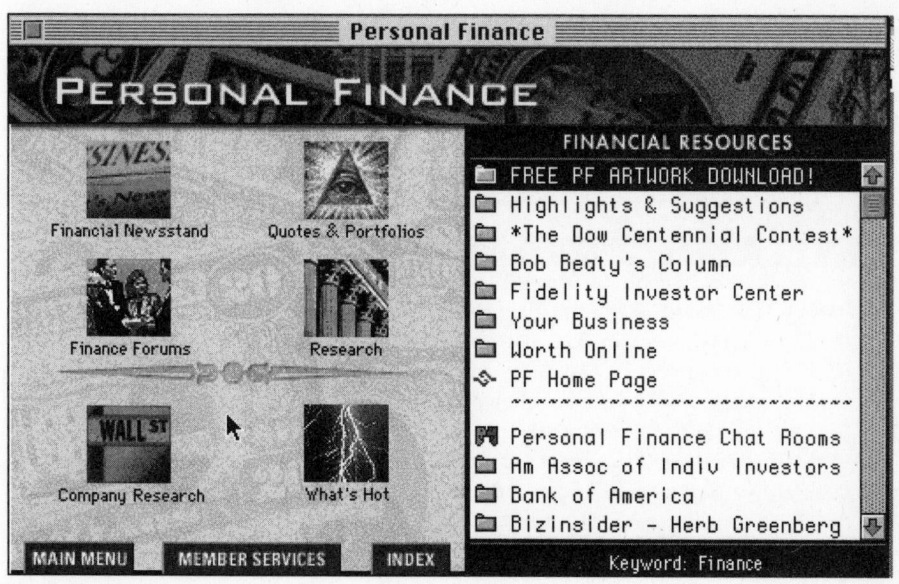

*The Personal Finance screen on America Online showcases specific sections and also lists everything that might be of interest.* (Courtesy America Online)

a news service that in much of the physical and financial worlds is as respected as Dow Jones, the publisher of the *Wall Street Journal*) and a button that lets me click for a download of Top Business Stories. I can also go to "Industry News" and click on a category such as Technology. This gets me another list of stories with sources that include Knight-Ridder/Tribune, PRNewswire, Business Wire, and Reuters.

This kind of groaning board of news isn't unique to America Online. Sign up with CompuServe for about the same price and type "go ENS" (for Executive News Service). Here an investor can consult Reuters, the Associated Press and AP Financial, Dow Jones, and the PRWire. The investor who's willing to spend a little bit more money—say $30 a month—faces an even wider set of choices.

Five years ago the question facing the investor was how to get any financial news at all for a reasonable cost. Now it's how do I pick?

First, it helps to realize that making this decision isn't some totally new and alien task for most investors. It's something we do everyday when we decide to subscribe to this paper and not that, or to listen to this financial broadcast and not that cable station. Making that decision is harder in the on-line world, though, because here the investor

*The "Business News" screen on American Online: Stories from sources such as Reuters and Knight-Ridder. (Courtesy America Online)*

will find scores of unfamiliar sources mixed with the familiar names. And journalistic and ethical standards are far looser in the still-being-invented electronic world than they are in print. It's not always clear what's a real news story and what's an advertisement or a self-interested financial promotion. But still, the process is analogous.

Browsing is one response to this wealth of unfamiliar sources. That, too, is an extension of how we handle information overload in the print world. Just keep in mind that most people browse in bookstores as a form of recreation or to kill time. It's not a very efficient way to look for information—especially when the electronic store to browse is far larger than even the super bookstore in the mall and is growing far faster. One list of new topics on just one version of the Internet—the World Wide Web—recently showed 349 new areas popping up in a single week.

Despite the adage about the informational relationship between books and their covers, it is far easier to judge a printed source by just flipping it over than it is to figure out an on-line area with a simple once-over. Let me give you a couple of examples.

The Investors Network on America Online sounds promising, if cryptic. Clicking on the

# So What's This World Wide Web Thing?

In the last year, the hip have gone from surfing the Net to browsing the Web and you're excused if you've become a little confused about the difference between the Internet and the World Wide Web. To simplify, the Internet is the highway. The Web is a vehicle for carrying information on that highway.

In the beginning the Internet was a network designed to send text and data. A user could send words and numbers, and by typing in words—commands written in UNIX—search for other databases, organizations, and individuals on the network. To do the hard work of finding data on the subject at hand, Internet users developed search software with the odd names of Archie and Veronica. Menus of databases were called "gophers." Using the gopher of the University of Michigan Department of Economics, for example, I could ask for a list of databases that might have economic information about U.S. inflation rates. I could type in the commands to connect my computer to the gopher (another computer) at the university and then, using more written commands, ask

*continued*

that gopher to search each database on the list for the information I wanted.

The World Wide Web turns that process into pictures. Instead of gophers, the Web is built around the "home page." Instead of typing in commands for a search, I can click on a button or key word on a home page to move deeper into the home page database or navigate to another home page database that sounds as if it might have what I want. While the Web can be considered just a visual interface for the Internet, its substitution of pictures and clicks for words and arcane code has made the electronic world of the Internet accessible to far more people than ever before.

name shows that the network itself has many parts, one with the intriguing sounding name of Top Advisors' Corner. That certainly suggests that some top investment gurus reside here. Well, they do, sort of. The screen shows a list of sixteen advisors. Some I've heard of, such as Geraldine Weiss, George Putnam, Stephen Leeb. Others I don't know. I can click on any of these names.

What does that get me? Certainly not the guru. This is actually just a collection of folders of back issues of each guru's newsletters. That could be useful in and of itself, of course, but the material in each offering is wildly uneven. In Stephen Leeb's folder I found just one issue of his newsletter, *Personal Finance*, which was nine months old. George Putnam's folder contained eight uploads from *The Turnaround Letter*. The most recent is just a week old. But these aren't complete copies of the newsletter—each lists just a single recommendation. I've spent twenty minutes—and I'm pretty good at checking areas out quickly—and I have nothing to show for my efforts except the knowledge that I don't need to go back here.

The browser will also soon run into the problem that I call "The seemingly familiar source." Morningstar, a familiar and reliable source of mutual fund data, also hangs out on America Online. The information here, which is directly from Morningstar, isn't bad; it's just not as complete as I expect. From a list of funds I can ask for one-page summaries of key numbers on performance and a brief description of the fund. I can even do a search by fund family or the manager's name. There's even a good user guide from Morningstar explaining the terminology that the summaries use. But again, there's no meaningful on-line help to tell the novice user what other kinds of searches might be useful or how to construct them. I miss the analyst's com-

# THE INSTANTANEOUS DELIVERY OF MOLDY INFORMATION

Just because it's on-line, don't assume that the information you are about to download is fresh. Many on-line providers post information only after lengthy delays. Some information vendors, especially those whose main, profitable business is producing print materials, put information on-line only after it has appeared on paper. A newsletter or magazine publisher, for example, might translate an issue into electronic form only after it has been created and mailed to subscribers. Which sort of kills all the advantages of electronic distribution, doesn't it?

But even services whose main business is providing information electronically can't be counted on to be as up to date as the distribution technology allows. Many, even if their product involves reporting on something such as stocks, where prices and fundamentals change daily, update their information only weekly or monthly.

So don't forget to consider the timeliness of the information that your investment style requires when you're putting together your plan for finding the sources you need on-line. Consider whether you need daily or weekly or monthly information. Decide how much of a time delay you can live with. Ruthlessly eliminate any sources you come across that provide information of the type you need but not with the frequency or freshness your system demands.

Actually, you shouldn't be totally ruthless about this. Given the speed with which the on-line world is changing, you should make a list of promising sources with stale information and revisit them, every three months or so. Some information vendors are slow to discover that it is constant updating that keeps electronic investors coming back for more— but they do get the message eventually.

mentary that I get in the print version. And I can't screen on all sorts of data that are readily available in the computerized versions of the database that Morningstar itself sells. I come away with the impression that, like many of the sources on-line, this one is a cut-down version of more expensive print and software products that is designed to give just enough to whet an investor's appetite for the real

# THE BEST AND THE WORST OF AOL

**B**esides The Motley Fool, what's good on America On-Line? First, check out the forum run by the American Association of Individual Investors. Reviews from AAII's Computerized Investing Newsletter focus on what to buy (in contrast to the Computer Corner on CompuServe, which tends to be better on how to run what you've bought). The section also offers some how-to's and good worksheets (see one entitled "A Worksheet for Evaluating Stocks"). Combined with The Motley Fool, this forum gives America Online two sound but different stock-picking philosophies.

The stock picker can use data from Morningstar to America Online's new company research section in the Personal Finance section. The 6,000-stock database essentially duplicates the fundamental information offered by Morningstar's DOS-based program U.S. Equities OnFloppy (see review in Chapter 3).

The Mercury Center, the on-line version of the *San Jose Mercury News*, shows how great an on-line "newspaper" can be. In my opinion, this is the best way available to keep up with high-technology and to understand the workings of Silicon Valley. The Center includes the day's business section with news on Silicon Valley companies and earnings reports, the computing section with columnists, hardware and software reviews, and semiconductor news, and the Tech Talk message board. The Mercury Center also provides access to Knight-Ridder/Tribune Business News.

America Online can also be supremely silly, however. The Personal Finance Software Center, hosted by Dave Wolf of PfSoftware, includes a limited library of software for doing basic tasks such as retrieving daily stock quotes from America Online using the Stock Quote Fetch program. The software is, by and large, elementary—lots of decimal to fraction conversions and loan calculators.

But the section does offer my favorite America Online piece of kitsch—Celebrity Picks. Last time I checked, the celebrity—who is, thank god, picking software and not stocks—was Julie Cialini, recent Playmate of the Year. With a click I can download a picture of her (clothed) and a conversation that finally wades through enough trivia to discuss MoneyMatter$ shareware.

thing. In other words, it's an advertisement masquerading as an information source.

## RULE ONE FOR BUILDING AN ON-LINE INFORMATION SYSTEM:
## SET A STRICT TIME BUDGET FOR BROWSING.

So here's my first rule for building an on-line system that serves your needs. Separate browsing for new sources from using familiar sources. Set aside a specific amount of time each week for exploring (don't underestimate how much time, and possibly money, browsing can consume).

For example, here's a record of an exploratory browse that I took. I started off by setting a time limit—an hour—and picking a region of the electronic world to explore, the Internet's universe of World Wide Web home pages. I started here because I'd heard about an interesting Web page coming out of the University of Texas. I typed the address into the navigator supplied by my Internet service: http://www.finweb.com/. (Don't worry about what this means. It's just a relic of the way the World Wide Web was developed. You don't have to know how to write computer code to use a word processor, either.) I find a list of sources on economics and finance managed by Professor James R. Garven at UT Austin. (See box on page 229 for a more complete description of this page.)

One of the sources listed on Garven's page is the GNN Personal Finance Center. (See the box on page 229 for a more complete description of this page.) By clicking on the name of the page the software sends me to this new site and saves me the trouble of typing the address (http://nearnet.gnn.com/gnn/meta/finance/index.html). At the GNN page I've got an entirely different list of resources to check out. (See how quickly this turns into a branching exercise that takes the user further and further into the maze?) I ask for a list called "What's New: Investment and Personal Finance." This turns out to be a list mostly of newsletters. Only a few sound interesting. A lot are just firsts—first Swiss bank on-line—that have a limited novelty value and nothing more. More turn out to be just extended ads. I can get a free sample by phone or e-mail or subscribe. Big deal.

So I return to Garven's page to see if any other branches seem more promising. I see a listing for Wertheim Schroder Equity Research and click on that page. The investment bank will give me a two months' free subscription to *Colloquium*—in hopes that I'll become a client. The sample issue that I can download is dated September 26, 1994, so out of date that I can't tell whether this would be a useful service. So I pass on this, too.

Then back to Garven's page. I skim it looking for anything of interest. I see a set of investment information from some organization called APL and I see the Securities and Exchange Commission's Edgar service, a depository of electronic quarterly and annual corporate filings.

But my hour's up. So I exit after adding the promising places to my automatic address list—again with a point and a click—so I can find my way back to them without even typing in the full address again.

Okay, but while this limit to my exploration may keep my time on-line (and frustration level) under control, the perceptive reader will notice that it is actually just adding to my problem. I've now got three or four new places to add to my list of on-line possibilities. And I've already noted that the problem is too many possibilities.

### RULE TWO: ON PAPER (YES, PAPER) DESCRIBE YOUR INFORMATION IDEAL.

For rule two turn off the computer and pull out a piece of paper. List (no more than) ten kinds of information you would like to have on-line. Include kinds that you already get from other sources, such as monthly data disks or newsletters. For me the list begins with news headlines and includes current quotes, changes in analyst recommendations, changes in earnings estimates, stock ideas, software reviews and help, Federal Reserve monetary policy, retail sales numbers, etc.

Don't be afraid to be very specific. Your list should, since every kind of investor uses different types of information, explicitly reflect your investment style. If you are a momentum investor, you might want an on-line source of charts that show some of the common indicators of price momentum. List that. Nothing, and I can't stress this enough, is too weird or too specific. If the on-line world can support a forum for people who hate the character Will Crusher on *Star Trek: The Next Generation*, it's likely to have what you want, too, buried in some obscure corner.

To get specific enough you'll have to do some really hard thinking about exactly what kind of investor you are. It isn't enough to say that you invest in stocks. You need to consider what kind of stocks you buy and sell, and most important, what kind of information determines your buy and sell decisions.

Why is this important? Let me show you. Prodigy's Strategic Investor service (really a way for the company to bundle a lot of information sources of interest to investors for a flat surcharge of $19.95 above the standard membership fee—see review at the end of this chapter) starts off with a page of hot stocks. A click of the mouse lets you choose among hot stocks from the New York and American stock exchanges, and the NASDAQ market. I scan the lists finding no name that interests me until I get to the NASDAQ section where ABC Rail Products, a stock that one of the newsletters I subscribe to has recommended, catches my eye. Another click pulls up a price volume chart of the stock for the last 54 weeks. ABC Rail Products is clearly outperforming the S&P on relative strength basis and has clearly broken above the 50-day moving average. The volume remains modest and I don't see any special trend in volume up or down. The stock now trades at $27, up from $13 a year ago.

Did you find that information useful? If you use technical analysis—the use of price and volume data from the past to predict future price movements—this information might be exactly what you want. If you buy stocks using

---

**TIPS ON THE TOOLS**

## THE BEST AND THE WORST OF PRODIGY

**S**trategic Investor is probably the single most impressive collection of investment tools available online—unless you are a technical investor in which case the service offers almost nothing of interest to you. Of course, it will cost you an extra $19.95 a month to use it, but for an investor who wants a lot of information on company fundamentals that's a very good deal. I've reviewed part of this program—the Stock Hunter stock screens and the Market Guide fundamental database—in Chapter 3.

But there's more to Strategic Investor. On the first page, an investor will find buttons for the charts of hot stocks (50 charts a day that the analysts at *Investor's Business Daily* think might outperform), and weekly features such as "Mutual Fund Close-up." At the bottom, the page spotlights company reports on five companies. Buttons along the side of the page will take the investor to company reports (Market Guide), Stock Hunter, fund reports, and money talk bulletin boards.

Clicking on fund reports allows an investor to type in a symbol (the page
*continued*

has a fund symbol finder) to get a report on an individual fund or to conduct a search by fund family, investment objective, or performance period (data for fund reports comes from Micropal). For example, if I look up the Crabbe Huson Special Fund, I get a page with one-month to ten-year performance (also versus S&P), charges and fees, inception date, and rank versus similar funds and all funds. Other pages give me the latest quote and a chart with five years of cash distributions and total return versus the S&P 500 (charts are 25 cents for Strategic Investor members, 50 cents for everyone else).

Many users hate Prodigy because every page comes with ads. For example, the first screen that comes up in the bulletin board section has a breathless announcement at the bottom in boldface. "Investors! Looking for unique growth opportunities? The Kaufmann Fund finds them for you." With a look button. I click look and get the ad: "The #1 performing mutual fund since the 1987 market low."

But I find it pretty easy to ignore the ad clutter—after all no one is forcing me to hit the "look" button. My problem with Prodigy is the bulletin boards themselves. They sum up the quasi-paternalistic attitude that characterizes Prodigy.

The board pages begin with a warning, prepared in cooperation with North American Securities Administrators Association, the organization of 50 state regulators and the Interactive Services Association. "Some postings may even be intentionally misleading, and the potential for investment fraud exists on-line, just as it does in other mediums. The good news is that with a little commonsense education, you can ensure your experiences will be positive," it reads. "It's important to keep in mind the following: Don't expect to get rich quick." "If something sounds too good to be true, chances are that it is." "On-line services do not validate claims." "The services rely mainly on their members to assess the value, importance or legitimacy of advice and tips passed along." "Don't buy thinly traded, little-known stocks without careful research." This all makes good sense but the message is, you're on your own.

I understand why no one rides herd on the chaos of the Internet—it's not a commercial service but instead a collection of cowboys strung together with wire. Prodigy, on the other hand, makes money from distributing messages. To pretend that it bears no responsibility for those messages is pretty lame.

a model called CanSlim—which looks for stocks with upward momentum, among other things—this information is useful, too, since it's produced by the analysts at *Investor's Business Daily*, the home of the CanSlim model. But if you invest based on earnings or assets or margins or some other piece of fundamental data, this section isn't going to help you much. In fact, my description of what I saw in the ABC Rail Products chart is probably pretty opaque. (This isn't to say that Prodigy doesn't have sources of fundamental data. See the complete review, please.)

An investor who makes decisions based on earnings would be better off in CompuServe's big section on earnings. Both I/B/E/S and Zacks, two competitors in tracking analysts' earnings estimates, can be found there. For 50 cents I can download a summary of earnings expectations from I/B/E/S. A complete detailed company report is $2 per company. The section gives samples of each so you know which one fits your needs, and it also has text files—"The Relationship Between Earnings Expectations and Stock Price," "Dealing with Your Broker's Recom-

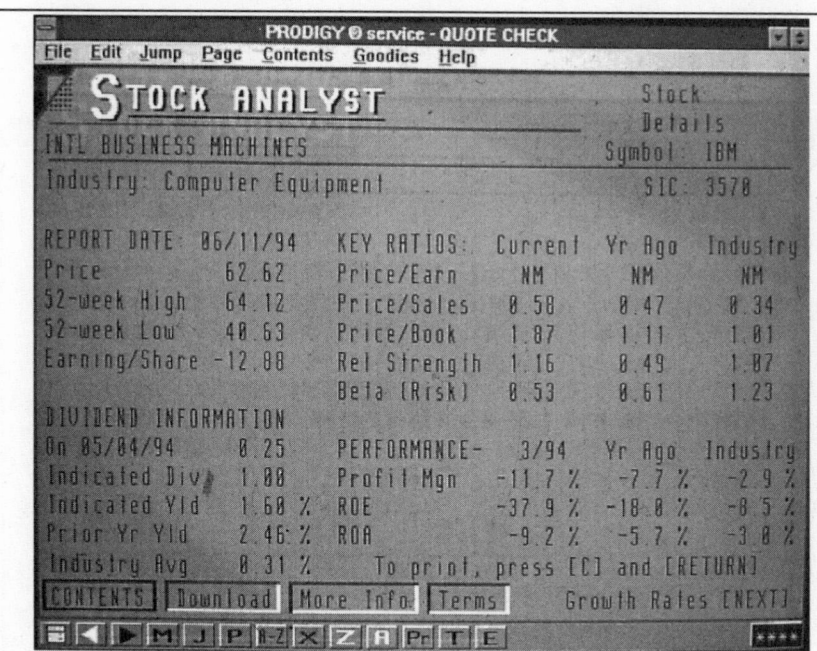

*Prodigy's Strategic Investor offers fundamentals, charts, stock tips, mutual fund data and more for $19.95 a month.* (*Courtesy Prodigy*)

mendations," and "The Importance of Trends in Consensus Earnings Forecasts"—that explain some of the ins and outs of using earnings expectations to make investment decisions. A momentum player might find this section useful to check Wall Street's expectations of future earnings growth; a technical investor would find this irrelevant; and some fundamental investors would find this information invaluable.

Is the Prodigy section better or worse than the one on CompuServe? It all depends on what kind of investor you are. So that's why you should be as specific as possible in drawing up your list.

Then divide your list in two. The first section will include all those types of information you don't get at all now. Finding those on-line will be your first priority. The second half will be composed of information that you already get from other sources. Here your task, and it has lower priority than the first, is to find better sources—and perhaps cheaper sources—on-line.

The "best of" tips that I've included in this chapter should give you a head-start. Fill in any parts of your list that you can now from those sources and by adding sources that you use already or have heard about. Your exploratory hours will gradually fill in the holes.

---

**TIPS ON THE TOOLS**

## The Best and the Worst of CompuServe, Part I

Besides Fundwatch Online by *Money* magazine (a good alternative to Morningstar on America Online) basic quotes, and the Investors and NAIC forums described in this chapters, try these services:

Get earnings estimates from I/B/E/S and Zacks, two of the information companies that track the earnings estimates of Wall Street analysts. Both services carry a surcharge. I/B/E/S (available in the Investments area under earnings) charges 50 cents a company for summary reports and $2 a company for detailed earnings report. You can pull up samples of both brief and extended reports so you know what you want.

Zacks (go to the Publications On-line area) provides one-page reports on earnings per share, broker recommendations, company versus industry growth rates, and a financial summary for $2.50.

Although I still have trouble understanding why anyone would want to read a magazine on-line, the Publications On-line area holds some useful resources besides Zacks. You'll find a few magazines here, such as *Fortune* and *IndustryWeek Interactive,* but most have moved their efforts to more graphically advanced services than CompuServe. Maybe the best feature is the ability to download a page from the *Value Line Investment Survey.* The cost is high at $5 a page, but probably worth it for the investor who has to have it now. (To download the page you'll have to first download a piece of graphics software, Adobe Acrobat. It's free, but line charges apply and it does take 16 minutes to download.)

Two areas in basic services not so much to avoid but to ignore: the Company Snapshot and the Financial Services Information Center. The company snapshot is basically an ad for more extensive and expensive information available in the surcharged areas. The Financial Services Information Center is just a listing of brochures and newsletters that you can order on-line and a list of mutual funds for which you can order prospectuses and investment kits on-line. The information is sent by the fund company free of charge.

## RULE THREE: NEVER REST ON YOUR ON-LINE LAURELS.

Don't be particularly concerned if you start with a source that turns out to be less than perfect. It will give you a benchmark to use in looking for something better. And that brings me to rule number three. An on-line investment system is always a work in progress and never finished. The smart investor realizes that information everyone knows isn't the most valuable kind and that the information sources everyone knows aren't the most valuable sources. New data might provide a temporary edge. And there's always something better out there. So start with whatever seems good, but always look for what's better.

This process will only work if you are willing to keep a completely open mind. Let me illustrate. Every mutual fund investor knows Morningstar's superb data and publications rating mutual funds. And, to the joy of the on-line investor, Morningstar is available on America Online.

Now, in the print world, *Money* magazine's mutual fund information is decidedly inferior to Morningstar's. But it won't pay to assume that this pecking order extends to the electronic world. Fundwatch Online by *Money* (available on CompuServe—Go Fundwatch) is surprisingly useful and comprehensive—indeed in some ways it's a superior product to Morningstar's offering. Using Fundwatch, an investor can screen 4,796 funds by objective, fees, performance, assets, management company, yield, and risk. For example, I ran a screen looking for funds that returned better than 5 percent in the last bear market. The list is, as I expected, dominated by currency and global/international funds. But if I were worried about the next bear market, I would be intrigued by such a list. I'm certainly impressed by Fundwatch's ability to produce such a list on-line. Morningstar, in contrast, reports on more funds on-line but won't allow me to build screens.

### RULE FOUR: STRUCTURE IS MORE IMPORTANT THAN VOLUME.

Comparing on-line information sources can be tricky. The beginner is likely to confuse more with better. Actually, the best source is the one that makes it easiest to find just the information you want—for the least cost in time and money. So rule number four is to look for structured information. Once you've found a quality source on-line, it's likely to overwhelm you with information unless it provides you with tools for separating the useful from the meaningless. And this tool has to be flexible. One investor's useful fact is another's triviality.

Let me go back to news again to demonstrate what I mean. On most news services I can search the news sources by company, industry, or keyword. For example, I can search America Online's news section with Intel as my keyword. That gets me thrity-eight stories as far back as December 1994. Some just mention Intel in passing. "Consilium Names New Marketing Vice President" comes up because Intel is a customer.

Now there's some kind of selection process at work here. But what? Reuters sure ran more than thrity-eight stories that mentioned Intel in the last six months—especially since the search is pulling up stories with only glancing relevance to the company. So I have to wonder if I'm getting all the news I ought to get.

On the other hand, I'd certainly like to get fewer stories like the Consilium one. I can add terms and connect them with *and, or,* and *not* to narrow the field. But I can't search by date, nor, as far as I can tell, limit or expand the time period covered by my search. I try the Help

# THE BEST AND THE WORST
# OF COMPUSERVE, PART II

**C**ompuServe's surcharged features can get pretty expensive very fast, but a few of them can be information bargains for the investor who needs high-quality, specific information—and can build a focused search. ADP Global Reports looks like such a bargain, despite its stiff fee. (Connect-time surcharge is $60 an hour during prime time and $30 off-peak and weekends, but there are no per-report charges. A typical report would cost around $1.18.) I've used it to find earnings information on international companies such as DESC S.A. de C.V., a Mexican auto parts maker. Also has auto search function. (Remember to capture files to your hard drive so that you can read them when you're off-line.)

The Company Screening function allows an investor to screen the 11,000 publicly-traded companies in the Disclosure database on a combination of thirty-nine criteria, such as five-year growth rates in sales, earnings, and net income. Surcharge is $15 per hour.

Investext strikes me as too expensive for most investors. A search that will list ten analyst reports by title costs $20; each page in the actual report costs $15. It's one way to get a copy of an analyst report on a company, but investors who can reach the Internet should try Cambridge Interactive's World Wide Web page (http://money.com), described in Chapter 3, as an alternative. Other investors may question how much Wall Street analyst reports are worth to begin with. And if all you need is a list, there's always good old print: Nelson's *Directory of Wall Street Research* is available at many libraries.

Finally, for the investor who wants to check out what another investment system is "thinking," Vestor provides a steady diet of buy/sell recommendations for $45 per hour. Each week this proprietary expert system uses twenty technical and fundamental variables to evaluate 7,000 stocks. You can ask Vestor for its recommendation on individual stocks, search the data base using your own criteria, and view Vestor's buy/sell recommendations for the week. The service claims that you can retrieve five different buy/sell recommendations in a minute or screen 6,000 stocks on fourteen criteria in two minutes.

function, but it doesn't provide me with any suggestions.

So here I have an editor who, like the one who decides what's on my front page every morning, determines what I know about. I know instinctively that even the "All the News That's Fit to Print" *New York Times* leaves out more than it runs on most days of the year. But on-line I can easily forget that the news or data is also edited—it isn't simply all the existing data ready to be consumed by me.

It's hard to get a feel for the parameters of editing on-line. I know that the news function on America Online makes me uneasy. Clicking on Technology, I get stories on the Czech stock exchange, Yugos as art, and a downgrade of mortgage pass-through paper. I expect a more selective filter than this. I don't think I want to read news edited in this fashion.

How do I go about finding an editor I trust? Starting with the names I know from the world of print journalism isn't a bad tactic. Granted that sometimes, as in the Morningstar section on America Online, the on-line version is not as good as the print version, but I can still rely on these organizations not to embarrass themselves on-line. Morningstar or Dow Jones have valuable names to protect.

Let me contrast America Online's news editor with the one that came with Apple Computer's beautifully designed but rather empty on-line service, eWorld. (I say "came" because eWorld is closing down in 1996.) Sign on to eWorld and enter an electronic village. The first screen is designed as a small community with a Newsstand, eMail Center, Info booth, Community Center, Business and Finance Plaza, and other functions represented as the buildings of a small town. Clicking on the skyscraper labeled Business and Finance Plaza makes the building yield to a full color screen with three icons (Corporate Intelligence, Dow Jones Business & Financial News, and eWorld Market Quotes).

I'm interested in news, so I click on the Dow Jones icon. This gives me a choice of editorial products: Front Page Business News, Market Updates and News, or Daily Newsletters (such as Dow Jones Asian News Update or Dow Jones Technology Update). All of these are products created by editors who are working, like their newspaper counterparts, to create a list of stories they think the reader will want.

I can also create my own newspaper by searching, just as I did on America Online. But Dow Jones and Apple have given me a much better set of editorial tools than I had on America Online. By hitting Company and Industry News, I get a browser with a list of headline topics, buttons for sixteen industries, and a search function. Hitting an Industry button replaces the general headlines in the browser function with a different set on the industry. Search gives me access to thirty days of Dow Jones news. (And a Help function that isn't much better or different from the one I disliked on America Online. It tells me I can use *or, and,* or *not.*)

I try searching on Intel again. This gives me forrty-four entries—more than the thirty-eight I got on America Online, even though I'm searching only the last month instead of the six months back to December 1994. I get Intel in today's market wrap-up story—it dropped 1⅞—and a story on May 15 about surging corporate profits that included a 44 percent increase in Intel's earnings. If I restrict the search by asking for items that mention both "Intel" and "earnings" I narrow the field down to just twenty-three stories. Browsing through fewer stories I notice one I hadn't seen before, from May 4, on the way the upbeat Hambrecht & Quist technology conference lit a fire under semiconductor stocks.

Is it worth moving up to the real thing by subscribing to Dow Jones' electronic news service itself rather than using the stripped-down version on eWorld?

**TIPS ON THE TOOLS**

## KEEPING UP WITH THE WORLD WIDE WEB

It's a frightening thought: currently 1,000 new web sites are added to the Internet every week. Even scarier: the pace seems to be accelerating.

Of course, for those who want to keep up, there's an Internet site to try. Originally operating out of Stanford University, Yahoo went independent this year. (Use your Internet browser to read the Yahoo home page at http://www.yahoo.com/new/). Buttons at the top of the page call up new sites, cool sites, headlines, the most popular sites, and (most interesting to me for what it says about the way some people use the Internet), a random sample of sites. One day when I checked the new category, it listed 1,013 addresses added during the most recent week. Be warned, however, that the new file is so large that it will certainly take more than 30 minutes to download (at 14,400 bps) and that it could overwhelm your machine's memory, causing a crash. I find the page of sites launching soon— CNN and the Rain Forest Action network, on one recent·day—the most interesting feature. The full-color sample home page designs give me a feel for the quality of the prospective site better than words can.

The decision should hinge on both the volume of news offered by each source and on the tools that each service offers to help structure all that information. Let's ignore the obvious volume advantage that goes to Dow Jones News/Retrieval Private Investor Edition and consider just its tools and structure. Click on the button for Business and World News Wires and search for news by subject, stock symbol, and company name. To this standard search engine, Dow Jones has added something called a "matrix search" that will let you hunt for news by mixing up to three categories from region, industry, topic, and stock symbol. For example, to see if I should hold on to my shares of Mexican auto parts maker DESC, I can search for stories that combine Mexico, auto parts manufacturers, and analyst opinions.

Unlike the news on America Online or even Reuters Money Network, I can search through extensive archives of past stories. Clicking on a button called Dow Jones Text Library gives me the ability to use a function called DowQuest to search through the last six months of stories from 550 publications such as the *Wall Street Journal*, *Barron's*, *American Demographics*, *Business Week*, *The Economist*, *Forbes*, various regional business publications, and trade journals. If that isn't enough, I can use the surcharged Dow Jones Text Service, which archives 1,300 publications back to sometime in the 1980s (the exact date depends on the publication: archives of the *Wall Street Journal* go back to 1984; press releases from the PRWire go back to 1989).

---

**TIPS ON THE TOOLS**

## MORE ON KEEPING UP WITH THE WORLD WIDE WEB

**Y**ahoo has a lot of entertainment value, but for investors looking for information, the page is too unfocused. Fortunately, a number of pages on the World Wide Web are devoted to keeping track of what's on the Internet specifically for investors.

Some of these pages are works of love, as it were, compiled by individuals for the benefit of the investment community as a whole. Douglas Gerlach, a sysop for CompuServe, has put together Douglas Gerlach's Investorama (World Wide Web address, http://www.investorama.com), a listing of the best resources on the Internet for individual investors. The page breaks down resources into eleven categories: NAIC, quotes, government, links, brokers, funds, 'zines, news, companies on-line, services, and home pages. Gerlach's page is itself cross-linked to other pages so that you can travel to anything that seems of interest simply by clicking on its name. "News" is the least interesting (it's just the Internet's misc.invest newsgroups). "'Zines" has some unusual stuff, such as the home page of the Red Chip Review (a free issue offer and some interesting articles from that small stock newsletter; address http://www.redchip.com).

FinWeb, managed by James R. Garven, a professor in the economics department at the University of Texas at Austin, is more focused on economics and finance than Gerlach's page (address is http://www.finweb.com/) Its list of resources is divided into five sections: Journals (home pages for Journal of Finance and ECONbase, and the electronically published "Studies in Nonlinear Dynamics and Econometrics"); Working Papers—in economics and finance; Databases—ECONData's economic time series, the Experimental Stock Market Page from MIT, and various quotation services such as QuoteCom and Security APL Co.; a list of other finance-oriented servers—the Federal Reserve Bank of Philadelphia (http://www.libertynet.org/~fedreserv/fedpage.html), the World Bank, and the RAND Corporation; and several miscellaneous sources. All of this can be accessed by clicking hot buttons from FinWeb.

O'Reilly Communications, an Internet pioneer, has set up the GNN Personal Finance Center (GNN stands for Global Network Navigator, address http://nearnet.gnn.com/gnn/meta/finance/index.html). The page's list of Internet Resources includes buttons for new resources and NCSA What's New, as well as the ability to browse by type of resource and subject. The week of September 5, the page was listing new resources from InvestorsEdge (including stock and mutual fund quotes and a free portfolio manager), *Money* magazine's MONEY Personal Finance Center, and Nikko Securities Co. (research reports and Japanese economic forecasts in Japanese and English). In the same week NCSA What's New listed sites such as Silicon Investor from VB-Webb Partners (http://www.techstocks.com/), Disclosure Inc.'s page for ordering financial statements (http://www.disclosure.com), and Micropal Financial Data Centre's mutual fund data page (http://www.cityscape.co.uk/users/bv32/).

But like Reuters Money Network, Dow Jones Private Investor Edition isn't just a news reader. The service combines news with in-depth financial information—analyst estimates from Zacks, five pages of fundamental data from Media General Financial Services on each of 5,400 companies, S&P profiles and estimates, and data on insider trading from Corporate Ownership Watch. (All these services are included in the monthly fee. Other databases, such as Disclosure's database of SEC filings and Investext's database of analyst reports, carry sometimes stiff surcharges.)

And again, the software comes with tools that help me structure this information. For example, I can create and track the day-to-day performance of a portfolio (but not track performance over any significant period). After typing stock ticker symbols into a portfolio, I can use the "Enhanced Current Quotes" function to get high, low, open, close, and volume numbers on all my stocks.

The software also integrates that portfolio function and its news service. A flag next to a stock listed in my portfolio indicates a current news story on the stock. So on September 10, I notice a flag next to the price of ABC Rail Products (down ¼ for the session on Friday). Clicking on news I get a current story on the company's announcement of expected earnings of 46–48 cents, and then a list of older stories that quickly fill me in on the background of this railroad equipment producer I've just begun to watch. One story tells me that the company expects to be buyer as the railroad supply industry consolidates and that it has already purchased a wheel-mounting business from General Electric. Another story reports on an interview with the company CEO. I get a price alert—a block trade at 21.75, down 1¼, of 27,000 shares. Investext abstracts are also on the list so that I can see that analysts from Paine Webber and Merrill Lynch have recently reviewed the company.

Going even further back—the menu is organized chronologically—I get a July 21 story reporting that three Kohlberg & Co. directors resigned after the leveraged buyout investment company liquidated its 25 percent share of the company in a secondary offering. This story also updates me on the 1991 leveraged buyout by management and the subsequent 1993 initial public offering. I also get an important story on the fall in price of the company's stock after the underwriters priced the secondary offering, which suggests that I might find a better price on the stock if I wait.

So now I face a decision. How should I get my news? On quality, I can rule out America Online. Its news editor simply isn't good enough. Dow Jones on eWorld is cheap (at the moment it's free, but the service won't last) and has a decent editor, but nowhere near the depth of information that Dow Jones offers in its own branded on-line service. And if I subscribe to Private Investors Edition, I can think about ending my subscription to Reuters Money Network since I get news, prices, research reports, and the like from both sources.

In fact, the decision will probably come down to one between Reuters Money Network and Private Investors Edition. Both provide a wealth of information presented in a clear structure that actually helps clarify decision making. Private Investors Edition certainly gets a nod on the sheer volume of news and hard information it offers (at a higher cost), but what may influence me more is the way the program structures that news. In the time I've tried the system, I've learned to appreciate the way in which the current-news flags draw me into the archive of older stories so that I can gradually learn more and more about the context for today's news.

This example is a decent outline for how I'd weigh one on-line service against another, but it's missing one crucial element—ease of use. Of course, by that term I mean the kinds of issues I've talked about elsewhere in this book: How long does the program take to learn, how reliable is the communications program, are the pull-down menus or icons arranged in a way that makes it easy to get where I want to go without a lot of detours or without having to work my way down too many menus?

Up until about a year ago Dow Jones would have dropped out of the running because it was just about impossible to use. I briefly subscribed to the Dow Jones News Retrieval service for individual investors, Market Monitor, paying $29.95 a month to get eight hours of service during off-peak hours, in January and February of 1994. Some days I couldn't get my modem to connect cleanly with the service—I'd get random strings of symbols mixed in with my messages and typing. Other days, I'd get on just fine, but found the Dow Jones language—arcane commands for each function—to access current news or for a search for older stories just about impossible. If I were a researcher using the system everyday, I assume I would have learned these commands in the same way that years ago I learned the commands to operate the early versions of WordStar. But as a casual user, I just couldn't get the hang of the system and I canceled my subscription. But in 1995,

Dow Jones introduced the Windows-based versions of their service—now called Dow Jones News/Retrieval Private Investor Edition—that has made all the difference in the world. Now the on-line news service that has always offered unparalleled depth in current and archived news is actually easy to use.

But there's one new ease-of-use issue that needs to get factored in to the decision process when we're discussing on-line services: automation. Does the on-line service allow you to customize its software so that it will automatically execute an entire list of tasks with just one key stroke or click from you?

Dow Jones Private Investor Edition, for example, gives me the ability to create a new button on the toolbar that lets me automate a simple task that I perform frequently. By clicking on the "Add toolbar" function under "Edit," I can create a new button (complete with an icon that I chose from a list of about fifty) that will enable me to update the prices and get news alerts on all the stocks in my portfolio by clicking on that button. No more opening layers of menus and scrolling through choices. I can also create a button if I'm interested in following the changes in earnings estimates reported by Zacks for a specific stock. So I can create icons for Intel and Coca Cola that, when clicked, pull up current estimates on those stocks.

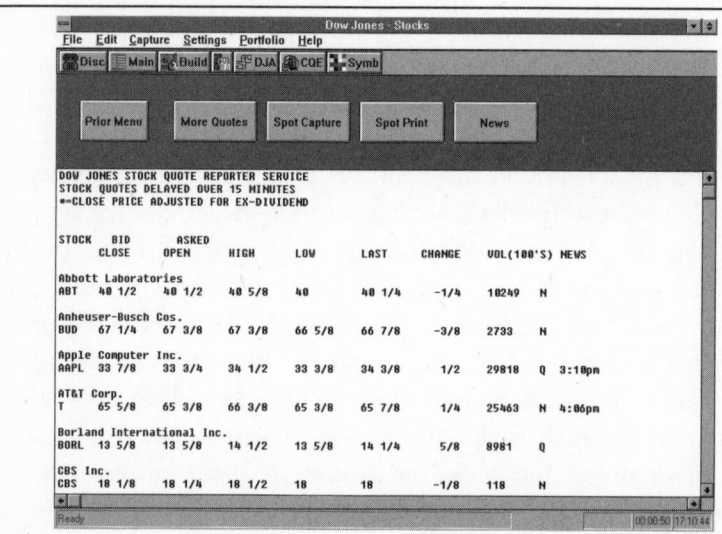

*Dow Jones News/Retrieval Private Investor Edition now uses a point and click interface to navigate its resources.* (*Courtesy Dow Jones Information Services*)

## Let an Agent Do the Dirty Work

Even that basic degree of automation saves me some work, but it pales beside the routines I can write for other on-line services, often using add-on software written expressly for that specific on-line service. You're likely to be seeing more and more of these programs and built-in routines—and you'll probably start hearing the more complex ones referred to as "agents." All kinds of programs now come with some kind of agent and the trend is likely to accelerate since both Apple (Apple Script) and Microsoft (Bob) are exploring the technology.

An agent is simply a software program, either freestanding or built in to a bigger program that fetches the kind of stories or information I've told it I want—without my supervision. Agents vary in their intelligence, with "stupid agents" able to do only exactly what they've been told to do and more "intelligent agents" able to exercise judgment and learn about my wants from examining past requests. Frankly, most current agents aren't very smart, but intelligent agents are clearly on the way, and a few of the current agents at least have the power to automate standing data requests. Even a good dumb agent can make an investor's life a lot easier. In the last year I've found useful agents for CompuServe, Prodigy, and the Internet, for example. (For a description of the new Internet agents, called spiders, see Chapter 9.)

Let me take the space here to tell you how one agent, PC Financial Network's Maximizer for Windows, works with Prodigy to download and chart stocks, to fetch current and historical quotes, to retrieve news and research from Pershing, a major Wall Street brokerage, and to keep a portfolio (with direct on-line trading if I want) all in one package.

Like most agents, getting this one hooked up correctly to the on-line service isn't as simple as it should be. Despite the fact that I'm already a Prodigy user with an established account, I have to exit the Maximizer program and access Prodigy manually to create an autologon nickname that changes the way I log on to the service.

That accomplished, I create lists (just like I did on Reuters Money Network) to tell the agent what quotes and company news I want regularly. I have to type in two lists—one for quotes and one for news— with pretty much the same companies. (Many times during this process I wish the agent were smarter so that I could avoid this painful duplication. Why can't the default simply assume that I want news on all the companies I ask for quotes on?)

But after that pain, the program does work as advertised. Using the slow 2400 baud modem in my laptop, I ask Prodigy for news and current quotes at 11:28 A.M. By 11:31 I have a clear spreadsheet style presentation of ticker symbol(but not name), last, net, open, high, low, volume (a big plus if you know what the average daily volume is), and date. I also get fifty-one news stories. The reader seems to be about as good as most are at finding stories that relate to my needs—none of the eight stories under the AAPL ticker symbol have anything to do with Apple Computer. The Gap story is an announcement of the regular 12-cent dividend. Most of the stories are from Dow Jones.

But some are actually valuable. I get a short notice that Brown Brothers Harriman analyst Robert Wilkes raised Motorola to buy from neutral, and I notice big block trades on Motorola and Intel.

Maximizer will let me download any of the investment forums on Prodigy—but it doesn't give me a way to automate reading the messages posted there or a way to separate the messages I'm interested in from those I don't care about. I haven't been able to find a tool that will let me do that on either Prodigy or America Online. CompuServe, however, provides Macintosh, Windows, and DOS versions of exactly that kind of program.

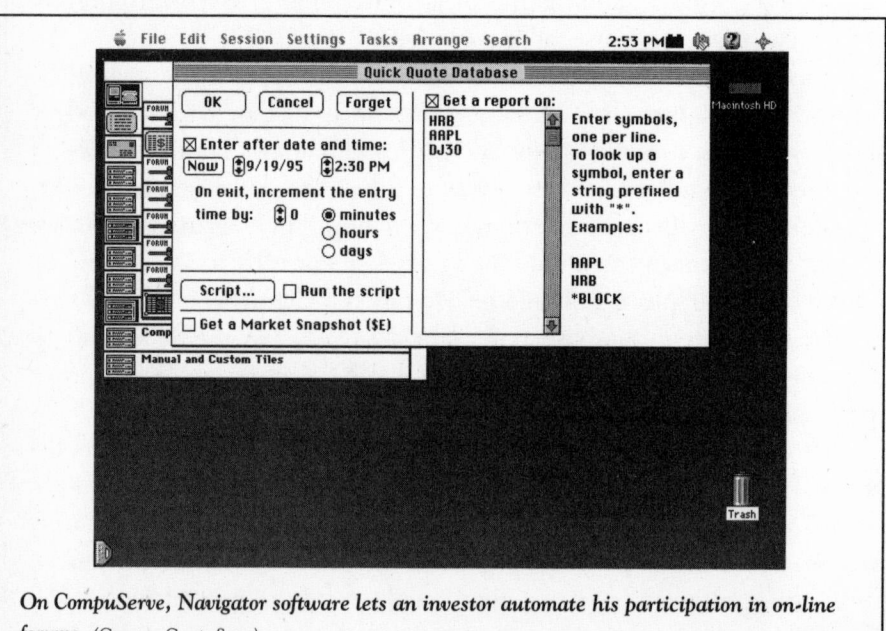

*On CompuServe, Navigator software lets an investor automate his participation in on-line forums.* (*Courtesy CompuServe*)

# BEST OF THE INTERNET I

**B**esides Edgar, the SEC's electronic depository of corporate files (address http://www.sec.gov) and Money.com (address http://money.com), both described in Chapter 4, the Internet is running over with good, bad, and mostly indifferent sources of financial information. These are among the best.

Interested in a complete and regularly updated list of brokerage firms in the U.S., Canada, Asia and Europe? Try Investment Brokerages Guide on the Internet (http://www.cs.cmu.edu:80/~jdg/invest_brokers.html) Compiled and updated by John Greiner at Carnegie-Mellon University, the list includes phone numbers, a brief description of services (including a notation if the brokerage is on-line) and a comparison of fees for several different kinds of trades for full service and discount retail and institutional firms.

Get key economic documents from the Philadelphia Federal Reserve Bank (http://www.libertynet.org/~fedreserv/fedpage.html). The bank's business outlook survey and its Mid-Atlantic manufacturing index are closely followed on Wall Street as indicators of basic strength in the economy.

The NETworth site (http://networth.galt.com) run by Galt Technologies—recently purchased by Intuit—offers information from mutual fund companies (prospectuses and performance data), Morningstar's database of more than 5,000 mutual funds, a real-time datafeed on market prices from Standard & Poor's, a weekly market outlook, and a listing (with some samples) of financial newsletters.

Morgan Stanley, an international investment bank that collects an extraordinary range of global financial information, has opened the Global Economic Forum on the Internet (http://www.ms.com). The World Wide Web site offers real-time economic analysis from economists in the U.S., Europe, Asia, and Latin America; performance statistics for developed and emerging markets updated daily (including Morgan Stanley's own benchmark EAFE and World indexes); historical charts and other data. The site was free through the end of 1995; the company was reevaluating that policy at press time. You'll need Adobe Acrobat to view the graphics, but you can download it from this page for free.

Using Navigator for the Macintosh, for example, I can create entire scripts that download quotes for the stocks in my portfolio, check to see if I have electronic mail and then download it, send any mail I've composed, and then check the forums that I've told the program I'm interested in visiting regularly—the Investors and NAIC forums, for example. When the Navigator signs on to these forums, it downloads a list of all message topics—in just the parts of the forum I've told it to check—and gets complete texts for those messages that I've highlighted in the prior session because they sounded intriguing. Doing all that takes the computer about twenty to thirty minutes, depending on how long I've let messages build up. I usually set the script's automatic timer to sign on to CompuServe at 2 A.M. or so. I can then view what my nets have caught in the morning at my leisure—and off-line, too, so I don't run up usage hours with CompuServe while I read the messages.

---

### TIPS ON THE TOOLS

## BEST OF THE INTERNET II

**P**AWWS, Portfolio Accounting World-Wide (http://pawws.secapl.com) is an attempt to create a comprehensive investment center on the World Wide Web. Run by Security APL, a provider of portfolio management software for professional investors, PAWWS combines delayed quotes, basic securities research, and three on-line brokerages (The Net Investor, National Discount Brokerage, and Jack White). Using PAWWS itself is free (although you will need to register), but some services—Ford Investment Services and Data Transmission Network, for example—charge subscription fees. For $5.95 a month, Data Transmission Network brings an investor company-specific news and earnings reports in real time; another $4 a month adds "Daybreak News" from national and international wires. (At press time PAWWS was about to add real-time quotes from North America Quotations.) You'll need a Netscape web browser to use the brokerage services. PAWWS lets the investor create a user name and an encrypted password for trading stocks. That's supposed to keep account numbers secure, but given the recently discovered holes in Netscape security, I wouldn't count on it. (For more on security and on-line brokerage services, see Chapter 7.)

IDD, the publisher of Wall Street industry journal *Investment Dealers Digest*, the *IPO Reporter*, *Nest Egg* magazine, and the Tradeline database (see review in Chapter 3), is offering bits and pieces of its information kingdom on its World Wide Web home page (http://nestegg.iddis.com/). The page includes articles from *Nest Egg*, a monthly calendar of important investment dates (the next numbers from Commerce on housing starts, for example), and data on mutual funds from Tradeline (performance leaders for periods as short as a week). Net Diver, IDD's collection of links with other Web pages of interest, is one of the most eclectic on the Web: the inclusion of the Internet Bartender's Guide seems curious unless the company believes investing (or reading investment information on the Internet, perhaps) drives people to drink.

Money and Investing Update from the *Wall Street Journal* (http://update.wsj.com) is still under development, but it's already a promising site that does more than deliver an electronic version of the *Wall Street Journal* the night before the paper hits the streets. Hot links in the stories are connected to files on a company's background, financal condition, and stock performance. Currently the site is free, although you'll have to register.

Want to be on the cutting edge of financial research and get solid investment information, too? Try the Experimental Stock Market run by the financial wizards in training at MIT (http://www.ai.mit.edu/stocks.html). Same day price and volume charts for 300 NYSE stocks and lots of intriguing data on the behavior of the market and individual stocks. J.P. Morgan, the international banking power, produces another cutting edge site (http://www.jpmorgan.com). Here investors will find an ongoing discussion of Morgan's proprietary Riskmetrics system for calculating the risk of fixed-income investments. The site includes Riskmetrics data that can be downloaded, as well as index data on commodities, currencies, emerging market bonds, and government bonds. And for the investor interested in the nuts and bolts of investing, Quote.com (http://www.quote.com) offers subscriptions to news from Reuters ($9.95 a month), analyst estimates from Zacks ($14.95 a month), and other data. With Quote.com's basic subscription ($9.95 a month), an investor can also download 200 quotes a day and keep 1 on-line portfolio up to date. More expensive subscriptions include more daily quotes, tracking on more portfolios, charts, and historical data.

# SHAREWARE

**A**dd cheap software to the list of great things available on-line. Some of this is freeware—programs written as a hobby and then donated to the world—but much of the best is shareware—programs available for a free trial with the understanding that if you like it, you'll pay the author a reasonable fee. Here are some worth checking out:

▪ **PFROI.** A solid portfolio manager that computes portfolio and security returns using internal rate of return (both before and after taxes). Registration $39. Look for it in the American Association of Individual Investors software library on America Online.

▪ **Capital Gainz.** Another good portfolio management program. Calculates gain/loss and tracks reinvested dividends. Look for it on PC Ohio bulletin board (216–291–3307 voice and 216–381–3320 modem).

▪ **Mutual Fund Manager.** This program will track a mutual fund portfolio and generate weekly charting reports. Look for it on CompuServe in the Investors Forum libraries.

▪ **Mutual Fund Tracker.** Test the buy and sell signals generated by this

## AGENTS SAVE TIME, BUT THEY KILL COMMUNITY

But while agents make it easier for investors to gather lots of information from the forums and chat areas of the on-line services, they actually make it harder to figure out what that information means. Let me show you want I mean . . . When I first signed up for my current Internet service on Pipeline, I was intrigued by Pipeline's "newsbot"—a news robot, get it?—that would allow me to filter the postings in one of the gabbiest sections of the Internet, the UseNet news groups. I can tell the newsbot which groups to check regularly (the "misc.investing" areas) and I can even ask it to search for news by subject, or keyword, or even by author. During a time when I was researching Intel, I asked the newsbot to pull up all references in these newsgroups to Intel. (Unfortunately, the program didn't give me any way to specify that the post must be in English. I'm still looking for someone to translate several seemingly intelligent posts in what I think is Swedish.)

But I've found that I don't use this newsbot very often. Random messages, even when on the subject and in English, aren't terribly useful. I don't know the speaker, nor the context, nor the reasoning behind a conclusion. By downloading pieces of interesting discussions I was getting just the illusion of information. I had data, but I couldn't interpret it.

Think about how you get useful information in a face-to-face discussion. The more you know about the individuals involved, the more information you can derive from their comments. You know Joe's agenda, so you can put his description of the new corporate plan in context. You understand that when he criticizes the budget, he's really talking about the cuts that his department has suffered. When Susan analyzes the projected sales figures, you know from other conversations and meetings what methods she

program using its "what if" function. Also on CompuServe in the Investors Forum libraries.

If the software libraries on CompuServe and PC Ohio, and at America Online's Motley Fool and American Association of Individual Investors don't have the shareware you want, try the Internet's Virtual Software Library (http://vsl.cnet.com), a database of 130,000 programs from the largest shareware and freeware archives on the Internet, combined with good tools for searching and downloading. All this has been packaged as a World Wide Web home page, so it's relatively easy to use. Registration is required, but it's free.

uses, how good those methods are, and how likely she is to have slanted her figures. I can state a general rule: The amount of useful information I derive from a such a session is directly proportional to the degree that all these people—myself included—form a community with a shared history.

## ON-LINE AS WELL, THE MOST USEFUL INFORMATION COMES FROM PEOPLE YOU KNOW

That's also true of the electronic meeting places on-line—and perhaps to an even greater degree since the method of communication in these forums has been reduced to printed words, leaving out all the verbal and nonverbal clues that help us shade meanings. The oft-repeated comparison between electronic and real communities is more than just metaphor or hyperbole. It captures an essential truth about what makes some of these places worth not just visiting, but belonging to. The discussion areas on the Internet and on Prodigy, CompuServe, and America Online were originally modeled on the discussions among CB radio owners and earlier direct-dial computer bulletin boards. These forums were intended to be places where like-minded individuals could meet to share opinions, news, and questions. They would be like a cocktail party or a town meeting or a small town general store. Sign on regularly and get to know the regulars. Become a regular. Join a community.

Most times now when I sign on to one of these areas I find it hard to recognize this original impulse. Many forums have degenerated into babble with too many new faces, too many bores who don't want to learn or follow any rules, and too many con-men and women who want to score a quick something, be it money or a cheap thrill. Sorting out the news from the useful information in areas like this simply isn't worth it—and I'm not even sure that it's possible. And, if my observations during the last year are any indication, once an area goes bad and enough jerks drive out the good people, it cannot recover.

Using an agent, unintelligently, only makes this problem worse. A good agent or collection of agents can make it easy for me to mine forum after forum for interesting topics. I probably don't have the time to visit America Online, CompuServe, Prodigy, and the Internet's UseNet groups if I have to do it manually. But with agents, I can download all these discussions when I'm asleep, filter them for interesting topics so I don't have to read every message, and then just read the messages I want. But while this lets me download lots of bytes, I don't think it gets me much information. Because my agent does all the communicating for me, I never become a member of any of these communities.

## Advice from Dysfunctional Communities

Let me show you what I mean by using the example of the investment forum called Money Talk on Prodigy. The board is divided into sections and I can select just those areas that interest me. If I sign on to Stocks, for example, I get a list of topics that have been discussed recently. I start with a topic where I already know the answer and click on "Intel to split when." That gives me the question and then I click "Read replies." "Record date was 5/19. Day split shares will begin trading is June 19."

That's straightforward enough. Next, scanning down the list, I pick a topic that's almost always trouble on the forums, penny stocks. This is a note on a penny stock, PERS, from Bob Monski to Bob Monski (reply-

**TIPS ON THE TOOLS**

# DON'T FORGET ABOUT BULLETIN BOARDS

In these days when all the talk is about the Internet and the World Wide Web, a service that requires an investor to dial up a dedicated phone number to get information from just one source seems positively anachronistic. But investors shouldn't neglect what once would have been called "electronic bulletin boards."

For example, try MoneyLetter Plus, the electronic version of *Money-Letter*. (To subscribe call 508-881-6252. The newsletter is also available through CompuServe. A subscription costs $49 for six months.)

MoneyLetter Plus is organized like a newsletter. There's "News from the Editors," market commentary, profiles of income mutual funds, and a model portfolio. In mid-March 1995, for instance, the newsletter ran a profile of the Strong Money Market fund, which had become *MoneyLetter*'s top money market fund in December by waiving fees and by guessing right on the economy. The Bond Market Insight feature issues buy and sell signals for bonds and bond sectors and recommends mutual funds for each strategy.

Two free bulletin boards worth trying are the Economics Bulletin Board, the deepest and most comprehensive single source of economic data in the electronic realm (202-482-2167 or 202-482-3870, or use the Internet gopher una.hh.lib.umich.edu) and the Federal Reserve's central data mine, run by the St. Louis Federal Reserve bank (314-621-1824 or Internet gopher town.hall.org.Federal Reserve Board).

In the pay-to-play realm, PC Ohio offers a tremendous wealth of investment data and investment shareware. Memberships range from $52 to $139 a year (216-291-3307 voice and 216-381-3320 modem).

The Free Financial Network bulletin board is one of the best bargains on-line: massive amounts of historical stock prices at reasonable prices (212-752-8660).

ing to his own posts) touting this stock with, he says $1.50 in cash a share and selling for 1.00. He recommends buying up to 1.09, "if you haven't already loaded up." He notes that the company has no business, just lots of cash. I know there's no way to keep stock touts off a service—and I don't even know if Bob Monski is a tout—but I'm disappointed that nobody bothered to flame this guy or at least call him to task by asking him to reveal his connections and affiliations. Exactly that happens on a fairly regular basis in the Investor's Forum on CompuServe. The Prodigy forum isn't doing a good job of policing itself. It's not acting as a community.

On the Internet I can find discussion groups in a network called UseNet on everything from coffee to an intriguingly named section called "christnet.dinosaur.barney." I leave that for another day, though, and go to the investment area, where I find areas named misc.invest, misc.invest.funds, misc.invest.stocks, and misc.invest.technical. I ask my software to get me the fifty most recent messages in misc.invest.stocks.

Some of the discussion is intelligent and well informed. I read an exchange of messages on how to play the expected success of Windows 95, (buying puts on AOL for example), thoughts on why the retail sector may be picking up (rotation from high-tech), and an informed refutation of the *Barron's* blast on Calgene. But there's too much here that I simply can't judge. One post recommends International Gaming Technology. "In agreement with my calculations, this stock is on the way to hit $22.00" What's the method? Is it one that I would find valid? Of course, I can ask, but that consumes time. I'd prefer to know before I start my discussion that we share at least a basic system on how to value stocks.

Now I can use an agent to download both the UseNet and Prodigy discussion groups, but is it worth it? A random list of messages won't give me much useful information. To turn these into useful investment tools, I'd have to spend time getting to know the people who post regularly, adding my own two cents from time to time so that my electronic neighbors get to know me, and building up that shared history that in my opinion defines a community.

## What Makes an On-line Site a Home?

Some forums are too diffuse, too random, too artificial—like the manufactured towns that suddenly spring up in America's suburbs—to reward that effort. That's exactly why I read The Motley Fool, hosted by David and Tom Gardner on America Online, the Investors and NAIC forums on CompuServe, and the AAII section on AOL instead of UseNet and Prodigy. It costs me money to subscribe to the on-line services that host these discussions among, mostly, nonprofessional investors. I could get the equivalent of these electronic communities on the Internet gratis. But instead, I fork over my bucks. In effect, I am willing to pay to talk to some people and yet I can't be bothered to talk to others for free. Why?

The answer is pretty simple: these are all healthy communities, sometimes because they are run by intelligent leaders and sometimes because a self-organizing community has developed that quietly enforces its own laws and rules of behavior. All of the four areas I read regularly, in fact, have strong personalities (sometimes individuals and sometimes collective) who control the level of discussion and keep the information content high.

I've already described The Motley Fool in chapter 2, so let me tell you about another on-line community, the Investors Forum on CompuServe.

I'm not much of a bond investor, but I like to keep up with that market and occasionally I add a bond to my portfolio. Over the years that I've read the CompuServe Investors Forum, I've learned to trust one of the forum's regulars, let's call her "Sue" so she won't get buried under e-mail, a Florida-based money manager on that subject. From reading her posts, I feel I know her conservative style of building a portfolio and I respect her level of skill. I've never met her, know nothing about her as a person. But as an investor she's a known quantity to me and I know how to interpret her comments on rates and maturities.

Fred is another familiar character. He's a sysop, a position peculiar to CompuServe among the commercial on-line services. The service pays him a fee to patrol the discussion on this forum, keep it moving, prevent abuses, add intelligent comment. He's not so much a CompuServe employee as a leader of this electronic salon.

Fred is fascinated by heavily mathematical, data-dependent studies. When I see him weighing in on a topic that someone else has posted, I ask my agent to get the entire conversation back to the beginning so I can see what has excited his interest. For example, in 1994 *Worth* ran a column by newsletter writer James Stack criticizing the studies that recommended a buy and hold strategy over an attempt to move in and out of the market to reduce risk. A CompuServe member I didn't know posted his attempt to reconstruct Stack's data. Fred responded in an effort to explain some discrepancies, which then started a short discussion on the effect on total return of even a few days of delay in following a buy or sell signal. But it's voices like Sue's and Fred's that keep this community a cut above other on-line areas.

As in real life, communities like this are hard to find. When you find one, my advice is cherish it—and work hard to become a member. The payback is worth it.

## Reviews

### America Online

America Online Inc., 8619 Westwood Center Drive, Vienna, VA 22182, 800-827-6364.

Versions available: Windows (version 2.5 requires 4MB RAM), Macintosh (version 2.6 requires 8MB of RAM).

Modem Speeds Available: 2400 baud to 28.8 kbps.

Cost structure: $9.95 a month for five hours ($2.95 each additional hour).

Internet and Web Access: Yes.

Technical support: 800-827-3338, 24 hours a day, seven days a week.

Strengths: Morningstar's mutual fund and stock information is a formidible one-two punch for investors. Add in earnings estimates from First Call and the sites by the Motley Fool and the American Association for Individual Investors, and America Online, which once trailed far behind Prodigy and CompuServe in serving investors, now matches up well with competing services. Possibly the strongest service for investors interesting in reading magazines and publications on-line: *Business Week, Investors Business Daily, Worth, Consumer Reports, San Jose Mercury News, Chicago Tribune, Orlando Sentinel,* and *New York Times.*

Weaknesses: News on the market is skimpy and slow. Markets-at-a-glance area gives major averages transmitted with a delay, but no indication of length of delay. (Everything besides the major averages is information from the day before.) General investor chat is not that well informed or useful. Lack of a software program to allow unattended downloading and then off-line reading of discussion in chat areas makes this service less convenient to use than CompuServe.

Special features: Once the best Internet connection and browser software of the three major on-line services; now CompuServe and Prodigy have just about caught up.

Tricks of the trade: America Online has been on an extended growth binge—it now claims five million members—that has made it frustratingly difficult to get on America Online at peak hours (anytime in the evening after about 6:30 until around 11). When the traffic jam seems endless, it's worth trying a detour. Everyone, of course, wants to sign on at the fastest modem speed possible—it makes everything from downloads to chat so much faster. But that also means that the fastest channels—phone numbers for connecting modems at speeds above 9600—get clogged first. Try a slower speed connection. Of course, all your communication with the network will be slower, but that's still less frustrating than not getting connected at all.

For investors, America Online has long been tall on splashy graphics and short on content. No more. Join a major upgrading to Morningstar's offerings on mutual funds and stocks with the addition of earnings estimates from First Call to the strong investment forums run by The Motley Fool and the American Association of Individual Investors, and America Online's offerings now almost match on CompuServe, traditionally the strongest on-line service for investors. Morningstar's mutual fund reports are now more detailed, including information on the top ten issues in a fund's portfolio. The company has also put much of the information found in its U.S. Equities product on-line. The service now offers financial statements on selected companies from the Securities and Exchange Commission's electronic database, Edgar, and from Disclosure, plus historical quotes from Prophet. Still, if I had to pick just one service—without regard for cost—for investment information, America Online, while clearly now worth consideration, wouldn't be my first choice. CompuServe has more information and its Investors Forum is still the best financial conversation on-line. Prodigy offers Market Guide, an unmatched database on company fundamentals. On the other hand, if cost is an issue, America Online probably goes to the head of the class: the service doesn't tack on extra charges for its investment information the way that Prodigy and CompuServe do.

The lack of an automated navigator makes this a cumbersome system to use for chatting with other investors (since you can't set the software for automatic and unattended downloading of discussions of topics that interest you during late-night hours for off-line reading at your convenience) and the service's current and historical quotes features are not the first choice of any software programs that I'm aware of.

## COMPUSERVE

CompuServe Inc., 5000 Arlington Centre Blvd., Columbus, OH 43220, 800-609-1674.

Versions available: Windows (version 2.0.1 requires 4MB RAM), Macintosh (version 2.4.1 requires 4MB RAM).

Modem Speeds Available: 300 baud to 28.8 kbps.

Cost structure: $9.95 a month for five hours ($2.95 each aditional hour).

Internet and Web Access: Yes.

Technical support: 800-848-8990, 24 hours a day, seven days a week.

Strengths: Among the big three, CompuServe is the least likely to frustrate an investor with constant busy signals. The company has done a good job of keeping its growth in membership from outrunning the number of available communications lines. Despite plain vanilla text treatment of menus, their intelligent design makes them easy to use without constantly jumping from list to list (a problem on Prodigy, for example). The service works with the best newsbot among the three major on-line services and includes an incredible array of news services. CompuServe also covers all the bases for fundamental investors with earnings estimates, historical quotes, and research from Standard & Poor's and Value Line.

Weaknesses: Surcharges for many services make pricing difficult to understand and make many services expensive. For example, S&P Online charges $1 for a company report, $2 for a master list menu with three choices, and $2 each for four investment ideas.

Special features: Despite lagging behind other services such as America Online in graphics and Internet access, CompuServe does the best job among the on-line services of providing ways to make access easy and routine. The navigators and other programs that allow the automated downloading of quotes and discussion topics, for instance, make it easy to adapt this service to any user's schedule.

Tricks of the trade: The computer corner of the Investors Forum is the best place on-line to ask other users for help on investment software— whether it's advice on what to buy or a technical question on how to download data for MetaStock. Software representatives often troll this area looking for comments and questions about their products. You can find most of the major companies in another forum on CompuServe, the Financial Software Vendors Forum.

It's an indication of how deep the investment information is on CompuServe that I can give just passing mention to Fundwatch by *Money* magazine, and the Investors and NAIC forums mentioned in the chapter above, and still not have space to list everything that CompuServe offers. If, as an investor, I had to limit myself to just one on-line service provider, this would be it. But be warned, many of the really useful features come with an extra surcharge on top of your monthly subscription.

Basic services—the free areas that come with your monthly $9.95 fee—include Basic Quotes (free current quotes by ticker symbol), a basic company snapshot (too basic to use for more than getting a mailing address), the Hoover Company Database (found on American On-line, too), and a few other items such as a loan analyzer and a very useful issue/symbol look-up function. There's not much available here to make the heart beat faster. Basic Quotes is the most useful feature and not an inconsequential one—a lot of investment software programs, from Quicken to Stock Analyst, use CompuServe to update prices automatically.

CompuServe doesn't really begin to shine until an investor enters the areas with extra fees (which can be quite reasonable or extremely expensive—always check the clearly posted on-line information about prices first.)

I've listed most of the specific functions that an investor ought to check out in the best and worst of CompuServe boxes in this chapter, but I haven't discussed two features that set CompuServe apart from its on-line competitors. CompuServe puts historical prices on-line. The fee structure that CompuServe has set up (5 cents a quote) makes this service too expensive for investors who are building databases for technical or statistical analysis (any of the CD-ROMs of data listed in Chapter 8 are a better deal). But for the investor who wants to check an occasional price, update a portfolio kept in software by adding all the paid dividends on an issue, or check on splits of an issue that the investor doesn't track regularly, then CompuServe's historical pricing area is probably the best computerized source.

CompuServe's Executive News Service allows you to build searches of the incredible set of news services offered: Associated Press, Reuters, PRnewswire, and Dow Jones. It also lets you set up clipping folders. The newsbot will automatically file all stories with INTC (for Intel) in an Intel folder, for example. Folders can also be built about topics.

### DOW JONES NEWS RETRIEVAL/PRIVATE INVESTOR EDITION

Dow Jones Business Information Services, P.O. Box 300, Princeton, NJ 08543, 800-815-5100.

Versions available: Windows (version 3.2a); Macintosh (version 3.2a requires 8MB RAM).

Modem Speeds Available: 2400 baud to 14.4 kbps.

Cost structure: Basic charge of $29.95 a month covers eight hours of off-peak (7:01 P.M.–6 A.M. weekdays, anytime on weekends) use of wide range of basic services. (6 cents per minute after 8 hours). Surcharges for other data providers such as Disclosure and Investext.

Internet and Web Access: None.

Technical support: 609-452-1511, 8 A.M.–midnight, M–F, 9 A.M.–6 P.M., Sat.

Strengths: A strong combination of in-depth archives of old stories and a flexible search program that can search for news by subject, stock symbol, company name, and matrix (a combination of region, industry, topic, and stock symbol) make this the best on-line news service for the investor who can live with its restricted hours. The program combines quote service and portfolio tracking with news stories in a way that gently guides an investor through a company's recent history.

Weaknesses: The manual I received gives a user almost no help in learning how to use the new Windows version. The user's guide lists the old, uniquely confusing Dow Jones commands for News Retrieval—although it does define what each function does—and I couldn't find any simple, comprehensive set of instructions about how to get the most out of the program. A tutorial would be helpful. The one guide that is customized for this version—a four-page folder—tells a user little more than how to install and set up a portfolio for prices and news. The program leaves the user alone to discover how to use it best. Although the interface of this Windows version is a vast step forward, the program still needs a little work. For example, the user can't look up symbols from the portfolio menu, so to enter new stock he or she either has to exit to "Symbol, look up" or have symbols already. An odd setup requires a user to build different portfolios for stocks and mutual funds (even equity funds).

Special features: Includes a general on-line encyclopedia, MCI mail, movie reviews, weather, and the Official Airline Guide.

Tricks of the trade: Don't assume all the surcharged services are too expensive for you. Some are. For example, Dow Jones QuickSearch, which generates a report on a company by combining data from enhanced quotes, Dow Jones news service, S&P, Zacks, Media General, Disclosure, Corporate Watch, and Investext, runs $49 per report plus extra charges for Investext pages. But others can be reasonable. Tradeline, from Investment Dealers Digest, with daily pricing back to fifteen years on 120,000 U.S. and Canadian issues (plus another 25,000 international issues) costs $5 per screening plus $.25 an issue plus $.05 a line on domestic stocks.

Finally the software has caught up with the content. After years in which users ran screaming from Dow Jones News Retrieval in despair, cursing its quirks and difficulties, Dow Jones has produced a program that is as easy to use as it is rich in resources for investors. This is now the best after-business-hours on-line service for news and financial data.

Just click on big, clear graphical buttons to get news from more than 550 publications (with archives stretching back into the 1980s in many cases); company and industry information from Zacks (earnings estimates); Media General Financial Services (price, volume, and fundamental data on 5400 NYSE, AMEX, and OTC companies); and Standard & Poor's. For more information see the description in this chapter.

## Dow Jones Personal Journal

Dow Jones Business Information Services, P.O. Box 300, Princeton, NJ 08543, 800-291-9382.

Versions available: Windows (version 2.0), Macintosh version scheduled for 1996.

Modem Speeds Available: 2400 baud to 14.4 kbps.

Cost structure: Basic charge of $12.95 a month covers one "edition" each day.

Internet and Web Access: None.

Strengths: You will get stories before they appear in the print version of the *Wall Street Journal*. For example, Personal Journal gave me news of the merger of the First Financial and First Data Corp (one of the stocks on my watch list) at 8:25 A.M. on June 13—before the market opened. I might have been able to use this information to catch part

of the stock's jump from $76.75 to $82. Markets section has good information on stock indexes for day as well as currencies and bonds.
Weaknesses: News reader seems very, what shall I say, selective. Some days
I got lots of stories on one of the companies on my news list and none
on any other company. Other days I got no stories at all. Special features: Besides creating a news list of ten companies, Personal Journal
will allow the user to build a similar list for favorite Journal columns and
features for regular downloading.

Not bad, but not very useful for the serious investor—it's too scaled
down. Only one "edition" a day is free—the next and every other access costs 50 cents. The software only allows me to get news on ten
companies and limits quotes to twenty-five stocks and mutual funds.
It's hard to imagine that any investor who wants to keep up with the
news would be able to live with these restrictions. Personal Journal is
probably best suited to the reader who finds the *Wall Street Journal* too
time-consuming to get through. The summary of business and world
news is adequate for the skimmer and the quotes that crawl across the
top of the screen in a ticker-like format do give the user a sense of the
market.

### eWorld

Apple Computer, Infinite Loop, Cupertino, CA 95014, 800-776-2333.
Versions available: Macintosh (version 1.1).
Modem Speeds Available: 2400 baud to 14.4 kbps.
Cost structure: $8.95 for 8 hours a month.
Internet and Web Access: Yes.
Technical Support: 800-775-4556 (6–8, M–F, PST).
Strengths: The eWorld town, the most attractive and intuitive opening
screen of any of the services, makes it easy and unintimidating to get
around in this service. Market update menu in Dow Jones area has
stories on market—topics on one day were Dow falls 43.23 to
4369.00, NYSE most actives at close, money rates, Treasuries end
lower. Daily newsletters from Dow Jones cover Asia and technology
quickly, but in depth. News browser has great search engine—cover-
ing last thrity days; it will often pick out stories skipped by other
browsers, even those with access to Dow Jones material. eWorld's
stock quotes function is fast and the format offers price-to-earnings

ratios, yields, and 52-week highs and lows besides the usual data. A portfolio function allows automatic updating of prices.

Weaknesses: There's not much *there* there, and the lack of content has kept the service from attracting many users, which in turn means that there's only a very small community of investors to talk to. Apple has decided to convert this service to an Internet gateway in 1996. Watch to see what survives the transition.

Special features: Since this service is owned and operated by Apple Computer, this is a great source of help for any Macintosh user. Apple promises next-business-day answers to technical questions posted on eWorld.

Tricks of the trade: eWorld's village interface characterizes the spirit of this on-line service. eWorld watches over its forums with the concerned eye of a small-town schoolmarm. That may make the service too constricting for some, but it does mean that content tends to be polite. This is a good place for a newcomer to on-line communications to get comfortable—the reception will likely be gentle—before trying the more rough-and-tumble world of the Internet.

Apple is converting eWorld to an Internet gateway so it's unclear what the service will eventually look like. Before the conversion, a user signing on to eWorld found himself in a small village. There was a Newsstand, eMail Center, Info booth, Community Center, Business and Finance Plaza, and more. To get to the kind of information you need, all you had to do was click on the appropriate building. Unfortunately, most of these buildings had very few tenants. Fortunately, some of them—Dow Jones news and a library of corporate reports—were rather useful to the investor. In the Business and Finance Plaza a click pulled up a screen with wonderful color graphics, but only four icons: Corporate Intelligence, Dow Jones Business & Financial News, eWorld Market Quotes, and KRT Business News (primarily news on currencies). The quotes function used the familiar "type a symbol get a quote" format. (A user could also set up a standing portfolio.)

Under the Corporate Intelligence icon, a user found a library of 3,500 10K's (the annual report every company files with the Securities and Exchange Commission). Hoover's Handbook also supplied very basic facts on 8,800 companies (address, phone, Website address, ticker and fiscal year-end were the most useful items), as well as more detailed profiles on a narrower universe of well-known corporations. Right now downloading a 10K is free, but eWorld plans to begin charging $5 to $10 per report sometime in the near future. (The reports are repackaged from the SEC's Edgar database with formatting that makes them easier to read with a standard word processing program. Whether it's worth paying the price for information that's free elsewhere on the Internet probably depends on how comfortable an investor is with the Internet.)

The Dow Jones page was one of the best news readers on-line— falling just short of Dow Jones News Retrieval itself and on a par with Reuters' WealthBuilder. Users got a choice of preselected story lists called Front Page Business News, Market Updates, and News. Or you could select news stories by company or industry, ask for editor's choice (top stories from Dow Jones publications), or request custom services, which provided daily e-mail of news and corporate reports. (Custom services were pricey—$50 a month to set up custom clipping folders for up to 5 companies, for example). All with neat and superior graphics.

### PC FINANCIAL NETWORK'S MAXIMIZER FOR WINDOWS

Ret-Tech Software Inc., 151 Deer Lane, Barrington, IL 60010, 800-729-6245.

Versions available: Windows only.

Requirements: Windows 3.1 or higher, 4MB RAM, Windows version of Prodigy, and 2MB free space on hard drive.

Cost: $54.90.

Guarantee: None

Demo or sample: None.

Technical support: 800-TALK-PCF, 8 A.M.–6 P.M., or Ret-Tech Software bulletin board at 708-382-4340.

User Newsletter or Online Forum: See Prodigy's Money Talk forum, Investment Tools topic.

Updated: Daily.

Strengths: If you have an on-line brokerage account with the PC Financial Network, this program will give you an extraordinary degree of communication with the brokerage firm, including daily views on the market and research from Pershing, the discount brokerage behind PC Financial Network. (For a review of this on-line brokerage see chapter 7.) The technical analysis part of this package is exceptionally strong, with more than twenty-one available types of study from moving averages to stochastics. In adddition, package includes daily and historical quotes and company news.

Weaknesses: Setup is likely to be slow due to the constant need to exit the program and enter Prodigy to verify exact names and addresses for Prodigy functions. Charts are the strength of the package, but data is expensive—about $5 a chart.

Tricks of the trade: Installation has one major quirk. Although the program is installed in C:\MAXWIN, the default path for data is C:\Pro. The user must tell the program where the data is installed, since, oddly enough, without instruction the program will not look in the default area (C:\Pro) but in MAXWIN. A warning: setting up the Maximizer to use the autologon function of Prodigy can remove basic system security. Now anyone can log on without the need for either ID or password. Autologon is certainly easier, but I wouldn't recommend it if your computer is installed in a location where the security of your Prodigy or brokerage account is an issue.

In theory this is a wonderful program. It works with Prodigy and the on-line brokerage PC Financial Network to give the user a complete package from downloaded quotes (current and historical) and technical charts to on-line brokerage, portfolio tracing, news, and research from Pershing, PC Financial Network's brokerage parent. In practice, the program is riddled with annoying failures that make setting it up more difficult than need be. Once over that hurdle, though, this program is a sound, basic all-in-one package for anyone who trades on-line with PC Financial Network. For those who don't have an account there, the program's functions are duplicated elsewhere more elegantly and more cheaply.

Signing on isn't as easy as advertised. I had to exit the program and access Prodigy manually to create an autologon nickname. I also had to know my Prodigy directory path (C:\Prodigy) in order to complete my communications setup—which meant I had to exit the program again and check file manager in Windows. The manual is not very good—it doesn't provide a straightforward explanation of how to use the different functions of the program.

To get news and quotes I have to create two lists of symbols. (Why can't the default simply assume that I want news on all the companies I want quotes for?) Again a problem. I have to use Prodigy symbols. No way to call up a list of them that I can see except by exiting the program, again, and signing on to Prodigy again. Once that problem is solved I get quotes (a clear spreadsheet style presentation of ticker, last, net, open, high, low, volume, and date) and news. The news reader is not particularly good at finding relevant stories for the ticker symbols I've provided—in other words, it's as good as most.

I can also add automatic access to Prodigy bulletin boards. Again, I have to exit program and enter Prodigy to get a list of the exact names of the bulletin boards I want. Quite a contrast to a program such as Navigator on CompuServe that gives me the choices from inside the program.

Technical charts are a strength of Maximizer, as you might expect, given that the program was written by David Rettger, the author of the MegaTech technical analysis program. Most all-in-one packages, such as Reuters Money Network, provide only a few kinds of charts and skimp on the number of indicators that an investor can use. Not Maximizer. Its MaxCharts function provides a library of twenty-five technical indicators. And for a program that's so clumsy about other features, MaxCharts is easy to use. A user sets chart parameters from a pull-down menu of choices—for example, by asking for 200 days and a volume and then moving the mouse arrow over the desired chart type and double-clicking. Simply moving the arrow over the chart type without clicking produces a blurb that describes this specific type of technical study.

Ret-Tech says that future versions will include e-mail management for Prodigy and the Internet.

## PRODIGY

Prodigy, 632 Broadway, New York, NY 10012, 800-776-3449.
Versions available: Windows (version 1.2) Macintosh (version 3.1).
Modem Speeds Available: 2400 baud to 14.4 kbps.
Cost: $9.95 for five hours of service. Additional hours are $2.95 each. No extra charges for e-mail. (The Value Plan at $14.95 a month offers unlimited access to core features and five hours of access to "Plus" features. The 30/30 plan at $29.95 offers 30 free hours of all Prodigy Features.) Strategic Investor accounts (an additional $19.95 a month) have unlimited access to Stock Hunter and up to fifty company reports per week. For non-Strategic Investor accounts company reports cost $1.95 each for Quick Reports and $3.95 for full reports.
Internet and Web Access: World Wide Web Browser requires 9600 or

higher modem. (World Wide Web Browser is a timed feature; hours spent on the Internet count toward your monthly time limit.) In addition, users of Prodigy's Internet access ramp have to sign a disclaimer testifying, among other things, that they're 18. As of early 1996, only the Windows version had full World Wide Web access.

Strengths: Strategic Investor provides relatively cheap access to the superb Market Guide database of fundamental information on more than 6,000 stocks—probably the best single source of this type online. Internet interface has solid well-designed bookmark feature that lets a user "remember" addresses of favorite Internet sites.

Weaknesses: Among the slowest of the on-line services with significantly longer lags between screens than either CompuServe or America Online. While users aren't quite as likely to get a busy signal as they are with America Online when they try to sign on, the service delivers significantly more busy signals than CompuServe. Investment information is heavily reliant on a few sources, *Investor's Business Daily* for stocks and *Kiplinger's* for personal finance and investment strategy. That's okay for investors who are attuned to those sources, but it can be a problem for stock pickers who don't subscribe to the momentum theories of *Investor's Business Daily*.

Special features: Ads everywhere. Every screen seems to have a sponsor. While no one is forcing me to click on any of these messages, I still find it annoying to be assaulted on-line, too.

Tricks of the trade: Investors who know how to run a spreadsheet can get around the limitations of the Stock Hunter screening program provided in Strategic Investor. Stock Hunter's set of tools is too weak to let you construct precisely the stock screen you need, but you can use it to first limit the universe by applying its basic rules, and then download the data on the stocks it picks out from Market Guide into a spreadsheet for further analysis. It's easy to write your own rules in Excel or Lotus. (See Chapter 9 for some suggestions.)

There's a kind of breathless tipster quality to Prodigy that results from more than just the constant yammer of ads from the bottom of the screen. For example, one day when I clicked on the Business/Finance icon, I started off with straightforward business and market news, like that on CompuServe or America Online: Dow down 16.25 at 4179.13, housing starts off 7.9, GM satisfied with Saturn, a sprinkle of personal finance advice, such as a story on the best values in credit cards.

But other buttons promise me more—and then really don't deliver. "Wall Street Edge: the Hottest Newsletter tips," one says. When I go to this item to read about the hottest newsletter tips, I discover that I've really called up an ad for a digest of investment newsletters called Wall Street Edge. The sample issue has lists of best stocks, low-priced stocks, mutual funds, new issues, options, market commentary, whispers (which turn out to be rumors).

The presentation is similar in the hot stocks area of Strategic Investor. I get fifty charts from *Investor's Business Daily* of what are called hot stocks. This is a list of stocks that the analysts there think might outperform the market. Now, I've got no objection to stock pickers going on-line and giving their opinions—that is exactly what The Motley Fool does. But Prodigy's approach leaves me a little uneasy. Adding up everything in the investing sections on the service I begin to feel like I've wandered into a room full of touts. For example, in Inside Track, I read Joseph Barthel of Fahnestock & Co. asking, "Is it time to take profits in IBM, Intel, and other top performing stocks?"

What exactly am I objecting to? I think it's the lack of interaction, for one thing. I can call anybody in CompuServe's Investors Forum on the carpet for his or her views and I can grill The Motley Fool. If I follow these areas enough, I'll even meet the same characters again and again. But here, I'm getting people presented as experts, telling me what to do, who aren't really on-line themselves. Can I ask Joseph Barthel about conflicts of interest, or e-mail him a week later to tell him his IBM call was wrong and ask why, or ask him to clarify something about his opinion I don't understand? No. This might as well be print—except that I can't call up the magazine and try to get the editor on the phone.

I don't think it's coincidence that Prodigy has the weakest on-line investors community among the big three services, either. The discussion isn't as informed, the personalities don't repeat as frequently, and the community isn't as cohesive as in the Investors Forum or The Motley Fool.

That said, I still subscribe to Prodigy. I just ignore its forums, news, ads, and touts, and keep my eyes on two high-quality data sources. First, the Fund Reports section (data from Micropal and updated monthly) allows me to pull up a report on a fund or search by fund family, investment objective, and performance period. Second, the Company Reports section (data by Market Guide) is the best single source of fundamental company data available on-line for such a reasonable price. (See my review of Market Guide, which is available through other vendors as well as Prodigy, in Chapter 3.)

## REUTERS MONEY NETWORK
### (MACINTOSH EARLIER VERSIONS ARE CALLED WEALTHBUILDER)

Reality Online Inc., 2200 Renaissance Blvd., King of Prussia, PA 19406, 800-346-2024.

Versions available: Windows (version 2.5), Macintosh (version 4.01).

Requirements: Windows version requires 8MB RAM, 20MB free space on hard drive, DOS 5.0 and Windows 3.1, and 2400 baud modem or higher. Modem for updating prices and information in investment databases and for downloading news.

Cost: Software plus membership plan. Software: Windows version $24.95 plus $7.50 shipping. Macintosh $49.95 plus $7.50 shipping. Windows CD-ROM $24.95 plus $7.50 shipping. Membership plans: $12.95 Gold or $19.95 Platinum per month. 30-days free on-line service with software.

Guarantee: 30-day money-back on software; cancel at any time and get refund for prepaid unused month of service.

Demo or sample: None.

Technical support: 610-239-0720 or through e-mail function of program (info@reality-tech.com).

User Newsletter or On-line Forum: *Reality Investor* mailed quarterly to subscribers. World Wide Web address http://www.moneynet.com.

Updated: Databases updated monthly.

See full review at end of chapter 2.

## STOCKTRACKER FOR COMPUSERVE

Virgil Corporation, 290 Green St, Suite 1, San Francisco, CA 94133, 800-662-8256.

Versions available: Windows (version 1.5).

Requirements: Windows 3.1 or higher and DOS 5.0 or higher; 4MB of RAM; CompuServe account.

Cost: $59.95 for software. On-line charges are those for CompuServe. Current quotes are free. Historical quotes are a nickel. Company reports, company news, price volume charts (50 cents a chart) all cost extra.

Guarantee: 30-day money back.

Demo or sample: None.

Technical support: 415-433-9025 (9–5, M–F).

User Newsletter or On-line Forum: CompuServe (Go Virgil).

Updated: Next update scheduled for 1997.

Strengths: Simple to learn because the program performs only a few functions. Just five tabs across the top—Portfolio, Stock, Edit, Options, Help—and just four icons down the side—Update Now, Get News, Get Report, Get Chart. The automatic update feature for prices is likely to be useful to investors who are frequent traders but don't need real-time data. The program notes the time of the next update on the system (all quotes are delayed by fifteen minutes); users can also disable this feature and update at times of their own choice. This too works off a list system, but unlike most programs it integrates the quote list and the portfolio so that you don't have to enter tickers twice. User can set alerts so that system will flag stocks that move above or fall below specified prices.

Weaknesses: Charts are horrible to look at and frankly just too hard to read. Vague tones and colors, no moving averages, an inability to toggle between logarithmic and arithmetic scales. Just one chart option—price and volume.

Tricks of the trade: The quantity, basis, and gain columns in the data for each stock make it tempting to use StockTracker to watch the performance of the stocks in a portfolio. But while an investor can follow individual stocks using this program, he or she can't track the performance of a portfolio since StockTracker doesn't offer any way to add up the performance of individual stocks (with different weights and different holding periods) to arrive at the performance of an entire portfolio.

This software provides an interface for CompuServe designed specifically for investors. It features automated securities pricing and direct access to company news, reports, historical pricing, and price/volume charts. All these features are, of course, directly available from CompuServe's own interface, but StockTracker makes using the investment information in that service a little bit easier.

Probably the biggest improvement that StockTracker offers is the spreadsheet style screen that puts everything about a stock on a single, graphically appealing page. Columns include news, symbol, name, basis, quantity, volume, high, low, last, change, change percent, value, and gain.

# 7

# The Electronic Broker

I confess. I used to suffer from electronic broker anxiety. There was just something about trusting two machines—my home computer and another sitting in the backroom of some brokerage somewhere—to buy and sell securities. I mean we're talking about real money here. What if one machine or the other bought the wrong stock, or failed to make a sale on time or didn't get me the best price?

But I'm getting over it. And I'm not alone. There are now 624,000 on-line brokerage accounts, up from 412,000 last year according to Forrester Research in Cambridge, Massachusetts. Forrester expects 1.3 million accounts by 1998. It doesn't take a rocket scientist to figure out why.

Using an electronic broker is simply too convenient; saves too much money in commissions; and gives me too much control over exactly how I buy and sell stocks. And I've discovered that if an investor learns a few rules about how to be an intelligent consumer of on-line brokerage services, there's no more reason to worry about an electronic broker than a flesh and blood one.

I went through the same process with the now ubiquitous bank cash machines—ATMs. First, I only used them to check my balances, then I withdrew money, and now I deposit checks, print out lists of what checks have cleared, and transfer funds from one account to another without worrying about the machine making an error. In fact, I often feel that I can trust the machine just a little more than I can some teller. The machine never gets bored, never gets distracted, and is never at lunch.

But the argument for doing more and more of my more routine trading without benefit of a human being is actually even more compelling than the one that has made the ATM a part of the American landscape. Sure, like the ATM, electronic trading is more convenient. I can do it on my schedule and at any hour. Want to place a trade at 2 P.M. for the next day's opening? No problem. Want to get an up-to-date list of every position in your portfolio on Saturday? No problem. Want to know if that dividend from American Electric Power is in your account, and ready to finance that purchase of shares in the France Growth Fund? No problem.

But electronic brokerage accounts come with an inducement that ATMs never offered during their infancy. Cash. I can save 10 percent on my commissions at Schwab by trading electronically using its Street Smart software. A stock that costs $55 to buy over the phone from a Schwab order taker costs just $49.50 electronically. And I can do even better. Buying those same 100 shares at $25 would cost me only $40 at PCFN, the Personal Computer Financial Network, and just $14.95 at E*Trade, two completely electronic brokerages. Schwab's own discount electronic brokerage, e.Schwab, would charge me $39. Think how attractive using an ATM would be if, besides 24-hour convenience, you got a $15 bonus on every $1,000 you deposited by machine instead of by teller?

That's a big inducement to calm my anxiety, but it isn't enough to make it go away entirely. I worry about the technology and the ability of brokerage firms—some established and some almost raw start-ups— to tame it. No teen-aged computer hacker has yet managed to penetrate one of these trading systems—or at least no one is admitting that this has happened—but I still worry about the security and privacy of my account. I know that computers do make mistakes—either because of some electronic glitch or because the human who programmed the machine didn't think of all the eventualities—and I worry about whether enough checks and cross-checks have been built into the system so that these errors are caught. And I worry, with good reason given recent events, about what is called the robustness of these systems. The entire NASDAQ market shut down twice in 1994 and once again in 1995 because their computer systems went down. At the end of May 1995, one electronic brokerage firm, E*Trade, went off-line for a week.

But, although these are real worries, there is a set of questions to ask and rules to observe that can identify the potential problem firms in the electronic brokerage community. These will help you become a better shopper for brokerage services of all kinds and to address some of the potential problems unique to the electronic providers before they cost you money.

## How Electronic Brokerages Work: The State of the Art

First, before we worry about how to shop for an electronic broker, let's start by looking at how three different systems work—two dedicated electronic brokerages, PCFN and E*Trade, and StreetSmart, the electronic trading system offered by Charles Schwab & Co.

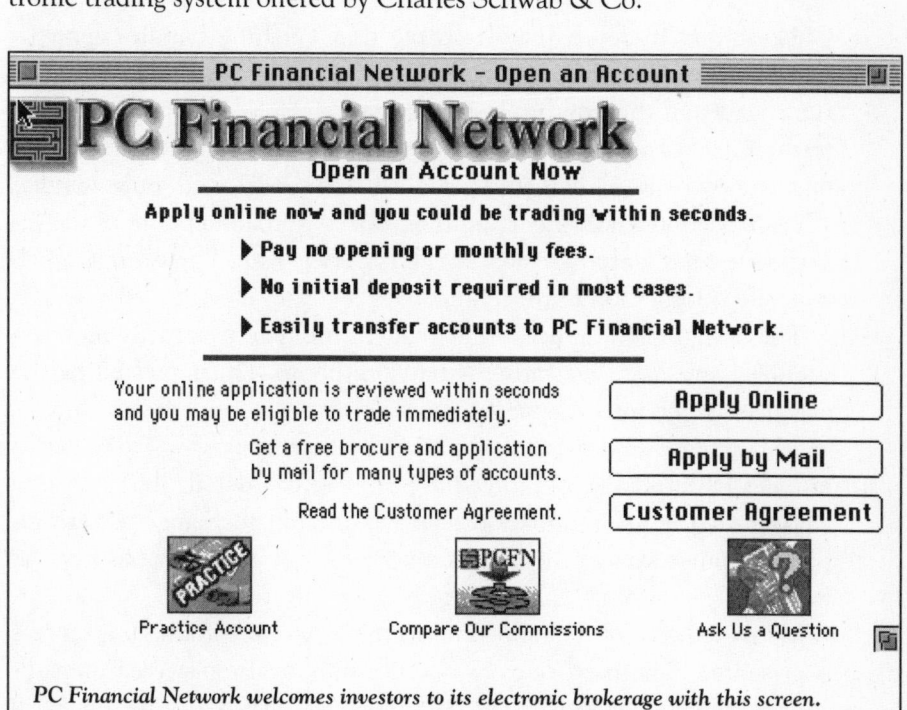

*PC Financial Network welcomes investors to its electronic brokerage with this screen.*
*(Courtesy PCFN)*

I reached PC Financial Network through Prodigy, although I could have also used America Online or CompuServe. After signing on to the service I typed "jump PCFN," which took me to the initial PCFN screen. Its look had more to do with Prodigy than PCFN. It was the typical cluttered Prodigy screen with an advertisement for the Maximizer Software program inside a starburst. I can order this software—which works with PCFN to give me the ability to analyze stocks—directly from this screen, now. (For a review of this software, see Chapter 6.) I can also click on "Learn about PC Financial Network," "Try a Practice Trade," or "Open Account Online."

I go to "Learn About." Who are these folks that I'm about to trust with my money?

Now I recognize that this is essentially marketing information designed to put a positive spin on everything, but it does offer some important information. PCFN is a service of the Pershing Division of Donaldson, Lufkin & Jenrette Securities Corp. Following Wall Street as I do that means something to me. I know the parent firms by reputation. But it probably means nothing to most potential clients. Wisely, PCFN gives those folks the option of asking for more information. Clicking on "In-depth Info" tells me that Pershing handles approximately 10 percent of the NYSE volume and 8 percent of all listed options, and that the firm has been around for fifty years. PCFN provides research from Pershing but doesn't make recommendations and doesn't make sales calls. PCFN was established in 1987 and now handles 170,000 accounts. Hitting a photo button downloads a photo of the investment representatives area at PCFN. Big deal. There's not much concrete information in this photo.

The design of the process that brought me here is actually more revealing—and more reassuring—than the photo. I'm impressed by the care that went into the structure of this information. It was intelligently arranged in a hierarchy so that the newcomer who knew Pershing and DLJ and PFCN didn't have to read the details, but someone who wanted more information could easily find it. Someone with either computer savvy or experience born of trial and error has been at work.

More evidence of that shows up in the way that information on fees is presented. The most obvious questions are again answered immediately. PCFN offers discounted commissions—and there are no extra fees to pay to Prodigy for accessing the service. But rather than presenting some static table of fees comparing the commissions on a limited number of combinations of shares and price at PCFN and other firms, the introductory screen again takes advantage of the fact that this is a computer screen and not a printed ad. A "commissions calculator" (my term not theirs) gives me the ability to ask what any number of shares at any price would cost at PCFN, Schwab, and Fidelity. One hundred shares at $24 a share would cost $40 at PCFN, $61.78 at a full commission broker, $55 at Schwab ($49.50 electronic) or $54 Fidelity ($48.60 electronic). I find it disingenuous that they don't list the cheaper discount brokers that do beat them on price, but this is a marketing document and it is perhaps too much to hope for.

## BASICS

# THE TERMS OF THE DEAL

**N**ot all sell or buy orders are the same, and while not all electronic brokerages will give you the ability to customize the terms of your order in all these ways, most do include at least a few of these possibilities. (None of these apply to mutual funds, where prices are calculated just once at the end of every market day.)

First, if you simply tell the brokerage to buy or sell without specifying a price, you've placed what is called a market order. The transaction will be conducted at the current market price. If it jumps a few dollars, you'll wind up buying at a higher price than you wanted, and the same on the sell side with falling prices. Market orders are especially risky when you're buying or selling thinly traded or volatile stocks.

To avoid that you can place a limit order. In this type of order you say that you'll buy 100 shares of Apple at $35 or better. If the current price is less than $35, the brokerage will execute your purchase. If it's above $35, it will wait until the price falls below your limit. Limit orders are generally placed either for the day or are good until canceled. A day limit may not be filled if the price that day doesn't drop below your limit, and will then be canceled.

Limit orders still leave an investor at the mercy of the market, although to a lesser degree than market orders. If the price of a stock hits the limit—say you've said you'll sell at any price above $35—you still can get

*continued*

whipsawed if the market moves unexpectedly after your price target has been reached. If after hitting $35 on one trade, the stock drops to $34.25, your brokerage will still execute your sell order. Same on a buy, where a stock could drop to your $20 limit and then rise to $21, the price at which the brokerage would buy. To narrow the price range further, you can use a stop-limit order, if your brokerage allows (and most electronic brokerages don't). A stop-limit order tells a brokerage to execute a buy or sell at a specific price once some target price has been reached. For example, a stop-limit buy might be stated like this: Buy 100 $35 stop $36 limit. To execute that order the broker would attempt to buy the stock at $36 or better once the stock had reached a price of $35. Not all exchanges will accept stop-limit orders.

On the downside, many investors give their brokers stop-loss orders (also simply called stop orders). This is a way to limit downside losses in the case of highly volatile stocks, options, or short sales. A stop-loss would tell a broker to sell a stock now trading at $35 if it hit a price of say $33. Stop-loss orders do offer downside protection, but setting the stop price too close to the current price can take an investor out of a stock because of a temporary movement in prices and result in excessive trading commissions. Most electronic brokerages won't accept stop-loss orders.

An account at PCFN stacks up favorably against non-electronic accounts on a number of features that matter. I can place limit and stop orders; buy stocks, bonds, and more than 500 mutual funds; and sell short. It also tells me that I can see real-time quotes—not quotes delayed by fifteen minutes—when placing a trade. I study the fine print. This means, I read, that when I enter an order I can get 100 free real-time quotes. I can't, however, simply use PCFN to get quotes on stocks that I track, unless I trade.

My portfolio at PCFN is priced daily. I can get on-line account information that includes the value of my portfolio, priced to market, and current cash balance, reports on the status of open orders, and a transactions report that lists past activity. (I can also download this information into spreadsheets and other financial software for further analysis.) The transactions report is especially important for worrywarts like me who want to double-check the accuracy of trades and portfolios. Because PCFN is linked to a major Wall Street firm, I also get a free report from Pershing's analysts daily, a weekend review, a look at market fundamentals, and a daily fixed income commentary from the same source. PCFN also provides free reports by selected Wall Street analysts. That's a lot of free information for a discount broker to provide. I do note, however, that unlike discounters such as Waterhouse, I don't get free reports from Standard & Poor's. Just as important in dollars and cents, all my cash will earn interest automatically in my choice of money market funds.

## IF YOU ALEADY TRADE WITH A DISCOUNT BROKER, YOU'RE PREPARED FOR ON-LINE TRADING

I can also try a practice trade to see just how complicated this whole process is. My first click gets me a list of products that I can trade—stocks, mutual funds, and so on. I click on "Mutual Funds" and get a list of types. (I don't like this method since it means that I have to figure out their system of categorizing funds.) I click on "Aggressive Growth," which is such a large category that it's divided in half alphabetically. I click on "A-M." Since this is just for practice I pick one of the first funds I see, Alliance Dividend Shares. (See what I mean by arbitrary categories—why is a fund that cares about dividends categorized as aggressive growth?) The screen tells me that I need to invest a minimum $1,000 initially. I select the fund for purchase by clicking on its name. A screen comes up that asks if I would like a prospectus before I buy or if have I already read one. I lie and say I've read it. I type in $1,000, the amount I want to invest. A new screen asks if I want to reinvest dividends. I click Yes. So far this is almost exactly the same process—same questions, same lack of advice—as the familiar one of making a buy or sell with an order taker at one of the discount brokers.

The screen now shows my order as it has been entered and asks if this is right. I click "Send" and seconds later my computer tells me that the order has been received at PCFN. I can now track it by selecting "Order Status" from the "Acct. Info" menu and selecting "Execution Reports."

Buying a stock is very similar. The first screen asks me for the type of transaction I'd like to perform: buy, sell position, sell stock, sell short, buy to cover. I have to specify stock by ticker or by typing name, so I type in "Apple Com" and the machine translates that into the stock's ticker of AAPL. With the symbol I get information on the current bid/ask prices. To buy, I type in the number of shares and the type of order (market, limit, stop, other). I select limit and a price of $42. Choice of "Good Till Canceled" or "Day" (I pick "Good Till Canceled"). Margin or cash. The system then recaps the order a second time (first is in box to right) and asks me to "Send" (if correct) or "Change." And that's it.

If this was a real trade, I'd get an on-line execution report, electronic trade notification in my Prodigy mailbox, and printed confirmation sent to my mailing address the next day.

Is this the state of the art? Pretty much. Fidelity On-Line Express (FOX) looks virtually identical to this. Schwab's Street Smart, too. Although both Fox and Street Smart demonstrate a few important wrinkles.

Here, in condensed form, is a virtually identical trade on Street-Smart (Version 2.0 for Macintosh). I want to buy $1,000 of Acorn International Fund (ACINX). Since StreetSmart is a freestanding software program rather than an on-line service such as PCFN, I can set up this trade off-line. I tell it to buy, fill in amount (it gives me the option of buying $1,000 plus commission of $35 or of buying $1,000 less commission, which is a neat reminder), asks if dividends are to be reinvested, and click at "Market" or "Limit." Then, as in PCFN, I get a screen that confirms my order before it is submitted (I can "Add Order," "Edit Order," or "Delete Order"). I click to submit. The software asks for my password and the modem dials into Schwab's computers. Type in my password and the modem dials. Almost immediately (five seconds, I'd say) I get a confirmation screen that says I've placed a day order for 100 shares at an estimated cost of $1035.10. Since this transaction is hooked up to my accounts at Schwab, the program also tells me I now hold a total of 474.911 shares of Acorn. Since mutual fund purchases get settled at end of the day prices, I won't be able to see the execution until after the market closes. When I sign on the next morning and ask for order status I see that it has been filled. I bought 64.267 shares at 15.56 with $35 commission.

## EVEN THE ON-LINE DISCOUNTERS ARE BECOMING— GASP!—FULL SERVICE BROKERAGES

Now, for the wrinkles. Both StreetSmart and Fox are trying to be more than just electronic order takers. Both Fidelity and Schwab are gradu-

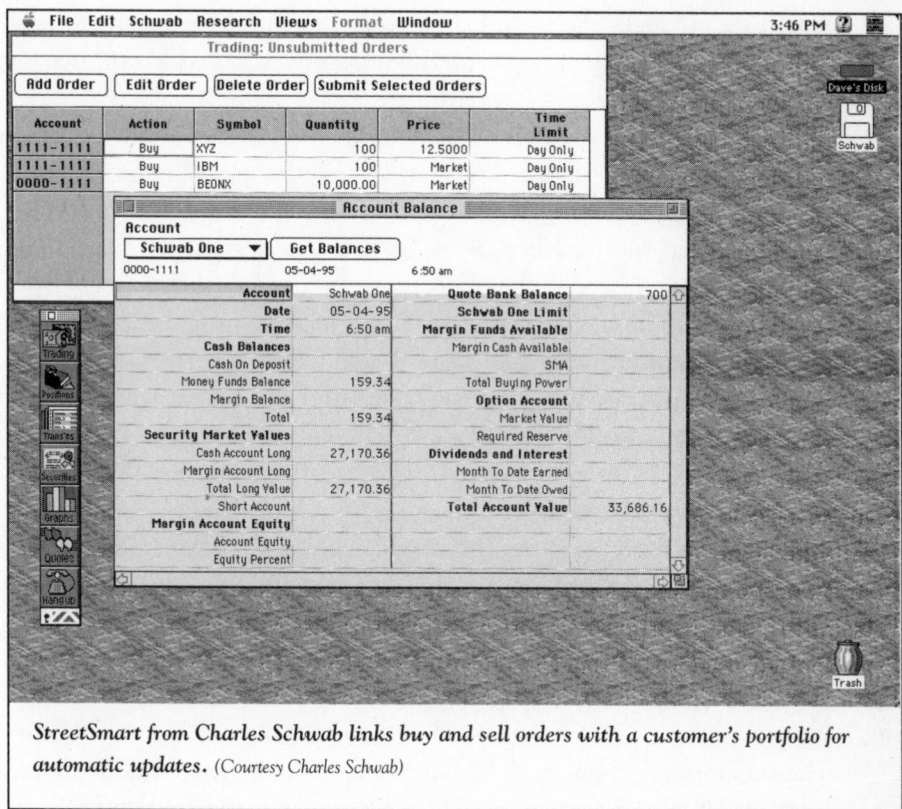

*StreetSmart from Charles Schwab links buy and sell orders with a customer's portfolio for automatic updates. (Courtesy Charles Schwab)*

ally turning their electronic broker programs into full function investment resources. (Schwab has also added a bare-bones electronic brokerage, e.Schwab. See review at end of chapter.) In some ways these two discount brokerage powerhouses are evolving into electronic versions of that full service brokerage I visited with my mother when I was fourteen. I hang around their electronic "office" because, besides buying and selling stocks, I can get information on stocks and the market, follow my account, and read analyst reports.

And there's a similar kind of business logic at work now. If executing a trade is basically a commodity, then firms have to compete on either price or service. Firms such as Schwab, Fidelity, and PCFN have decided not to be the cheapest in the market and instead decided to compete on service. If you follow the marketing logic of firms like Schwab and PCFN, you'll be influenced by the add-ons, essentially bells and whistles that provide real value to the investor, but all of which are available in other ways. PCFN has hooked up with Ret-tech, the com-

pany that produces the technical analysis program MegaChart, to provide an on-line charting and information service called Maximizer for
Windows (see review in Chapter 6).

Schwab gives the investor access—for additional fees—to Dow Jones
News Retrieval and Standard & Poor's MarketScope. Windows users of
StreetSmart's latest revision for that operating system (version 3.0) also
get the Reuters Money Network.

The advantage here to the investor is convenience. I can access Dow
Jones information or Standard and Poor's reports through StreetSmart
and its communications protocols. I don't pay any start-up fees or
monthly minimum—just for what I use. And the system works well. I
pull down the Company Reports menu and ask to download a company
report on ADBE, Adobe Systems. StreetSmart connects without problems and downloads without problem. Two minutes later—it takes that
long for my printer to output the eight-page report—I have Standard &
Poor's data and opinion on this software company.

## BUT DON'T LET THE BELLS AND WHISTLES DISTRACT YOU FROM PRICE

These kinds of add-ons make it hard to figure out the specific trade-off
between price and service. Not that figuring out the trade-off is easy
even without these add-ons. Take price, for example. On the surface it
seems like this is one area where it should be easy to figure out the winner. If Schwab charges $55 to trade 100 shares of a stock selling at $50
and a deep discount broker such as Aufhauser & Co. charges $35, isn't
Aufhauser cheaper by $20? And if Pacific charges just $25 for the same
trade, isn't it the cheapest? Well, not exactly. Schwab doesn't charge a
handling fee, for example, to send you a confirmation of the trade in
the mail. Aufhauser does—$2.50—so the difference there is actually
$17.50.

That's only one of the charges that can change the price half of the
equation. It costs $35 to start up an IRA at Aufhauser, but nothing at
Schwab and Pacific. Aufhauser also charges $50 to close such an ac-
count, Pacific $35, and Schwab nothing. Fail to do enough trades and
inactivity fees can trip in—$25 at Aufhauser and $50 at National Discount. Generally, it's true that the deep discount brokers such as Pacific, National Discount, and Aufhauser are cheaper than discount
brokers such as Schwab, Fidelity, and Quick & Reilly, who are in turn

**BASICS**

# COMPARING COMMISSIONS

**C**ommissions depend on the number of shares in a transaction and the price per share—which makes comparing commissions among brokerage firms difficult. These tables suggest relative costs for a $2,000 and $8,000 trade.

**– $2000 Trades –**

| Firm | 400@$5 | 200@$10 | 100@$20 | 50@$40 |
|------|--------|---------|---------|--------|
| Accutrade | $ 48.00 | $ 48.00 | $ 48.00 | $ 48.00 |
| Aufhauser | $ 37.49 | $ 27.49 | $ 27.49 | $ 27.49 |
| Brown | $ 29.00 | $ 29.00 | $ 29.00 | $ 29.00 |
| E*Trade | $ 14.95 | $ 14.95 | $ 14.95 | $ 14.95 |
| Fidelity | $ 57.15 | $ 57.15 | $ 48.60 | $ 48.60 |
| Lombard | $ 36.50 | $ 36.50 | $ 36.50 | $ 36.50 |
| National | $ 33.00 | $ 33.00 | $ 33.00 | $ 33.00 |
| Pacific | $ 33.00 | $ 33.00 | $ 33.00 | $ 33.00 |
| Quick & Reilly | $ 50.00 | $ 50.00 | $ 49.00 | $ 49.00 |
| Charles Schwab | $ 57.60 | $ 57.60 | $ 49.50 | $ 49.50 |
| Jack White | $ 45.00 | $ 39.00 | $ 36.00 | $ 34.50 |

**– $8000 Trades –**

| Firm | 1600@$5 | 800@$10 | 400@$20 | 200@$40 |
|------|---------|---------|---------|---------|
| Accutrade | $ 48.00 | $ 48.00 | $ 48.00 | $ 48.00 |
| Aufhauser | $ 95.50 | $ 61.50 | $ 37.49 | $ 27.49 |
| Brown | $ 29.00 | $ 29.00 | $ 29.00 | $ 29.00 |
| E*Trade | $ 14.95 | $ 14.95 | $ 14.95 | $ 14.95 |
| Fidelity | $ 98.10 | $ 92.43 | $ 92.43 | $ 92.43 |
| Lombard | $ 36.50 | $ 36.50 | $ 36.50 | $ 36.50 |
| National | $ 33.00 | $ 33.00 | $ 33.00 | $ 33.00 |
| Pacific | $ 33.00 | $ 29.00 | $ 29.00 | $ 29.00 |
| Quick & Reilly | $ 79.00 | $ 79.00 | $ 79.00 | $ 79.00 |
| Charles Schwab | $ 108.00 | $ 92.88 | $ 92.88 | $ 92.88 |
| Jack White | $ 81.00 | $ 57.00 | $ 45.00 | $ 39.00 |

Commissions include electronic trading discounts and per trade handling fees where applicable.

cheaper than the full service brokers such as Merrill and Prudential. But not always and not for all investors and not always for all trades. Academic studies have shown that, especially on the over-the-counter market, not all brokers get the lowest possible prices on purchases for investors or the highest possible on sales. It's quite a puzzle these days. Picking a brokerage firm based on price now requires finding the best match between the pricing structure of a brokerage and the services that you need as an investor with your investment habits.

Unfortunately that's the simpler half of the equation. After all, it's only possible to compare prices if brokers are providing comparable service. For example, I can buy no-load mutual funds through Charles Schwab; but although I can buy load funds through Aufhauser, the firm doesn't sell no-load funds; and Brown & Co. doesn't sell any funds at all. Want to buy a zero-coupon bond? Jack White sells them; Brown doesn't.

Or how about talking to an account representative if you have a question? *Smart Money* magazine surveyed how long it took to get a human being on line at the various discount brokerage firms. Best were PCFN and Jack White, at 8 and 12 seconds respectively. Worst were E*Trade at almost 14 minutes and Pacific Brokerage Services at almost 2 minutes. How much is your time worth and how does that figure into the comparison of cost/service among brokerage firms?

Evaluating and then picking an electronic brokerage does present unique problems for an investor. Although I can ask questions about the ratio of account representatives to customers and about policies on mailing confirmations that will tell me something useful about the level of service I can expect from a brokerage, it's much harder to evaluate two other crucial aspects of an electronic brokerage. I'll call the first reliability and the second security.

When brokerage firms still consisted of scores of white-shirted men at desks in dozens or perhaps hundreds of offices, it required a sizable investment to start a firm. That kept turnover in the brokerage industry down and limited the number of new firms that could build a national presence. Today, all it takes to open a brokerage firm is some phone lines, an agreement with an existing clearing firm for trades, and an advertising budget. Which means that not all brokerages that open their doors on-line have enough capital to provide a high level of service if a lot of customers come pounding on those doors.

# Checking a Brokerage Firm's Credentials

It's *relatively* easy to check out the credentials of an individual broker. You can call the National Association of Security Dealers disciplinary hotline and ask for the record on any broker by name (Securities and Exchange Commission actions against firms and brokers are available on the Internet at http://www.sec.gov). That's by no means foolproof—the NASD database isn't particularly complete. Another route is to check a document called the uniform termination notice (U–5), which is available from the office that regulates securities in your state. That will give you a glimpse at a broker's employment record and insight into the reasons for any dismissals.

Those methods aren't perfect, but they're a lot better than anything you can do to check on a securities firm you've never heard of. At the least honest end of the securities business—the realm of the cold-call boiler rooms and the bucket shops—starting a new firm is a well-established way to bury disciplinary actions and legal judgments. Even though the brokers at the new firm may have long track records of questionable dealings at the predecessor firm, the new firm will turn up clean.

That's a real problem for investors in the on-line world, because so many of the companies starting on-line brokerages aren't familiar names. So you have two options. First, deal only with on-line firms with established reputations. That won't insure that you don't get a bum stock tip or get hit up to buy an inappropriate investment, but the truth is that problems such as manipulating stock prices using client accounts is far less prevalent at firms that want to protect their long-established image. Second, you can research not the unfamiliar firm itself, but its principals. Any firm should be willing to tell you the names of its officers down to the level of vice president. You can check those individuals for their brokerage industry track records. One bad apple probably shouldn't stop you from trading on-line with a firm, but you should ask the company for an explanation. If, on the other hand, your search turns up a number of individuals with violations in their past, you should do your trading elsewhere. Investing is fraught with enough unavoidable risk. Who needs to go looking for trouble?

## YOU DON'T WANT TO GO ON-LINE WITH JUST ANYBODY

The on-line trading community got a taste of this problem at the end of May 1995 when E*Trade, an on-line brokerage firm in Palo Alto, California, went silent for five days. Two power outages caused the problem, according to E*Trade. The first knocked their computers out of service for about one and a half hours. A day later, a second outage fried the firm's telecommunications link to Sprintnet, the phone service that connected the brokerage to CompuServe, AOL, and their own dial-up network. The phones kept working, but the increased volume of phone calls from investors who couldn't execute their trades on-line overwhelmed the system and the staff.

A regrettable series of accidents, but why should it have shut down the electronic brokerage? Certainly, a firm should have a backup power system—maybe even a backup site that can handle traffic if the main computers go down. Certainly, a firm should have alternative communication systems so that one power surge or even a fire can't prevent customers from reaching their accounts. E*Trade claims to have learned its

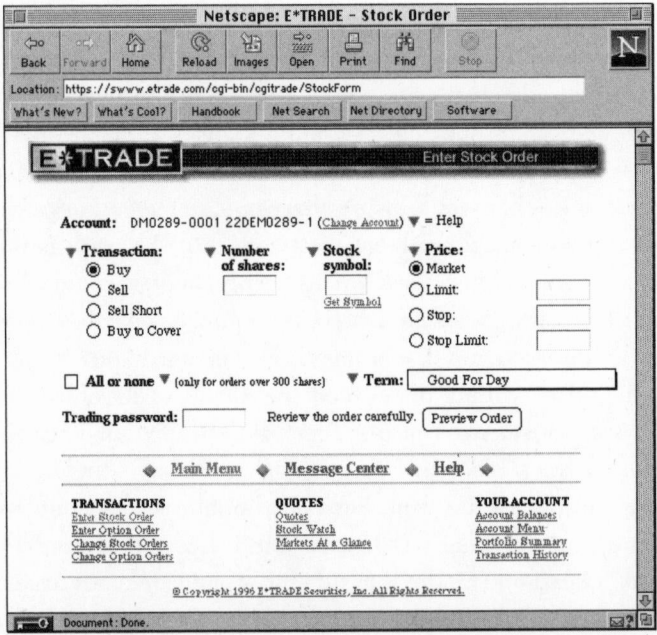

*E*Trade has joined the growing number of brokerage firms providing trading over the Internet.* (Courtesy E*Trade)

lesson. In the wake of the incident the firm added six people to bring its systems staff up to eighteen and promised to install better backup power. Yet it's still hard to believe that the whole problem wasn't caused by too much growth and too little planning. The company, which now claims 30,000 accounts, doubled its customer base in 1994 and was predicting another doubling for 1995.

An investor could always call up a firm such as E*Trade or PCFN and ask questions about their backup systems for power and communications. (And I expect that the surest indicator of potential trouble would be if an investor couldn't find anyone to talk knowledgeably about the issue.) But I have another suggestion that suits my conservative nature better. I'd like any electronic brokerage firm I do business with to be able to handle trades using a phone/human backup, if worse came to worse. It was a sign of the trouble to come at E*Trade that it took them fourteen minutes to answer their phones—without any emergency—in *Smart Money*'s survey. Similarly, PCFN's ability to come out on top in this category—just eight seconds—makes me feel good about my ability to stay in touch with my account at this electronic brokerage.

Of course, it's difficult to try out all the competing systems. Some, such as PCFN and E*Trade, do offer guest accounts that let an investor try a dummy trade. Others, such as Schwab, Quick & Reilly, Fidelity, and Brown & Co., require an investor to set up an account with the brokerage firm first. At these firms electronic trading is just one optional method of conducting a trade, along with talking to a customer service representative on the phone, using a Touch-Tone phone to place orders, and, in several cases, visiting an office and making a trade face to face with a human being. But there's still nothing that says that you can't open an account at the minimum and then try out the firm before moving substantial money into the account.

## HOW SECURE ARE YOUR ON-LINE TRADES?

Security is even harder to judge. When it's working well, it's invisible. When a firm trips up—by allowing an unauthorized stranger access to your account, for example—the problem isn't exactly publicized. An investor has the right to know, however, how secure each trade is and each account. He or she wants to know that the system will catch mistakes made by the investor in entering an order or fraud by an unautho-

## TIPS ON THE TOOLS

# BASIC SECURITY

You've probably seen the scene in a recent movie. A group of near-genius hackers bust into some computer network by using a sophisticated computer and software to crack the security codes used by—pick one—a bank, the phone company, illegal drug-dealers, nasty arms traders. Of course, it's possible to break into a heavily secure system like that. A French hacker recently hooked up a string of workstations to run random numbers until he broke the encrypted security code in the World Wide Web browser Netscape.

But that isn't the way most accounts get broken into or how most passwords are stolen. Most fall into unauthorized hands because of human carelessness. A telephone company employee recites a password to a caller masquerading as a security consultant. An investor secures a brokerage account behind a password using his or her initials or birthdate. I write down my account access numbers in my Rolodex. You give your credit card number over the phone to a stranger claiming to be verifying an order that you don't exactly remember making.

To paraphrase an old Carl Reiner–Mel Brooks routine, "Bernice, don't do that." Besides avoiding

rized person trying to use the account. He or she wants to know that no one can steal information about personal finances, trading habits, or stock ownership from the system for use in any way.

Any on-line system should at least make you feel like the brokerage company is trying. PCFN, for example, says its system is secure since two separate passwords are required to reach an account—one to get on the on-line service such as Prodigy that provides the gateway to PCFN, and the other to access PCFN itself. Of course, if an investor sets Prodigy for autologon, anyone can get on-line without a password, and if an investor picks a simple password, such as a birthday, the second level won't provide much security, either. But then, no system can protect your account if you're careless or stupid.

But this kind of visible effort doesn't guarantee anything about the security of the computer network at the brokerage. It won't tell you anything about how often the system changes its own passwords so that outsiders can't simply dial in to the main computers that keep records of every investor's portfolio. It doesn't tell you anything about how difficult or easy it is for someone to intercept your communication with the brokerage and gain access to your account numbers and passwords.

The truth is that no computer system in the commercial world is totally secure. Determined hackers routinely break into America Online and steal passwords and account numbers. Lore has it that hackers have even repeatedly gained access to the account used by company founder Steve Case. In early September 1995 two Stanford University students cracked the security codes in Netscape, the most popular World Wide Web navigation software, and then published the method on the Internet itself. For days anyone with solid computer skills had a shot at intercepting credit card numbers transmitted on the Internet in commercial transactions.

That shouldn't stop you from using on-line brokerages (although you should recognize that the Internet is less secure than on-line services, which are in turn less secure than dial-up systems), any more than the knowledge that people counterfeit currency prevents you from using paper money. But it does suggest that you should keep careful paper records of your transactions and check all confirmations and account statements thoroughly for accuracy.

Trading on-line you face two dangers. First, you can make a mistake in entering an order using the firm's computer interface. Second, someone can steal your account number and password. That would allow them to trade your account and probably transfer money electronically to another account.

I worry about making a mistake in an electronic trade. One day, trying to place an order through Schwab's StreetSmart for shares of Intel, I got a cryptic message from the brokerage firm. The trade, it appeared, couldn't be executed because it was "out of the market," whatever that

---

the obvious errors, though, you should also change your passwords from time to time. That way, even if someone does breach the security of a system you're using, the damage to you will be limited in time since the password that has been compromised will no longer be valid. Give some thought to creating a secure password. Obviously avoid simple codes such as initials or birthdates, names of children or spouses or pets, and company names. Mix numbers and letters—the combination is harder to break than either alone. Don't use the same password for all your accounts so that if one falls, all will. And if you must write passwords down, keep those jottings in a secure place—especially if you're using a computer in a place where you don't control access—such as your office.

meant. Since Schwab lets me call a human representative as well as trade electronically through the same account, I simply phoned, asked what action had been executed, and resolved the problem. If I had been using the firm's e.Schwab system, which limits my queries to e-mail (or charges a $5 fee), or an electronic brokerage such as E*Trade, my first resort would have been to try to resolve this problem using e-mail. How long would it have taken? I've had almost immediate response when I've sent e-mail to Schwab through StreetSmart on other issues, but I don't know how quickly I could have resolved this issue. I strongly advise anyone about to sign up with an electronic brokerage that limits your access to human representatives—either by charging fees or by being extremely slow to answer the phone—to try out the firm's e-mail response time repeatedly before committing a significant amount of cash.

Electronic theft should be a non-issue. In the pre-electronic age, the securities laws clearly made brokerage firms reponsible for losses if they allowed an unauthorized person to trade your account—just like a bank is reponsible for the loss if it accepts a forged check. (That's not to say that a brokerage firm wouldn't give you an argument before making good on the loss.) Unfortunately, responsibility when the trades are done electronically isn't nearly as clear. If you want to read some scarey legalese, read the fine print on some of the applications for electronic trading. One that I've seen comes with a disclaimer that says that the firm will employ various methods of authentification (to make sure that the person claiming to be you is really you), such as asking for a password. In signing up for the account you agree that this is a reasonable effort at authentification and that as long as the brokerage firm has employed one of these methods, you, and not the firm, are responsible for losses.

I've asked various securities lawyers and regulators to clarify this issue and their responses all boil down to this: Electronic trading is a new frontier of the law and some brokerage firms are pushing the boundaries harder than others. I would urge you to talk about this issue to any electronic brokerage firm you are considering and ask for their policy on loss responsibility and security procedures in writing.

Of course, even finding a firm that agrees to accept the old definition of responsibility still doesn't give you protection from inconvenience. Having your account number stolen can turn your affairs into a quagmire of forms and explanations. You could spend days closing compromised accounts and arguing with everyone who did business with the thief operating under your name. At some point, part of your assets could be frozen while everyone figures out who was to blame.

Frankly, this kind of theft is much more likely to affect accounts traded on the Internet than accounts handled through proprietary dial-up networks. (If it's not obvious to you how your transactions are handled electronically, ask.) Although no computer network is safe from high-tech intrusion, the Internet, because of its nature as a distributed network, is a lot more vulnerable. The brokers doing business on the Internet have attempted to prevent this kind of security breach by requiring that investors use a World Wide Web browser that encrypts passwords and account names. In theory that means that no one without the key to the system—a very large randomly generated number—can capture your account number and password from the system. But in practice that security isn't exactly secure. The software that most on-line brokerages (those on PAWWS, for example) use for this purpose is exactly the NetScape browser that has been repeatedly breached in the last few months. It's probably impossible to build a system that can't be breached, but you as an individual can take some simple steps to keep the possibility that you'll be a victim to a minimum.

## THE MOST LIKELY CRIME WON'T INVOLVE HIGH-TECH HACKING

Hacking by high-tech criminals, as popular as it is as a subject for current movies, isn't the greatest danger to investors using electronic brokerage services. As hackers have demonstrated to the phone companies over and over again, it's far easier to cajole a human being into giving up a password than it is to hack a computer. And it's far more likely that you'll type in a mistake than it is that you'll be the victim of some high-tech global ring of computer geniuses. A recent e-mail posting from Steve Case, the president of America Online, stressed this point. Computer hackers have attempted to get individual account passwords by posing as America Online employees and sending customers e-mail asking them to reveal their passwords. In one scam, the hacker claimed that a virus had infected the American Online database containing customer passwords and asked the customer to e-mail his or her password to help repair the damage. Amazingly some customers did as they were asked. In a truly secure system no employee of the on-line service or the brokerage firm should have access to your password. No one with a legitimate purpose would ever phone you or e-mail you and ask you to reveal yours.

On-line brokerage firms can offer lower commissions than those that operate over the phone or take your money in real offices because they've eliminated human beings from most mundane transactions. But good on-line brokerage firms realize that unsupervised machines increase the risk of theft and fraud—and simple mistakes. Rather than cutting the number of employees to the absolute minimum required to keep the machines running, they retain some human beings on the payroll because they are the most reliable, up-to-date security devices they can find. Let me take you backstage at PCFN to show you what I mean.

The tower that houses the Personal Computer Financial Network rises from the battered streets of Jersey City like an alien monolith. By this time the company was supposed to have similarly high-rise neighbors. Planners, real estate developers, and politicians were once predicting that the back offices of Wall Street would soon migrate across the Hudson River from the expensive real estate of lower Manhattan to the wide open spaces of New Jersey. Thousands of the essential but less glamorous workers of the securities industry—the people who keep the books, send out the statements, and check the trades—would soon fill these streets at lunch hour. It didn't quite happen that way. Today, PCFN's nearest financial neighbor does a steady business from behind a storefront that boldly announces, "Checks Cashed, Money Orders, Food Stamps."

In its isolation the office towers remind me of one of those fragile frontier towns, so new that the pine sap is still oozing from the lumber in the buildings, which sits on the prairie waiting, hoping for the railroad to come and the farmers to arrive. The comparison is totally fitting, as it happens. Launched in 1988, PCFN represents the frontier of stock trading.

Upstairs on the 11th floor, today's business fills only one-quarter of the floor and lots of empty cubicles stand ready for future employees. Fifty, maybe sixty young men and women sit in front of terminals watching a stream of orders flow by—buy, sell, short, long, stocks, options, bonds, all cross their screens. K. Blake Darcy, a veteran of the securities industry and chief operating officer of PCFN, seems ancient. No one working here seems much over twenty-five.

The floor is strangely hushed for anyone familiar with the hubbub of a typical Wall Street brokerage firm. No loud sales pitches to a client in Westchester. None of the edgy jokes about great stocks or deals about to go sour that help brokers relieve their tension. In most firms brokers this age would be feverishly making cold calls trying to build up a list of clients. I don't hear a one.

What are all these people doing? This is an electronic brokerage. Nobody human is actually taking any orders.

Darcy and I stop to peer over a shoulder. David, a sandy-haired man in his late twenties, spends a moment reading a screen, punches a key to pull up another, and then sends that data on its way.

David is part of the human safety net at PCFN. He's checking orders to see that they conform with a customer's past trading history. A transaction by an investor who has never traded options but is suddenly buying them by the fistful would pop up on David's screen. So too would a trade by an investor who wants to sell more Westinghouse stock than he owns and one by an investor who owns AIG but seems to be selling AIP. If the trade seems questionable, David phones the customer to confirm it.

PCFN and other electronic brokerage firms don't offer this kind of tour for every customer; you really can't visually inspect how thorough a job a brokerage does to protect your money before you sign on. But you can and should interview them. And, of course, if you can't easily get ahold of someone to interview, write the firm off. You're trying to give them money and they still can't spare a moment to talk with you? Ask how many customers they have per account representative (in case the electronic system breaks down). Ask about backup systems. Ask about how they verify orders (and how many people scan them) and how quickly you'll get a confirmation slip. Ask about their NASDAQ record and about violations and complaints. Any brokerage owes you this basic information. If you're not comfortable with their answers, move on. There are plenty of other brokerage firms out there who want your money.

## A LIST OF BROKERAGES OFFERING ELECTRONIC TRADING

### ACCUTRADE, INC.

**800-882-4887;** Technical support: 800-555-4137

**Stock commissions:** $48 minimum up to 1600 shares, then $.03/share.

**Mutual fund commissions:**
Free for over 400 funds in AccuFunds system
$27 for other funds

**Features:**
Touch-tone quotes and trading: PC quotes and trading through Accu-
trade for Windows
Limit orders
Margin accounts
Options
Bonds
Pink sheet and foreign stocks
No-fee IRA accounts with no inactivity fee

The firm's software, Accutrade for Windows, uses direct-dial, toll-
free number for access to accounts. The new version of the software,
which was scheduled for release in February 1996, will allow investors
to obtain quotes (real-time quotes cost $20 a month, delayed quotes
are free), place trades, monitor an account, and track investments. Its
"Program Trading" feature is designed to let investors create and execute automatic trading strategies. The Basket Trading feature will
allow investors to group stocks in a basket and buy or sell the entire
basket at once.

### K. Aufhauser & Co., Inc.

**800-368-3668;** Technical support: 212-246-9431

**Stock commissions:** Below 400 shares, $24.99; for larger trades,
$.02/share or $800 annual Internet account with $0 commissions.

**Mutual fund commissions:** $34 fee $0–4999

**Fees:** $25 annual inactive account fee; $20 fee to set up account;
WealthWeb account free or $20 a month for real-time quotes

**Features:**
Touch-tone quotes and trading: PC quotes and trading via Internet
WealthWeb page (http://www.aufhauser.com)
Limit orders
Margin accounts
Options
Bonds

WealthWeb requires a NetScape-secure Internet connection. The page provides a daily research report from Market Guide, access to Aufhauser's securities database, and real-time ($20 a month fee) and 20-minute delayed (free) quotes. In 1996 Aufhauser plans to offer the entire Market Guide database as a pay-per-view service.

## BROWN & CO.

**800-225-6707;** Technical support: 800-822-2021

**Stock commissions:** $29 for up to 5,000 shares; $29 plus $.01 a share for more than 5,000 shares.

**Fees:** PC Line free up to 5 minutes, then $.45/minute.

**Features:**
Touch-tone quotes and trading; PC quotes and trading via direct-dial
  PC Line
Limit orders
Margin accounts .
Options
Bonds

## E*TRADE

**800-786-2573;** Technical support via CompuServe (76703,2064), America Online (E*trade), and Internet (etrade.com)

**Commissions:** $14.95, add $.01/share for trades of exchange-listed shares exceeding 5,000 shares

**Fees:** Add $15 per transaction for broker assistance; $5 for stock certificate transfer; Touch-tone service charges $.27/minute with free 12-minute credit for each trade.

**Features:**
Touch-tone quotes and trades; and PC quotes and trading
Limit orders
Margin accounts

Options
Bonds

**Problems:** There have been some complaints about service in the Internet's misc.invest.stocks and on CompuServe.

**See review** following this listing of brokerage firms.

E*trade is available through CompuServe and America Online, or directly through the brokerage firm. Minimum balance to open an account is $2,000. E*trade provides delayed and real-time quotes ($30), automatic portfolio updating, and watch lists that can be used to track stocks that aren't already owned by the investor. Internet service began in early 1996.

### FIDELITY BROKERAGE SERVICES

**800-544-9375;** Technical support: 800-544-0296

**Stock commissions:** $38 minimum

**Mutual fund commissions:** No fee on more than 200 funds

**Features:**
Touch-tone quotes and trading; PC quotes and trading through Fox (Fidelity On-line Express)
Limit orders
Margin accounts
Options

**See review** of Fox on-line trading software at end of this chapter.

Information on Fidelity accounts and the mutual funds offered by parent Fidelity Investments are also available through American On-line, Prodigy, and Microsoft Network (all by going to keyword Fidelity), and on the Internet (http://www.fid-inv.com).

### LOMBARD INSTITUTIONAL BROKERAGE

**800-688-3462;** 800-688-6500: Technical support: 800-688-6896

**Stock commissions:** $.02/share, with a minimum of $34

**Mutual fund commissions:** No added commission on no-load funds

**Fees:** Shipping and handling $2.75/trade

**Features:**
Touch-tone quotes and trading; PC quotes and trading via Internet web
  page (http://www.lombard.com)
Limit orders
Margin accounts
Options
Bonds

Trading using Lombard's World Wide Web page requires a secure browser such as NetScape version 1.22 or the forthcoming version 2.0. From Lombard's page, account holders can get real-time quotes and intra-day graphs on stocks, portfolio updating, and news and company reports. In 1996 Lombard is planning to offer real-time company specific news.

### NATIONAL DISCOUNT BROKERS

### 800-888-3999

**Stock commissions:** NASDAQ: $25 ($20 via automated phone service or on-line); non-NASDAQ: $28 plus $.01 each share above 5,000 shares

**Mutual fund commissions:** Varies with fund

**Fees:**
$3 handling/trade if you don't use their market makers
$.02/share on listed stops and stop limit orders

**Features:**
Touch-tone quotes and trading; PC quotes and trading via Internet
  page http://pawws.secapl.com
Limit orders
Margin accounts

Options
Bonds

**Problems:** There have been some complaints about service in the Internet's misc.invest.stocks.

National Discount Brokerage will accept only stock trades through its on-line service. The Touch-tone service will accept trades in stocks and options. All other transactions require a human broker. Using the World Wide Web page requires a secure browser such as NetScape.

### The Net Investor

### 800-638-4250

**Stock commissions:** Net value account: for trades up to 3,000 shares, $33 plus $.027.

**Mutual fund commissions:** For no-load funds and trades up to $15,000, $35

**Features:**
PC quotes and trading via PAWWS World Wide Web page at
   http://pawws.secapl.com
Limit orders
Margin Accounts
Options (but not online)
Bonds

A division of Howe Barnes Investments Inc., a New York Stock Exchange member firm; $5,000 is required to open a Net Value account (another option requires $10,000). A NetScape secure browser is necessary to trade. Free delayed quotes plus free real-time quotes for investors who conduct 8 or more trades a month. Portfolio tracking and updates through PAWWS.

### Pacific Brokerage Service

### 800-421-8395; 213-939-1100

**Stock commissions:**
$29 up to 5000 shares; above 5000 shares, $29 plus $.01/share.

**Fees:**
$4 handling/trade

**Features:**
Touch-tone quotes and trading; PC quotes and trading
Limit orders
Margin Accounts
Options
Bonds

**Problems:** There have been some complaints about service in the Internet's misc.invest.stocks.

### PC FINANCIAL NETWORK

**800-825-5723**

**Stock commissions:** $40 minimum

**Mutual fund commissions:** $40 minimum (500 funds available)

**Features:**
PC quotes and trading via Prodigy, Reuters Money Network, CompuServe, and America Online.
Limit orders
Margin accounts
Options
Bonds

**See review** at the end of this chapter.

### QUICK & REILLY

**800-634-6214**

**Stock commissions:** $37.50 minimum

**Mutual fund commissions:** On no-load funds ($1–$15000) commission is 0.51% of principal

**Features:**
Touch-tone quotes and trading: PC quotes and trading via QuickWay
Limit orders
Margin accounts
Options
Bonds

QuickWay provides delayed quotes (its screen lets an investor monitor up to eighteen stocks at once), portfolio tracking and updating, alerts on stocks that have hit buy or sell targets, and a similar feature, Option Watch, designed for options traders. A $1,000 deposit is required to open an Option Watch account.

### CHARLES SCHWAB & CO.

### 800-442-5111

**Stock commissions:** For StreetSmart 10 percent off Schwab's regular rates; for e.Schwab $39.

**Mutual fund commissions:** 10 percent off Schwab's regular rates

**Fees:** With e.Schwab talking to a human representative by phone costs $5 per call.

**Features:**
Touch-tone quotes and trading via StreetSmart and e.Schwab
Limit orders
Margin accounts
Options
Bonds

**See review** of StreetSmart at end of this chapter.

Any investor with a Schwab account can use StreetSmart and get a 10 percent discount on trades. Schwab's deep discount on-line service, e.Schwab, limits an investor to electronic trading—talking to a human representative costs $5—but cuts commissions to a flat $39. You can preview both systems at Schwab's World Wide Web page (http://www.schwab.com).

## MURIEL SIEBERT & CO.

**800-872-0711:** Technical support: 800-822-2021

**Stock commissions:** Value rates (for trades of less than $8,000) $37.50 minimum. Shares rates (for trades above $8,000) $.03 a share with minimum of $75. Ten percent discount for trading by Touch-tone phone or computer.

**Mutual funds:** 400 no-load funds without transaction fees; other funds $39.50 minimum commission

**Features:**
Touch-tone quotes and trading; PC quotes and trading via direct-dial
  Siebert OnLine.
Limit orders
Margin accounts
Options
Bonds

Using Siebert OnLine software (a demo is available and the software is currently free to investors who open an account at Siebert of at least $10,000; although the firm says this is a limited offer—the software normally costs $49.95), an investor can obtain real-time price quotes and current news, verify account positions, and track and update account value. A watch list feature lets a user monitor the prices of up to 27 securities at once.

## JACK WHITE & CO.

**800-233-3411**

**Stock commissions:** $33 minimum plus $.03/share below 2000 shares; above 2000 shares $33 plus $.02/share

**Mutual fund commissions:** 350 funds available without commissions

**Features:**

Touch-tone quotes and trading; PC quotes and trading via PAWWS
World Wide Web page at http://pawws.secapl.com. Ten percent discount for Touch-tone or PC trading.

Limit orders

Margin accounts

Options

Bonds

Jack White offers some innovative programs for investors tired of
fees and big spreads. It will try to match buyers and sellers of load mutual funds, thus saving them that sales charge, and it will also arrange
after-hours trades, also through matching of buyers and sellers.

## REVIEWS

### E*TRADE

E*Trade, 1 Embarcadero Place, 2400 Geneg Road, Palo Alto, CA
94303, 800-786-2575.

Electronic address: Internet (http://www.etrade.com), America Online
(ETRADE), CompuServe (GO ETRADE).

Requirements: E*Trade Navigator requires modem, 750K free hard
drive space, windows 3.1 or higher.

Cost: NA.

Guarantee: NA.

Demo or sample: NA.

Technical support: 9–8. through Internet, America Online, and CompuServe.

User Newsletter: None.

Strengths: Cheap. Cheap. Cheap. It's hard to beat a flat $14.95 for a
trade.

Weaknesses: You get what you pay for. Don't expect that you'll be able
to reach an E*Trade representative by phone within a reasonable
length of time.

Tricks of the trade: Be patient, the menus make this system very slow.

Definitely get E*Trade's Navigator software or use the Internet version. Both have an easier-to-use interface than you'll get with E*Trade on CompuServe or even America Online.

E*Trade is about as bare bones as an electronic brokerage gets. And maybe a little too much so. When the firm went off-line for five days, company spokesman Michael Amaya, vice president of marketing and a seven-year Schwab veteran, placed the blame at the feet of two power outages in south Palo Alto. The first knocked the firm's electricity for about niney minutes and the second fried their telecom connections to CompuServe, AOL, and their own network. But that doesn't explain why the firm didn't have backup systems or add the human capacity to handle investors by phone. And certainly the firm's explanations of the problem on forums such as CompuServe's Investors Forum weren't exactly models of clarity or contrition.

You can do business with E*Trade via CompuServe, America Online, the Internet, or E*Trade's own system. The prices are the same on each venue: $14.95 per trade for listed shares; trades of more than 5,000 shares carry a 1 cent per share surcharge.

The CompuServe route gets you into a plain text system with menus. Type 20 for an order menu, then type 21 for a stock order, then 211 to buy stocks. Working through all the levels of the menu can take a while. It took me about five minutes to place my first order. The system prints out the order for confirmation on the screen and won't trade until the user confirms it. At the same time, the system generates an order number and states when the order was placed. Until April 1995 the price quoted at verification was on fifteen-minute delay. That's been upgraded to real-time pricing.

The system has a few bells and whistles. A company analyzer function gives the investor access to CompuServe's information from S&P, Disclosure, etc., at the usual surcharges. A news section has dividend and split announcements, earnings announcements, and 52-week high/low alerts.

E*Trade's own software, e*TRADE Navigator for Windows 3.1. (free—plus shipping—to account holders) addresses one of the major disadvantages of using this brokerage directly through either of the online services. Using Navigator, an investor can download stock prices and study them off-line (avoiding usage charges), and then go back online to make a trade.

## Fidelity On-line Express (FOX)

Fidelity Brokerage Services, 161 Devonshire St., Boston, MA 02110,
   800-544-9375.
Versions available: Windows 2.1.
Requirements: Windows 3.1, 3.2MB of free space on hard drive.
Cost: $49.95.
Guarantee: 30-day money back.
Demo or sample: Demo available at Fidelity's World Wide Web page.
Technical support: 800-544-0246.
User Newsletter: None.
Strengths: Fox's TurboTrader is an extremely robust trading engine that
   never got hung up in my ten tries. Research from Standard and Poor's
   (pretty common with electronic brokerages currently) and Telescan
   (unusual) make this a rather complete information and trading desk.
   And, of course, you get the Fidelity service organization, a trifle bu-
   reaucratic for me, but definitely one of the best in the business.
Weaknesses: You can get lost in the hierarchies of this program's menu,
   and the fact that it's only Windows-like means that Fox is harder to
   navigate (and not as pretty) as programs such as StreetSmart. Fidelity remains one of the more expensive discount brokerages, even
   after the 10 percent discount for trading with Fox.
Tricks of the trade: On security, compare carefully electronic brokerage
   services that use an on-line service and those that use their own dedicated gateway. If you share an on-line account with other family
   members, be sure that you can set up separate passwords to prevent
   children, for example, from accessing your investment accounts.
   Many of the on-line services give you up to five screen names per account, each with its own password possibilities. One suggestion: use
   one of these to access your on-line brokerage and nothing else. That
   way you can restrict access easily and also change the password frequently without inconveniencing other family members.

   With version 2.1 of FOX, mutual fund giant Fidelity Investments has
closed most of the distance separating its electronic brokerage software
and Charles Schwab's StreetSmart. Most, but not all. Like StreetSmart,
FOX now offers access to Dow Jones News Retrieval and Standard &
Poor's Marketscope. And FOX offers Telescan, a powerful fundamental
and technical analysis program StreetSmart doesn't include.

But FOX isn't fully a Windows program (Fidelity calls it "Windows-like") and that means difficulties installing the program for computer neophytes. The program actually installs as a DOS program and then the user constructs the FOX icon and loads it onto the Windows desktop. While the procedure isn't too difficult, it does take three pages in the manual to explain—which means that a lot of potential users will have trouble.

Still, most investors aren't opening Fidelity accounts to get FOX, but instead are using FOX to access their existing mutual fund or brokerage accounts. And on that level FOX works just fine. Downloading account information is easy once a user gets accustomed to the fact that opening an account gives only the last balance and position downloaded and not current details—for that an investor has to click "Connect with Fidelity" and ask for account or transaction information.

From the transaction menu investors can get the value of their portfolio—either a summary or in position-by-position detail. Transaction history shows deposits, buys and sells, and dividends and interest payments (and reinvestment). The portfolio analyzer is decent: it offers an asset analyzer, capital gains update, customized reports, and a form for reporting schedule D information for tax time. Like Quicken and StreetSmart, FOX isn't great at tracking lot sales for tax purposes. The designation of a specific group of shares purchased at a specific time and price (as opposed to other shares of the same stock purchased at a different price) is important to minimize a gain or maximize a loss for tax purposes. Just as in the other programs, to track lot sales in FOX you'll have to manually designate lots with slightly different names.

Fidelity seems to have installed enough lines and servers to keep response crisp. Ten tests of the system failed to produce a single busy signal or hangup.

## PC FINANCIAL NETWORK

PC Financial Network, 1 Pershing Plaza, Jersey City, NJ 07399; 800-825-5723.

Versions available or electronic address: Prodigy, America Online, CompuServe, and Reuters Money Network.

Requirements: On-line account.

Cost: Free.

Guarantee: N/A.

Demo or sample: Do a dummy trade on any of the on-line services.

Technical support: 800-825-5720 or e-mail.

User Newsletter: No, but free research from Pershing.

Strengths: A well-designed computer interface that answers all the first-time user's questions, combined with a solid, established brokerage firm. PCFN offers an extremely wide range of accounts (money market, IRA, SEP, margin) and transactions (shorting, stop limits, check writing). An unusual plus for an electronic brokerage account: free research on stocks, bonds, and the market in general.

Weaknesses: Since PCFN operates through three of the major on-line services, your electronic connection with your brokerage account is dependent on your ability to access these services. (You can't use the phone either since the firm doesn't currently offer Touch-tone trading.) While that probably ensures that your electronic connection is safe from anything but a major catastrophe, it also means that you can't count on easily dialing in during the busy evening hours on America Online and Prodigy.

Tricks of the trade: PCFN provides 120 days of transaction history. If you want more than that—and you probably will for tax returns and portfolio management, remember to download that history periodically into a separate file on your computer.

You may never have heard of these guys, but PCFN combines one of the most thoughtfully designed brokerage interfaces with some long-established Wall Street muscle—the service is owned by the Pershing, a major Wall Street clearing firm that handles approximately 10 percent of NYSE volume, and which in turn is a division of Donaldson, Lufkin & Jenrette, a member of the NYSE that dates back to 1959. PCFN itself dates back to 1987, making it one of the oldest electronic brokerages.

I accessed PCFN through Prodigy. (It's also available thorough CompuServe, Reuters Money Network and America Online.) The opening screen offers me three choices: Learn about PC Financial Network, Try a Practice Trade, and Open Account Online. Investors should note that this is the only on-line brokerage (that I know of) that allows you to begin trading immediately without first sending a check to the firm to put a balance in your account. PCFN sets a limit for that first trade of $2,000. A complete description of the interface and how it works appears earlier in this chapter.

PCFN's connection to Pershing makes this offering a little different from Fidelity, Schwab, and the other electronic brokerages that are connected to a discount brokerage firm. PCFN provides daily research and market views from Pershing as well as free stock reports from selected Wall Street analysts. As you might expect from a discount brokerage, the firm does not recommend individual stocks.

### STREETSMART

Charles Schwab & Co., 101 Montgomery St., San Francisco, CA 94101, 800-334-4455.

Versions available or electronic address: Windows (version 2.0), Macintosh (version 1.0); Schwab Web page http://www.schwab.com.

Requirements: Windows requires 8MB RAM, 8MB free space on hard drive and Windows 3.1 or higher. Macintosh requires System 7 or higher, 4MB RAM, 5MB free space on hard drive. Both versions require modem.

Cost: $39.90.

Guarantee: 30-day money back.

Demo or sample: Downloadable demo on Internet at http://www. schwab.com or free from any Schwab branch.

Technical support: 800-334-4455 (6–7 PST, M–F, 8–4:30 PST, S and S).

User Newsletter: None.

Strengths: Adaptable connection with other software, StreetSmart will export data to Excel, Quicken, Lotus 1,2,3, Tax Exchange or any program that reads ASCII-formatted data. Schwab's first-rate service extends to support for StreetSmart. Their 800-number answered on the first ring when I needed help in setting up Dow Jones News Retrieval and S&P Marketscope.

Weaknesses: While the software uses the very reliable CompuServe for quotes, the program does not have a look-up function. To find a ticker, you'll have to use the printed S&P directory provided with the program—which of course will go out of date.

Tricks of the trade: While you can theoretically access all your Schwab accounts on StreetSmart, in reality you may have trouble if your household runs several accounts under different names—for example, if you have an IRA in your name and your spouse has one under his or her own name. One way around this problem is to set up StreetSmart to access joint accounts and then sign up each spouse with power of attorney to the other's accounts. If that kind of arrangement isn't suited to your household, set up separate StreetSmart accounts (each with its own password) for each of you. On a more technical note, downloading stories from Dow Jones News Retrieval requires modifying the size of the disk cache to prevent the loss of stories. Set the size of the cache to at least 64KB.

Schwab seems to be trying to turn StreetSmart into the only software that its customers will ever need. I'd like it better if, instead of adding more services, they fixed a few annoying problems in the basic program.

Mind you that my criticisms begin with a general admiration of StreetSmart. The on-line buying and selling are easy to use and allow adequate confirmation to avoid mistakes. Execution is fast, and I've even done a sale or two between the buy/ask spread—unusual even with a human broker. The presentation of prices is clearer than Quicken and the system seems to have enough line capacity so that I get few busy signals or hangups—important since Schwab has set up the software so that most of the time you spend on StreetSmart is off-line, and only after everything is set up does an investor call up Schwab.

The bells and whistles are useful, too. Some investors will find the package of Dow Jones News Retrieval, S&P Marketguide, and Reuters Money Network (on Windows versions only), all the investment information they'll ever need.

But don't throw away all your other software just yet. StreetSmart charges premium prices for bundling this information—a company report from S&P is $5. And StreetSmart still has major holes. For example, the software is difficult to use for pricing fixed income instruments such as Treasuries. When I first set up my accounts on StreetSmart, it downloaded the wrong information on the price and sale of a zero-coupon Treasury. Just as frustrating is the program's accounting functions. While I can easily get StreetSmart to calculate a capital gain or loss on a security, I can't get it to calculate total return—using internal rate of return, for instance—which severely limits the usefulness of this program as a portfolio management system for any investor who buys stocks with dividends or bonds that pay interest. (In fact, it takes some work to get StreetSmart's gains/losses calculation to work correctly. Beware of reports that show unrealized gains and losses on securities that were sold long ago.)

Final summation: a great front end for trading on Schwab, but you'll still need other software for reasonably priced investment information and to keep track of the results of your investing.

In January 1996 Schwab rolled out e.Schwab, an electronic brokerage account for investors who felt comfortable enough using a computer to abjure all human contact. To use e.Schwab you have to open a special e.Schwab account at Schwab (even if you have an existing Schwab account, but you can maintain an e.Schwab and a regular account at Schwab at the same time). Commissions on e.Schwab are capped at $39 for up to 1,000 shares, no matter the price of a share. But you can't use a Schwab office, and talking to a Schwab representative will cost you $5. Instead you can ask questions, get help, etc., via e-mail. My experience with StreetSmart suggests that e.Schwab's e-mail function will be pretty efficient. The software is free (shipping and handling cost $6.95).

# 8

# Timing Is Money: The Art of Technical Analysis

Computers were meant for technical analysis. Using a computer to do the heavy-duty number crunching and chart preparation that lie at the heart of technical analysis lets an investor produce precisely the chart that he or she wants exactly when it's wanted. And that chart can be resized in order to study a short period in more detail or to find a long-term pattern in a long stretch of data. Indicators can be modified and combined to find the exact analytical tool that best reveals the future course of the stock. Drawing tools let an investor find trends and cycles that might forecast the future.

But the newest technical analysis programs try to do much more than that. Programmers are starting to build rudimentary "artificial intelligence" that captures some of the wisdom of the experienced technician into this software. No one has yet put a "black box" with the sophistication of the multimillion-dollar programs invented by the rocket scientists at Wall Street firms like Morgan Stanley on the desk of an individual investor. Still, the day when a technical analysis program selling for $495 or less "thinks" for an investor is on its way.

That could turn technical analysis from the preserve of cagey veterans and full-time number nerds into a tool for the individual investor who can't find the time to learn the difference between slow and fast stochastics. Just how close are we to the point where a machine can act as your investment partner?

A great paper chart book, like the ones produced by Ned Davis Research, is a treasure. (As it should be, since this charting service costs $10,000 annually.) Let's say that I want to gauge the future direction of the current stock market. I might begin with chart S7 illuminating. Here the technicians at Ned Davis have drawn the course of the Standard & Poor's 500 stock index from 1926 to the present. An investor can clearly see the huge dip of 1932, and 1973–1974 bear market, and the 1987 crash. So far this is nothing more than a graph of prices—the raw material for all technical analysis.

But these technicians then add a few simple lines to the chart and turn it into an interpretive tool. They draw a trend line through the high points of the S&P's seventy-year history and another through the

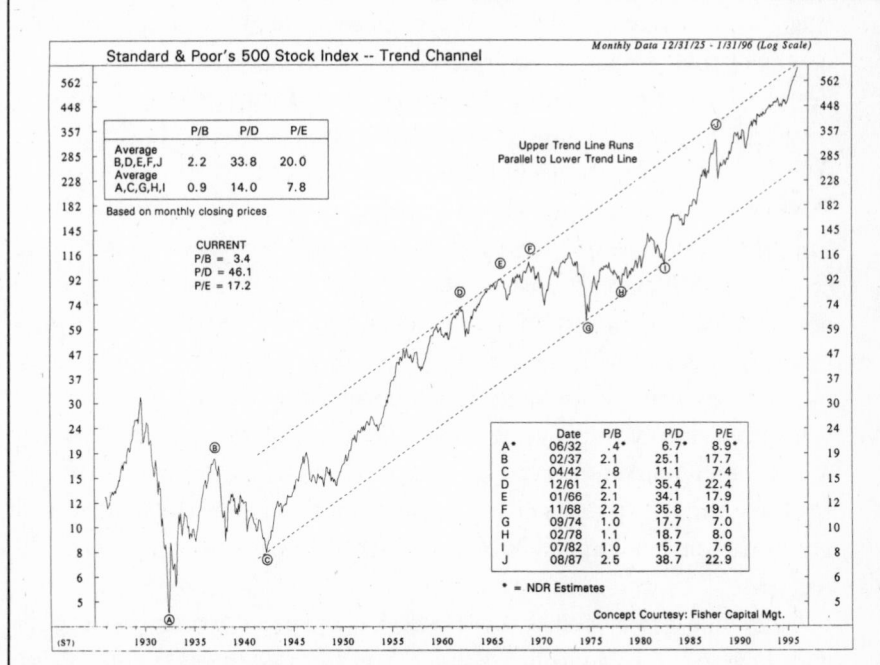

*Even a simple chart like this one from a chart book shows the character of the market.*

(*Courtesy Ned Davis Research*)

low points. Suddenly the price history of the market shows a steady upward trend that vacillates inside a band. Short periods that look like terrible markets, such as 1973–1982, don't break the trend at all; they still follow it upward, close to the lower boundary of the channel.

Now, it's easy to separate great investors' markets from terrible ones, or from the just so-so. The market from July 1982 through August 1987, when the market moved from the bottom of the channel to near the top was one of the greats. November 1968 through September 1974 was one of the worst. And the current bull market has generally been just okay—the S&P has moved up at about the historical average, without significant interruption. But because the market began this bull so far to the topside of the channel, the climb really can't compare with the 1982–1987 move from bottom to top.

That's all history, of course. But the chart also gives an investor, if not an explicit prediction, at least a suggestion for how to invest now. It's clear that the market can approach the upper boundary of the channel and stay there for a considerable length of time. It did so for a decade beginning in the late 1950s and ending in 1968. It's also clear that the relatively recent past, which shows little of the choppy ups and downs of that decade, is unprecedented. Looking at this chart, an investor who has been out of this market would think twice about suddenly jumping in. It's easy to see that this is a picture of a market with far more downside potential than upside.

Want other perspectives on the market? Look at other ways of charting prices. For example, chart S23 studies the year-to-year percentage change in the market. Historically, it's wise to sell when the year-to-year change is greater than 27.8 percent and then falls, the Ned Davis researchers say. On the other hand, it's time to buy when the market has been dragging downward and then picks up enough to move upward from deeply negative territory toward zero. The specific buy signal? When a market that has been headed downward moves up enough to pierce the negative 9 percent barrier. On this chart, the market isn't yet in the danger zone called "overbought," but it's headed in that direction.

Or to take a third perspective, look at chart S215, which tries to produce buy and sell signals by tracing the number of stocks trading above their 30-week moving average. (A *moving average* is an average built on a period of days or weeks that, by smoothing short-term variation, reveals longer-term trends. For example, today a 50-day moving average averages yesterday's prices and the previous 49 days. Tomorrow, the average will include today and the previous 49 days—thus lopping off the oldest day of data.) After studying market history, the technicians at Ned Davis Research believe that when 70 percent of the stocks in the Standard & Poor's index are trading above their moving average of the last ten weeks, that's a sign that the market is overbought—an investor should sell. When the percentage is less than 30, that's a sign that investors are too pessimistic about the market—so an investor should

---

### BASICS

# WHAT IS TECHNICAL ANALYSIS?

**A**t its simplest, technical analysis looks at the behavior of past prices and a few other factors, such as trading volume, to predict future prices. In contrast to fundamental analysts, a pure technician doesn't consider data on sales or price-to-earnings ratios or profit margins. Technical analysis holds that the course of future prices can be forecast by looking at the behavior of prices in the past. To that end, a technician spends his or her days looking for patterns in the behavior of past prices that one technical theory or another says are predictive of future price movements.

A technician has a choice of dozens of tools, but the vast array breaks down into a few categories. Breakout tools track market trends and monitor when a security price penetrates a trend on either the up or down side. In analyzing the general direction of the market or an individual security, technicians using these tools often draw trend lines, which connect highs with highs or lows with lows, and channels, which combine a pair of trend lines to track movement within a band. Breakout tools also indicate levels of support and resistance.

Pattern recognition also studies the figures created by the movement of a security, but instead of looking for a trend, this method tries to match the current price and volume behavior to well-known formations such as the head and shoulders, double and triple tops and bottoms, rectangles, diamonds, and wedges. Profits result when the technician finds a pattern in formation and buys or sells in anticipation of its completion.

Other tools study the movement of the market in regular cycles or waves. Technicians who use these methods believe that like waves in water, waves in the market occur at regular and predictable intervals and sizes.

buy. Right now, this indicator, like the previous one, says that the market isn't yet in overbought territory—after a brush with 70 percent, the market pulled back into the low 50s. Still, like the other charts, this one suggests that we're much nearer a top than a bottom.

Technical analysis software makes it possible—and simple—for an investor—hooked up to a source of price data—to build exactly this kind of chart. For example, using MetaStock, here's how I go about building Ned Davis's rate-of-change chart. I start by clicking the MetaStock icon in Windows and then, once I've got the program's opening screen, I click on "Tools" and then on "Downloader," MetaStock's automated method for getting price data from CompuServe. I select S&P 500 by clicking on it and then click on "Download prices" in the main menu. The software automatically dials up CompuServe (or the data vendor of my choice), downloads the figures for daily open, close, high, low, and volume, double-checks the data for accurate transmission, and then signs off.

Returning to the main MetaStock menu, I click on "New" and, using

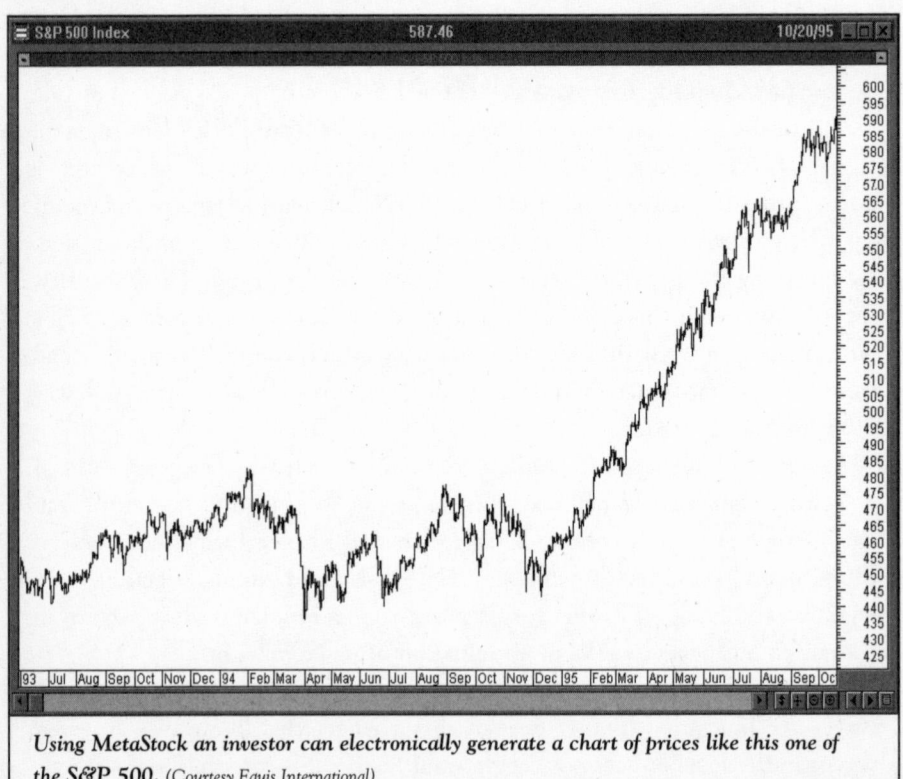

*Using MetaStock an investor can electronically generate a chart of prices like this one of the S&P 500. (Courtesy Equis International)*

the program's "Smart Charts" feature, click on "S&P 500." That gives me a basic bar chart (so-called because each day's prices are graphed as a bar where the bottom indicates the day's low, the top the day's high, and a little flag at the day's close) of the S&P for the time period I've specified (in this case from June 1993 through October 26, 1995).

Then I go to the top of the screen and the pull-down menu of indicators. I scroll down until I get to "Rate of change." I click on it with my mouse, and holding down the mouse button (the cursor changes from an arrow to a hand that grasps the words "Rate of change"), I drag it to the window that already shows the S&P line chart. When I release the mouse button, I get a red line tracing the percentage change in the S&P index. Going over to the side of the screen, I pick an icon that looks like a long dash. This is a drawing tool that lets me draw a straight horizontal line at any level I want. I pick the 27.8 percent "sell" level the Ned Davis technicians chose. I then repeat the process to draw a "buy" line at their –9 percent level.

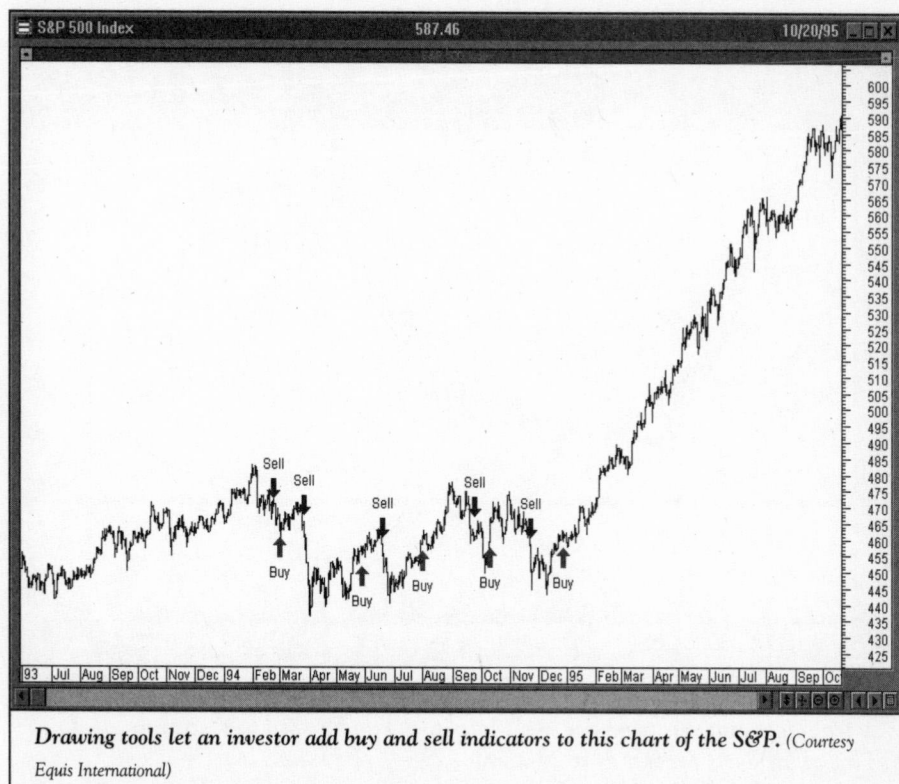

*Drawing tools let an investor add buy and sell indicators to this chart of the S&P. (Courtesy Equis International)*

The chart shows me a clear buy on July 8, 1994, as the rate-of-change line moved through the –9 percent line like a knife through butter. About a month and a half later, on August 29, the rate-of-change line gave a clear sell as it broke into overbought territory by crossing the 27.8 percent line.

## BETTER THAN PAPER: EXACTLY THE CHART YOU WANT, WHEN YOU WANT IT

Software, such as MetaStock, MegaChart, Telechart 2000, Windows on Wall Street, Supercharts, and Wall Street Analyst, has certain advantages over the paper charts. For example, I can suddenly decide to chart any individual stock that I become interested in using exactly the technical tools I think are most revealing. I can create a simple chart of the price of Motorola (still using MetaStock) and apply two simple technical tools—trend lines and moving averages. No ordering a paper chart

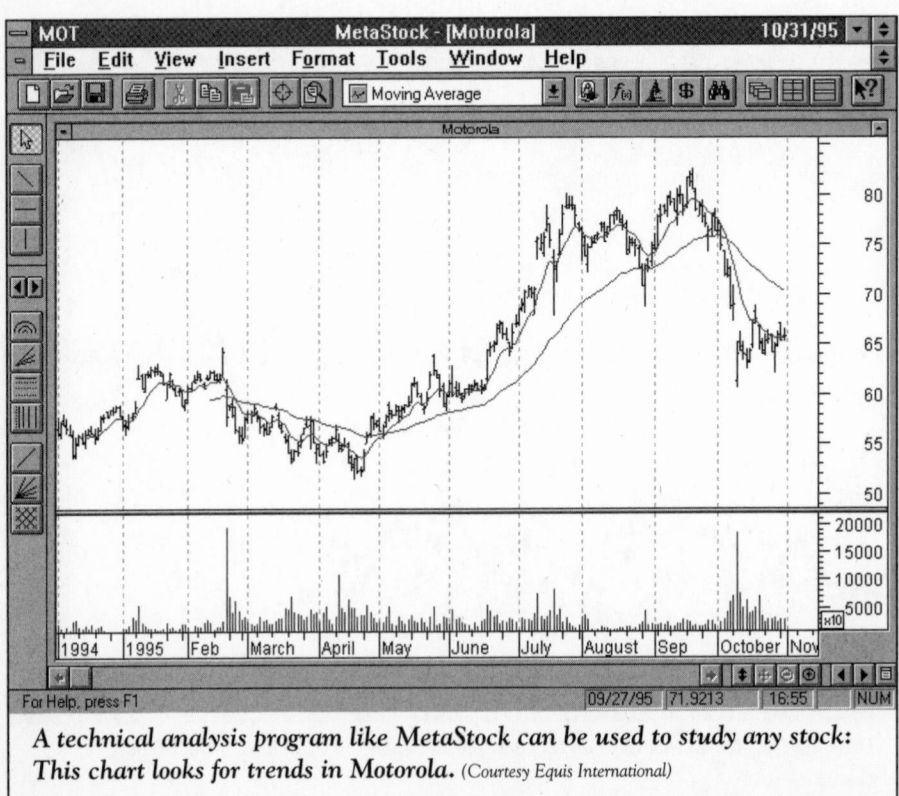

*A technical analysis program like MetaStock can be used to study any stock: This chart looks for trends in Motorola.* (Courtesy Equis International)

and waiting for it to be delivered. No disappointment if the charting service doesn't chart the stock I want or use the indicators that I think most appropriate.

The price of a share of Motorola has climbed from a recent low of $51 on April 19, 1995, to a high of $82.50 on September 19, 1995. (I get that date by simply moving my cursor over that point on the chart; MetaStock then automatically reads out the date and the price in the lower part of the screen.) The stock has since fallen to a low of $60 before recovering slightly.

I then apply a few simple tools to see what insight into the future I can wring out of this data. First, I want to study the trends in Motorola's stock price. So, using the program's simplest drawing tool, I connect all the tops to each other and all the bottoms with each other beginning with the April turnaround. The pattern's not perfect, but I do have a stock moving up, both in its highs and lows, relatively consistently inside a channel. Until July. Then I get two violations of the trend line, one on the top and the other on the bottom. Both are significant.

On the upside, on July 12, Motorola literally jumps through the top of the channel. For that day on the chart, if you look closely you can see a gap between the high for July 11 of almost $71 and the low on the next day of nearly $73. Also, looking at the bottom of the page where another chart shows trading volume for the day, I can see a big spike in trading around these dates. For the next few days, Motorola stays above the high trend line and it looks like the stock may not only be establishing a new high but setting a new trend for a further climb.

## TIPS ON THE TOOLS

# THE DAILY DATA GRIND

**F**or the dedicated technical analyst, monthly data delivery won't do. There's no point to watching the trends of the market with data that's weeks old at best. While your wallet will thank you if you buy your historical data on disk or CD-ROM (see Tips on the Tools: Buying History, in this chapter), generating profitable buy and sell signals with a technical analysis program requires daily data delivered by modem. Here are some sources with notes on cost, top modem speeds, data format, the breadth of

*continued*

market coverage (stocks, mutual funds, NYSE, NASDAQ, etc.), and, for those who want their historical data fast, and cost be damned, the starting date for historical data.

### COMPUSERVE (800-848-8199)

Top modem speed: 14,400 bps
Other delivery formats: None
Cost: $.03 per quote per security
Data formats: ASCII, comma and tab delimited, MetaStock
Stock data: All exchanges (high, low, close, volume) since 1982
Mutual funds: All (NAV, price, distributions), back 13 years
Futures and options: 250 futures, all options back 13 years
Indexes: More than 200, back 13 years
Additional notes: International data limited to Canada

### CSI (800-274-4727)

Top modem speed: 14,400 bps
Other delivery formats: disk, CD-ROM, tape
Cost: By modem: $.10 per month per security. By disk: $.20 per month per security for first 500, $.15 for 501–1,000, $.10 over 1,000 securities
Data formats: CSI format (provided software converts data to other formats) and MetaStock
Stock data: All NYSE and NASDAQ since 1980, 700 AMEX stocks since 1980 (open, high, low, close, volume)
Mutual funds: More than 1,000 (NAV and price) since 1986
Futures and options: All U.S., back to either 1942 or 1982, overseas futures since 1968
Indexes: 50 back to 1928
Additional notes: Canadian stock data since 1995. Windows version of data management software is scheduled for mid-1996.

### DIAL DATA (800-275-5544)

Top modem speed: 9600 bps
Other delivery formats: None

Cost: $.02 per quote per security. Fixed packages available (for example, stocks for $19.99 per month)

Data formats: ASCII, comma and tab delimited, MetaStock

Stock data: All exchanges (open, high, low, close) since 1970

Mutual funds: 4,300 (NAV, price) since 1986

Futures and options: All U.S. and Canadian; futures back to 1963, options back to 1993

Indexes: 250 back to 1970

Additional notes: 16,000 quotes per connection limit. International data on 6 countries, 3,000 stocks. Fundamental data also available.

## Dow Jones News Retrieval (800-815-5100)

Top modem speed: 14.4 kbps

Other delivery formats: None

Cost: Fixed rate Private Investor package $59.95 per month (up to 5 hours per month access from 7:01 P.M.–6 A.M.)

Data formats: ASCII, comma delimited, MetaStock

Stock data: All exchanges (high, low, close, volume) since 1973

Mutual funds: 5,000 (NAV) since 1973

Futures and options: More than 50,000 since 1973

Indexes: 1,800 since 1973 (includes non-equity indexes)

Additional notes: Most complete international coverage of any vendor— 20,000 stocks.

## DTN Wall Street (800-475-4755)

Top modem speed: N/A

Other delivery formats: Satellite or cable TV

Cost: $37.95 a month plus start-up fee of $295 (payable after free 30-day trial)

Data formats: ASCII, MetaStock

Stock data: All exchanges (high, low, close, volume)

Mutual funds: 4,500 (NAV prices)

Futures and options: All

Indexes: Dozens

*continued*

Additional notes: Also through DTN: S&P Stock Guide Database (additional $18 a month). Data includes fundamental information on NYSE, AMEX, NASDAQ stocks—company descriptions, SIC codes, dividend yields, rates, institutional holdings, latest prices, historical ranges, trading volumes, and sales history. Updated weekly and transmitted 3 times a week. DTN recently launched DTN Spectrum, which adds charting, audio/visual alarms, and additional fundamental data to DTN Wall Street's regular offerings.

## FinComm (212-838-6324)

Top modem speed: 14,400 bps
Other delivery formats: None
Cost: Prices are available on bulletin board (212-838-6324)
Data formats: ASCII, comma delimited (software for conversion to other formats provided)
Stock data: All NYSE and AMEX since 1992, 5,000 NASDAQ since 1990 (high, low, close, volume)
Mutual funds: 2,000 (NAV, price) since 1992
Futures and options: none
Indexes: 91 since 1992
Additional notes: 10,000 quotes per day limit. Requires Internet connection. No international data.

## Iverson Financial Systems (408-522-9900).

Top modem speed: 28.8 kbps
Other delivery formats: Disk and tape
Cost: $0.0025 per data item per stock per day; $0.02 per index per day; minimum order $100
Data formats: ASCII, comma and tab delimited, MetaStock
Stock data: All exchanges (open, high, low, close, volume, dividends, shares outstanding) since 1981
Mutual funds: 4,300 (NAV, price, distributions) since 1987
Futures and options: 203 with varying starting dates
Indexes: More than 600 with varying starting dates

Additional notes: Discounts available for large orders, international data limited to Canada

### PINNACLE DATA CORP. (800-724-4903)

Top modem speed: 34 kbps

Other delivery formats: disk and CD-ROM

Cost: Various fixed rate packages available (for example, $299 for history of indexes and breadth)

Data formats: ASCII, comma and tab delimited, MetaStock

Stock data: None (ARM's index since 1965, Hines ratio since 1983, OFX ratios since 1983)

Mutual funds: None

Futures and options: 50 since 1969

Indexes: 30 since 1901

Additional notes: No international data; 300 business and economics data items back to 1945

### PROPHET INFORMATION SYSTEMS (800-772-8040)

Top modem speed: 19,200 bps

Other delivery formats: disk, CD-ROM, and Internet

Cost: Complete historical stock database $195; updates $29 per month; complete historical mutual fund database $195; updates $29 per month

Data formats: ASCII, comma and tab delimited, MetaStock, Technical Tools

Stock data: 3,000 NYSE since 1982, 1,000 Amex since 1982, 6,000 NASDAQ since 1982. All open, high, low, close, volume.

Mutual funds: 6,000 funds since 1988

Futures and options: 200 with varying start dates back to 1959

Indexes: More than 100 with varying start dates

Additional notes: Little international data—5 indexes; updates and charting offered on World Wide Web (http://www.prophetdate.com)

*continued*

**TELECHART 2000 (800-776-4940)**

Top modem speed: 14,400 bps

Other delivery formats: Historical data available on CD-ROM for $29

Cost: Daily updates $0.005 per security per quote with $.99 a day maximum charge. Telechart software $19.

Data formats: Telechart 2000 (software converts to other data formats)

Stock data: 2,300 NYSE, 840 AMEX, 4,800 NASDAQ since 1984. All open, high, low, close, volume.

Mutual funds: 4300 (NAV) since 1988

Futures and options: None

Indexes: More than 130 since 1988

Additional notes: No international data

**TELESCAN (800-324-8246)**

Top modem speed: 9600 bps

Other delivery formats: None

Cost: Unlimited non-prime time $25 per month, up to 5 hours per month $9.95. $29.99 activation fee. Also requires QuoteLink software ($29.95).

Data formats: ASCII, comma delimited, MetaStock

Stock data: All exchanges since 1988 (open, high, low, close, volume)

Mutual funds: 2,500 (NAV) since 1988.

Futures and options: More than 1,000 current contracts

Indexes: More than 500 since 1988

Additional notes: No international data

But that isn't what happens. On August 18, Motorola breaks below the trend line of highs and over the next few days breaks through the low side of the channel, too. The stock then rallies, but, significantly, doesn't climb back up to the upper trend line before taking a dive straight through the bottom trend line. Another big spike in volume, which then stays heavy for the next few days, indicates that a large number of investors are selling their Motorola. The sentiment on the stock seems to have changed.

Could an experienced technician have seen the breakdown coming? Probably. When the stock attempted to establish a new, higher trend line in the middle of July, volume almost completely dried up. No one was buying at those levels. The rally from the downside breakthrough on August 29 didn't look convincing, either. Volume once again dried up. There's simply a lot more enthusiasm for selling at these levels than for buying.

And an experienced technician wouldn't have been analyzing the stock with just one set of tools. For example, he or she might have applied another simple tool, the moving average. The longer a period a moving average uses, the less sensitive it is to daily fluctuations and the further the trend that it describes lags current events. Some technicians put that lag to use by tracking a moving average against the daily price movements of a stock. When the price line crosses over the moving average line, that often indicates a change in the stock's direction. In the Motorola chart, the price line (the most volatile line in the illustration) crossed over the 50-day moving average (the least volatile of the three lines) on April 25, creating a buy signal. Acting on that wouldn't have

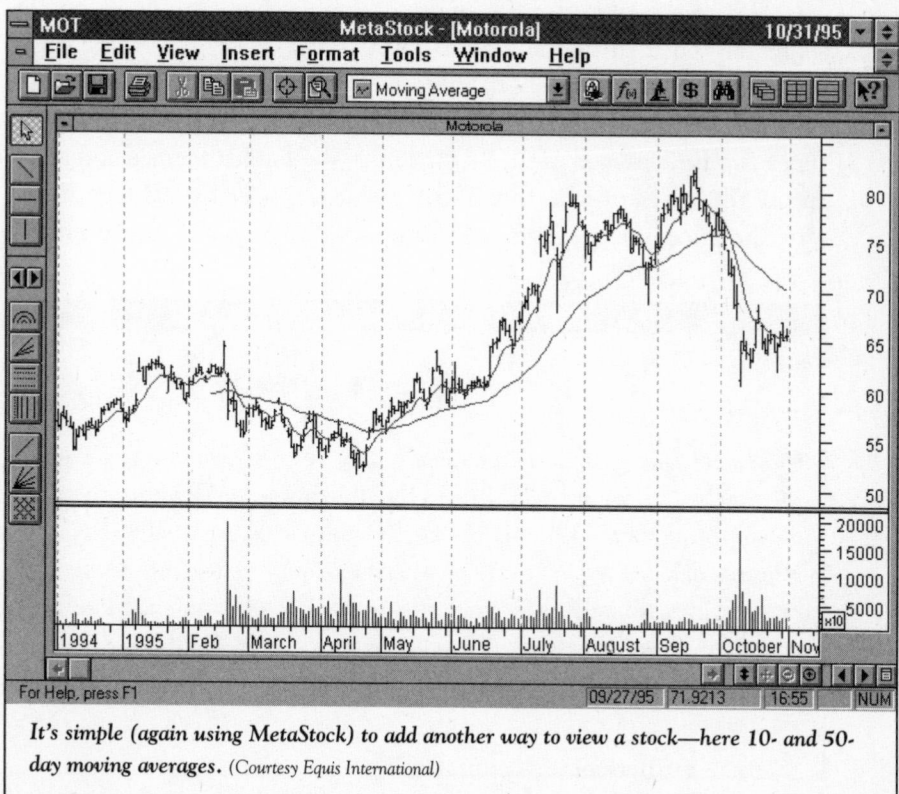

*It's simple (again using MetaStock) to add another way to view a stock—here 10- and 50-day moving averages.* (Courtesy Equis International)

put an investor in at the absolute recent bottom of April 19, but acting on the signal would have captured most of the subsequent upturn. In the same way, the crossover on August 28 gave a strong sell signal, one confirmed by a second crossover on September 29. The subsequent downturn of the moving average itself gives further confirmation of the sell signal.

Of course, a 50-day moving average wasn't the only choice. The same illustration above also shows a 10-day moving average (the line with medium volatility). Notice that it generates buy and sell signals a lot more frequently. An investor following that line would have bought on July 19, sold on August 1, bought on September 5, and sold on September 22, a period during which the 50-day moving average issued just one sell signal, on August 28. Which strategy would have been superior? The answer would differ for different investors, depending on how many shares each individual was buying and selling and on transaction costs. As a rule of thumb, however, shorter moving averages pay off better for investors with larger positions. A $5 a share move on 10,000 shares is certainly a lot more profitable than a $5 move on 100 shares, after deducting transaction costs.

Some technicians plot both a relatively long moving average, such as 50 days, and a shorter moving average, then follow the crossing of those two lines as well as the crossovers of the longer average and price. In the case of Motorola, the 10-day average crosses the 50-day shortly after the price line does, thus confirming the buy signal in late April.

---

## TIPS ON THE TOOLS

# BUYING HISTORY

To keep any system of technical analysis up to date, you'll have to buy timely data via modem. But to build your system's history the first time, downloading data on-line is the costly alternative, especially if your system requires data for a good hunk of the past history of several indexes and a lot of securities. Instead, buy your historical data on disk or, more and more commonly, on CD-ROM. The diving price of CD-ROM delivered data makes it possible for you to buy all the history you need at reasonable prices.

But before you rush to buy, consider if your computer system will be able to store all the data the vendor will deliver. For example, Stock Data's database of 9,000 stocks and securities eats up a lot of hard drive space. Daily data for all three major exchanges takes up 35MB per year (approximately 135K a day).

(Besides the primarily disk- and CD-based vendors below, see also the historical data on CD-ROM from daily data suppliers Prophet Information Systems and Telechart 2000 listed in the previous box.)

## Eagle Data (317-293-2696)

Top modem speed: N/A
Other delivery formats: Disk
Cost: $39 for one market; $190 for complete database
Data formats: ASCII
Stock data: None (breadth data, indices, inflation indicators, etc., back to 1885)
Mutual funds: None (4 fund indicators back to 1954)
Futures and options: None
Indexes: Daily market

## Momentum (800-379-0206)

Top modem speed: N/A
Other delivery formats: CD-ROM
Cost: Initial CD-ROM $99. Quarterly update $20. Annual subscription to quarterly updates $60.
Data formats: ASCII, MetaStock
Stock data: All NYSE and AMEX since 1989 and 5,000 NASDAQ since 1989 (open, high, low, close, volume)
Mutual funds: None
Futures and options: None
Indexes: 4 Dow Jones indexes—Industrials and Transportations back to 1897, bonds back to 1923, utilities back to 1934.
Additional notes: No international data

*continued*

**STOCK DATA CORP. (410-280-5533)**

Top modem speed: 19.2 kbps

Other delivery formats: Disk, CD-ROM, e-mail

Cost: On disk all NYSE, AMEX and NASDAQ stocks $250 a year, mutual funds $60 a year; on CD-ROM all stocks $69.95 for any five years of data (add mutual funds for $50)

Data formats: SDC format. (Provided software can convert data into formats for MetaStock, Computrak, AIQ, Supercharts, Technifilter, Savant, ASCII, and Spreadsheets.)

Stock data: All exchanges since 1987 (open, high, low, close, volume)

Mutual funds: 4,800 (NAV only) since 1993

Futures and options: None

Indexes: 200 since 1987

Additional notes: No international data. Comes with Tactician software that will create simple charts (with none of the drawing tools and only a small fraction of the indicators in full technical analysis programs) and will screen only such data as gain or loss, minimum percentage of change, minimum volume, and minimum price. Internet address: http://www.stockdata.Inter.net/

This may seem cut and dried—read the chart, buy or sell—but experienced technicians know that even the most reliable indicators generate false buy and sell signals. That's why they turn to other indicators for confirmation. Look at another period on the Motorola chart, that of February to April 1995. Using either the 10-day or 50-day moving average would have produced at least three false buy signals. After each, the stock, instead of heading higher, moved lower. Volume would have even confirmed these buys. Of course, an investor following them would have lost money on each trade—and more important, might have lost interest in Motorola completely just before the stock's April upturn.

Rather than blindly following the buy/sell signals generated by this one indicator, or even two in conjunction, the experienced technical analyst would try to put Motorola in context. How does the stock compare to other technology issues? Is the sector as a whole showing strength that might turn Motorola's churning of February and March into a steady climb? What's the direction of the market as a whole? Is Motorola attempting to advance while the market as a whole is falling backward?

In this case, a quick look at the charts for Intel—another semiconductor maker—and the NASDAQ composite index since the over-the-counter market is heavily weighted with technology stocks—indicates that Motorola is actually lagging as the technology sector and the NASDAQ market in general move upward. Seen in this light, the churning of February and March seems evidence, not that the stock is directionless, but that it is building a base for a possible advance.

## NEXT, PUTTING THE "EXPERT" IN THE SOFTWARE

Notice how often the phrase "experienced technical analyst" comes up? It's a clue to the reason why more investors don't use technical analysis—and why many of those who do don't make much money. Techni-

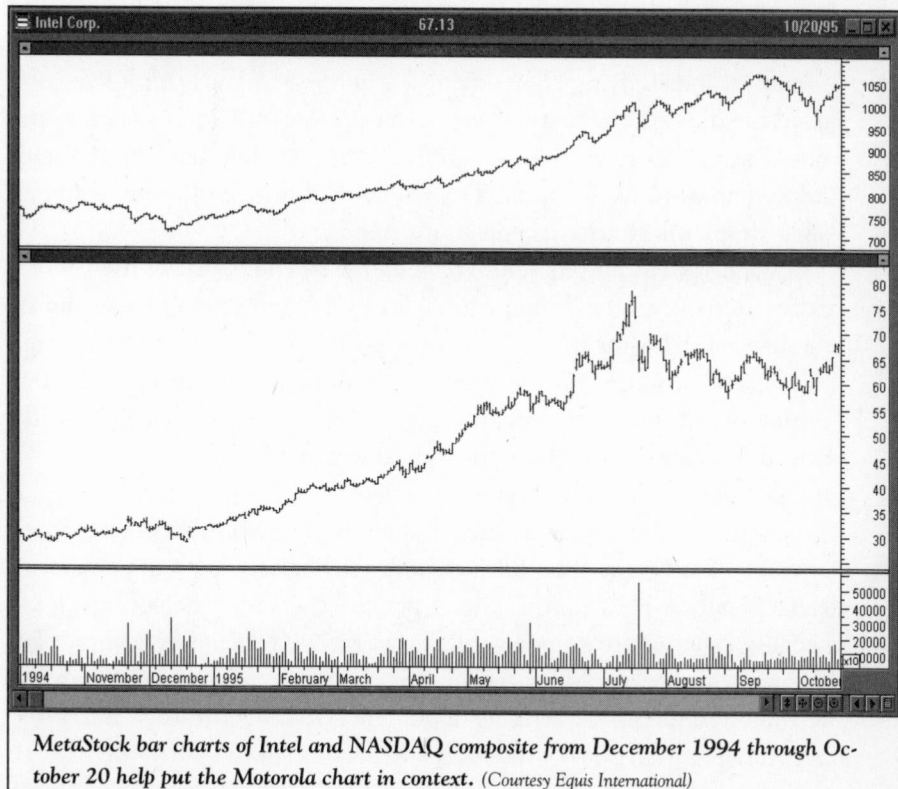

*MetaStock bar charts of Intel and NASDAQ composite from December 1994 through October 20 help put the Motorola chart in context.* (Courtesy Equis International)

cal analysis is hard. Interpreting charts is an art that takes years to master. It takes an expert eye to find a pattern in a chart in the first place. Only the technician who has studied the behavior of that pattern in all kinds of markets can use it to make money in the markets.

To an extent I performed some sleight of hand when I took you from the Ned Davis paper chart to the computer version drawn in Meta-Stock. I used all the experience that the Ned Davis technicians compiled to guide me in generating and interpreting those charts. Why did I pick the "rate of change" chart for the market as a whole? Because they knew it was significant. How did I decide that overbought territory began at 27.8 percent and oversold at –9 percent? Because they had discovered a valid historical pattern.

In the case of Motorola, why did I pick 50-day and then 10-day moving averages? Why did I concentrate on crossovers as buy and sell signals? Why did I look for confirmation? Basically, because I've read books by the masters of technical analysis such as Martin Pring's *Technical Analysis Explained*, Alexander Elder's *Trading for a Living*, and Gerald Appel's *Winning Market Systems*.

I consider myself a technical neophyte. I've been reading some of the literature and studying charts for about two years now. I think I've got a good handle on how to use some of the simpler indicators—such as the ones I described above—but I certainly can't claim to have built a trading system or to have explored all the tools that one of these technical analysis software packages puts in my hands.

In fact, I often find myself overwhelmed by the power of these tools. Supercharts gives me 77 indicators, for example. Many of these can be modified. Do I want to use 10 days or 25? Do I want to use a weighted average or unweighted? Exponential or normal? And even once I've settled on an indicator and picked parameters I feel comfortable with, how do I know this is the right indicator to be looking at now in this market—or that my interpretation is right?

Compare using a good technical analysis program such as MetaStock or Supercharts to a good fundamental stock analysis program such as NAIC's Stock Selection Guide. I praised the Stock Selection Guide because its structure helped guide a user through the analytical process. Even a beginner would learn something useful by filling in the data the program required and thinking about the questions it raised. But while Supercharts and MetaStock—and programs like them—are superb tools for the experienced analyst, they don't help the novice much. In

## Do You Need Real-Time Data?

Technicians themselves can be divided into categories depending on the time frame they use to study the market. At the shortest end lie the day traders. These technicians use real-time intraday (that is, the tick-by-tick prices of securities when the markets are open) to rapidly turn over their positions. A day trader can hold a position for only a few hours in the endless search for temporary mispricing of a security. This technique demands constant attention, and can in my opinion only be successfully executed by full-time traders. It's hard for a nonprofessional to execute this strategy successfully. Signals are generated frequently, which increases transaction costs, and the profit on a single share is likely to be low, which means that it requires a sizeable capital stake to make real money.

For these reasons, individual investors who pay higher commissions than professionals and who have difficulty getting the best prices on trades operate at a disadvantage when executing a short-term strategy. Real-time data feeds and software to produce the short-term buy and sell signals this strategy requires cost significantly more than end of day data and software.

Investors with longer time frames—those who look for trends that unfold over weeks—or patterns that take months to complete—don't need real-time data or systems.

fact, they're likely to thoroughly confuse anyone who hasn't already mastered the art of technical analysis.

And this isn't because Supercharts or MetaStock, to take two programs with big followings, are bad programs. MetaStock, especially, is in fact just the opposite—it's one of the best Windows-based pieces of software of any kind that I've ever run. The icons are relatively self-explanatory, the menus arranged in logical hierarchies, the tools themselves easy to use by simply pointing and clicking. And MetaStock's "click and learn" interface, which defines a term, lists a date, or reports a price when a user moves the cursor over a chart, is a marvel to use. No, the problem is simply that technical analysis is a difficult art to master.

So the current generation of technical analysis software has set out to help the beginner- and intermediate-level technician get better investment results and conquer the mysteries of technical analysis. To do that

## DO YOU KNOW WHERE YOUR DATA IS?

Little is more aggravating than trying to call up a chart or transfer information only to discover that you don't know where your software has stored the data. That's a problem with all DOS and Windows software, but it's a particularly big problem with data-intensive programs like those used in technical analysis.

I recommend that you take a few moments to map how your program organizes its data files. That's less complicated than it sounds. For Wall Street Analyst, for example, it would consist of a list with just a few names—stock data: c:\omega\data\usstock and c:\omega\data\canstock; mutual fund data: c:\omega\data\mutfund; and index data: c:\omega\data\index. Keep that list either taped to your computer or in a computer file that you can access while your technical analysis program is open. Then you won't have to stop a data transfer or a charting session to find the file name you need to retrieve or store data.

some programs, such as Meta-Stock, have added functions that help a user find the "right" indicator. Other software companies, such as Omega Software, the maker of Supercharts, have built whole new programs, Wall Street Analyst, in this case, to guide the less-experienced into the world of technical analysis (and then, in the case of Omega, added that module to the existing Supercharts program). Relative newcomers such as MarketArts have built their technical analysis software from the ground up with the idea of guiding users through technical analysis.

Does it work? The results are, shall we say, interesting. These programs confront two fundamental trade-offs. First, it's difficult to write a single program for both the experienced and beginning user. At some point, the effort to make the program "easier" to use for the beginner can start to frustrate the experienced user who finds it "dumbed-down" or restricting. The routines added to help a beginner, for example, can strike the experienced user as pointless and time-wasting restrictions on navigating the program. Second, these programs must walk a fine line between developing functions that help the user find the best investment system for him or her in this market and functions that "tell" the user how to invest. Let's explore how three software companies are approaching these problems.

## MetaStock: The Investor Is the Expert

MetaStock exemplifies one approach: Equis International, the company behind MetaStock, has spent considerable time and effort making its software as easy to run as possible, but in content and tools has basically continued to cater to the experienced user.

For example, MetaStock for Windows provides an "Explorer" function. I'm going to stick with two of the indicators we've used so far to demonstrate how this feature works. Under "Tools" I click on "Explorer" and then click on "New" to start an exploration. This gives me a template to create a spreadsheet. I have buttons that let me name each column and specify what data (either a raw number such as price or a calculated number such as a moving average) I want in that column. The user can either learn how to write these data requests in MetaStock's language or, by clicking on "Function," cut and paste the desired statements into the template. For this example, I'll ask that column A be the most recent closing price, column B the most recent value of the 20-day moving average, and column C the most recent value of the relative strength index—which will give me buy and sell signals, much like those generated by the rate of change indicator. Despite its name, the relative strength index compares a stock, not to other stocks or indexes, but to its own past price change. It's calculated from the average upward price change and the average downward price change. I ask the Explorer to look at a dozen stocks and three indexes this way.

What does the table show me? (I choose to limit the number of stocks and indexes in this Exploration to a handful I've been following lately. Theoretically, I could look at the entire universe of stocks this way—or at least all those I've bought data on.) Quite a lot, actually. First, the relatively experienced investor—or one who has read the description of the relative strength index in the back of the MetaStock manual—knows that stocks tend to top out at a relative strength of 70 and bottom at a relative strength of 30. Motorola, interestingly enough, is now at 46.9. It's still got a way to fall, it seems. Microsoft, a stock I've been watching for signs that it's near a top, is getting close if I look at relative strength (57.4), but its closing price is still comfortably above the moving average so the stock probably hasn't topped. This one bears watching, though. And so does CitiCorp. The bank looks as if it's near a top (relative strength of 61.2). The stock's moving average is approaching its closing price—another sign of a stock that's fully loaded. CitiCorp might be ripe for selling.

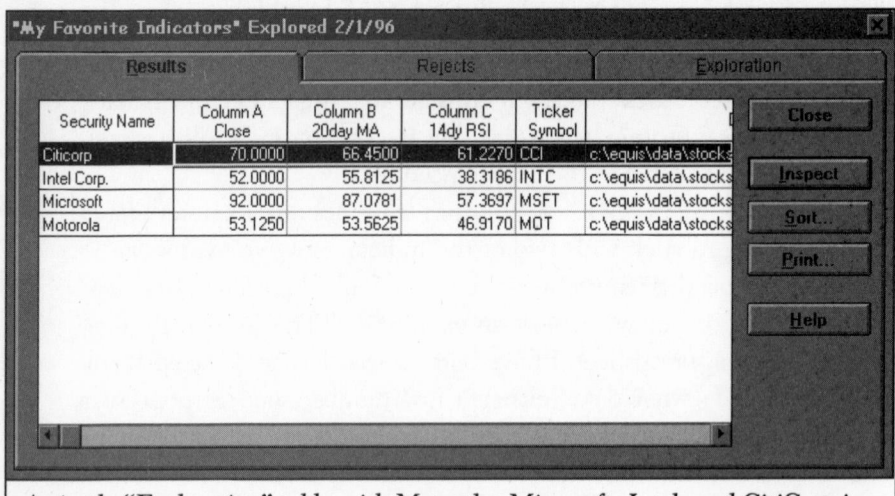

*A simple "Exploration" table with Motorola, Microsoft, Intel, and CitiCorp in MetaStock lets an investor scan for promising patterns.* (*Courtesy Equis International*)

By clicking on CitiCorp and then on the "Inspect" button at the right of the screen I can look at data on CitiCorp for a longer period. I can see that the stock's relative strength index was at 68 as recently as October 16. Shortly after that date, the stock's moving average crossed the price line. I can also see that the relative strength index was lower than it is now on October 26, when it hit 31.6.

If I had used a larger sample of stocks and indexes in this exploration I would probably want to sort this database from high to low on price, or moving average, or relative strength looking for the best buy or sell candidates. And, of course, since it's relatively easy to set up an exploration, I can go through this process with other indicators. MetaStock comes with a dozen explorations already set up and ready to go: binary waves, long-term bearish, long-term bullish, MACD buy signal, price and volume breakout, and others. It's easy to use any of these to identify promising candidates for further study. And in fact, the investor relatively comfortable with technical analysis is likely to find this a very useful tool.

But the beginner still has to do a lot of work. The spreadsheet still requires interpretation—in even my simple example, I have to understand the relationship between closing price and moving average and the significance of relative strength. Working through the preset explorations might be a useful way to learn about technical analysis, but this isn't an "instant" way to pick winners or a fully developed trading system.

## WINDOWS ON WALL STREET PRO:
## EDGING TOWARD THE BLACK BOX

Windows on Wall Street Pro from MarketArts Inc. takes MetaStock's Explorer a step further with a feature called SmartScan Plus. (Only the Pro version of Windows on Wall Street contains SmartScan Plus.) Like Explorer, SmartScan is a way to sort an investor's entire database to find stocks that have formed potentially important technical patterns. Like Explorer, SmartScan comes with predefined trading systems that a beginner can use to generate buy and sell signals immediately. (An advanced user can modify these templates and create new ones.) But unlike Explorer, SmartScan generates charts with brief explanations of how to interpret these indicators.

MarketArts has tried to make Windows on Wall Street as easy to operate as possible. The first screen has just four buttons along the side—securities, charts, research, assistant—which makes approaching the program unintimidating. Clicking on "Charts" produces a screen that shares the basic organization of MetaStock, but may be a bit easier to use because it relies on more words and fewer ambiguous icons. A menu bar across the top again reduces the program to a few functions: the ever-present "File" and "Edit," "View" (a list of ways to format the screen), "Plots" (moving averages, indicators, price volume plots, custom indicators, plot line styles and scaling), and "Tools" (the technical methods grouped into categories such as trend lines, regression lines, etc.). For the icon-addicted, a row of cryptic icons sits along the top under the menu bar. Another row of icons occupies the side of the screen. One pictures a grainy Sherlock Holmes examining charts. That's SmartScan. I click on it to pull up the SmartScan dialog screen.

Ignore all the other details and look at the lower left-hand corner of the illustration. There you'll see the heart of SmartScan—a box that allows an investor to scan for Percent Change, Trading Systems, or Custom Alerts, or some combination of those.

Percent Change is simple. Using the box to the immediate right, a user can ask the program to scan the entire database looking for stocks that have changed in price or volume (or both) by any specific percentage. For example, type in 3.00 in the box labeled "Close" to find stocks that moved up or down by 3 percent or more today (or in the number of periods that you specify at the top of the dialog). Leave the next two boxes blank, but fill in "Volume" with 75 percent. That tells SmartScan to look for stocks with big changes in price and big changes in volume—a combination that could signal a major change in the direction of the stock or a breakout. If you then also click on "Display Chart If Signal" before hitting OK, SmartScan will produce charts for all the stocks that meet these standards. (Which can result in quite a pile-up on the screen if you've set the standards too loosely.)

So far SmartScan is pretty much like Explorer on MetaStock, but now let's move from the "Percent Change" box to "Trading Systems." First click on "Template Directory." That will give you a list of all the preset trading systems in Windows on Wall Street and any that you've designed as well. For this example I'll stick to an indicator that I've already discussed, relative strength. I choose that preset trading system from the templates, and then, by clicking OK, ask SmartScan to look

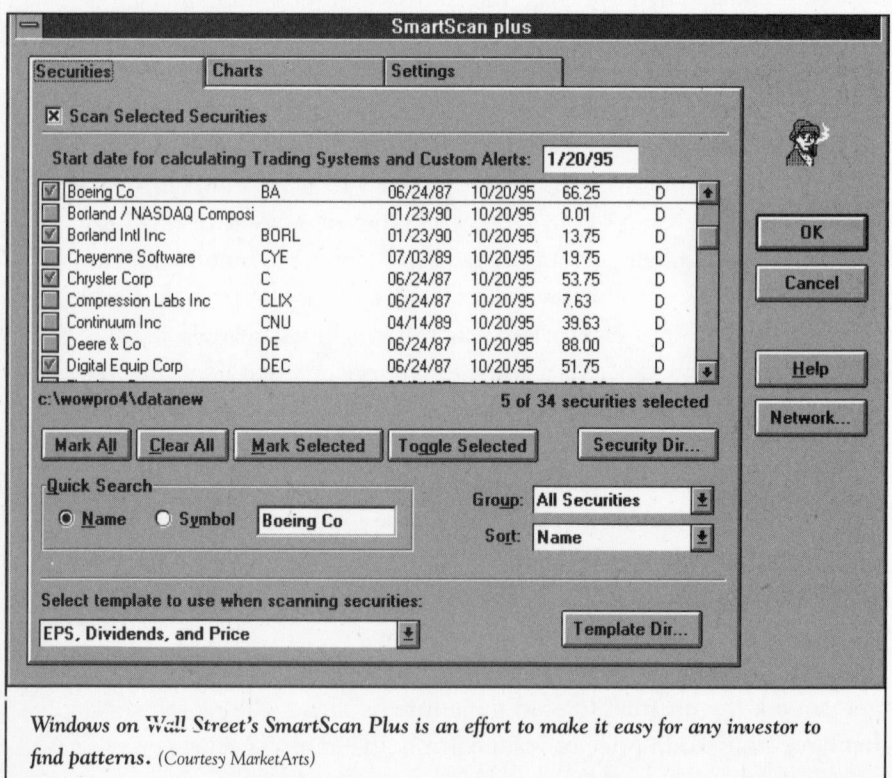

**Windows on Wall Street's SmartScan Plus is an effort to make it easy for any investor to find patterns.** *(Courtesy MarketArts)*

for any stock with a relative strength alert because it has broken through the 70 percent level into overbought or fallen below the 30 percent level to oversold. One stock and its chart pops up: Boeing.

Here's what SmartScan gives me: at the bottom of the page a price plot of Boeing, in the middle a relative strength chart for Boeing, and at the top a chart that I don't know much about, the slow stochastic. On the bottom price plot colored diamonds mark the points at which the relative strength indicator and the slow stochastic issued a buy or sell signal.

The bottom chart is generating complex signals without too much work on my part. The program is using relative strength and percentage change in price (as indicated by the slow stochastic) to generate clusters of signals at temporary bottoms and tops. I don't have to be especially visually acute to pick up the way that diamonds cluster around May 16, June 27, August 1, August 22, and August 19 at low points in the price cycle. These are points when I should have bought, according to this system. A similar cluster in early June marked a top for the stock. Single diamonds at September 5 and October 10 indicate sell signs.

But while SmartScan has found a system that seems to fit Boeing, and which I can now adopt, I really don't know if this is the best system that I can use to make money on this stock. And should I extend this system to other stocks? Should I follow these recommendations?

Windows on Wall Street has edged an investor close to "black box" territory here. An investor can use SmartScan that way: Pick a pre-designed trading system, apply it to the market or some part of the market, and then buy or sell faithfully on the system's recommendations. The investor won't really understand why the system is generating those signals. All he or she will know is the input (price data) and the output (buy or sell). The system will remain a mystery—a black box—that simply spits out results.

An investor doesn't have to treat SmartScan that way, of course. Instead it can be a "gray box." The system does tell an investor how it is producing alerts—that's what the text that the program's "learning mode" puts on a chart tells the user—and it is possible to modify the system's rules (for example, an investor can create a new alert that combines relative strength with the rate of change in price). Most important, an investor can use Windows on Wall Street's "Profit/System Testing" feature to see how well this trading system would have done in the past and compare it to other systems.

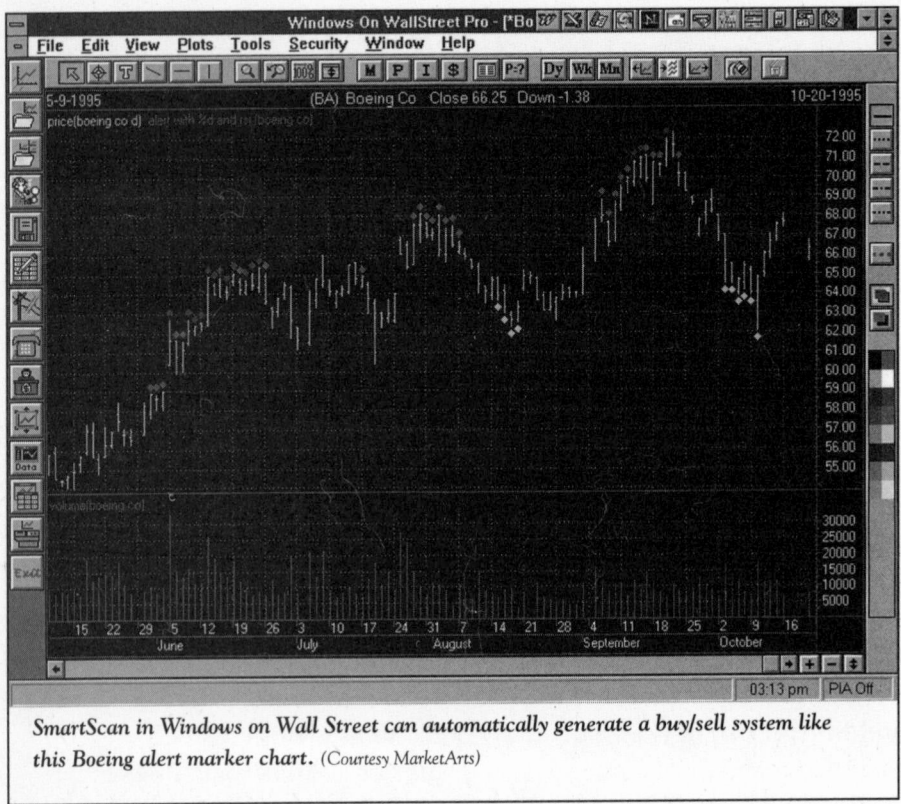

*SmartScan in Windows on Wall Street can automatically generate a buy/sell system like this Boeing alert marker chart.* (*Courtesy MarketArts*)

I can turn on the profit-testing feature either from the main menu bar or from inside SmartScan. By clicking "Print Profit Report" in the extreme lower right, I can generate a report on how the relative strength indicator that is now telling me to buy Boeing has done in the past. From the Boeing report, I can see that from May 1992 through October 1994, this system gave me net loss of $310 on an initial $5,000 investment, for an annualized rate of return of about −6 percent. Interestingly, about 75 percent of the trades the system suggested turned out profitable. But the quarter that went bad were real stinkers. The average profitable trade earned just $120. The average loser cost $432.

It may be difficult to decide between technical analysis programs based on the number of indicators they offer or their ability to keep your price data clean, but a technical analysis program without a good system-testing feature comes close to being useless. Fortunately, it's relatively easy to list the qualities of a good systems testing function. There's just really a single important issue: Does the system-testing feature allow you to test the results under reasonably realistic circumstances?

For example, Windows on Wall Street asks an investor to set a commission rate (either in dollars or as a percentage), to set the dollar amount of the first trade, to trade long and/or short, and to deduct margin interest. You can also include any limit rules (trailing stop, maximum loss stop, and break-even stops).

It also goes one crucial step further and asks what price the system should use in calculating the profit or loss on the trade. Let me explain why that's critical. Say on August 28 the program generated a buy signal. At what price should the test assume the stock was purchased? Your database probably doesn't include every tick (the price of the stock at five-minute intervals), but just high, low, close, and open. Did you hypothetically buy at the low or at the high? The choice obviously makes a tremendous difference. (Beware of any system or investor who claims to buy always at the day's low.) Well, how about the closing price? No investor can be certain to get the stock at its last price for the day. Opening price the next day is a safe and realistic alternative.

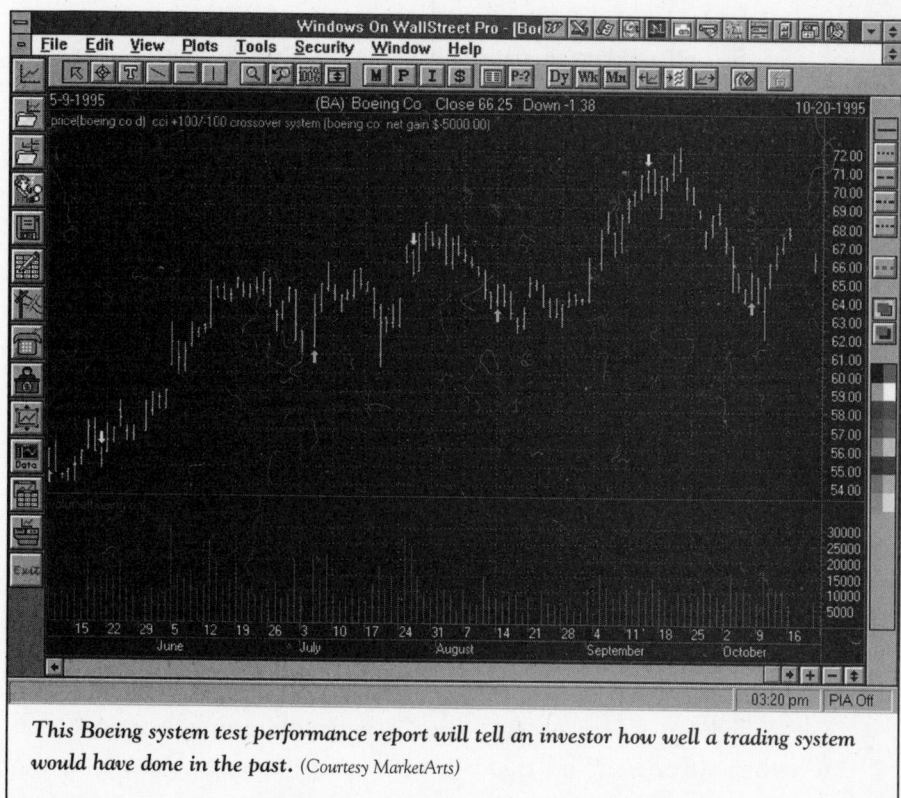

*This Boeing system test performance report will tell an investor how well a trading system would have done in the past.* (Courtesy MarketArts)

## THE CD-ROM REVOLUTION

In 1995 producers of technical analysis programs joined the CD-ROM revolution. The combination of a medium that will hold years of data and programs that constantly cry out for more information is a natural.

Two long-term producers of technical analysis software have been first out of the blocks. TeleChart 2000 puts twelve years of data on 14,400 stocks, mutual funds, and indexes on CD-ROM. Daily updates for the stock database cost $2.45 a day (with additional fees for other data updates). Best of all, the data format is compatible not only with TeleChart's own technical analysis software, but also with Windows on Wall Street, Nirvana's OmniTrader, MetaStock, and The Candlestick Forecaster.

Omega has put its Wall Street Analyst on CD along with twenty-five years of data. Downloads cost $19.95 a month (plus $35 sign-up fee) and Dial Data is the sole provider. Data format is compatible with other Omega products and with all the programs (including TeleChart 2000) listed above.

You know that you'll be able to duplicate that timing in the future, so it's reasonable to use that price for testing the system.

## WALL STREET ANALYST: THE "SMART" PROGRAM

Wall Street Analyst is the "smartest" technical analysis program I've run. Its strengths and weaknesses pretty much sum up the state of the art of artificial intelligence in technical analysis programs designed for the individual investor.

The program certainly oversells its technology. The box announces "Stock charting software so advanced, your broker may start calling you for advice!" One of the opening screens that flash by during installation notes that the program includes a "Fuzzy logic rule base of classic technical and fundamental analysis methods." Fuzzy logic, along with chaos theory and fractals, is one of the current buzz terms among Wall Street's heavy-duty number crunchers.

But try not to let the hype turn you sour too quickly. The program combines the type of chart scanner employed by MetaStock and Windows on Wall Street and a simple but actual honest-to-god artificial intelligence program—the sort called an expert system—into a very interesting learning tool. Whether anyone should trade on it is another issue. Describing the program reveals some of its strengths and weaknesses.

Wall Street Analyst calls its SmartScan/Explorer function either "The Automatic Analyst" or "ChartScanner," depending on whether you're running the program in its diskette version or the CD-ROM Wall Street Analyst 2 update. Like SmartScan, ChartScanner searches through your entire database of charts to look for stocks that show buy or sell signals.

ChartScanner produces two different kinds of reports—one similar to that produced by SmartScan, and the other a result of a simple artificial intelligence module. Let's say I run ChartScanner on Microsoft (ticker symbol MSFT). First, I get a page that gives me an alert on any indicator I ask ChartScanner to use—just like SmartScan. Second, I get what the program calls "Expert Analyst Alerts," both technical and fundamental and long term and short term.

Using the disk version of Wall Street Analyst, I get to the chart for Microsoft by clicking, "Go To" from the menu bar. The chart that comes up is the standard bar chart for prices with stochastics of various sorts in chart at bottom. I can, of course, do the normal things to modify and examine this chart using the tools menu or icons along the side.

But I can also go to "Analysis" on the menu bar to ask the program's artificial intelligence what to make of this chart. Under the Analysis menu I find "Indicator," "Expert Analyst," "Show Commentary," "Show Fundamental Data," and "Show Expert Analyst Outlook."

Clicking "Show Commentary" produces comments on the chart—pretty much like Windows on Wall Street gave me. Some are really helpful. Some are just jargon. I can also click on "Show Fundamental Data" to create a "Fundamental Data Report" with data on the stock's beta, book value, current ratio, dividend rate, earnings per share growth, net profit margin, and other fundamental data.

Clicking on "Show Expert Analyst Outlook" puts illustrations of bulls and bears on the screen. For Microsoft the long-term technical outlook box shows a growling bear. The short-term technical outlook pictures a second bear. The final box, for fundamental outlook, however, contains a bull. Clicking gives me a written explanation for each of these predictions. For example, "The long-term trend is down. ADX levels are declining, suggesting a choppy market ahead."

What's behind these picks and pans? "Expert Analyst" uses a kind of intelligence in making its comments. Expert Analyst examines the market and the stock and then modifies the indicators it uses to perform its predictions based on a judgment about the character of the

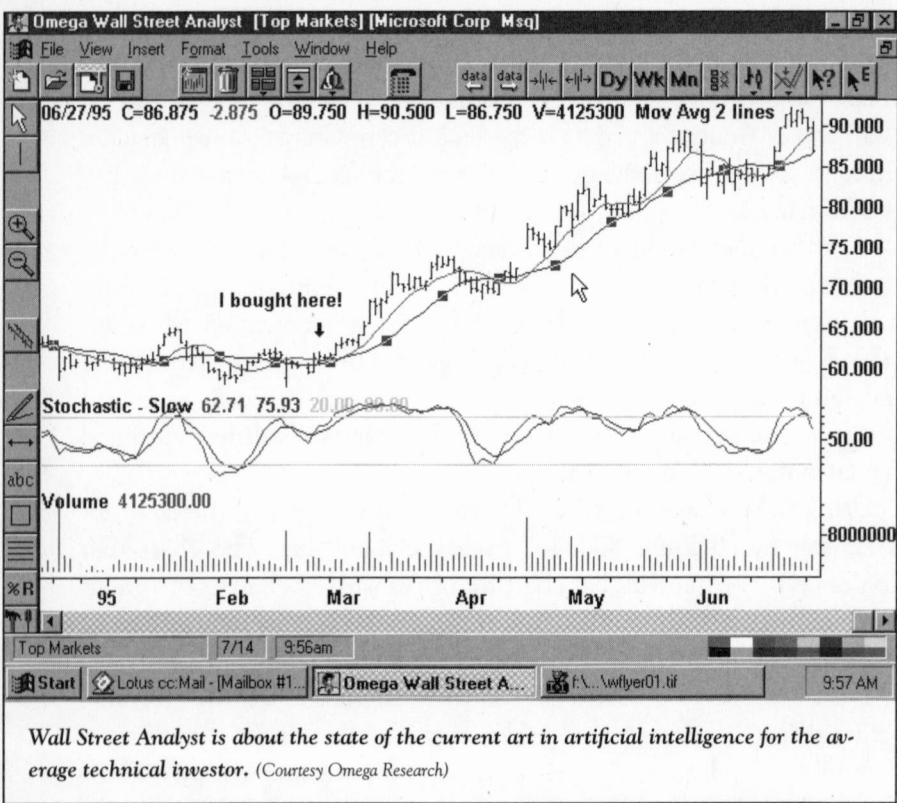

*Wall Street Analyst is about the state of the current art in artificial intelligence for the average technical investor. (Courtesy Omega Research)*

market. Basically, the program uses the ADX indicator (ADX measures the strength of the current market trend) to decide whether or not the market is showing a strong trend or whether it's non-trending and choppy. In trending markets, Expert Analyst places its emphasis on indicators such as moving averages, including Bollinger bands, which have a strong track record of predicting continuing price movements. In a non-trending market, Expert Analyst emphasizes overbought/oversold studies such as stochastics. To calculate bullish and bearish ratings, the program applies a simple numerical calculation that assigns bullish and bearish points to each indicator and then modifies the total with confidence factors to increase or decrease the importance of individual factors.

Should an investor trade on that system? It's not sufficiently sensitive to market conditions and uses too few confirming indicators for my taste. But it is still a useful tool. A beginner can learn a lot by watching the expert at work and comparing his or her own analysis to the machine's. More advanced technicians almost certainly have developed trading systems that are more complex—and I hope more profitable—than this one. For them an expert is a fellow investor who can be engaged in debate when predictions differ.

But Wall Street Analyst is a breakthrough. The program has put artificial intelligence on the desk of individual investors at a reasonable price and with minimal effort. In the next chapter I'll look at programs that put more advanced intelligences inside home computers—as well as exploring the kinds of programs that we're likely to see in the future as the current revolution in electronic investing continues.

## Reviews

### AIQ Trading Expert

AIQ Systems, 916 Southwood Blvd., Incline Village, NV 89452. 800-332-2999.

Versions available: DOS (version 3.2), Windows (version 2.1).

Requirements: DOS version 640K RAM, 11MB free hard drive space, DOS 3.0 or better. Windows version 2MB RAM, 11MB free hard drive space, Windows 3.1 or better. To install either version with basic data you will need at least 15MB of free hard drive space. Installing the S&P 500 stock data will require an additional 11MB.

Cost: DOS $996, Windows $996.

Guarantee: 30-day money back.

Demo or sample: 30-day trial for $88 refundable deposit.

Technical support: 702-831-2999, 7:30 A.M.–4:30 P.M. PST, M–F; America Online at AIQonline@aol.com.

User Newsletter: Monthly, $99 for annual subscription.

Updated: Program is updated at least once a year (cost is usually about 15 percent of original purchase price). The program will accept data updates from Interactive Data Corp., Dial/Data, Telescan, and Dow Jones News/Retrieval. Adding the data transfer utility DTU Pro, from AIQ, will allow the program to read data from Signal, PC Quote, CSI, MetaStock, and CompuTrac.

Strengths: A trading system that seems to have all the bases covered. The Expert Rating signal rates the market as a whole and each stock you track on a scale of 1–100, using technical signals at the end of every day. AIQ also generates a fundamental rating for each stock based on a combination of fundamental data specified by the user.

Trading Expert also produces an action list of all the stocks with recent high ratings that have been confirmed by price action. Lastly, "Profit Manager" advises an investor when to sell a profitable position.

Weaknesses: It's not that Trading Expert doesn't track profits and losses from its trading suggestions and recalculate the value of portfolios, but it's not as good at it as I'd expect from a program that is so thorough about everything else. It's harder than it should be to get a feel for how well this trading system is doing. Testing the system's performance on historical data is also harder and less rigorous than the rest of the program led me to expect.

Tricks of the Trade: AIQ lets an investor analyze sectors of the market as well as individual stocks. The investor specifies which of the stocks he follows that should be put into a sector, choosing industry groups from either the S&P or *Investors Daily* industry lists. That will let you compare the relative strength of an individual stock with that of its market sector.

With the AIQ Trading Expert an investor is taking a step into the land of black box investment systems. The core of the program is its expert ratings, which grade a stock's potential for moving up on a scale of 1–100 and do the same for possible downward movements. The program generates those rankings by using a form of artificial intelligence called an "expert system," which looks for historically meaningful patterns in the technical indicators for each stock. The program puts each stock though a kind of questionnaire, where the questions are about whether the technical pattern of the stock and the market match or don't match patterns in the past that are associated with movements in stock prices. By adding up the answers to each of these questions, the program arrives at a expert rating for the stock. Ratings of 90 or more are considered significant signals for trading.

The program's screen looks much like that of any other technical analysis program with a standard bar chart of a stock's price in the upper window and a lower window that can be used to display any of the program's extensive library of technical indicators. Values for those indicators are listed in a table along the right side, which culminates in the expert rating box.

An investor can use this rating in two ways. First, Trading Expert will screen through all the stocks an investor follows to find those that are now showing ratings of 90 or more. Second, an investor can pull up a single stock and search for all those dates when the stock's expert rating was 90 or more.

Trading Expert doesn't force investors to accept this advice completely on faith. In either screen mode you can call up a list of the technical indicators that led to the expert rating, along with explations of the indicators.

Very few technical analysis programs let an investor consider fundamental data and analysis in making investment decisions. AIQ's Expert Trader does. (The dedicated technician can ignore fundamental data easily since it's handled through a separate progam, the Fundamental Data Interface.) Unlike some technical programs that provide just a few items of fundamental data, AIQ lets an investor download up to twenty items. (Investors who use Telescan can pick 25 data categories from the 200 that program offers.) An investor can then construct a fundamental rating for each stock by combining the stock's rankings on fundamentals. The exact fundamental data fields included and the weight given to each in calculating a fundamental ranking are set by the investor.

Rather than delivering a stripped-down demo version, AIQ will let you try the complete program for thirty days (after that point the program becomes disabled unless you pay for it). This will give you a real chance to see if this box is for you.

## ASPEN GRAPHICS

Aspen Research Group, Glenwood Springs, CO 81602, 800-359-1121.
Versions available: Windows (version 3.0).
Requirements: 16MB RAM and 340MB free space on hard drive. With a 486 machine, Aspen Research recommends a math co-processor.
Cost: Start-up up fee $350. Then $350 a month for Aspen Graphics. Options include real-time MESA studies ($30 a month).
Guarantee: None.
Demo or sample: Free demo.
Technical support: 303-945-2921; fax 303-945-9619; bulletin board 303-945-0381
User Newsletter: On-line Forum, Internet address: Regular newsletter for subscribers.
Updated: Real-time updates through AspenInfo Stations. Unlimited

free historical data via the dial-up Aspen Host Network. Compatible with data from ComStock, Platt's, Signal, Bonneville, and Knight-Ridder.

Strengths: Easy to set up screen with charts at top of screen and raw data in tabular form at bottom—useful for checking accuracy of data. The program also allows the investor to remove the gaps in these charts created when no shares trade. Compressed tick-by-tick data makes it possible to construct a chart with any time period—including intraday charts. It's simple to build a study for one stock and then apply it to another—just type in the new symbol. No rebuilding necessary. Historical prices are both cheap—that is, free—and extremely inclusive—every tick from every exchange.

Weaknesses: Certainly more program than the average investor who uses technical analysis needs. If you don't do day trading, you're paying for functions and data you don't need.

Tricks of the trade: Don't be chauvinistic when it comes to calendars and data. Not all markets are open on the same days and a program that treats data from a holiday on the Tokyo market as if it the market were open will seriously throw off any trading system you develop. Aspen Graphics allows the user to automatically adjust for holidays on a exchange-by-exchange basis. For less sophisticated programs, it's a good idea to save a backup data set before every download. That way if the software fails to pick up a holiday, you can fix the problem either by editing the most recent data (if that's easy in your software) or by going back to the original data.

Sure, it's expensive and eats hard drive space like a hungry tiger, but this is what it takes to play with the traders. This street-quality quote station will put real-time pricing information—trades, bids, asks on minute-by-minute basis—on your desktop and then allow you to create customized quote pages for following the market, using either preformatted templates or the software's quote editor.

As a trader's product must, this can create spreads, baskets, and custom alerts. The user can set alarms—visual or audio—for an unlimited number of symbols on self-defined conditions that can be anything from simple price levels to complex formulas. (Formula language can be pretty sophisticated—absolute value, standard deviation, moving average, weighted moving average, if, thens, and, ors, and true/false are all included.)

Once you've created your own screen environment—I put statistics and news along the bottom—it's easy to create charts in any format and any time interval. Since Aspen delivers the price of every stock at every tick (compressed on your hard drive), an investor can study a chart in as much or as little detail as desired—tick to tick or week to week, both are just as easy. The "rescale box" lets me move to different data ranges for historical charts, and the program's macros enable me to build charts with multiple symbols and recall favorite technical studies I've created without reentering the formulas. The interface is simple to use with good pull-down menus for changing studies, scale, and time periods. The charts "feel" good—the screen is clean, the charts clear and easy to read. The toolbox is solid—predefined studies include all the basics with moving averages, momentum, MACD oscillator, relative strength, and cumulative volume.

An "Account Watch" module tracks profits and losses in real time for an unlimited number of accounts, with up to 100 positions per account.

## THE CANDLESTICK FORECASTER

International Pacific Trading Co., 1010 Calle Cordillera, Suite 101, San Clemente, CA 92673. 800-444-9993.

Versions available: DOS (version 2.1), DOS master (version 4.5).

Requirements: 1MB RAM (4MB recommended), 6MB free space on hard drive, math co-processor recommended.

Cost: DOS version $249; DOS master $800.

Guarantee: 30-day money back with 15 percent restocking fee.

Demo or sample: Free by calling 800-444-9993 or on CompuServe "Go Fiven" and scroll to Library 8.

Technical support: Toll-free 800-444-9993 for first six months, then 714-498-5152 or CompuServe "Go Fiven" and look for International Pacific Trading Company tech forum.

User Newsletter, On-line Forum, Internet Address: *The Rice Paper* newsletter is free to registered users.

Updated: Every 3 months. Upgrades free for six months after initial. Accepts updated data in ASCII, Signal, MetaTech Pro, MetaStock, and TeleCharts 2000 formats.

Strengths: Extremely large library of candlestick patterns and a very poweful system for matching past and current patterns. A basic library of other technical indicators can be superimposed over the candlestick charts to compare buy and sell signals. The program comes with an easy-to-run tutorial that will get a user up and running.

Weaknesses: This is a niche product. The investor who doesn't regularly use candlestick forecasting as part of technical analysis won't be able to exploit the full power of this program.

Tricks of the trade: Definitely try the demo first. It will give you the full flavor of this methodology and let you see if this is a tool that you'd like to add to your toolbox.

In principle, Japanese candlestick charts aren't that different from traditional bar charts. The latter indicate high, low, and closing prices for a stock on a specific day. Japanese candlesticks begin with a box drawn between the opening and closing prices. But that's not the end of the information these charts present—they manage to pack an incredible amount of information into relatively simple figures. For example, if the closing price is above the opening price, the body of the box is colored green (in this program); if the close is below the opening, the box is colored red. A line extending from the box, called the shadow, represents the difference between the high and low prices and between the open and close. If the shadow extends above the body of the box, it indicates that buyers lacked the strength to sustain new highs. Below the body of the box, the shadow indicates sustained strength. The length of the shadow indicates the market's reaction to prices. And the location of each candlestick in relation to the preceding one signals the market trend.

It takes a while to learn how to read all this information. For example, while an ascending line of green candlesticks would indicate an upward trend in a stock, an investor's reaction to the pattern would vary depending on the characteristics of the accompanying shadows. A chain that ends with long shadows above the bodies could indicate that investors are taking profits in the stock.

So a good candlestick program needs to pass two tests. First, it should present the candlesticks themselves in a clear, easy-to-read graphic format that makes it easy to see, study, and manipulate patterns. Second, it should include a large library of patterns and make it easy to scan the current market to see if any of the patterns that have proven useful indicators in the past match current conditions.

The Candlestick Forecaster passes the first test. The candlesticks and shadows are easy to read and clearly resolved. But the graphics of this program aren't significantly better than others produced by more general technical analysis programs when they display candlesticks.

It's on the second test that the program really struts its stuff. The basic DOS version comes with a library of more than 700 candlestick patterns. The program uses artificial intelligence—the manual claims that the software combines an expert system and a pretrained neural network—to look for matches between the current market and that library of patterns, and then offers comentary on the possible meaning of the matches that it's found. (The master edition includes 1,000 patterns.)

For example, here's the program's commentary on a candlestick called the "Gravestone Doji Line." (Candlestick forecasting was invented to predict turning points in the Japanese rice markets—hence the sometimes odd-sounding names.) "Possible reversal" the screen notes in lavender. "This candle is created when the open, low, and close are all equal and below the high. While it can sometimes be found as a market bottoms, it's forte is in calling tops."

Using a combination of the F5 and F6 keys, an investor can scroll through all the pattern matches that the program finds in the current market. The investor who wants to combine these with other technical indicators can go to "Setup" to establish commands for calling up favorite indicators such as relative strength. Simple function commands let the user superimpose technical measures such as a moving average on top of the candlestick chart, extremely useful for comparing signals from different indicators.

The difference in price between the basic and master edition is certainly not insignificant, but the dedicated charter of candlesticks gets a couple of very helpful tools. CandleWatch will automatically scan up to 600 charts looking for patterns. CandleVision will back-test a single chart and generate a profitability study.

International Pacific Trading Company plans to introduce a Windows version in July 1996.

## CLARITY

Papyrus Technology, 14585 Big Basin Way, Saratoga, CA 95070, 800-628-6435.

Versions available: Windows (version 3.07).

Requirements: 16MB RAM and 100 MB free space on hard drive. Papyrus recommends a 486/66 or better PC.

Cost: $995.

Guarantee: 30-day money back.

Demo or sample: Free demo.

Technical support: 408-867-9801, 9–5, M–F, PST.

User Newsletter, On-line Forum, Internet address: http://www. papyrus.com.

Updated: Daily by modem; data import and export in ASCII format.

Strengths: Too many valuable and in some cases unique features to name. The program can set price alerts to "ring" through other Windows applications such as Word, WordPerfect, and Excel. It can sort foreign exchange information by currency, bank, or cross-rates. A statistics feature allows an investor to examine the relationship between two stocks and see if their movements are related using standard deviation, best fit, and direction of correlation. The account statement function allows construction of actual or hypothetical portfolios and automatically marks all open positions to market.

Weaknesses: Cost. This program isn't worth the price for investors who don't day trade. One other caveat: data stored in only one time-frame format. So if you want to build daily charts, they don't get built from tick prices. Instead the program stores only daily prices. This means that an investor can go up, from ticks to day, but not down, from days to ticks.

Tricks of the trade: A good technical analysis program—Clarity or Meta-Stock, for example—allows the user to examine the raw data behind the charts in spreadsheet format. Regular checks of the data in this form are the best way to turn up errors in transmission, corrupt files, and missing or redundant dates. Any of those can make the most sophisticated trading system useless.

Modesty isn't Clarity's strong suit. The program calls itself the ultimate charting and technical analysis program for real-time traders, and claims that this is the most advanced charting and technical analysis program in the PC world.

But then, Clarity delivers what is among the most advanced technical programs for real-time traders and what is certainly the most beautiful program I've seen.

I'm not sure that there's any way to verify the program's claim to work with "unlimited" number of charts, quote pages, tickers, and time scales, but I wasn't able to overwhelm the program's desktop. As with Aspen Graphics, a user can customize the desktop to display just the tools an individual uses for trading. I put tickers across the bottom, bond yields and interest rates in a box at top, and still ran charts. The program would have let me create a number of customized desktops and then call up the appropriate one. Desktops not in use still update automatically.

I couldn't find an indicator (Clarity comes with thirty different candlestick patterns, for example) or charting style that Clarity didn't offer. I had the option of charting in ticks, minutes, hours, days, weeks, and months. Screens could be customized with spreadsheets, tickers, news, news keyword search, custom quote pages, snap quotes, portfolios, account statements, and spread analysis.

Perhaps surprisingly for a program with so many tools, Clarity's charting system works off the standard data entry box. I typed in the symbol of what I wanted to chart, added the time frame, clicked on the name of indicator, made a choice of moving averages, choose overlay or not, and then clicked on OK.

The programmers have decided to pack the graphics side of the program, too. Of course, Clarity comes with the standard set of drawing tools that you'll find on MetaStock (tools for creating support and resistance levels, channels, grids, arcs, cones, parallel trend lines, horizontal bands, etc.), but it adds a few wrinkles. A color-bar feature indicates not only the spread between high and low on a day, but the direction of a stock's movement: blue in upper half if up, red in lower half if down.

And, in tribute to those who understand that technical analysis isn't a science but an art, the program's "paint box" allows a user to apply any color that the monitor can produce to the charts, not just a limited range of preset colors.

## MegaTech Chart System

Ret-Tech Software, 151 Deer Lane, Barrington, Il 60010, 708-382-3903.
Versions available: DOS (version 2.03).
Requirements: 640K RAM, 1.5MB free space on hard drive, DOS 3.3 or higher, modem.
Cost: $175.

Guarantee: None.

Demo or sample: Free by calling 708-382-3903 or download from the Ret-Tech bulletin board at 708-382-4340.

Technical support: Ret-Tech bulletin board 708-382-4340 (also source for free programs to manage other data formats).

User Newsletter, On-line Forum, Internet address: Ret-Tech bulletin board at 708-382-4340.

Updated: By modem from Prodigy, Signal, or Knight-Ridder.

Strengths: The basics done straightforwardly and solidly. MegaTech combines a well-thought-out tool set with a reasonably easy to use interface. Setting up a chart will be relatively easy for the user with a familiarity with some of the basic concepts of technical analysis.

Weaknesses: The program comes with an adequate array of predefined indicators, but although a user can modify those provided, an advanced user will be frustrated since the system does not allow the creation of new indicators. The beginner may need a little more time to get up to speed on MegaTech—the program doesn't provide any preset chart templates.

Tricks of the trade: MegaTech's indicator on indicator function lets a user build new technical studies on the foundation of earlier construction. For example, you can plot relative strength for a security (or the market as a whole) and then, using this function, plot the moving average of that relative strength indicator—a good way to look for breakouts, or breakdowns—in your system's basic indicators.

Dave Rettger, a former trader on the floor of Chicago Board of Trade, built this system well. Although MegaTech hasn't seen a major overhaul since its introduction, it still gets the job done—and still boasts a few functions missing from most of the competition. The program's unique indicator on indicator function is complemented by an impressive ability to customize alerts for high and low price or volume breakouts, and a hard disk space-saving method for storing charts that makes this one of the most efficient technical analysis programs at managing data. A welcome alternative for investors who don't own computers with huge hard disks.

## METASTOCK

Equis International, 3950 South 700 East, Suite 100, Salt Lake City, UT 84107, 800-882-3040.

Versions available: DOS (version 4.52), Windows (version 5.1); both versions include Downloader software.

Requirements: DOS version requires 8MB RAM and 12 MB free space on hard drive. Windows version requires 4MB RAM and a minimum of 5MB free space on hard drive (which will run MetaStock without Help, the tutorial, sample data, Downloader, etc.). To install completely count on needing about 12MB of hard drive space.

Cost: $349 for DOS and Windows versions.

Guarantee: 60-day money back.

Demo or sample: Free demo.

Technical support: 801-265-9998, 8 A.M.–5 P.M.. M–F; fax 801-265-3999; on-line CompuServe (Go Equis), America Online (Equis), Prodigy (Money Talk), and the Internet (http://www.equis.com).

User Newsletter, On-line Forum, Internet address: Free newsletter, *The Equis Monitor*, published quarterly. On-line forums on CompuServe (Go Equis), America Online (Equis), Prodigy (Money Talk), and the Internet (http://www.equis.com).

Updated: By modem using Downloader module.

Strengths: Few programs are as well thought out and then executed as MetaStock is—it's almost a joy to navigate the screens. MetaStock's data format and formula language have become de facto standards, making moving data back and forth from other programs to Meta-Stock simple and ensuring that most how-to articles on technical analysis are written for the MetaStock user. While I have found technicians who prefer other programs and even former users who now prefer a competitor, I've never heard anything but praise for the quality of the company behind MetaStock. Equis International wins consistent kudos for customer support and helpfulness.

Weaknesses: MetaStock RT ($495), the program's real-time version for the intraday trader, hasn't kept pace with the end of the day Windows program. It still relies on an older DOS interface. The company is planning an update for 1996. Hold off till then—or look to other Windows packages for an intraday trading program.

Tricks of the trade: If you want to test your trading system or quickly teach yourself the ins and outs of technical analysis, try the "Learn-As-You-Plot" feature added to the latest Windows version (5.1) of MetaStock. Make buy and sell decisions on any historical chart and then move to the next time period to see how you did. Use Meta-Stock's ability to keep multiple data windows open at once to test a system and see what would happen if you changed simple parameters, such as moving from a 10-day to a 50-day moving average. Also explore how different systems do in up and down (and non-trending markets.) Some systems that are great at buy and sell signals in a trending market go to pieces when the market turns choppy. You'll be able to see this at work if you use 1994 as an example.

The standard for the intermediate to advanced technician involved in end of the day trading, MetaStock is a wonderful combination of technical tools and the quality software design. The program's starter booklet and tutorial will let the beginner start to use the program for simple charting after just an hour or two.

MetaStock gives an investor two ways to do almost everything. There's the long but individually customizable method, and there are shortcuts and quick routines that capture about 90 percent of the program's flexibility. That two-level approach makes the program a good fit for the technician who wants to build a customized trading system from the ground up—the program's language for writing systems and alerts is powerful and flexible—and for the beginning or casual user of technical analysis who just wants to use relatively standardized tools to either learn the field or confirm some other method of stock picking.

For example, charts come in three formats: Charts, Smart Charts, and Layouts. Smart Charts are the most convenient—they automatically save any changes. There are two ways to plot indicators as well: by choosing from the Insert menu or by dragging from the Indicator Quick List. To use the Quick List just grab an indicator from the menu and drag it to the chart window where you want to apply it. A dialog window then automatically opens that asks for parameters such as time periods. Then click OK.

Few other technical analysis programs have used the drag and drop capabilities of Windows so thoroughly. To apply an indicator simply drag it from the menu list and drop it either in a window already filled with other indicators—in which case it just becomes another line in that study—or drop it in an empty window or drag it to the title bar and drop it there to create a new inner window. To have an indicator plotted on something other than price (for example, to have moving average plotted on relative strength) simply drop the moving average indicator on the relative strength line that you've already created.

MetaStock's programmers have made it possible for an investor to ignore menus and toolbars part of the time. Commands are often embedded in on-screen objects themselves. Clicking the right-hand mouse button while the cursor rests on an object such as a trend line displays a shortcut menu that can be used to manipulate an object or modify an indicator. In addition, clicking on the Help icon and then on an indicator generates definitions and tips on using the indicator.

I've described the process of creating charts in MetaStock in this chapter, so here I'd like to add just a few words on the program's data management features. MetaStock's Downloader sets the standard for what an automatic data management program should be. The program is more than just a modem manager. It allows the user to view the data in spreadsheet format to look for problems if there are any and to modify data. The Downloader also conducts several error-checking routines after every download of data. The program automatically looks for more than 100 possible error conditions, including missing data, invalid dates, invalid high-low close relationships, and then, using the test function, generates an error report. When I downloaded data on Fidelity Magellan, the program noticed that Magellan had distributed capital gains since I last updated and asked if I wanted to correct my past data for it. One final and minor feature exemplifies MetaStock's thoroughness. The Downloader's browse feature let me pause in the middle of adding data on a new security to look up an unfamiliar stock symbol without having to exit the routine and click on another menu. At the end of 1995, Reuters, the parent of Reality Online, bought Equis International, the maker of MetaStock. It will be interesting to see how and if Reuters combines the technical analysis of MetaStock with the news delivery of Reality Online's Reuters Money Network.

### OmniTrader

Nirvana Systems Inc., 3415 Greystone, Suite 205, Austin, TX 78731, 800-880-0338.
Versions available: Windows (Version 2.1).
Requirements: 4MB RAM, 10 MB free space on hard drive, Windows 3.1 or higher.
Cost: $395.
Guarantee: 60-day money back.
Demo or sample: Free demo.

Technical support: 512-345-2592; fax 512-345-4225; CompuServe (e-mail to 72662,2166).

User Newsletter, On-line Forum, Internet address: Free *OmniTrader News* ($99 a year); on CompuServe "Finven."

Updated: Software updated once or twice a year (updates cost $99–$149). Free updates available via modem from Nirvana OnLine. Nirvana Data Collector software ($79) handles downloads of daily price data from Telescan or Dow Jones News/Retrieval, but Omni-Trader will read data files in Telechart, MetaStock, AIQ, CSI, and Omega Research formats as well. The company also sells historical data on CD-ROM.

Strengths: Amazingly easy to use and navigate for a program with so many features and so much information. The credit goes to a well thought out chart screen page that puts almost the entire trading system in one simple-to-access place and then adds lots of explanatory help. Beginning with a "black box" buy-sell recommendation, Omni-Trader gently guides the user through deeper and deeper levels of explanation so that, at the end, the technical factors behind the decision have been thoroughly explained for you.

Weaknesses: OmniTrader, which will handle either daily or weekly data, is not designed to be a real-time trading system or to execute intraday trades. Investors who need a day trading system should look elsewhere. Also this program is a purely technical one: it offers no method for integrating fundamentals with technical analysis.

Tricks of the trade: OmniTrader comes with two practice modes, Game Mode and Lab Mode. Game Mode helps you learn your way around OmniTrader and technical trading in general using a single security. Lab Mode expands the game to a collection of securities. Lab Mode comes with enough data so that you can run a few months of trading in just an hour or so. To its credit, both Lab Mode and OmniTrader stress that the point of this exercise is as much psychological as technical. Good traders know that part of making money in the market is learning how to buy when the signals say buy but your heart says no.

Like AIQ Trading Expert, OmniTrader is a trading system that uses some of the techniques of artificial intelligence to generate buy and sell signals. Such systems tend toward "black boxes"—that is, they tell you what to do without telling you precisely why. Certainly OmniTrader has that flavor—it doesn't explain the details of the "voting" process that results in the system emphasizing some technical indicators for some securities at some times. All that the user knows is that Omni-Trader sorts through more than 100 trading systems to find those that are the best for any specific security. But the program also goes further than most to explain trading systems and indicators. For OmniTrader to work for you, you'll still have to trust the program to a great degree, but at least the program stops to explain the outlines of its work along the way.

The program is organized around tasks—and the "Chart" task is the key one of those. The main screen in Chart puts a big price/volume chart in the middle of the page (to move from one chart to the next, simply click on the stock in the "Focus List"), and then surrounds it with trading systems and explanations. A "Voting Line" box at the bottom of the page lists all the indicators that the program has looked at for a specific stock with the day-by-day buy or sell signals that each recorded. A "focus list" in the upper left lists all the stocks in your portfolio and indicates which currently show buy or sell signals—along with a numerical rating of the strength of that signal. Below that, a "performance box" tracks the results of the system's trades for the stock currently being charted.

The chart itself, like MetaStock's, provides object-oriented help. Click on either a green or red box on the chart and the program's "chart assistants" explain what the chart is showing at that moment. In addition, click on any signal on the voting line and the system will explain it, too. For example, on December 30, 1994, the advisor says "Buy Wells Fargo" with 92 confidence because of a commodity channel index peak, a Williams %R peak, a trend line reversal, a Trix Momentum Peak, and a Momentum peak without weekly confirmation. Clicking on the name of any system in the "voting line" produces a display of the security in that system.

Other tasks besides "Chart" include "Profile" (which lets you customize your trading style as aggressive, for example); "Update" (reprices your portfolio and confirms pending buy/sell orders); "Test" (back-test symbols and optimize systems); "Signals" (generates the current trading recommendations); "Compare" (ranks the signals, but unfortunately is limited to showing two charts at a time); "Orders" (sets up brokerage accounts and submit orders); and "Portfolio" (sets up accounts and edits portfolios).

An investor would probably want more detail in tracking a portfolio than OmniTrader offers, but otherwise this is a complete end-of-day trading system at a reasonable price.

## PERSONAL ANALYST AND PERSONAL HOTLINE

Trendsetter Software, 2024 N. Broadway, Suite 310, Santa Ana, CA 92706, 800-825-1852.

Versions available: Personal Analyst Macintosh (version 2.1) and Personal Hotline Macintosh (version 6.9).

Requirements: 2MB RAM and 5 MB free space on hard drive; Personal Hotline requires 2.5 MB RAM, and 5 MB free space on hard drive.

Cost: Personal Analyst $395; Personal Hotline $595.

Guarantee: 30-day money back.

Demo or sample: None.

Technical support: 714-547-7275 (7 A.M.–4 P.M. PST); fax 714-547-5063; on-line on America Online (e-mail Trendsetter), CompuServe (e-mail Jeff Borowitz 73320,1015), eWorld (e-mail Trendsetter), and Internet (e-mail trndsetter@aol.com).

User Newsletter, On-line Forum, Internet address: On-line forum on America Online (keyword TS).

Updated: Programs are upgraded approximately once a year. In the past updates have varied in cost from free to $89. All products are scheduled for upgrade to PowerPC versions by the end of the summer 1996. Data updates from Dial/Data, Dow Jones News/Retrieval, CSI, and CompuServe.

Strengths: A solid list of indicators, decent graphics (although not quite as eye-popping as on some of the newest Windows programs), good help to explain the indicators, and a very solid system for screening to find the best trades.

Weaknesses: Some of the less pricey and simpler programs in Trendsetter's lineup don't offer all the basics required for success in trading. If you want to build your own indicators, check carefully to see if the version will support their construction. Examine the program to see if it will track and report profits in sufficient detail and with enough accuracy for you. (Most investors will probably need the high-end Personal Hotline). If you want to do intraday trading you'll have to move up to Professional Analyst ($595), which accepts a data feed from Signal.

Tricks of the trade: Personal Hotline relies on an undisclosed trading
model to help guide an investor to the best trades. But remember
that you don't have to take the program's advice—you can start a regression line at a different point, for example. Before you decide to
trust the program's brains completely, throw it a few challenges. Use
the shift key to select your own starting points for analysis and compare the results. Keep trying to beat the program—rather than becoming its slave.

The Macintosh user doesn't have many options when it comes to
picking technical analysis software. Fortunately, Personal Analyst is a
good solid program. It's ill suited for the aggressive trader who wants to
build a system and track the results (no profit and loss report for example), but this program will get the job done for the investor who wants
to add a technical tool to his or her other stock-picking methods, or
who wants to use technical analysis to trade in and out among a portfolio of regularly followed stocks.

Two features make Personal Analyst especially appropriate for those
tasks. "Equiview" charts display two years of closing prices on a single
security and automatically draw a linear regression line through the
data (a straight line that is the "best" fit through all the data points) to
show the standard deviation for each year. "Multiview" charts compare
two sets of closing prices for two securities—and automatically draw
linear regression lines and calculate standard deviation and correlation.
The linear regression line gives you the trend, and the standard deviation indicates both how strong the trend is (how much variation exists
within it) and how much risk there is in that trend (how likely it is
that you'll take a big loss while the trend, generally, continues upward.)

Drawing tools are good—Personal Analyst lets the user draw and
then move trend lines—and the program generates bar, candle, line,
point and figure, multiview and equiview charts. Predefined indicator
selection is adequate: 30 indicators include simple and exponential
moving averages (not weighted), Bollinger bands, envelopes, Fibonacci, Gann and regression analysis, advance/decline line, MACD,
on-balance volume, relative strength, and stochastic oscillator.

Trendsetter offers its technical analysis software in so many versions
and at such different price points that it almost makes up for the general
paucity of Macintosh software for the technician. I can't stress enough
the value to the Macintosh user of buying from a company that concen-

trates on the Macintosh. Trendsetter is now in the process of producing PowerPC versions of its software. The new versions are being rewritten from scratch with all new code, says Trendsetter's Jeff Borowitz. That should make them as fast and as easy to use as the owners of Apple's PowerPCs expect.

### SUPERCHARTS

Omega Research, 9200 Sunset Drive, Miami, FL 33173, 800-422-8587.

Versions available: Windows (version 3.0), Windows CD-ROM (version 3.0).

Requirements: Windows and CD–ROM versions require 4MB RAM, 4MB free space on hard drive, Windows 3.1 or higher; 8MB if running Windows 95.

Cost: $249.95.

Guarantee: 30-day money back.

Demo or sample: Free (800-422-8587).

Technical support: 305-270-8674, 1 P.M.–10 P.M., M–F, fax 305-270-9560. Internet, http://www.omegaresearch.com (e-mail to tech-supp@omegaresearch.com).

User Newsletter, On-line Forum, Internet address: World Wide Web, http://www.omegaresearch.com; techsupp@omegaresearch.com.

Updated: By modem from DialData. Historical data (up to 25 years of historical price and fundamental data on CD-ROM updated quarterly) costs $14.95/quarter for DialData subscribers and $50 a quarter for nonsubscribers).

Strengths: The CD-ROM version provides an immense amount of data—up to 25 years on more than 7,000 securities. And Omega has provided an ingenuous way to make life a little easier for your hard disk. Historical data arrives on CD-ROM and stays there—your machine will read it from the CD-ROM rather than downloading it to your hard drive. Updates will go on your hard drive. When you need the data, the program merges the two sources.

Weaknesses: A small but vocal percentage of Supercharts users complain of glitches in the program and shoddy technical support; the on-line forums contain a steady stream of their angry messages. That's troubling, but the tone of Omega's replies in the three months I monitored is also worrisome. The company seemed by turns defensive and arrogant. Many of the replies were unsigned, from members of the technical assistance staff—Omega is the only software vendor that I've seen resort to this dodge on-line. The best gloss that I can put on what I've seen is that Supercharts is a very complex program whose programmers haven't been able to clearly show users how to accomplish all the tasks they need to perform. In other words, it's not as easy to use as it should be. That, of course, doesn't explain the company's occasional hostility toward its customers.

Tricks of the trade: Note that downloading new fundamental data writes over prior data. If you want to create a file of historical fundamental data, you'll carefully have to copy and rename the old file before downloading new data. The program does not come with fundamental data. That is supplied by your choice of data vendor—if your data vendor supplies fundamental data, that is. This version of Supercharts, however, will allow you to view and use fundamental data.

A player (along with MetaStock, Telechart 2000, and Telescan) in the current wars to add new functions and provide cheaper data, Supercharts is a complete technical analysis system flexible enough to be used either to study individual stocks or to create and then track complete trading systems. The newest updates—which combine CD-ROM for data storage and Windows for an interface—give you immense amounts of historical data and some really nifty tools for using it. For example, the program's "Expert Analyst" function now can forecast stock movements using either fundamental or technical data. The forecast comes as either a written report or as buy, sell, and hold signals.

For the user who wants to use the program as a trading system, Supercharts comes with useful "paint bar" and "show me" functions. These functions allow the user to see visual alerts for any trading system. Used in conjunction, the paint bar will change the color of a bar or mark a line with a dot when one of the conditions selected by applying "show me" has been met. For example, you can ask "show me" to look for a signal such as a breakout or island reversal. Or to find bars that show increasing or decreasing momentum. "Paint bar" will mark each of those instances with a colored dot or by changing the color of the bars.

Supercharts comes with impressive abilities to calculate the results of any trading system. A user can specify a number of trading methods— break-even, profit target, trailing—define exit and entry signals, account of commissions and margins loan interest, calculate the maximum draw down, and generate a profit/loss report. One weakness—the program will not compare trading systems against each other.

Drawing tools are among the best. Personal Analyst lets the user draw and then move trend lines—and the program generates bar, candle, candle volume, line, and point and figure charts. Predefined indicator selection is ample: seventy-seven indicators include simple, exponential, and weighted moving averages, Bollinger bands, cycle lines, envelopes, Fibonacci, Gann and regression analysis, advance/decline line, island and key reversal, MACD, momentum, on-balance volume, relative strength, stochastic oscillator, and up/down tick difference.

A real-time version of Supercharts is scheduled for 1996.

### TELECHART 2000

Worden Brothers Inc., Five Oaks Office Park, 4905 Pine Cone Drive, Durham, NC 27707, 800-776-4940.

Versions available: DOS (version 3.0).

Requirements: 540K RAM, 5MB free space on hard drive, DOS 3.3 or higher, modem.

Cost: $29.00 for software; data costs 1/2 cent per symbol per day with daily charge for any number of symbols capped at 99 cents. Downloads using a slower than 9600 baud modem incur a surcharge.

Guarantee: 30-day free trial with $15 data credit.

Demo or sample: Free trial of complete system.

Technical support: 800-373-2055 (9 A.M.–10 P.M., M-F and 10 A.M.– 5 P.M., S); fax 919-408-0545.

User Newsletter: Free *Daily Electronic Worden Report* is downloaded automatically with each day's chart data.

Updated: By modem from Worden Brothers database.

Strengths: An amazing combination: straightforward, easy to learn, and damned inexpensive, and yet packed with enough indicators and charting tools to do real technical analysis. The manual is very, very good—clear and complete on what each function does, how to do it, and why to do it. Commentary in *Daily Electronic Worden Report* on the patterns in the market provides a dialog likely to keep the user's technical skills growing. Data format is readily transportable to other major technical analysis packages.

Weaknesses: I had a mixed experience with technical support. One out of my three calls for support resulted in a wait of five minutes on hold. The other two were answered promptly.

Tricks of the trade: Leave yourself plenty of time to update the data that comes on TeleChart's historical database on CD ROM. As promised, the update was free, but it took me almost four hours to bring the database up to the moment (the download added 76 days of data) and then to calculate all the necessary adjustments due to splits and corrected prices. All that time, of course, I couldn't use my computer for anything else. Also consider how much historical data you'll be using regularly. The program gives the user the option of moving just one year of data to the user's hard drive—that takes up 58MB. Moving fifteen years worth would eat up 790MB. Most investors don't regularly draw charts that need more than a year of data.

Worden Brothers has decided to virtually give away its program—for $29 a user gets the TeleChart 2000 program and 100 years of historical stock data. Daily data isn't expensive either, just 1/2 cent a day per symbol with a maximum fee of 99 cents a day for any number of symbols.

But that's really only the beginning of the good news about this program. TeleChart is a powerful technical analysis system with a full library of indicators and a reasonable set of drawing tools. An investor can chart relative strength, moving averages, envelope channel, linear regression, price rate of change, time segmented volume, on balance volume, volume, stochastics, Wilder's RSI, MACD/momentum, and balance of power. Still, don't expect this DOS program to match all the drawing tools and features of Windows programs such as Metastock.

The addition of a CD ROM full of historical prices makes TeleChart even more valuable—if a bit harder to use, since the core program and the CD are not seemlessly integrated. Once it was up and running, however, I could screen using price, average volume rank, market cap rank, relative strength, and earnings growth rank—and then sort on any of these criteria as well.

## TELESCAN

Telescan Inc., 10550 Richmond Avenue, Suite 250, Houston, TX 77042, 800-324-8246.

Versions available: Analyzer DOS (version 3.0), ProSearch DOS (version 4.0), and Telescan Investors Platform for Windows (version 1.0).

Requirements: DOS version requires 2MB RAM, 5MB free space on hard drive. Windows version requires 4MB RAM, 6MB free space on hard drive.

Cost: Investors Platform for Windows $395. See review in chapter 4 for full cost.

Guarantee: 30-day money back on software.

Demo or sample: Preview on Internet at http://www.telescan.com.

Technical support: 800-324-4692.

User Newsletter, On-line Forum, Internet address: Free quarterly newsletter, *Telescan News*.

Updated: Daily by modem from Telescan.

Strengths: No program provides a better combination of fundamental and technical tools. Measured against other purely technical programs, Telescan's features put it solidly in the middle of the pack. But Telescan's fundamental tools and data are unsurpassed. The combination is impossible to beat for the investor who lives with a foot in both camps.

Weaknesses: The pure technician will find Telescan's tool box relatively meager and its tools robust but somewhat underpowered in comparison to programs that concentrate on technical analysis. Telescan is pricey, too, even now, when it's dropped its frustrating division between prime and non-prime time. Customer service was slow the three times I called during the middle of a weekday afternoon. I was on hold seven minutes during the longest delay.

Tricks of the trade: Take a tip from technical programs that emphasize studying a single stock by using multiple indicators to produce several charts of the security and then stacking them on top of each other for easy comparison. Telescan will let you do the same thing with a technical chart on the top of the page and a fundamental chart below. For example, plot the ratio of a stock's yield to price in the bottom screen and chart a moving average in the top window to compare valuation with momentum. With Telescan, an investor can create historicalf ranges for a stock's valuation on fundamental data, just as the technician does with price and volume. (For a review of Telescan's fundamental stock analysis features see Chapter 4.)

Fundamental investors who use technical charts to confirm their investment decisions can't find a better program than Telescan. Nothing else on the market combines good charts with such deep data on company fundamentals. It's not clear to me, however, that the program works quite as well for investors who want to use technical signals to build a trading system.

Telescan certainly has enough analytical power for the investor who wants to study charts. Charts can be displayed in six different ways— the standard bars, lines, point and figure, and candlesticks, as well as in 3-D. The trend line function holds adequate drawing tools for sketching in trend lines, parallel trend lines, speed resistance lines, least squares, Fibonacci fans, and price and time zones. The user can set charts for arithmetic or logarithmic scaling. And with more than 100 market indexes in its database, there's more than enough data for comparing individual stocks with the market or an industry group.

Telescan does a reasonable job of integrating its technical and fundamental information. From a graph window you can access earnings estimates, quarterly earnings, news from Reuters, annual reports, analyst reports and opinions from Standard & Poor's and MacroWorld.

But while Telescan amazes me by providing fundamental data and tools that I can't find anywhere else, in the technical arena I feel that I'm dealing with a scaled down set of tools. The indicators menu, for example, lists just commodity channel, cycles, directional movement, MACD, momentum, moving average, parabolic time/price, stochastics, trend line market, volatility, and Wilder RSI. Certainly not shabby, but fewer than you'll find in programs that serve just the technician.

The technician who wants to build a trading system will find Telescan even less adequate. For instance, the program lacks the detailed reporting systems of profit and loss that are necessary to track how well a system is performing. Comparing even Telescan's fundamental features to that of a trading program such as AIQ Trading Expert illustrates the problem. Telescan's fundamental tools and data blow the other program away, but Trading Expert quickly turns fundamental data into a simple rating number that makes it easy for an investor to integrate fundamental data into a trading system.

Finally, as with so many other programs, your perception of Telescan's quality will depend on the kind of investor you are. No matter what your methods, you're likely to appreciate the simple Windows design—a big improvement over the DOS version—and the very useful Help feature. But this program has the most to offer the investor who combines fundamental and technical analysis (it even has enough fundamental features to make it a top choice for the investor who relies solely on fundamentals). The pure technician may be happier else-where, however.

### WALL STREET ANALYST

Omega Research Inc., Omega Research Building, 9200 Sunset Drive, Miami, FL 33173, 800-556-2022.

Versions available: Windows (version 2.1), CD-ROM, called Wall Street Analyst 2CD (version 2.1).

Requirements: 4MB RAM required (8MB recommended), 30MB free space on hard drive, DOS 5.0 or higher, Windows 3.1 or higher.

Cost: $49.95.

Guarantee: 30-day money back.

Demo or sample: None.

Technical support: 305-270-0174 (1 P.M.–10 P.M. EST M–F); fax 305-270-9650; Internet at http://www.omergaresearch.com; e-mail tech-supp@omegaresearch.com.

User Newsletter, On-line Forum, Internet address: Forums on AOL, CompuServe, and Prodigy;Internet at http://www.omegaresearch.com

Updated: Daily by modem from Dial Data. Historical CD database is updated quarterly ($14.95 a quarter for Dial Data subscribers and $50 a quarter for non-subscribers).

Strengths: One of the few technical programs to supply some funda-mental data—although categories are limited to earnings, beta, and other basic information. CD-ROM version comes with twenty-five years of data—an incredible resource for anyone doing long-term market studies. And since the program uses the data from the CD-ROM rather than downloading it to the hard disk, the program takes up relatively little hard drive space to store all this information.

Weaknesses: Not buggy, but glitchy. My copy had a tendency to hang up. The downloader failed more frequently than it should have. This is especially a problem because Omega sometimes provides less than genial technical support. Certainly some of the exchanges that I've seen on CompuServe suggest that the company's customer service representatives need a vacation. Data suppliers effectively limited to Dial Data for CD-ROM version since only their data will integrate seamlessly with the data already on the CD.

Tricks of the trade: With every update the program writes over old fundamental data so that a user will never have more than the most recent period on CD or hard disk. Combine the resulting temporal shallowness of data with the meager categories offered and most users who care about fundamental analysis will conclude that they have to buy a program that specializes in this sort of analysis and sign up for a more comprehensive data service.

Good, but not as good as it should be, Wall Street Analyst combines a selection of basic technical tools with a limited but useful artificial intelligence feature—but then mars the package by making the software more difficult to operate and navigate than it needs to be. Add in a distressingly large number of error messages and this program starts to feel like one rushed to market before all the quirks were ironed out.

Let me take a concrete example that will give you the flavor of the problem. The programmers who wrote Wall Street Analyst put a lot of effort into adding Help features that will explain the various technical indicators supplied by the program. Either by clicking on Help itself or by using the program in learning mode, a user can easily put an explanation of the indicator on the screen. Great technology. The equal of anything in MetaStock or Windows on Wall Street.

But the execution is lousy. Here's what I get when I ask for a definition of stochastics: "A stochastic function based on the tendency of price action to accumulate near the highs in an uptrend and near the lows in a decline. The SlowD is a smoothed average of the SlowK." That's helpful?

I've discussed the program's two most innovative features, ChartScanner and Expert Analyst in the chapter above, so let me just run through the basics here. Graphics are crisp and clear, and charts are, if not beautiful, easy to read with good definition of points and lines. Indicator selection is a notch below the package that comes with MetaStock or Omega's own Supercharts. The program does include standards such as momentum and MACD, moving average, envelopes, relative strength, various stochastics, and volatility.

In summary, the experienced technician will probably want a more powerful program than this. For the beginner the choice may boil down to this program or Windows on Wall Street. I'd give the nod to Windows on Wall Street for ease of use and sound design—even if Wall Street's Expert Analyst is currently the best teaching use of artificial intelligence in a technical analysis program.

### WINDOWS ON WALL STREET AND WINDOWS ON WALL STREET PRO

MarketArts, P.O. Box 850922, Richardson TX 75085, 800-998-8439.

Versions available: Windows on Wall Street Windows (version 2.1), Windows on Wall Street Professional (version 4.0).

Requirements: For Windows on Wall Street 2MB Ram required (4MB recommended), Windows 3.1 or higher, DOS version 3.3 or higher, modem, on-line account with data vendor. Windows on Wall Street Professional requires 4MB RAM (8MB RAM with CD–ROM database), 5MB free space on hard drive.

Cost: Windows on Wall Street $49, Pro $179.

Guarantee: 90-day replacement if defective.

Demo or sample: Free demo.

Technical support: 214-783-6793; fax 214-414-6798; Bulletin board 214-414-7982; Internet e-mail to Support@WallStreet.Net; World-WideWeb at http://www.wallstreet.net/marketarts.

User Newsletter, On-line Forum, Internet address: CompuServe (Go Finven); Internet at http://www.wallstreet.net/marketarts.

Updated: By modem from CompuServe, Dial/Data, Dow Jones. CD database updated quarterly ($14.95/quarter with annual subscription, $49.95 a quarter without annual subscription).

Strengths: It's worth it to pay the extra cash for the Pro version to get SmartScan. This tool makes it easy to search your complete database of stocks on price change, volume, or any technical indicator, and to create alerts. Windows on Wall Street uses MetaStock language for writing indicators and alerts, which makes it easy to port formulas from that program and sources such as "Technical Analysis of Stocks and Commodities" magazine. The trading system testing feature allows the investor to figure commissions, margin costs, limits, and end or beginning of day prices into projections of system performance.

Weaknesses: Downloading from CompuServe worked perfectly with a stock such as CitiCorp, but I got a "symbol not recognized" when I asked for data on the S&P 500. The on-line research function is a dinosaur. It uses a plain text interface with CompuServe or Dow Jones News Retrieval. Better to use the on-line services' own software, which provides graphic interfaces that are much easier to navigate. Windows on Wall Street comes with very little historical data: about one year's worth of daily historical price quotes for 206 stocks, 210 mutual funds, and a few indexes.

Tricks of the trade: Although the program supports importing from most competing technical analysis programs, it will not import the tab-delimited form of ASCII, which makes it extremely difficult to transfer data from Supercharts.

A pleasure to use with simple menus arranged in logical hierarchies, relatively few indecipherable icons, and a good array of the right tools. Graphics are crisp and clear and drawing tools are easy to operate. I was able to draw a regression line without reading the manual within five minutes of loading my first chart, and figuring out how to zoom in and out to study a section of a chart was just as simple. This is one of the best technical analysis programs for the beginner. A good selection of basic and not-so-basic predefined indicators and trading systems will get the novice up and running quickly.

At the same time, it's got all the tools and graphics to keep the experienced technician happy. Charts can be loaded into twenty-three predefined chart templates, such as price and volume, candlestick, or bar chart templates. It's easy to create your own templates, too, by saving the studies or indicators performed on any security as a template file. No need to plot individual indicators for every new chart.

Windows on Wall Street comes with thirty predefined and forty-three customizable indicators. (Predefined indicator templates include Price Rate-of-Change, Price and Volume Trend, Relative Strength Index, Stochastic Oscillator, MACD, Momentum, On Balance Volume, Volume Oscillator, and Open Interest.) In addition, the program supplies sixty-seven control functions for building your own indicators—simply cut, paste, and fill in a few variables. Windows On Wall Street also provides ten predefined trading systems.

The program's "Personal Assistant" function lets an investor perform unattended downloads of data and automated batch printing of reports.

# 9

# The Cutting Edge: Where We're Going from Here

My crystal ball is in the repair shop—it seems to spend a lot of time there—so I can't tell you precisely what the world of electronic investing will look like in five years. I don't know, specifically, what new products from new companies will appear on the market, or what new technologies or investment techniques will find their way into software for the home. But I do know that the forces that have brought the individual investor financial information on the Internet, electronic brokerages, desktop news readers, historical stock databases on CD-ROM, and technical and fundamental analysis programs such as MetaStock and the Stock Selection Guide have no means become exhausted. More personal computers will be on home desks next year than this. They will come with faster chips, more memory, bigger displays, and larger hard drives.

That in turn will keep the revolution roaring along. Software makers will continue to put more powerful and sophisticated features into cheaper and cheaper packages. Companies that now write programs only for the professional market will migrate versions of those programs to individual desktops—or new competitors will. Technologies that have been limited to the researcher deep in some financial laboratory or the professional Wall Street number cruncher will reach the market first in versions that only the most computer and financially literate of individual investors will be able to use, and then in popular versions with simplified interfaces that do much of the work for the user.

Many of the changes that this revolution will introduce will be evolutionary. A product will add a feature that improves upon existing ways of analyzing investment data or collecting information. But other changes will mark major breaks with the existing state of the art. They won't simply improve an existing method, but instead will allow investors—or perhaps force them—to rethink how best to understand the financial markets.

I don't claim to be able to identify all of the new approaches that are likely to come down the software pike in the next few years. But in four areas I've seen the vanguard of change. Programs already on the market are leading the way toward (1) new graphical ways to organize and understand investment information; (2) a massive expansion of the available universe of investment information; (3) the migration of new financial strategies from professional to individual investors; and (4) new applications of the latest in artificial intelligence.

## THINKING IN CHARTS

Nothing better exemplifies the increasing power and sophistication coming to mass market investment software than the newest release of the CD-ROM version of Quicken Deluxe, which hit the market in November 1995 (version 5.0 for Windows; Quicken had not released a Macintosh version as this book went to press). Intuit, of course, added the usual upgrade improvements—more shortcuts and a better way to view an investor's entire portfolio—intended to convince existing users that they had to open their wallets for the new version. That all falls into the category of evolutionary change, I'd say. (I've described this part of the program in my review in Chapter 2. But the program is also the best example I've seen of the way that the graphic power of the current generation of personal computers will change how investors organize data.

Quicken Deluxe includes a feature called Investor Insight. This service lets you get news stories and price quotes for any stock or mutual fund on your watch list. For either $9.95 a month (for 10 securities), or $19.95 for 50, Investor Insight provides news stories from Dow Jones, PR Newswire and Business Wire, and five years of quotes for stocks and mutual funds. So far that's basically what Reuters' Money Network provides—with limits on the number of securities an investor can follow that Reuters doesn't impose. Like Money Network, Quicken lets an investor use all that price data to build simple price volume charts and even overlay basic indicators such as the 200-day moving average or trend lines. These charts won't do the job for any fan of technical analysis, but they do show the ebb and flow of an issue's price over time.

But if you think of these graphs just as charts, you're missing the point. They're really a brand-new way of organizing information for the investor. Like the charts built by MetaStock, Quicken's charts are interactive. But instead of giving me definitions of indicators or prompting me about the parameters of constructing a chart as I move the cursor over it, as MetaStock does, Quicken turns its charts into a way to keep track of my investment actions and study the relationship of market action and news. As I move the cursor down the price chart

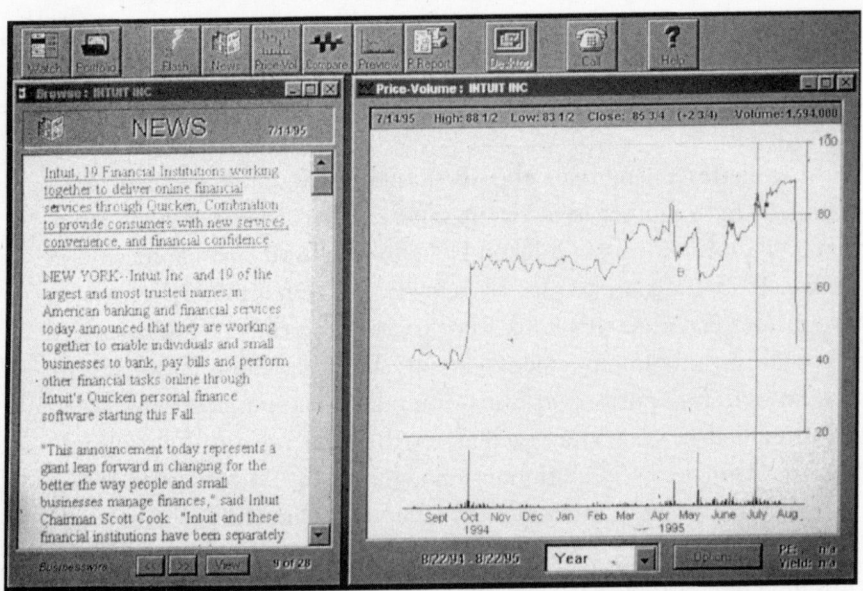

*Quicken's Investor Insight uses charts to visually integrate historical prices and news.* (Courtesy Intuit)

line and cross a hot spot (indicated by a colored dot on the chart) I get a symbol that tells me I bought (or sold) this stock on this date. Clicking on the dot tells me when I bought, how many shares, what price, total cost, and the account involved. I different color dot tells me that there's a news story on this issue for that day. Clicking on that spot on the chart pulls up the story.

Seems like a simple tool, doesn't it? But consider the new ways that it lets me think about my investments. I can now easily track how news has moved the price of a stock. I can see how much of a lag is typical, how quickly the market discounts an event, and how often a stock moves up ahead of the public announcement. I can also track the relationship between price activity and my buying or selling patterns. I can see if I tend to buy too soon—after the quick spike that often follows an event but before a stock settles back down a bit. I can check to see if I overreact to news by selling on emotion. All this in a simple chart.

A few years ago I saw a demonstration of the prototype of a software program that used virtual reality to organize information about all the stocks on the market. A user would give the program a list of the parameters that governed buy and sell decisions. For example, I could tell the program to track earnings per share growth, and earnings surprises, and sales growth, and profit margin, and market share, and changes in management, and price and volume movements. For each parameter, I'd tell the machine how much change had to occur to trigger an alert.

Sounds traditional enough, so far. After all, many of the technical analysis packages come with the ability to generate alerts and alert lists. But it was the way that this prototype handled the information that was intriguing. Instead of a list or a brief message along the bottom of the screen, this program generated a three-dimensional playing field that displayed all the stocks in the universe the investor watched. Each was indicated with a shape such as a diamond or a column. When any stock triggered an alert, it might start to spin, or pulse, or grow in size. The investor operating a joystick could fly through this space to examine individual instances up close and get more information about an individual stock and the conditions that had drawn attention to it. Flying over the landscape from a distance, an investor could quickly zoom in on any change.

The prototype for this program was about as big as a dentist's chair and required a viewer the size of the headset an optometrist uses to check your vision. That's a far cry from the simple interactive charts used by Quicken, it's true, but they both speak to the same need. As the amount of information available to investors increases, investors will need radically different ways to quickly scan it, to eliminate the irrelevant, and to focus on the pertinent. And as great as the increase in the amount of information available to investors has been over the last five years, we are really just at the beginning of a true explosion in the amount of data any investor can put on a desktop.

## ALONG CAME THE SPIDERS

How do I know that we're just at the beginning of an explosion in investment information? A spider told me so.

Spiders are a new kind of search software written for the Internet's World Wide Web and Usenet newsgroups. There are around a dozen different brands of them at the moment, with more appearing every week, but they all work in roughly the same way. For example, here's how I used the "Excite" spider produced by Architext, a Mountain View, California, company founded in 1993 by six Stanford University graduates, to look for information about Silicon Graphics.

I signed on with my Internet provider at about 4:30 P.M. on a Sunday and typed in Architext's World Wide Web address (http://www.atext. com). Architext's Web page tells me about their spider and how to use it. Using Excite I can search the World Wide Web (or the Usenet newsgroups or both), either by concept or keyword to find the Web pages most likely to have the information I want. Thinking of the spider as an agent you send out on the network is a decent analogy. You tell your agent what you want to find and, depending on how smart that agent is, it comes back with a list of good, indifferent, or bad matches.

I tell the spider to look for Silicon Graphics on the Web. In a matter of a minute or two I've got a list of ten pages, ranked by the spider on the probability that the page will match my request. At the top—an 86 percent probability—the spider has listed a page from Silicon Graphics that summarizes 1994 press releases from the company. Next down is a listing for a page with current headlines. The spider even summarizes the first one: "Silicon Graphics and Avid to Deliver Products for Multi-Billion Dollar Broadcast and Post-Production Markets." Just below that there's a page with company releases on current financials, and then the Web page produced by the company's investor relations depart-

# THE WEB'S SPIDERS

The World Wide Web's spiders come in a number of different species. There are those that simply search the Web looking for pages that match the keyword or concept that you've typed in using a software-only search. These simply scan the words in the first hierarchy of the Web page, looking for a reference that fits your request. There are those that add human editors to the process. Instead of just searching the terms on the Web page, these services use human beings to index existing Web pages so that the spider knows something about the content of each page. Some spiders and their human editors have mapped more of the Web than others.

One final difference: some spiders search only the free sections of the Internet—a few will look through proprietary databases. Of course, those searches cost money. Right now all spiders, except those searching proprietary databases, are free to all users. How long that will last is anyone's guess. The economics of the Internet are fluid and will be until someone figures out the best methods for making money on what began as a free network of widely distributed information and computers. Here's a list of some current spiders and a brief description.

Architext, Mountain View, CA
http://www.atext.com
Claims that it can retrieve a million pages a day. Human editors review and search for the most interesting pages.

Infoseek, Santa Clara, CA
http://www.infoseek.com
A subscription service ($4.95/month for 50 queries) that offers a one-month free trial of its spider that will search proprietary databases.

The Internet Sleuth, Baltimore, MD.
http://www.intbc.com/sleuth/
A spider that finds other spiders, Internet Sleuth generates a list of hyperlinks to other specialized spiders that you can use for your searches.

*continued*

Lycos, Pittsburg, PA
http://www.lycos.com
One of the oldest spiders, out of Carnegie Mellon University, this one can be slow (because of high volumes), but offers brief excerpts from each page's contents so that you can judge how well it fits your search.

Magellan, Sausalito, CA
http://www.mckinley.com
A mid-1995 start-up that uses what it calls "smart spiders" that learn to shun some sites and favor others. Human editors add judgments.

Open Text, Waterloo, Ontario
http://www.opentext.com
At the moment the most precise spider, this one can search for individual words and use Boolean logic and word-proximity descriptors to limit your search to just the most likely sites.

WebCrawler, San Francisco, CA
http://www.webcrawler.com
America Online's proprietary spider can also be used by anyone on the Internet.

ment, where I can, the spider summarizes, check out the latest financial reports, earnings releases, press releases, stock price, and investor information. Ending the list, the spider has added a page with press releases from the company dating to 1993. All I need to do to go to any of these pages is to click on the name of the page. The spider has already created the Internet link to take me to any of these addresses.

The Internet and its robots aren't finished with me, however. While I've been on-line with Architext's spider, the newsbot that came with my Internet connection has been busy, too. Weeks ago I had programmed it to send me a copy of any exchange on the Internet about Silicon Graphics that it found in any of the investment newsgroups on Usenet. Today, it downloads a seven-message exchange that begins with a technical comparison of the major families of microprocessors, written by an engineer at Silicon Graphics. Most interesting to an investor in the company, is that he estimates current growth rates for the proprietary chip from subsidiary MIPS that Silicon Graphics uses in its graphics workstations. Like some other investors, I'm worried that if the chip isn't building volume, the company won't sink the research and development money into it necessary to keep up with Intel's efforts on its Pentium line of chips. His data gives me some comfort: volumes should double in 1995. The rest of the messages aren't worth even a quick scan—a couple of pleas for information from investors upset at the stock's recent fall in price and a pissing match between an engineer at Silicon Graphics and one at Convex, a competing maker of powerful computers just acquired by Hewlett-Packard.

Spiders are likely to be everywhere very soon. Quicken Deluxe 5 for CD-ROM comes with an Internet connection and a collection of spiders including Excite, Infoseek, and Lycos. So far most of them can only retrieve information from the free portion of all the computerized data on-line. But that situation will gradually change. Some fee-for-data services have already signed up with one spider or another. And various companies, ranging from start-ups such as Digital Cash to Visa, are hard at work to develop a cheap and secure way to conduct financial transactions over the Internet. Several schemes are already in trial and the big barrier—making handling the transaction cheap enough so that users can buy just what they need (perhaps a dollar's worth of data about a company)—seems likely to succumb to the eventual economies of scale as electronic transactions grow on the Internet.

What happens when more information than investors have ever dreamed of becomes available easily and cheaply? They demand better analytical tools.

## TRICKLE DOWN: TOOLS FROM THE PROS

Reviewers often get to test the next new hot rod before it's actually available to the public. Because I've been writing a book on investment software, several firms that specialize in advice and data for professional money managers have let me try some of the programs that they sell or lease to the folks who handle billions of dollars in pension funds or university endowments or mutual funds. I don't know if any of the firms that market this software for this professional audience plan to bring a version to the individual investor, but I do know that very little now prevents them from doing it. In the last year or two big investment advisors such as the Frank Russell Co., Ibbotson Associates, Barra, Wilson

Associates, and Wilshire have all moved their software to Windows. These professional programs are now running on the same operating system used by millions of individual investors on their computers—and the computers sitting on many of those home desks are just as powerful as those used by the investment professionals.

Let me tell you about two programs that I've tried that I would love to use as an individual investor. Both fill gaping holes in the array of information and analytical tools available to the individual investor.

First, there's the I/B/E/S Express software produced by the Institutional Brokerage Estimate Service so that their clients can track the daily ebb and flow in Wall Street's opinion of future earnings. The version I tried gave me a database of all analyst estimates of earnings per share and changes in estimates for 4,883 U.S. stocks. (A user can also buy data for Asia/Pacific, European, Canadian, and emerging markets stocks.) Let me tantalize you just a bit.

The first screen, called Alert USA, lists all the companies in the universe of 4,883 for which analysts have changed their earnings estimates. I can pick any period—the current quarter, for example—and then rank the stocks by the number of changes in the period. When I ran that screen May Department Stores topped the list with six changes. The Gap, which has moved from the mid-$30s to near $45 a share since I ran this screen, came in at number five with five changes in estimates.

By double-clicking on the name of a stock, I can generate a report on a particular company that gives broker-by-broker estimates including date, previous estimates, when reviewed, and the direction of any change in opinion. I can also get a consensus report on any stock that will tell me how Wall Street as a whole views this security. I can also do the reverse and choose to follow just a single analyst whom I think is particularly well-informed about the companies he or she follows. With a couple of clicks I can sort the universe to find all the companies that analyst follows.

Like most powerful tools, I/B/E/S Express requires a skilled operator. For example, I quickly learned how to generate an obviously useful screen called a Forecasted Growth Report. It listed the growth projections for all 4,871 stocks in the universe. Then, using the screening function, I looked for stocks with an estimated 12-month forward growth rate of greater than 200 percent. The list of what Wall Street is expecting to be super-growth companies came to just 108 stocks. Of course, I wouldn't rush right out and buy just any of these. Some estimates should be taken with a grain of salt. For example, Vitesse, a maker of specialized computer chips, is coming off a 24 cents a share loss in 1994 and analysts are projecting a 480 percent pickup in earnings over the next 12 months. Is this a buy? I'd feel more comfortable if the company's total following on Wall Street added up to more than just three analysts.

Right now I get my earnings estimates company by company by downloading them on CompuServe from I/B/E/S or Zacks or as part of Market Guide on Prodigy. But I can't screen for changes in estimates or follow individual analysts this way—nor do I get changes in estimates as they happen. Wall Street's traders constantly know more than I do about the state of opinion on the Street. (As this book went to press, Zacks Investment Research, an I/B/E/S competitor, launched Analyst Watch on the Internet [http://aw.zacks.com] which offers much of this information for $30 a month.)

I can imagine using I/B/E/S Express to follow the stocks that I own, to time my purchase of stocks currently on my watch list, and to find new candidates for purchase. (Unfortunately, it costs $10,000 a year.) I'd love to link a trading-oriented package like this to one such as CORR and the CORR Optimizer PT from Ibbotson Associates, which concentrates on asset allocation.

Ibbotson's software fills another major gap in the offerings available to individual investors. Although solid academic research indicates that as much as 90 percent of the return to investors is linked to the kinds of assets they pick rather than the specific choices they make in those asset classes, there's virtually nothing on the market that will help investors put together the most efficient portfolio. (The best available program is noted in the box "Investing on the Efficient Frontier.")

## TIPS ON THE TOOLS

# INVESTING ON THE EFFICIENT FRONTIER

**P**rosper (Version 1.04 for Windows only, requires 4MB RAM and 12MB free space on hard drive) from accounting giant Ernst & Young can't match the power of Ibbotson's software, but for $44.95 it gives investors a good tool for understanding the trade-offs among a mix of assets in a portfolio, especially one targeted toward your eventual retirement.

*continued*

Ignore as many of the financial planning worksheets as you can (you've seen most of them if you're a Reuters' Money Network user since Reality Online produces both packages) and go to the kernel of the program's value by clicking "Planning" on the toolbar. Here you'll have to fill out a Risk Profile ("Move the slider bar to the location that best describes your risk tolerance"), which, annoyingly, doesn't define its terms very well. (I fit the category "aggressive growth investor" because I want to outperform the market—who doesn't?—and I'm willing to take losses as large as 20 percent of my capital—over what period?)

From there, go to "Budget." Here I have to fill in my budget and balance sheet in more detail than I'd like. Finally, on to Goal Manager. Set up the program to deal with retirement plans and current portfolio. When I've done all this I find that I need to build a $3.8 million portfolio by 2018 to give me the inflation adjusted-equivalent of $90,000 in current income.

Now comes the payoff. So how can I get to $3.8 million given what I've told the program about my current assets and expected annual savings? The "Strategy" button will let me explore some of the alternatives.

I click on "Expected Return." My current portfolio, states the program, after looking at the asset classes in my portfolio, needs to return 13.56 percent (if the future is like the past) to get me close to the nest egg I require at retirement. My actual portfolio allocation isn't that far off though—the machine projects its return at 13.40. If I put more money into international equities (bringing that class to 20 percent of my portfolio) I can increase my expected return to 13.73 percent a year. I could also take less risk—by lowering my exposure to growth and international stocks—and lower my return to 12.30 percent.

But how efficient is each of those mixes? Which one gives me the best mix of high return and low risk? Maybe I'd be better off going with the more conservative mix and increasing the amount I save each month?

Well, clicking the bar graph icon in the upper right-hand corner of the asset allocation widow gives me a set of graphs that takes me a distance toward an answer. One, the graph of the efficient frontier, shows me risk (measured in standard deviation) versus return. For example, my current portfolio is located at the intersection of 13.4 return and almost 16 risk. That means that two out of three times, my return will fall between 29.5 percent (13.5 plus 16) and –2.5 percent (13.5 minus 16).

But I can now ask the program to optimize that portfolio—and to my surprise it suggests that by changing my mix of assets I can move my portfolio to the intersection of 13.59 percent returns and 15.14 risk. Basically all the program suggests for me is a fine-tuning—a little less aggressive growth and a little more international. To double-check the results, I can then graph that suggested asset mix against portfolios composed solely of long-term growth stocks, aggressive growth stocks (what the program calls "maximum capital gains"), and international stocks. Compared to a portfolio of growth stocks alone, for example, the suggested portfolio roughly yields the same return over the last ten years but with less of a drop in 1987 and 1991. It slightly underperforms the aggressive growth portfolio, but shows much less volatility.

The program comes with a manual that does a good job explaining the theory behind efficient asset allocation. (To order, 800-821-2610.)

The process is called "optimization." In a nutshell, it uses the best research of the last forty years—what collectively falls under the name of Modern Portfolio Theory—to mix and match different assets to produce the mix that gives an investor the best return for the least risk. The mix will take into account the investor's time horizon and tolerance for risk. An investor who wants to lock up money for just five years and who can't afford more than a 10 percent variation in return will wind up with a very different mix of assets than an investor putting money away for thirty years, who is willing to suffer through bigger variations. But both optimizations will recommend the mix that results in the highest return possible under those conditions.

I tried only a demonstration version of the Ibbotson program, but even that was impressive. Here's the scenario CORR begins with: Mr. and Mrs. Peterson schedule an appointment to discuss their portfolio. They have $50,000. They're in their forties and plan to retire in twenty years. They aren't satisfied with current return but don't want to take on more risk. Their current portfolio is 55 percent in S&P 500 stocks, 30 percent in long government bonds, 15 percent in short 90-day Treasury bills. As their advisor you tell the Petersons that adding a "risky" aggressive growth class such as U.S. small stocks can actually reduce risk by increasing return. CORR can then generate the portfolios and charts that prove this case.

# THE STYLISH INVESTOR

The mutual investor convinced of the value of building a properly balanced portfolio quickly runs into a big problem. It's difficult to identify the exact investment style of any particular mutual fund. Certainly the fund's own name and description are misleading. Sogen International is really a global fund, for example, and the categories applied by the big fund raters such as Morningstar and Lipper Analytical Services can be just as bad. Morningstar classes the Acorn fund as a small cap domestic fund—even though as much as 30 percent of its portfolio has been in international stocks in the relatively recent past.

The big institutional money managers and advisors such as Ibbotson and Barra have recently attempted to tackle this problem using a technique called style analysis. Pioneered by Nobel Prize–winning economist William Sharpe, style analysis attempts to categorize funds on the "if it quacks like a duck, it's a duck" theory.

Rather than taking apart a fund's portfolio to see what kinds of stocks and bonds a fund holds—and then categorizing the fund—style analysis looks at a fund's performance and tries to find the mix of market indexes that most closely matches a

The proof is overwhelming. The charts clearly show that the current portfolio is taking on more risk and getting less return than the optimal risk or return portfolios. The Petersons could get either the same return with less risk or more return with the same risk.

With their current portfolio, the Petersons can expect a return of 7.63 percent annually; the expected standard deviation of their return, one way to define risk, is 15.89. Now, if the Petersons dump all their S&P 500 stocks, add enough small cap stocks to bring that asset class up to 30 percent of their portfolio, increase long government bonds to 70 percent, and sell all their short-term Treasury bills, they can keep exactly the same return but lower their risk to a standard deviation of 9.52. And if they really want to get the top returns with the least risk, they should restructure their portfolio further toward small cap stocks (now 75 percent of the total) with 25 percent still in long-term governments. The standard deviation soars to 38.68, but returns climb to 16.7 percent.

## BRAINS IN A BOX

I'd welcome a chance to add tools like CORR or I/B/E/S Express to my toolbox. But I don't think those tools will end my search for an edge on the financial markets and my fellow investors. After all, when I am able to buy these programs a lot of other people will be, too. And while I believe that I'll find ways to turn these tools to my advantage—which my fellow investors don't have the discipline or the time or the knowledge to match—I'm well aware that these tools really aren't going to tell me things about the market that no one else knows. So in the last few months I've begun building my own artificial stock market expert.

Artificial intelligence has been slow to catch on in either professional or personal investing, but now I see traces of it everywhere. That's because artificial intelligence experts have changed their approach to building machines that "think." To simplify radically, the first generations of machines fell into the category of expert systems. The idea was to tell the machine all the rules that led to successful investing and then let the machine do it. This effort never really caught fire— because no successful investor could articulate all the rules that led to success and because the

fund's behavior. For example, the performance of the Acorn fund might best be matched by a mix of the Morgan Stanley emerging markets index and the small cap Russell 2000 stock index.

Finding this match is still the domain of professionals able to afford $5,000 software packages and the monthly performance data for funds and indexes that Sharpe's mathematics demands. But Advisor Software Inc. in Orinda, California, now offers a database of fund styles—the end result of the calculation—for individual investors. Each fund's style is described in terms of cash, four fixed income categories, six equity categories, and a foreign index. For example, at the end of October 1995, the database showed the Fidelity Magellan fund's style as being 49 percent large value stock, 34 percent medium growth stock, 10 percent small growth stock and 8 percent foreign. The software, Style Advisor, with data on 4,000 funds, costs $95 (800-738-6369). The company also runs a World Wide Web page (http://www.advisorsw.com) where investors can find the styles of individual mutual funds at no charge.

professionals on Wall Street never took to the idea that they could be duplicated by a machine.

But the current approach to building an artificial intelligence faces neither of those problems. The new tools are called neural networks

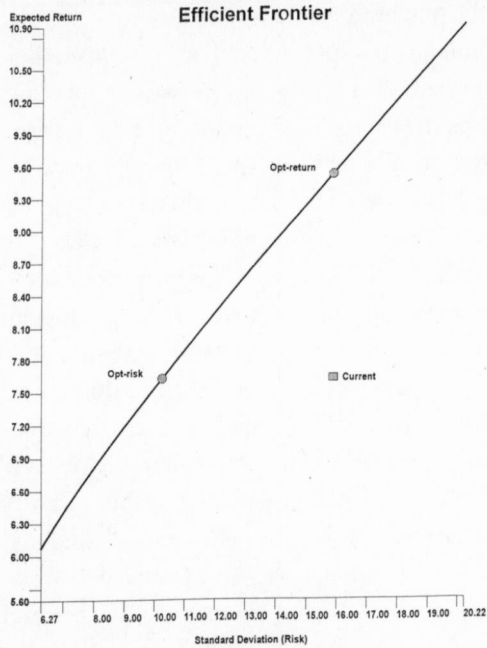

*An "optimizer" such as Ibbotson's* CORR *searches for the best mix of risk and return.* (*Courtesy Ibbotson Associates*)

and genetic algorithms. These start from the principle that the market is a complex place that often seems orderless to human beings. Although there may be order here—the patterns are hard to perceive. Maybe a computer, with its incredible speeds and vast patience at routine tasks, can find some of those patterns. Simplifying again, the current approach is best called pattern matching.

To do that researchers have built machines that "discover" a pattern by looking at part of the data universe, apply it to another part of the data, see how well it explains the data, and then change that pattern to find one that may fit just a little better. The advantage the machine has is that it can try pattern after pattern with immense speed. And the machine never gets tired or frustrated in the search, no matter how often it fails.

One of the major questions absorbing the attention of researchers in artificial intelligence is how to best build that repetitive search. They are looking for ways to maximize the efficiency with which the machine arrives at a final pattern, as well as to improve the fit of that final choice. Two methods currently account for a large part of the research. The one called neural networks is modeled on recent theories of how the brain works. A neural network computer tries to find a way to connect all its nodes—by analogy to the way that the brain may organize itself as we grow and learn—so that the direction and strength of the connections will produce the right answer. The second, genetic algorithms, uses an evolutionary model. Hundreds or thousands of computer programs that might be able to solve the problem are created. Those that don't come close to generating a correct answer are killed. Those that do are allowed to reproduce—with a random change introduced into the program, in much the same way that random genetic mutation changes a biological system. For generation after generation, programs strive to solve the problem, die or reproduce, and try again. Eventually they "breed" a good solution.

I haven't yet seen an investment program incorporating genetic algorithms in a product for the individual investor, but neural networks have been around for nigh on ten years. For most of this time they've been written in arcane software languages and required programming skills that I don't have. But recently I've started to see neural network programs written in Windows that tout their ease of use. I decided to see how difficult it would be to put one of the current generation to work on solving a perennial thorn in the side of mutual fund investors, the question: Does anything in the past performance or characteristics of a mutual fund predict future performance?

Neural Connection from SPSS Inc. (version 1.0 for Windows only, 4MB RAM required, 8MB RAM recommended, 4MB free space required on hard drive) is daunting straight out of the box, especially if you make the mistake of opening the shorter manual—the one entitled *Applications Guide*—first. It unfortunately folds open to a diagram of the Multi-layer Perceptron that immediately introduces the mathematics of nonlinear functions. I've written an entire book about neural networks and I still find the theory behind this type of artificial intelligence hard to digest. However, you don't need to understand how a neural network uses multiple layers of nodes joined by connections of different strength to "think" in order to run this program. Neural Connections' NetAgent function will handle most of the details of neural network management without any help from the user.

Neural Connection takes some of the mystery out of artificial intelligence by treating neural networks as just another problem-solving tool.

The program comes with three neural network models—the Multilayer Perceptron, the Radial Basis Function, and the Kohonen Network—as well as three standard statistical tools—a Closest Class Mean Classifier, Regression Analysis, and Principal Component Analysis. The juxtaposition of neural networks and statistical tools allows a user to throw both at a problem.

But while having six tools in my Neural Connection tool set means that I don't have to pretend every problem is a nail because all I own is a hammer, it does require me to start by analyzing the nature of my problem. Neural Connection's manual sorts problems into two groups: classification and prediction problems. In a classification problem I want to know what group an individual belongs to—for example, I can think of my mutual fund problem as one where I want to know whether a fund is an outperformer—one that outperforms its peers. And there are prediction problems. In that case I'd want to be able to predict the likelihood that a fund will be an outperformer.

To begin designing my network I click on NetAgent. It asks me about my problem: "Are you classifying or predicting outputs." I think I want to classify these funds. NetAgent then asks me to select a method, either linear statistics or a neural network (I pick neural network), and NetAgent selects the appropriate neural network tool, the Radial Basis Function. I then type in the name of my data file, "mutual funds," which I've transferred to Neural Connection from a Microsoft Excel spreadsheet (annoyingly, Neural Connection will only accept data from Excel version 5 or better). NetAgent asks me to confirm that these parameters are correct.

Unlike statistical analysis, which demands that I know the best tools to apply to wring the secrets from this particular problem (see "Statistics and Damn Statistics" in this chapter), a neural network will learn how best to weigh the data so that it most accurately categorizes all these funds. But I can't use all my data to train the system, because then I won't know how this solution fits new data—the system will have learned how best to treat one data set, but that method won't necessarily work for all the data. So I have to divide my data into three parts, a set for training the network, a set for validating the training (to make sure that the network doesn't overtrain), and a set to test the performance of the trained network. (You're probably already getting the picture: Neural networks demand lots and lots of data.)

Here's what I've given the program to work with. My total data set

# STATISTICS AND DAMN STATISTICS

The investor looking to build original investment screens or find an underexploited corner of the market ought to put a statistics program in the toolbox. Most investors, and I count myself in this group, didn't take enough statistics courses during our educational careers to feel comfortable with the ins and outs of regressions and correlations, but fortunately even the most high-powered programs in this category have become relatively easy to use. The best will guide you to the optimum methods for finding patterns in your data—and then turn that data and those patterns into revealing graphs.

Mathematica (for Macintosh and Windows and eighteen other platforms, 6MB RAM required but 10MB recommended) is one of the easiest to use. The company has developed a finance pack with specialized tools for calculating bond sensitivity measures such as duration and programming examples for constructing Markowitz efficient portfolios and moving averages. (Wolfram Research, 800-965-3726, $995)

Statistica (for Macintosh and Windows, 4–8MB RAM required) comes with a disappointingly disorganized manual, but the program itself is relatively simple to operate. A user who has some grounding in basic statistics should be able to get up and running despite the handicap. (StatSoft, 918-749-1119, Windows $995, Macintosh $695)

SPSS, maker of Neural Connection, offers a library of statistics programs and graphic mapping software for Windows. The program's tutorials speed up the learning process for each, and the modular design lets the user buy only those statistical and mapping functions that he or she needs. (SPSS, 800-543-2185, prices vary)

consists of 453 mutual funds that invest in large capitalization growth stocks. At random I divide that into three roughly equal parts. Many's the neural network—or other system—that produced skewed results because of some bias in how the data was chosen. For each fund I've got data (for the period ending in August 1994) on performance (five-year performance, three-year performance, one-year performance), fees and expenses the fund charges, fundamental characteristics and changes in them over the last three years (current beta, three-year-prior beta, percent change in beta, current net assets, three-year-prior net assets, percent change in net assets, current price-to-earnings ratio, three-year-prior price to earnings, percent change in price-to-earnings, current price-to-book ratio, three-year-prior price to book, percent change in price to book, turnover), and data on the tenure of the fund manager. Performance for 1995 is the last crucial piece of data—this is stated as either outperform or underperform depending on whether the fund beat the Russell 1000 Growth Index for the period.

I've done this exercise before using just an Excel spreadsheet. By creating systems of ratings (using weighted mathematical combinations of parts of the data) and then combining those ratings, again using weighted values, I've designed a system that I believe sheds some light on a fund's future performance. The neural network I'm trying to build will do exactly the same combining and weighting, only instead of using a combination of statistical analysis, trial and error, and intuition to figure out the best way to combine it all to most accurately predict the best funds, now the neural network will learn that best combination.

For the training run, I give the computer the data on the funds through August 1994 and the 1995 performance. The neural network will organize the data to predict what it already knows—future performance. In the final run it will use the system that it built to classify out- and underperform.

I tell the program to begin the training run with a click of the mouse. When, after four minutes, training is completed, I use the validation data to fine-tune the network. Then, with a third set of clicks, I set the trained network to work on the test data. The results are interesting: the program tells me that the network, as now trained, correctly identified 68.3 percent of the funds in my sample as underperformers or outperformers. I've now got an application that I can use to pick better than average funds.

But note that I don't know two things. I don't know whether the combination of factors that the network picked that identified 1995 winners from 1994 data will hold for any other year. In a great year for growth stocks such as 1995, maybe high betas are good indicators that a fund will outperform. They'd probably lead to underperformance in a down market such as 1990. For me to feel confident in this system, I'd have to run it with data for a lot more years with very different characteristics. This isn't a problem unique to neural networks, however. Any investment system must deal with the possibility that the future will not be like the past.

And I don't know that this is the highest accuracy that I can get out of this program. Neural networks are very sensitive to undetected patterns in the data. For example, like most linear statistical models, neural networks assume that the data in each field is normally distributed; that is, most of the points heap together into a peak in the middle, and then taper off at the same rate to either side. But mutual fund returns are not actually normally distributed—more funds underperform than statistically should. I can use the Analyze function of Neural Connection to create distribution graphs of each data field and then click on a Weighting function to make the distribution of each variable more normal. When I do this and, beginning from scratch with a completely naive network, train the network again, the accuracy of my predictions goes up to 70.1 percent. From my final sample of 150 funds, the program has identified 37 that will outperform.

Looking at the results in the program's spreadsheet, I realize that a large number—18 to be exact—of these funds outperformed by anywhere from just a few tenths of a percentage point or a couple of points. Another ten are mistakes—they didn't outperform in 1995. A final nine are really interesting—they outperformed by at least five percentage points. Perhaps if I redesign the data set so that only funds that outscore the others by five percentage points are listed as outperformers and maybe if I ask for the probability that a fund will outperform, the system will work better. And I could also run the data through one of the program's other neural networks, the Kohonen Network, to preprocess the data and reveal any clusters that might be influencing the final results. That might improve the accuracy of my system.

Neural networks aren't the last word in computerized investing. When I last went to the annual "Fuzzy Day" conference sponsored by the Society of Quantitative Analysts in New York, the audience of Wall Street's most committed number crunchers was abuzz with talk of chaos theory and genetic algorithms. Physicists from the government laboratory at Los Alamos, New Mexico, had raised money from a big Swiss bank and were using neural networks or chaos theory or something to beat the commodities markets. Two kids had left MIT to run a hedge fund using some kind of cutting-edge system. No one had any concrete numbers and no one with a system was explaining it in detail, of course. But the air was full of possibility. Someone, somewhere was going to figure out the market.

Doyne Farmer, one of the former physicists from Los Alamos turned portfolio manager, dismissed that idea as hopelessly naive. "We have no idea what kind of a system the stock market is or how complex it might be." A solution that explains how all the variables are related is, at best, far distant. But, Farmer continued, the good news is that investors don't have to figure the financial markets out to the last decimal point. "You can make an awful lot of money just by being right a little bit more than fifty percent of the time."

And, I'd add, by being just a little more disciplined, a little more up to date, and a little more knowledgeable than other investors. That's the edge that electronic investing promises, even in its current imperfection. And that's good enough for me.